JOHN
MILTON

A reader's guide to his poetry

MARJORIE HOPE NICOLSON

Farrar, Straus and Giroux
NEW YORK

Contents

Preface

To know the poetry of John Milton is to have a liberal education. His own word in his famous definition is even better—a "generous" education. Since I have taught Milton's poetry to students for nearly forty years, I know that the teacher of Milton today faces problems quite different from those I first encountered. Until the Depression, we could take for granted that the majority of college students had studied some Latin, often entering with "four units." Most of them knew at least a little classical mythology, since the old "College Board Examinations" stressed such knowledge. And many, if not all, had some knowledge of the Bible. From the time of the Depression, this situation changed drastically. Most colleges lowered their admission requirements; the College Entrance Board began to offer others than the "Old" and the "New Plans," and the requirements in literature became much less specific than they had been. During the intervening years, the average college student has known no Latin, and since reading the Bible in public schools is prohibited by law in many states, and attendance at Sunday School less common than it used to be, many students, I have found, are quite unfamiliar with even the most famous Biblical stories and often recognize no classical allusions. Recently this situation has been changing somewhat for the better, through the growing emphasis in colleges upon "Humanities" and "Great Books" courses, in which the classics and frequently the Bible are required reading. Yet there has been no time during forty years when I have not found it possible to interest students in reading Milton, and through such reading, helping them enrich the somewhat sparse literary education to which many of them have been subjected.

But let me grant at once that teaching Milton is more difficult than teaching Shakespeare, in part because Milton drew his materials and formed his style much more self-consciously than did Shakespeare from the classics and the Bible. The young student often finds Milton's style perplexing and his many Biblical and classical allusions more difficult still. T. S. Eliot's strictures upon Milton's poetic influence are well known. In 1936 he warned modern poets against modelling themselves upon Milton, indicating that he was not alone in his opinion, but that the "true jury of judgment is that of the ablest poetical practitioners of my own time." That judgment was in effect: "Milton's poetry could only be a serious influence for the worst upon any poet whatever." ("A Note on the Verse of John Milton," republished in *On Poetry and Poets,* pp. 138-42). Mr. Eliot's criticisms were made on various grounds, as his later so-called "recantation" shows. I am not quarreling or agreeing with him, but merely using his remarks as a point of departure, in order to point out some characteristics of the "Miltonic style" which at first make the reading of his poetry difficult for modern students. Mr. Eliot was saying in effect that the language of poetry should be less far removed from the language of prose, that it should be more conversational and employ more of the language of everyday, as Dryden in his time and the authors of the *Lyrical Ballads* in theirs also felt. Milton, on the contrary, believed that the languages of poetry and prose were poles apart, and deliberately made them so. What are some of the characteristics of style that made his poetry consciously "poetic"?

One characteristic, particularly of his earlier styles, is Milton's use of archaic words, in which he was following the example of Spenser, whom he admired greatly. Spenser, too, might have written of Sabrina (*Comus* 827), *"Whilom* she was the daughter of Lo-crine," using a form already obsolete in the language. When Milton said:

> But come, thou goddess fair and free
> In heaven *yclept* Euphrosyne,
>
> (*L'Allegro* 11-12)

he was quite aware that the old form of the past participle had passed out of English well before Spenser revived it. Milton's fondness for archaisms of this kind occasionally led him into trouble. In his lines on Shakespeare, he said:

> Or that his hallowed reliques should be hid
> Under a star-*ypointing* pyramid,

which is an impossible construction, never known in English. Other archaisms are found in Milton's spelling. Since most readers of this volume will be using modernized texts, I shall not enter into this except to say that the spelling-archaisms, when they exist, are analogous to the kind of "quaintness" familiar even in our day in such phrases as "Ye olde Coffee Shoppe." Archaisms, however, are largely confined to Milton's early poems and are never as frequent as they were in Spenser.

Modern readers of Renaissance literature are frequently puzzled by words that sound archaic to them, though were not so in their time. These must not be confused with deliberate archaisms. We should gladly put ourselves to school and increase our vocabularies by adding words and phrases used by our ancestors, many of them entirely familiar to those who have read or heard the King James' Version of the Bible. Language is constantly changing, and we must not be surprised to find that many words familiar to us in one sense had a different meaning in the Renaissance. Any student of Shakespeare knows that "fond" and "silly" had other connotations. "Ay, me, I *fondly* dream," we read in *Lycidas,* and know that it meant "foolishly," or "vainly." When Milton writes of the shepherds in the *Nativity Ode:*

Perhaps their loves or else their sheep,
Was all that did their *silly* thought so busy keep,

he was not insulting the shepherds, but merely implying that theirs
were "simple" thoughts. When he described Mirth in *L'Allegro* as
"buxom, blithe and debonair," he was not suggesting that the charm-
ing girl was over-plump, but merely that she was "sprightly" or
"lively." "Sad," might mean "sorrowful," but it might also mean
either "serious" or "heavy." Often a word or phrase familiar in
the Renaissance has disappeared entirely from our language be-
cause the object it described is no longer known. When the "jocund
rebecks" sound in *L'Allegro,* we have to use a glossary to learn that
a "rebeck" was a fiddle.

I call your attention particularly to words which our Renais-
sance ancestors used in their Latin meaning, rather than our mod-
ern, or which could be used in both senses with an interesting
double-play. When Milton wrote in the *Nativity Ode,* "O run, *pre-
vent* them with thy humble ode" (line 24) he was not suggesting
any attempt to "hinder" or "stop" the arrival of the Magi with
their precious gifts. He was using the word modestly in its Latin
sense, "arrive before them," because he was an unknown young
singer and his gift much more humble than theirs. When he said in
his sonnet on Fairfax, "Thy firm unshaken *virtue* ever brings Vic-
tory home," the word *virtue* has the double meaning of "physical
strength" and "moral excellence." One of the best examples of the
double meaning of a word in its original and derived sense is

> Let none *admire*
> That riches grow in Hell; that soil may best
> Deserve the precious bane.
>
> (*P.L.* I. 690-92)

Admire carries the Latin meaning of *admirari,* "be astonished,"
"wonder at," and at the same time rebukes the more modern con-
notation "regard with approval," and so leads up to the paradox
and oxymoron of "precious bane." The word *fame* should be
watched. In most instances it is pejorative, associated, as in *Lyci-*

das, with the famous passage in the *Aeneid,* known to every school-
boy, in which *Fama,* ("Rumor,") flies over the housetops, spread-
ing rumor.

Inevitably Milton's vocabulary reflects his long training in Greek
and Latin, but this is no more peculiar to him than to any other
Renaissance writer, except that Milton is more "learned" in his
vocabulary than Shakespeare, for example. But Milton's vocabu-
lary can be and often is extraordinarily simple, as in *L'Allegro* in
which the words are largely of Anglo-Saxon origin. "Laughter
holding both his sides" is as Anglo-Saxon as any true-born English-
man could wish. Indeed, so far as vocabulary is concerned, the
language of the early poems is often as "conversational" as even
T. S. Eliot could desire. So too is much of the language of *Paradise
Regained.*

The difficulty modern readers may find at first with *Paradise
Lost* arises less from vocabulary—by the time you reach it, you will
be familiar with most of the words—than from sentence-
structure. And here Milton is, indeed, classical and particularly
Latinate. The syntax of many sentences is framed on classical
models, the constructions of which sound strange to the ears of
readers unversed in Latin. Take, for example, the opening lines of
Paradise Lost. The first words are, "Of man's first disobedience
and the fruit of that forbidden tree." But what is the construction?
We do not know until line 6, when we find the verb in *"Sing,* Heav-
enly Muse." Our normal English order is first the subject, then the
predicate, then the object. Latin sentences incline to be periodic,
with the verb at the end. When you begin to read *Paradise Lost,* I
suggest that you turn to Gilbert Murray's *The Classical Tradition
in Poetry,* and read the first pages and the section in which Mr.
Murray analyzes in close detail the first twenty-six lines of *Paradise
Lost,* in such a way as to make us realize the extent to which Milton
and other Renaissance poets loved the traditions of the past and
strove to use their native language as Homer and Virgil had used
theirs.

This matter of "tradition" is of utmost importance, so far as Milton is concerned. Like other Renaissance humanists, he loved the classics and wished to treasure up in his own poetry the glory that was Greece and the grandeur that was Rome. He was writing for an audience of readers who had been trained, like himself, upon classical literature. Shakespeare may have had "small Latin and less Greek," but he had a great deal more Latin than most college students today. Perhaps Donne "banished the gods and goddesses" from his poetry, but neither Milton nor Shakespeare had any desire to do so. Most Renaissance authors loved the lore of mythology and took for granted that their readers did also. Everyone in those days was familiar with the classical pantheon, and knew both the Greek and Roman names of the gods and goddesses and what each symbolized: Zeus (Jupiter, Jove) the king of the gods, and Hera (Juno) the queen; Athena (Minerva) the goddess of wisdom; Aphrodite, (Venus) the goddess of love and beauty; Ares (Mars) the god of war; Phoebus Apollo, the god of the sun as well as the god of music. And there were dozens more major and minor deities, about whom the schoolboy of Milton's and Shakespeare's time knew the involved pedigrees and interrelationships by marriage, as well as the many love-affairs in which classical deities seem constantly to have been engaged. Heroes were equally familiar. They all knew such tales as the *Odyssey,* the *Iliad,* the *Aeneid,* and could have charted the progress of the Trojan War, the wanderings of Odysseus, the adventures of Aeneas. They grew up on such tales, as other generations of children have grown up on fairy tales or *Mother Goose*—or characters in the "comics." It is never too late to build up something of a classical background, and if the reader who is beginning the reading of Milton has had no such background, this is an ideal time to learn it and share in the great tradition that has marked our culture for hundreds of years. There are dozens of books in which the classical stories are retold, dozens of translations of the famous works of Greece and Rome—some of them little classics of English prose and poetry, as well as faithful adaptations and translations. There are annotated editions of Milton's works which explain all his allusions, though brief notes cannot take the place of reading the stories for oneself and becoming more and more familiar with them.

The same thing is true of that other goodly heritage Milton has transmitted to us, the literature of the Bible. Whatever one's religious faith—or lack of it—every student who sincerely wishes to appreciate English literature must know the Biblical stories that have been constantly on the lips of English and American poets, novelists, dramatists, essayists. Fortunate the child who has been required to learn Biblical passages in youth, so that they echo in his ears all his life. But, again, it is not too late. Anyone may become familiar with the Biblical stories in the Old and New Testaments most frequently used by great English and American authors. I recommend that you use the King James' Version of the Bible, rather than any of the modern revisions, not only because it is great literature in itself, but because it is written in the language used by Milton and his contemporaries. The sections of the Bible most frequently referred to by Milton are the first chapters of Genesis, the Book of Job, the story of Samson in Judges, the four Gospels, and, underlying all, the Psalms and the Revelation according to John. If you know these well, you will have the general background for most of Milton's poetry. There are dozens of Biblical references and allusions, many of which an annotated edition of Milton will explain sufficiently, but the basic tales I have mentioned and the great poetry of the Psalms, Job and Revelation are so pervasive that annotations alone are not enough. Let the reader of Milton take this opportunity to make up for deficiencies and limitations in his own education. It will prove, I assure you, not a task but an increasing delight. To know the poetry of John Milton is indeed to have a liberal, a generous, education.

In preparing this volume I have had in mind particularly three groups of readers: the general reader, who may have read no Milton, or, at most, the Minor Poems and possibly the first two books of *Paradise Lost;* the undergraduate, often reading Milton for the first time; the English teacher who is not a "Milton specialist," but who must teach Milton in a "survey course" or in a course in Renaissance literature from Spenser to Milton. I have quoted from a modernized text, and recommend the use of such a text, in order that the beginning reader need not face the unnecessary barrier of unfamiliar spelling, punctuation, capitalization. The teacher, at least, should have on his or her desk, and use constantly, the best modern annotated edition of Milton: *John Milton, Complete Poems and Major Prose,* edited by Merritt Y. Hughes; a copy of the Bible in the King James' Version. (I recommend particularly *The Holy Bible, A Reference Edition with Concordance,* American Bible Society, New York, which also contains a valuable glossary of words that have changed in meaning); a good reference book on mythology, (preferably *The New Century Classical Handbook* or *The Oxford Classical Dictionary*). Douglas Bush, *Classical Influences on Renaissance Literature* will also prove helpful. Such older standard books as Bulfinch's *Age of Fable* are still valuable. Since Milton scholarship has become so formidable that only a specialist can be expected to know its vast scope, I have appended a selected bibliography including all works to which I have specifically referred as well as a few others.

I may make two other remarks, one addressed chiefly to the teacher, the other to my colleagues in the academic world who are "Milton specialists." Because of my long experience in teaching Milton in high school, in undergraduate colleges, and in graduate universities, I have ventured to suggest some of the devices I have found valuable in trying to transfer my own love of Milton to my students. The teacher will find such suggestions implicit, at least, in the sections on *L'Allegro* and *Il Penseroso,* on *Comus, Lycidas,* and the introductions to *Paradise Lost.* To "Milton specialists" I add that I have deliberately avoided the use of footnotes, except on rare occasions, and that I have entered into scholarly and critical controversies only when it was absolutely essential. This volume makes no pretense of being a "contribution to Milton studies," in the sense in which we scholars think of such contributions. Finally, if I have not always seemed to acknowledge indebtedness to learned articles of the last twenty years, it is not because I do not recognize the value of those articles but usually because—thanks to my long experience as a teacher of Milton—I had developed my interpretations of various works before the articles appeared. I mention only one example: as early as 1924 I was opposing the idea of "digressions" in *Lycidas,* showing its tripartite structure and its water-imagery. If there be doubting Thomases among you, I can and will summon up a cloud of witnesses from among the hundreds of students to whom I have taught Milton, all of whom I have threatened to haunt if they ever teach "digressions" in *Lycidas.*

I
THE EARLY YEARS

The Education of a Poet

Early in his life Milton felt himself "called," as his theologically-minded generation would have expressed it, to be a poet. Wordsworth, who had much in common with Milton, dated specifically the moment at which he became aware of his own "calling," during a summer vacation in his Cambridge years, after a night spent in "dancing, gaiety, and mirth." Returning home as the sun rose upon a morning "glorious as e'er I had beheld," he recalled that

> to the brim
> My heart was full; I made no vows, but vows
> Were then made for me; bond unknown to me
> Was given, that I should be, else sinning greatly
> A dedicated Spirit.
>
> (*Prelude* IV. 333-37)

At approximately the same age, when he too was a Cambridge undergraduate, Milton expressed his desire to be a great poet. In the "Vacation Exercise" he was writing in the light vein fitting for the occasion of an academic holiday, but interrupted his address to his "native language" to say more seriously:

> Yet I had rather if I were to choose,
> Thy service in some graver subject use.

The following twenty-five lines show that he intended the "graver subject" to be an epic in the classical mode: a poem leading now to the "thunderous throne" of the gods, then down to earth with "kings and queens and heroes old." Homer is obviously his master, the *Odyssey* his model.

A year later he returned to the same theme. Writing to his friend Charles Diodati, of whom we shall hear more, Milton again suggested the theory of poetry which was to be his throughout life. He would be numbered, he wrote, among those poets

> who demi-gods and heroes praise,
> And feats performed in Jove's more youthful days,
> Who now the counsels of high heaven explore,
> Now shades, that echo the Cerberean roar.

The *Odyssey* is again his model and his master again Homer who

> led, of yore,
> His chief of Ithaca from shore to shore,
> Through magic Circe's monster-peopled reign,
> And shoals insidious with the Siren train.

With his classical background, Milton took for granted that there was a hierarchy in poetry (as, indeed, in everything). Highest in the scale was the epic, treating of gods and "heroes half-divine," the composers of which were not only the greatest poets but also teachers and prophets. Below the epic, though still in high place, was drama, which to Milton implied tragedy, modeled upon Aeschylus, Sophocles, Euripides. The lyric occupied a lower place in the scale, though still an honored one, practised as it had been by such poets as Pindar and Ovid, Sappho and Alcaeus, Horace and Catullus, Theocritus and Virgil.

The young man did not labor under any delusion that he would write a great poem in youth. Homer's epics were to him the productions of a reverend master, mature and blind. Virgil had written eclogues and bucolics well before he had attempted the *Aeneid*. Although Milton felt that he had been born a poet, he agreed with

Ben Jonson—and indeed most of his contemporaries and predecessors—that "A good poet's made, as well as born." And so he set himself a long apprenticeship of *learning* to be a poet.

"A Pigeon of Paules"

Milton was as fortunate in his family as in his education. Of his mother, Sarah Jeffreys Milton, we know little except that she came from a respected and fairly well-to-do family, and that her son later spoke of "the esteem in which she was held, and the alms which she bestowed." (*Second Defence of the English People*) She died in April 1637, shortly before her son set off on his foreign travels. Of the father, for whom the poet was named, we know much more. The elder John Milton was a scrivener—an occupation for which we have no exact modern counterpart, but of importance in the seventeenth century. "The scrivener's profession," Professor Ernest Brennecke Jr. writes (*John Milton the Elder and His Music*, p. 48) "was a comparatively prosaic one, combining the services that are today performed by attorneys' assistants, law stationers, and notaries, services that were especially important in an age when illiteracy was more prevalent among the well-to-do than it is today. Scriveners drew up and witnessed wills, leases, marriage settlements, and suchlike legal documents, and they often did some money lending and trading in securities on the side." That the profession was a lucrative one in the elder Milton's case, we may deduce from the generosity which he devoted to the education of his gifted son.

Milton's father was a scrivener by profession but he was also a musician of parts, a composer of some note, and well acquainted with many in the world of music and the arts. In a Latin poem, "Ad Patrem," in which he was urging his father to permit him still more time for leisurely study, the poet subtly reminded him that both father and son were artists in their different fields:

thyself
Art skilful to associate verse with airs
Harmonious, and to give the human voice
A thousand modulations, heir by right
Indisputable of Arion's fame.
Now say, what wonder is it if a son
Of thine delight in verse, if, so conjoined
In close affinity, we sympathise
In social arts, and kindred studies sweet?

An artist himself, the elder Milton carefully planned and directed the education of his son.

Many years later Milton wrote in *The Reason of Church Government:* "My father destined me from a child to the pursuits of literature . . . and had me daily instructed in the grammar school, and by other masters at home." Milton's early education was a combination of the curriculum traditional at English "public schools" (in America we would call them "private schools") and of private tutoring at home. Since the records of St. Paul's school in Milton's time have been lost, we cannot tell at what age he became "a Pigeon of Paules," as the boys were called by inevitable association with the pigeons that flocked about the great Cathedral. He might have entered as early as his seventh year, though it is more likely that his first schooling was under tutors at home. He remained until the end of the eighth form, the normal time for graduation. Going to school in Milton's time was a rigorous experience. The boys were required to arrive at seven o'clock, having breakfasted at home and walked to school in the cold gray dawn of London mornings. Fortunately for Milton, he lived only about three blocks (as we would say) from St. Paul's. The first session lasted from seven until eleven, the second from one to five. The day opened with prayer. One of the most interesting of many books on seventeenth-century education is Charles Hoole's *A New Discovery of the Old Art of Teaching Schoole* (ed. E. T. Campagnac), in which there is a vivid picture of the beginning of a seventeenth-century schoolday. Although Hoole was writing about schools smaller than St. Paul's, which numbered one hundred and fifty-three students, the situation was probably not much different. The Scriptural lesson for the day was read aloud by one boy, and followed by the others in four languages: the youngest boys read in English, the next forms in Latin, the next in Greek, and the grave and reverend seniors in Hebrew. "English," as we think of it to-day, was not taught as a discipline in seventeenth-century schools. Latin was the common language. In the four lower forms, the boys' time was spent in learning Latin grammar and conversation, in reading simpler Latin literature and in writing essays and themes in Latin, following models assigned to them. The study of Latin continued throughout the eight forms, but in the fifth Greek was added and during the last year most boys had a smattering of Hebrew. The modern languages were not taught in English schools, but the elder Milton saw to it that his son learned French and Italian, probably at home with private tutors. In the Latin poem addressed to his father, Milton wrote:

> when I had opened once
> The stores of Roman rhetoric . . .
> Thyself didst counsel me to add the flowers
> That Gallia boasts; those too with which the smooth
> Italian his degenerate speech adorns,
> That witnesses his mixture with the Goth.

Because of his own feeling for Italian culture, Italian was emphasized, and the young man learned the Tuscan language so well that, before he went to Italy, he was able to write Italian sonnets with a high degree of facility. Milton and his classmates must have learned at least the rudiments of mathematics, but as Donald Clark has shown in *Milton at St. Paul's School,* pp. 3-4:

In Imperial Rome and in Renaissance England all seven of the Liberal Arts were honored as the basis of a liberal education, but in both periods the mathematical arts of the quadrivium (Arithmetic, Geometry, Music, and Astronomy) were honored more than taught. The core, flesh and skin of the educational apple were comprised in the linguistic arts of the trivium (Grammar, Rhetoric, and Logic). Hence in Milton's boyhood, his father might have boasted, quite correctly, that he was giving his son a sound "trivial" education.

By the time Milton left St. Paul's for Cambridge, he had become a good Latinist, reading and speaking Latin and composing in it as readily as in English—perhaps even more readily. He had at least a fair knowledge of Greek and he knew a little Hebrew.

We must not leave this period of Milton's early life without passing reference to subtler memories Milton took with him from St. Paul's. Nearly a half-century later, reminiscences of his school days recurred in *Paradise Regained* (IV. 213-21). In the description of the child Jesus in the Temple are echoes of two lovely prayers which the boys at St. Paul's knew by heart, one supposed to have been composed by John Colet, the founder of the school, and the other—still recited by Paul's boys—by the Renaissance humanist Erasmus in an imaginary colloquy between himself and Gaspar, a schoolboy. Both prayers were addressed to Jesus "as a boy twelve years old."

One echo we should like to hear is silent. John Donne was Dean of St. Paul's Cathedral from 1621-1631. During his first four years, Milton was still one of the schoolboys. Did the young poet listen to the eloquence of the poet-preacher under which strong men were said to have fainted? We do not know. We can however be fairly certain of memories of the Cathedral in *Il Penseroso:*

> But let my due feet never fail
> To walk the studious cloister's pale,
> And love the high embowéd roof,
> With antique pillars massy proof,
> And storied windows richly dight,
> Casting a dim religious light.
>
> (ll. 155-60)

Here are the pillars and arches of St. Paul's Cathedral, the painted glass of the windows, particularly the great rose-window which the boys could see from their schoolrooms, and the cloisters familiar to generations of "Paules Pigeons" who often studied there. In the lines that follow, Milton—true son of his father—remembered the organ of the Cathedral, of which the organist during six of the years of Milton's studentship was John Tomkins, who was closely associated with Milton's father, particularly as a composer of airs for Ravenscroft's *Whole Booke of Psalmes*. His music may still echo in *Il Penseroso:*

> There let the pealing organ blow
> To the full-voiced choir below.
> In service high and anthems clear,
> As may with sweetness, through mine ear,
> Dissolve me into ecstasies,
> And bring all heaven before mine eyes.
>
> (ll. 161-66)

With these memories of the Cathedral and its music, we may consider for a moment one matter which has been deliberately omitted until now. Milton's father, although he came from a Catholic family, was a Puritan. When the Civil War broke out in England and families were often divided into passionate camps of "Royalist" against "Puritan," Milton deliberately threw himself into the Puritan camp and devoted nearly twenty years of his life to the defense of the party which had put a king to death and established a new form of government. For many years some historians read over Milton's loyalty to party into his poetry and some critics, from Samuel Johnson to T. S. Eliot, interpreted his poetry through the spectacles of their own royalist and Anglican prejudices. Milton became not only "the Puritan poet," but the "stern Puritan." Particularly here in America, we can find Milton critics reading into *Paradise Lost* the kind of "Puritanism" associated in this country with Pilgrims as stern as the rockbound coast on which they landed.

Thanks to such historians as William Haller (*The Rise of Puritanism; Liberty and Reformation in the Puritan Revolution*) and various others, we know today what a broad word "Puritan" really was. Whatever we may later learn of Milton's political convictions, we must not think of the family "Puritanism" in any sense as negativistic denial of beauty or grace in living. Later in the century, some Puritans defaced cathedrals, broke the "storied windows richly dight" and forbade music in their religious services. These were not the Miltons. The young poet attended a Church school, sheltered by a Cathedral. He loved the "service high and anthems clear" which could dissolve the hearer into ecstasy. There was no difference between the education of the young John Milton and that of any Cavalier gentleman's son except that Milton was more fortunate in his musician-father than were many of his schoolmates.

Over one of these students we must pause for a little—the closest friend Milton ever made, Charles Diodati. In the "Lament for Damon" which Milton wrote in memory of his friend who died tragically young, he said:

> Thyrsis and Damon . . . from childhood had pursued
> the same interests and were most affectionate friends
> . . . . Now Damon represents Charles Diodati, who
> through his father was descended from the Tuscan
> city of Lucca, but in all else was an Englishman—
> a youth who, while he lived, was outstanding for
> genius, learning, and every other splendid virtue.
>   (Hughes ed. p. 132)

Charles Diodati, like Milton, was fortunate in his family, which was of much greater distinction, as well as more aristocratic, than the Miltons. In Italy the family went back for several generations (Donald Dorian, *The English Diodatis*), and numbered names of some prominence in Italian history. Among the Diodatis were several members with a strong Protestant leaning who in time broke from Roman Catholic Italy and migrated to the freer air of Protestant countries. One group—distinguished in theological history—settled in Switzerland, another in England. Theodore Diodati, father of Milton's friend, was a physician of note, trained at Leyden. He established an enviable practice in England, where he was physician to many families of the aristocracy. Through the association between the two boys, the Milton family became well acquainted with various other foreigners resident in London, particularly with musicians, and Charles seems to have joined in the music at the Milton home. Charles Diodati received most of his elementary training at St. Paul's, probably entering in 1617 or 1618 and proceeding to Oxford in 1623. One year Milton's junior, he was senior to him in school and evidently the more brilliant of the two. After their paths divided, the boys wrote each other frequently. To a modern student, it seems incredible that they wrote largely in Latin, and often in Latin verse. (Two of the extant letters of Diodati to Milton are in Greek.) Diodati left St. Paul's for Trinity College, Oxford, in 1623, Milton for Christ's College, Cambridge, in 1625. The education these young "Paules Pigeons" had received so far may not seem to us a "liberal" education—almost lacking as it was in many of the subjects we emphasize today. But in Milton's case, it had already laid the basis for the kind of poet he wished to become: he was a fairly expert Latinist, reading, speaking and writing a language that was far from dead, indeed the one truly international language of educated men everywhere in Europe. He had read many Latin authors, setting himself and being set to learn and imitate their styles. He was competent in Greek, which had opened to him another great world of literature. He knew enough Hebrew to read simpler passages of the Bible in the original. He was well versed in music and he knew some French and Italian very well indeed. Thanks to his father, his St. Paul's masters, and his tutors (particularly one tutor, Thomas Young, to whom he wrote an elegy) John Milton at the age of seventeen was already very familiar with the two worlds from which he drew his poetry—Latin and Greek classics, and the Bible.

"The Lady of Christ's"

I suspect that Milton would agree that the important formative years of his education were those at St. Paul's rather than the period he spent at the University. Like Bacon and many another writer of the seventeenth century, Milton was disillusioned at Cambridge. It is interesting to see that in the one work in which he dealt professionally with the subject of education, his tractate *On Education,* written in 1644, much of the theory and practice he condemns had its counterpart at Cambridge, while the kind of academy he envisions is based in large part on St. Paul's School. From the fragmentary references in Milton's works to Cambridge, it would seem that Milton resented much in both the social and academic situation he found in the University.

The name "Paules Pigeons" had been shared by many boys. Milton's Cambridge nickname, "The Lady of Christ's" was peculiar to him. There were various reasons that the sobriquet might have been given him, the most obvious of which was his physical appearance. Milton was fair in complexion and slender in build. More ink than necessary has been spent on the trifling question—*how* fair—one modern German scholar going so far as to assert that he was an albino. The tempest in a teapot was precipitated in Milton's own time by one of Milton's mud-slinging adversaries, Alexander More, who in attacking Milton's political principles, attacked also his moral character and his physical appearance. He implied that Milton's blindness made him as ugly as Homer's fearful one-eyed Cyclops. Milton replied: (*The Second Defence of the English People*—Hughes p. 824)

> I do not believe that I was ever once noted for deformity by anyone who ever saw me, but the praise of beauty I am not anxious to obtain. . . . My face, which is said to indicate a total privation of blood, is of a complexion entirely opposite to

the pale and cadaverous; so that, though I am more than forty years old, there is scarcely anyone to whom I do not appear ten years younger than I am.

To Alexander More's taunts about Milton's puny stature, Milton replied peremptorily:

My stature certainly is not tall, but it rather approaches the middle than the diminutive. Yet what if it were diminutive, when so many men, illustrious both in peace and war, have been the same? And how can that be called diminutive which is great enough for every virtuous achievement? Nor, though very thin, was I ever deficient in courage or in strength; and I was wont constantly to exercise myself in the use of the broadsword as long as it comported with my habit and my years. Armed with this weapon, as I usually was, I should have thought myself quite a match for anyone though much stronger than myself.

When Milton became a schoolmaster for a short time, he saw to it that his boys were as well trained as he had been in both fencing and wrestling.

Milton's contemporary biographer, John Aubrey, that snapper-up of unconsidered trifles, reported: "He had Auburn hair. His complexion exceeding fair—he was so fair that they called him the Lady of Christ's College. Oval face, his eye a dark gray." On the question of Milton's stature, Aubrey, as so often, is as amusing as he is irritating: "He was scarce so tall as I am—*quaere, quot* feet I am high: *resp.* of middle stature." Portraits of Milton—three authentic, others dubious or imaginary—do not solve the problems. Aubrey said that Milton's widow preferred above the others "his picture when a Cambridge scholar, . . . for the pictures before his books are not at all like him." The picture his widow preferred shows a very oval face, large eyes and hair which might or might not have been auburn. The sitter was certainly slender and delicately made, though by no means frail.

Although his physical appearance is the obvious explanation for his nickname, there is a second possibility that will later lead us to one of Milton's early recurrent motifs—his theory of chastity. During Milton's undergraduate years, there is little question that he found much dissoluteness among his fellow students. Let us remember that St. Paul's was not a boarding school, and that Milton had always lived at home under the protection of an affectionate, cultivated, mildly Puritan family. Cambridge was his introduction to ways of living which boarding-schools boys might have encountered earlier. As we shall see, the young Milton believed that chastity was as essential for a young man as for a young woman. Many of his more sophisticated Cambridge acquaintances may well have considered him a "sissy" for this reason if for no other.

The combination of attitudes provoked by his delicate physical appearance and by his temperance is implied in Milton's direct reply to some of his classmates in his Sixth Prolusion, which, with the "Vacation Exercise" were part of the student entertainment of 1628 which Milton had been chosen to write:

> Some people have lately nicknamed me the Lady. But why do I seem to them too little of a man? I suppose because I have never had the strength to drink off a bottle like a prizefighter; or because my hand has never grown horny with holding a plough-handle; or because I was not a farm-hand at seven, and so never took a midday nap in the sun—last perhaps because I never showed my virility in the way these brothellers do. But I wish they could leave playing the ass as readily as I the woman.
>
> (Tillyard, *Milton*, p. 29)

Perhaps in his heart Milton was more proud than ashamed of his nickname, since Virgil had also been called by one that may be translated, "Miss Virginity."

If we seem to make more of an undergraduate nickname than it warrants, it is because the very characteristics that set Milton apart from one group of undergraduates are highly significant in Milton's development as a poet and in his theory of poetry. The "uncessant care" and devotion to a "thankless Muse" inevitably alienated him from many students who—as in other generations—considered the undergraduate experience primarily as a period for fun and freedom from family restraint. Milton had not only been made a student by his masters at Paul's—he was a natural student who loved study for its own sake.

The curriculum he found at Cambridge was not designed as a seed-time for poetry. "How ill does that place suit the votaries of Apollo!" Milton wrote impatiently of the University, like Shelley and many other English poets who protested against their university education. As at St. Paul's the Cambridge emphasis was primarily upon the trivium, though that alone would not have disturbed Milton, since it was basically his own. His reaction was somewhat that of his earlier contemporary, Francis Bacon, who resented the fact that the universities remained impervious to the new breath that was stirring with the "new science" which outside university walls began to replace the "old learning." In large part, Milton's protest against what he called in *Of Education* an "asinine feast of sow-thistles and brambles" agreed with Bacon's, who insisted that the chief enemies of learning were the learned men themselves, spiders, as Bacon called them, who spun cobwebs of learning out of their own substance. The course of study at Cambridge, which had remained unchanged for many years, was still dominated by scholastic philosophy. There were no "electives." The curriculum was hidebound and conservative, and many of the hurdles which marked the progress to a degree were almost the same as in the period of the University's foundation. Scholastic logic and disputation were basic requirements. During his undergraduate years, Milton must have been required to defend as many theses as Martin Luther once nailed to a church door.

A modern "composition teacher," accustomed to "drawing out" of students whatever students presumably have in them, might try the experiment of setting some of the subjects assigned at Cambridge, on which Milton's papers are extant:

Whether Day or Night is the more excellent.
On the Music of the Spheres.
In the Destruction of any Substance there can be
no Resolution into First Matter.
Learning makes men happier than does Ignorance.

On the Platonic Idea as Understood by Aristotle.

That Nature is not subject to Old Age.

Let the teacher be sure to add that each thesis must be attacked or defended in strict accordance with the rules of scholastic logic, that each must be adorned with all the allusions and learning gained through an expensive preparatory and University education. And last—but by no means least—let him make abundantly clear that all these themes must be mellifluously expressed in Latin—usually in Latin verse. O tempora, O mores.

An "asinine feast of sow-thistles and brambles," this may seem to modern students. But if, as we incline to believe, the academic exercise, "Whether Day or Night is the more excellent" caused Milton to write *L'Allegro* and *Il Penseroso,* the exercise was not set in vain, and the strenuous training in logical disputation left its mark upon Milton, as upon many seventeenth-century writers. Debate is an integral characteristic of his poetry; we find it in the speeches between the Elder and Younger Brother and between the Lady and Comus; in the Council Scene in Hell in Book II of *Paradise Lost;* in Samson and his chorus of "Job's Comforters," in Samson and Delilah, Samson and Harapha. *Paradise Regained* is an extended debate between Christ and Satan. Long trained in upholding a given side of an argument, whether or not it was sympathetic to him, Milton could always give the "opposition" excellent speeches. The Lady wins the debate—but Comus' are the more beautiful and persuasive lines, as are Delilah's in her debate with Samson. Milton was as impatient as Bacon of scholastic logic, but Belilal's speech in the Council Scene and Adam's masterly soliloquy in Book X of *Paradise Lost* would have been far less brilliant without Milton's knowledge of such logic. The long study of rhetoric and oratory at both St. Paul's School and Christ's College is shown persistently in all Milton's major works. *Areopagitica* is the greatest classical oration in the English language, as great as any written by Isocrates, who was Milton's model. All the speeches in the Council Scene, I suspect, had their classical models in the historians or the rhetoricians, as did the oratory by which the dread commander Satan aroused and inspired his fallen troops. The true poet can transform even scholastic logic to pure gold.

Since Christ's was a small college, numbering about two hundred students—not much larger than St. Paul's School—Milton must have made many acquaintances. Of his relationship with Edward King, in whose memory he wrote *Lycidas,* we shall speak later. But he made no such intimate friend as Charles Diodati, with whom he continued to correspond. One of those letters—this one in verse—tells of an episode of which we might not otherwise be aware. In 1626, during his second year, Milton was "rusticated" (we would say "suspended") from the University for a short time. Because Milton mentioned to Diodati "the threats of a stern master," some biographers have attributed the rustication to Milton's revolt from the tutor to whom he had been assigned, William Chappell, and have read into it various differences between tutor and student in academic or religious ideas. On the other hand, Milton may merely have been guilty of some minor infraction of the University regulations which had been unchanged for so many years that they were as antiquated as the almost medieval curriculum. As one reads accounts of them, one does not wonder that Milton and other students were "sent down" but rather that any of them ever managed to remain in residence. It is in this Latin verse-epistle to Diodati that Milton wrote impatiently, "How ill that place suits the votaries of Apollo." With the characteristic bravado of youth, Milton insists that he has no regret at being banished from the reedy Cam and the "naked fields" nor is he homesick for his "forbidden rooms." Instead of distasteful exercises, he is free "to give my leisure up to the placid Muse; and books, which are my life, have me all to themselves."

From his rustication Milton returned to follow the prescribed curriculum for several years. No matter how he rebelled—kicking against the pricks is implied in various of his writings—he apparently performed all the necessary tasks and jumped the proper hurdles successfully, since he proceeded B.A. in March 1629 and M.A. in July 1632. During these seven years he was studying, reading, and writing exercises assigned by tutors and others which he set himself. In his sonnet for his twenty-third birthday not long before he took the Master's degree, Milton indicated discouragement that he had accomplished so little:

How soon hath Time, the subtle thief of youth,
Stolen on his wing my three and twentieth year!
My hasting days fly on with full career,
But my late spring no bud or blossom show'th.

Compared with Keats or Shelley at the same age, Milton had indeed produced little and published nothing except the lines on Shakespeare that appeared in the Second folio of 1632. But in addition to numerous exercises in Latin prose or verse that he wrote to order, Milton had written various exercises of his own—Latin elegies on the deaths of the Bishop of Winchester, on the Bishop of Ely, on a Vice Chancellor, in lighter mood two poems on the death of Hobson, the University carrier, and in more personal vein, "On the Death of a Fair Infant," lines occasioned by the death of his niece, daughter of his sister Anne. Far more important than these was "On the Morning of Christ's Nativity," composed at Christmastime in 1629, which, if not entirely great, has greatness in it. If we follow Professor Tillyard and transpose the perfection of *L'Allegro* and *Il Penseroso* from Horton to Cambridge, we must feel that at the age of twenty-four John Milton need have made no apology for his poetic performance.

The Horton Period

In July 1632 Milton received his Master's degree and returned to his father's home though not to the house in Bread Street where he had been born. The elder Milton, now nearly seventy, retired from his profession as scrivener, had purchased or leased a house in the country at Horton, seventeen miles due west from London. Horton was and remains a small village. In Milton's time it numbered only about three hundred persons. It was of somewhat more importance in those days, since it was on a main post road through which nearly a hundred coaches passed daily. Watered by tributaries of the Colne river, it was rich and fertile country, yet only two hours' ride from London. Of the buildings Milton knew, only the church is now standing, a church old even when Milton was young, since it dates back to at least the thirteenth century. In Horton the poet settled with his mother and father for a placid five years of study, learning to be a poet.

Probably the transition from Cambridge to Horton was not quite as simple as it seems. The elder Milton was an indulgent father, but even he must have been startled when his elder son, after seven years at the University, indicated no intention either of entering a profession or of making his own living. The younger son Christopher had proved much more practical. He had gone up to Cambridge during the last two years of his elder brother's residence, but left, announcing that he intended to study law; he was admitted to the Inner Temple in the autumn of 1631 at the age of sixteen. John—seven years older and with two degrees—had no plans except to learn to be a poet. The family seemed to have taken for granted that he would take holy orders, the profession for which his long years of study particularly qualified him. But Milton had definitely decided against the Church. Years later in *The Reason of Church Government,* he wrote:

> The church, to whose service by the intention of my parents and friends I was destined of a child, and in mine own resolutions: till coming to some maturity of years and perceiving what tyranny had invaded the church, that he who would take orders must subscribe slave and take an oath withal, which, unless he took it with a conscience that would retch, he must either straight perjure or split his faith; I thought it better to prefer a blameless silence before the sacred office of speaking, bought and begun with servitude and foreswearing.

The law Milton, dismissed as definitely as the Church. We do not know the date of the poem "Ad Patrem" to which two references have been made. Like E. M. W. Tillyard (*Milton,* p. 384) I should put it stylistically a little later, but the subject-matter fits well enough into this particular period. In deft Latin, Milton pays high tribute to his father as a fellow-artist, and as a parent who has devoted himself to the education of his son. Then as if replying to the natural impatience of a father who was also a practical man of affairs, Milton said:

> thou never bad'st me tread
> The beaten path, and broad, that leads right on
> To opulence, nor didst condemn thy son
> To the insipid clamours of the bar,
> To laws voluminous and ill observed;
> But wishing to enrich me more, to fill
> My mind with treasure, led'st me far away
> From city din to deep retreats, to banks
> And streams Aonian, and, with free consent,
> Didst place me happy at Apollo's side. . . .

Whether or not this poem played any part in the decision, altercation was over and Milton settled down for five leisurely years at Horton. Much later he described this period in his life:

On my father's estate, where he had determined to pass the remainder of his days, I enjoyed an interval of uninterrupted leisure, which I entirely devoted to the perusal of Greek and Latin authors; though I occasionally visited the metropolis, either for the sake of purchasing books, or of learning something new in mathematics or in music, in which I, at the time, found a source of pleasure and amusement. In this manner I spent five years till my mother's death.

During this period he came of age as a poet. If *L'Allegro* and *Il Penseroso* were not written at the end of his Cambridge career, they were composed early in the Horton period, followed by *Arcades,* then by *Comus* and finally *Lycidas.*

In 1637, Sarah Milton died. The plain stone in the chancel of the Horton church bears the inscription, "Here lyeth the body of Sara Milton, the wife of John Milton, who died the 3rd of April, 1637." No details about her death have come down to us, although we know that the plague was abroad in England in 1636 and 1637 and that it had spread to Horton. During the following August occurred two other deaths, important in the history of English literature for different reasons. On August 6, Ben Jonson died at the age of sixty-five. The day after he was buried in Westminster Abbey, a vessel went down in the Irish Channel, carrying to death nearly all on board, among them Edward King. King had entered Christ's College within a year of Milton, like him had proceeded to the M.A. and, after Milton left, had remained as fellow and tutor. Unlike Milton, he had taken holy orders intending to enter the ministry. In November, when Milton learned that a volume of poems was being planned "in token of love and remembrance by his sorrowing friends," he wrote an elegy which he dated November 1637. The poem we call *Lycidas* (Milton did not use the title in the first edition) appeared in the memorial volume, published a month or two later. The poems were in Greek, Latin and English. Milton's was the last of the poems, whether by chance or because the editors realized that it was the artistic climax of the volume.

The epilogue of the poem—signed simply "J.M."—concluded with the line, "Tomorrow to fresh woods and pastures new." As Milton wrote the words they were merely the conventional conclusion of a pastoral elegy. We like to find a double meaning, for Milton was about to set out on a journey to Italy—and, he hoped, Greece—again financed by his indulgent father. We might consider the Italian journey the climax to long years of study and leisure, which began with tutors and St. Paul's School. But since it ended more abruptly than Milton had anticipated, with the death of Charles Diodati and rumblings of an incipient Civil War in England, we shall consider it, not as the end of "The Education of a Poet" but as the beginning of "The Training of a Statesman."

Juvenilia

Paraphrases of the Psalms

"This and the following Psalms were done by the Author at fifteen years old," Milton noted when he included paraphrases of Psalms 114 and 136 in his *Poems* of 1645. To most modern readers such exercises seem barren and sterile—if not works of supererogation. Why should any poet, young or old, have felt that he could improve upon the Psalms of David, great poetry in the original and in the King James' translation? Certainly the fifteen-year-old Milton did not improve either version. But whatever they may be as literature, paraphrases of psalms are important historically. The fact that the earliest poems Milton kept and published were such paraphrases would indicate at once, if we did not already know it, that he came from a Protestant family.

"The singing of the Psalms of David in metre," wrote William Allan Neilson ("The Scottish Psalter," in *The Bible and its Literary Associations,* ed. Margaret B. Crook, p. 333.), "is singularly bound up with the history of Protestantism. Not only was this practice a factor in the spread of the Reformation, but in the more than three-and-a-half centuries which have since elapsed, the rise and fall of psalm singing have been a sort of thermometer measuring the rise and fall of Puritan zeal."

The custom of psalm paraphrase originated very early in Protestant sects among the followers of Wycliffe and Lollard in the fourteenth century. Under Queen Elizabeth, the singing of psalms in parish churches was permitted within certain limits. From the middle of the sixteenth century the practice was common in such homes as the Miltons'. Indeed, there was a specific reason that young John Milton would have tried his hand at paraphrase just when he did. About 1621 the elder John Milton had contributed three settings for paraphrases to a volume that became standard for many years, the *Whole Book of Psalms,* compiled by Thomas Ravenscroft, music-master at Christ's Hospital, and a close associate of the elder Milton. The Ravenscroft volume was a sequel to one that had long been standard in England, settings of the Psalms by Thomas Steinhold and John Hopkins, which had gone through many editions since its publication in the sixteenth century. "During what one may term the Golden Age of psalm singing," writes Ernest Brennecke (*John Milton the Elder and his Music,* p. 99), "almost every English composer of note tried his hand at harmonizing these tunes. The result is a body of hundreds of little compositions, fascinating to hear today and extremely valuable in the history of the development of harmony."

Psalm paraphrase never achieved an important place in the history of literature, even though Wyatt, Surrey and other poets had tried it. As the seventeenth-century Thomas Fuller said, such versifiers were "men whose piety was better than their poetry, and they had drunk more of Jordan than of Helicon. Sometimes they made the Maker of the tongue speak little better than barbarism, and have in many verses such poor rhyme that two hammers on a smith's anvil would have made better music." (Quoted, Neilson, p. 335.)

Milton's youthful verses are no better and no worse than the majority produced by paraphrasers. Did his father set either of them to music? one wonders. He might have set Psalm 136, the metre and refrain of which would lend itself to music:

Let us with a gladsome mind,
Praise the Lord, for he is kind,

> For his mercies eye endure,
> Ever faithful, ever sure.

He could hardly have set the other, Psalm 114, since as Professor Brennecke points out, the metre is not adapted to any known music of the time:

> When the blest seed of Terah's faithful son,
> After long toil their liberty had won,

Milton himself surpassed these early efforts in the mature paraphrases of Psalms 80-88, written in one of the most singable metres familiar in the anthology to which his father had contributed. Professor Brennecke suggests that Milton may have written them at this particular time "as a memorial act of filial reverence, for it took place almost exactly on the first anniversary of the scrivener's death." But these early paraphrases, like all Milton's juvenilia, were exercises set by the young poet to himself, and all of them were to come to fruition in his later minor or in his major poems. The greatest paraphrases of the Psalms of David ever written are not in any anthology: they are embodied in the texture of *Paradise Lost*.

If I have paid more attention to these first exercises than their literary importance warrants, it is less because they are an introduction to the poet than that they serve to remind us of the happy youth Milton spent with a family that often sang together and invited friends to sing with them. President Neilson, remembering his own Scottish youth in a family not very different from Milton's, may say the final word on this matter (pp. 337-340): "To attempt literary criticism of these artless verses is impossible to anyone who learned them before the service of praise was diluted with 'human hymns' or the 'kist of whistles' was permitted to drown the failures of the quavering voices that strove vaguely if pathetically to scale heights beyond their reach. To such a one these verses and the melodies to which they have so long been sung bring back memories and emotions that render impossible an aesthetic judgment. . . . Generation after generation the rhymes and rhythms, often awkward but endeared by long association, have imprinted themselves on the ear and memory of every Presbyterian Scot. . . . They have been sung on thousands of Saturday nights like the cotter's described by Burns."

On the Death of a Fair Infant

During his first year at Cambridge, Milton wrote at least five elegies. The other four in Latin were probably exercises set by tutors, since they memorialized the deaths of public figures: The Beadle and the Vice Chancellor of Cambridge, Lancelot Andrewes, Bishop of Winchester, Nicholas Felton, Bishop of Ely. But the epitaph on the death of a child was not a task set by a master. The "fair infant" was Milton's niece, Anne, daughter of his older sister Anne, who had died ten days after her second birthday. The rate of infant mortality was so high in the seventeenth century that few families escaped the death of a child. Milton's parents had lost their first before John's birth. John was probably too young to have remembered his sister Sarah, who lived less than a year, though he must have remembered Tabitha, who died in her third year when he was eight. To our ears, Milton's epitaph, charged as it is with mythological allusions, and pagan rather than Christian except in three stanzas, seems too weighty a craft on which to send the soul of a baby even across the Styx. There was good authority among classical poets Milton knew for letting earth rest gently upon the fragile dust beneath, a mood reflected by Ben Jonson in his lines on his dead daughter:

This grave partakes the fleshly birth
Which cover lightly, gentle earth.

The ceremonious formality of the over-elaborate mythology is lightened somewhat by the conceit Milton employs in the first four stanzas: the little flower was so lovely that Winter was tempted to kiss her rosy cheek, a conceit which might have been charming if the young versifier had not felt it necessary to develop it at too much length through the legends of Aquilo and Orythia, Apollo and Hyacinth—myths, let us remember, more immediately familiar to his contemporaries than to us. But Milton was still only a young student, bred in an academic tradition that elegies should be formal, impersonal and learned. He has not yet the emotional maturity nor the sureness of technique that will lead him to adapt his materials more perfectly to his subject. Milton must have felt its lack of success, since it is the only one of the extant English poems he did not include in the *Poems* of 1645.

We who read it with critical hindsight may find in it some anticipations of the more familiar Minor Poems. Milton was experimenting with English metres in which he was probably still much less adept than in Latin verse. He used the stanzaic form which he will better employ in the introductory stanzas of *On The Morning of Christ's Nativity,* rhyme royal, a seven-line ab, ab, bcc, iambic pentameter with a final alexandrine. Although the poem belongs officially to the *genre* of funerary elegies, it approaches the ode that Milton begins to establish in the *Nativity Ode.* There are vague anticipations of *Lycidas* in the young poet's attempt to rise from paganism to Christianity, from mortality to immortality. Like a musician, the young poet is practicing, exercising his fingers and his voice to increase both his facility and his control. He is still a student, still an amateur. But all this practice was important in the development of the craft and art of a great poet.

At a Vacation Exercise

The general background for these lines, delivered at Cambridge at the end of Easter Term 1628, when Milton was nineteen, has been suggested in the biographical account of young Milton. Modern college students, particularly those who have attended residential colleges, can understand the occasion, even if the language sounds strange to them. Often in our colleges there is an occasion on which the students are given, or give themselves, "liberty hall," to put on student plays or skits, satirizing the curriculum, particularly the "required courses." The end of Easter Term, marking the beginning of the Long Vacation, was such an occasion at Cambridge.

As presented that afternoon or evening, the "Vacation Exercise" was in three parts. The first was Milton's Sixth Prolusion, on the subject, "Sportive exercises on occasion are not inconsistent with philosophical studies," Then followed the English verses, and a final section which has been lost. Much of the fun of the occasion lay in the Latin portions in which the other students would have recognized puns and classical tags and general parody on various styles of rhetoric which they had been forced to imitate. Fellow-students would have chortled, too, over the last section of the English verses, a "spoof" in pantomime on their "required courses." Here the Aristotelian categories are personified, with Ens, "Father of the Predicaments" and his ten sons. All these escape us, as our own collegiate satires will escape our descendants three centuries from now. But we can understand the address to his "native language," which must have surprised the dons and students of Cambridge, since it is a much more personal expression than they would have expected to hear.

"Here I salute thee," Milton addresses the English language. Publicly he professes that in time he hopes to use that language in the service of poetry. He distinguishes carefully among kinds of poetry in which it will be used:

> Not those new-fangled toys and trimming slight
> Which takes our late fantastics with delight.

We must be careful not to read into "our late fantastics"—as some earlier critics did—such styles as "Euphuism" or "metaphysical poetry." "Euphuism" was a movement in prose style, and Milton is speaking specifically of poetry. And the "metaphysicals"—

not yet so called—were far from "late." They were very active at the time Milton wrote. Probably Milton's reference was specific, to some group of Cambridge students who had made themselves famous or infamous by a style peculiarly their own.

Milton wishes to use the "richest robes" of the English language for some "graver subject." As I have suggested, the themes are those of the epic: above the "wheeling poles," at the door of the classical Heaven on Olympus, we find the gods before the throne of Jupiter, listening to the music of Apollo. Descending from Olympus, we pause momentarily—as we shall in *Comus*—over another of the realms into which mythology divided the universe, Neptune's seas and waters, the seas sailed by "long-tried Odysseus." As in the classical epic, we descend too, from gods to heroes, and recognize the central scene in the *Odyssey* in which Odysseus heard his own story sung by the minstrel Demodocus, at the palace of Alcinous. Here is Milton's first public confession of faith that he has been "called" to prepare himself for writing the "highest" and "gravest" of all the kinds of poetry—the epic.

On the University Carrier

These two poems are both "occasional" and "light" verse. Milton was only one of many students who contributed lines on the death of a "campus character." Thomas Hobson had been the "University carrier," who drove the weekly coach between Cambridge and London for sixty-seven years, from 1564 until almost the day of his death, January 1, 1631. He had carried the post and he had carried the young gentlemen—not only Milton and his fellow-students but in some cases their fathers and their grandfathers. Always on hand for generations, he must have seemed indeed "an immortal carrier." Ironically, it seemed he had died because he had been forced to take a vacation, forbidden to drive to London where the plague was raging.

Many who would never have heard of the Cambridge carrier know his name which has passed into usage in the phrase "Hobson's choice." In addition to driving the coach, Hobson kept the local livery stable, and when young or old came to hire horses, he made each comer take the horse nearest the door—hack or thoroughbred—so that "Hobson's choice" is no choice at all. That the phrase had wide currency throughout the seventeenth century is shown by the fact that Steele devoted part of *Spectator* 509 to Hobson and the phrase. It is customary to say that in the "Carrier" poems, Milton was trying his hand at "metaphysical" verse. We mean little more than that Milton was using "wit" here in a sense different from that we usually find in him. Like his contemporaries —metaphysical and other—Milton frequently puns on serious subjects, and plays with various meanings of words. The "wit" in the Hobson poems is far from subtle; it is intentionally obvious. Milton and other students used the kind of wit Hobson himself could have understood and appreciated. The rhymes, too, are simple, a large majority monosyllabic. The puns and paradoxes could readily have been appreciated by the probably unlettered carrier: "While he might still jog on and keep his trot"; "nor would with ale be quenched"; "If I may not carry, sure I'll ne'er be fetched." Even the academic puns are on a simple level: "Too long vacation hastened on his term."

The first poem is more successful than the second, because Milton builds it around a simple basic figure: Death, with whom Hobson had sparred for many years (driving the London coach was not without perils in that time) had finally met up with him, but the change would have seemed imperceptible to the old traveler. Not infrequently during his life, when his "girth" (saddle girth) had broken, or his coach had been mired, Hobson had been forced to spend the night at a roadside inn. This time Death in the form of an inn-servant, had showed him a room, taken off his boots, and put out the light. To all intents, "Hobson has supped and newly gone to bed."

On Shakespeare

It seems peculiarly fitting that the first poem Milton ever pub-
lished should have been his tribute to Shakespeare. The lines ap-
peared in the Second Folio of Shakespeare's works in 1632—how
and why we do not know. Milton was completely unknown as a
poet and could hardly have been solicited to write them. Probably
he contributed them, in the hope they would be selected for pub-
lication. Whatever the reason, this little poem has become the
most familiar of all the dedicatory verses in the Second Folio, hold-
ing a place in literary history only a little lower than the most
memorable contribution in the First Folio, Ben Jonson's "To the
Memory of my Beloved, the Author, Mr. William Shakespeare."
In form this is an epigram in heroic couplets. Milton's basic figure
had also been used by Jonson: "Thou art a monument without a
tomb," but Milton did not necessarily borrow it from Jonson. Both
were using one of the most familiar commonplaces of literary trib-
ute, never more succinctly phrased than by Horace: "Exegi monu-
mentum aere perennius" ("I have built a monument more lasting
than bronze"). Most often used as tribute to an author the phrase
was equally fitting for an artist, sculptor or architect, as in the
epitaph of Sir Christopher Wren in St. Paul's Cathedral, which he
had rebuilt after the Great Fire, as he had rebuilt so much of Lon-
don: "If you seek my monument, look about you."

Shakespeare, says Milton, needs no monument of stone, no pyra-
mid, to preserve his "reliques." His works are his monument. The
sepulchre he had raised for himself so transcends any of marble
that we might raise for him "that kings for such a tomb would wish
to die."

Milton speaks of Shakespeare as a poet by "nature" whose "easy
numbers flow" "to the shame of slow-endeavoring art." Such was
the almost unanimous opinion of the seventeenth century, con-

tinuing well down into the eighteenth. Shakespeare was a poet by "nature," Jonson a "learned" poet, and a poet by "art." Jonson had gone further than most of his contemporaries when he concluded his dedicatory poem with the lines beginning,

Yet must I not give Nature all; thy Art
My gentle Shakespeare, must enjoy a part.

In *L'Allegro,* too, Milton's passing tribute is to "sweetest Shakespeare, Fancy's child," who warbles his native woodnotes wild. Here he is obviously thinking of the romantic comedies and of Jonson's "learned sock." But we shall find that Milton was much more profoundly moved by Shakespeare than perhaps even he knew. Again and again in *Paradise Lost* Shakespearean lines echo in his ears and spring to his lips in paraphrase. And in spite of his tribute to the romances, the lines he paraphrased were from tragedies, by which he had been deeply moved.

Early Odes

It has become customary to call *On the Morning of Christ's Nativity* the *Nativity Ode,* although that was not the title Milton used. Different as it is from most of its classical and English predecessors, I think Milton was consciously writing an ode in this case, and—more than that—that the group of youthful poems that follow for some time are all experiments in the ode tradition. So I shall interpret them. It is interesting to know that shortly before he wrote *On the Morning of Christ's Nativity,* Milton had bought a copy of Pindar. The volume, now in the Harvard Library, is closely annotated in Milton's hand. (D. M. Robertson, *Pindar: A Poet of Eternal Ideas,* pp. 26 ff.)

The term "ode" is a broad one with a long history. (An excellent treatment of its background and development in this period is Carol Maddison, *Apollo and the Nine: A History of the Ode*). Literally the Greek verb from which it is derived meant "to sing," so that the term "ode," as used by Renaissance poets, was not necessarily more specific than the Latin "carmina" (from Latin "to sing"), which it gradually displaced. Even among classical writers, the ode had taken very different forms in the hands of its chief practitioners. Pindar was the father of them all, Anacreon in Greece and Horace among the Romans, his most distinguished sons. The greatest body of Pindar's works did not survive. Of the ten categories which he is reported to have used, ranging from hymns and threnodies to drinking songs, and songs for processions of maidens, only one group—songs for victories in great games—was rediscovered in the Renaissance. "Pindaric" implied to Milton and his contemporaries, in addition to other qualities, lofty choral poetry, with a formal elaborate structure, dividing itself into the three main parts of strophe, antistrophe, and epode. Later in Milton's century Cowley attempted to imitate the structure in his *Pindarique Odes,* much more popular in his time than in ours. More familiar to most students is Ben Jonson's adaptation in "To the Immortal Memory and Friendship of that Noble Pair, Sir Lucius Cary and Sir H. Morison." Here Jonson uses the tripartite division with another vocabulary: "The Turn, The Counter-turn, The Stand." Dryden's "Alexander's Feast" is in many ways the most "Pindaric" of our English odes in its exalted and stately moods and to some extent in its elaborate formal structure. Milton is not writing a Pindaric Ode in "On the Morning of Christ's Nativity," though I think he adapted the form in some of the shorter poems.

The odes of Anacreon are so different from those of the Pindar we know that it seems almost impossible for one *genre* to include both. Probably Anacreon was following some aspects of the Pindar we have lost, Simple soft songs in theme, structure and style, intended for one voice, not for chorus, their themes are youth, wine and women, roses, dancing—basically "carpe diem." But "Anacreon," as he was known to the Renaissance, included many songs Anacreon had not written, covering poets of nearly one thousand years. He and his imitators wrote in the soft Ionian mode, not in the Doric as Pindar had done. The usual Anacreontic was a short song in simple meter, and while some followers made it longer and even strophic, it bears no relation in theme, structure or mood to the *Nativity Ode*.

If Milton was writing an ode, it was Horatian rather than Pindaric or Anacreontic. Horace had not intended his odes to be sung, either by chorus or solo voice, though he did intend them to be read aloud. Horace's forms—he had many—are not stately orchestral Pindarics. Many of his odes are in quatrains, some in couplets. Pindar was poet and prophet; Horace was an ethical teacher. His lessons are essentially simple, not themes of lofty heroism, but the need of virtues necessary in everyday life: responsibility, self-control, moderation, decorum. His contribution to the history of the ode lay less in structure and style than in the ethical lesson he inculcated in it. More Horatian than Pindaric or Anacreontic, Milton in *On the Morning of Christ's Nativity* establishes a form that is peculiarly his own and peculiarly English —a form which was to be more influential in England than any other.

On the Morning of Christ's Nativity

On his twenty-first birthday, December 9, 1629, Milton came of age legally. On Christmas Day of that year he came of age poetically. All the earlier juvenilia we have glanced at—as well as many Latin poems that have not been mentioned—were exercises. *On the Morning of Christ's Nativity* may still have been exercise and practice to the young poet, but unlike the earlier verses, it is poetry in which if not full perfection, there is greatness. Milton has told us—or rather he told Charles Diodati—when and how he wrote the poem. Diodati was spending the Christmas season in the country, evidently among friends to whom Christmas was more "holiday" than "holy day." He had written Milton describing the festivities which included a great deal of wining and dining. That the Puritan Miltons spent Christmas differently, we can tell from Milton's first amusing sentence in his Sixth Elegy: "On an empty stomach I send you a wish for the good health of which you, with a full one, may perhaps feel the lack." He continues "How well you report the splendid feasts and the hilarious December—the festivals that do honor to the heaven-forsaking God—the sports and pleasures of winter in the country and the French vintages quaffed beside merry fires."

Diodati seems to have apologized in his letter that festivity had not proved compatible with devotion to the Muse. Milton replied: "But why do you complain that poetry is a fugitive from wine and feasting? Song loves Bacchus and Bacchus loves song." Ovid, he reminds his friend, wrote his worst verse when he was living in banishment among men who had no banquets and no wine. Classically trained as they were, both young men knew that there had been two main traditions in ancient poetry, one long associated with eating, drinking and making the most of time. "For such poets," says Milton, "grand banquets are permitted, and frequent potations of wine."

But Milton had tasted of another dispensation and was following another poetic tradition. Here, as in the "Vacation Exercise" he implies his "calling" to the high task of epic poetry to which in time he hopes to aspire: "But he whose theme is wars and Heaven under Jupiter in his prime, and pious heroes and chieftains half divine, and he who sings now of the sacred counsels of the gods on high, and now of the infernal realms where the fierce dog howls, let him live sparingly like the Samian teacher Pythagoras and let herbs furnish his innocent diet. Let the purest water stand beside him in a bowl of beech and let him drink sober draughts from the pure spring."

In the lines that follow Milton implies one aspect of his poetic creed which becomes increasingly important as his theory of poetry develops: that there is an important relationship between the life and character of the poet: "Beyond this, his youth must be innocent of crime and chaste, his conduct irreproachable and his hands stainless. His character should be like yours, O Priest, when glorious with sacred vestments and lustral water, you arise to go into the presence of the angry deities." The phrase, "his youth must be chaste," takes us back to that nickname, "The Lady of Christ's" but let us leave that problem until we come to *Comus.* The two sentences involve the conception of the poet-priest and the poet-prophet, which lies behind Milton's major poetry. To be sure, all that he is saying here is inherited tradition, in no way original with Milton. Some critics indeed feel that the Sixth Elegy is only another rhetorical debate, like the Prolusions, another intellectual skirmish with Diodati. This may indeed be Il Penseroso replying to L'Allegro Diodati. Yet in spite of the lightness of tone of the opening lines, we should remember that Milton was writing on Christmas Day—a holy day—and that he had just finished *On the Morning of Christ's Nativity.* I think we may take this section of the Sixth Elegy as seriously as Milton intended it to be taken by Diodati. Two weeks after his twenty-first birthday—a time of resolutions in many young lives—Milton was vowing that he would be a "dedicated spirit."

In the last lines of the Elegy he tells Diodati about the poem he has just written: "I am singing the heaven-descended King, the bringer of peace, and the blessed times promised in the sacred books—the infant cries of our God and his stabling under a mean roof, . . . I am singing the starry sky and the hosts that sang high in air, and the gods that were suddenly destroyed in their own shrines." This poem, Milton says, came to him with the first dawn of Christmas Day. It is his "birthday gift to Christ."

The poem begins with a four-stanza introduction in rhyme royal, the metre Milton had used in his epitaph on his niece. As usual in the odic tradition, the poet announces his theme and the occasion for which he is writing. This is the birthday of the Christ Child, prophesied, so Christians believed, by the "holy Sages" of the Old Testament who had foretold the coming of the Messiah. On this day Jesus was born of "wedded Maid and Virgin Mother." In the phrase we find two figures of speech of which Milton was fond, particularly in youth. The first is *chiasmus,* a charming figure that has almost disappeared from modern style. The word, from the Greek letter Chi, corresponding to our X, implies "crossing." In Milton's figure we see that the two adjectives are "crossed" with the two nouns they modify. We should expect, "Virgin Maid" and "wedded Mother." The crossing results in the second figure, *oxymoron,* a form of paradox, on the surface a contradiction, basically true. The coming of Christ to earth heralds, to the Christian, the Redemption and the Atonement. By the sacrifice of Christ, man will ultimately be saved, released from his "deadly forfeit," the penalty of death incurred by Adam and Eve for mankind. Notice the word "peace" which concludes the first stanza, and watch the way in which Milton will use both the word and the idea of peace, as part of the structure of the "Hymn."

The second stanza, with its blazing light, looks forward unconsciously to *Paradise Lost.* Always to Milton—as to many another poet—God the Father and God the Son are symbols of light. Like other Renaissance poets Milton could play upon "Sun" and "Son" with utmost reverence. Christ has temporarily laid aside his glory, to come to earth and live the life of a man among men. Notice the contrast in the last two lines of the stanza between "everlasting day" and "darksome house of mortal clay," and watch Milton's use of darkness and light throughout the poem in something the way we shall find in *L'Allegro* and *Il Penseroso.*

In the last two stanzas of the introduction, the youthful poet charmingly and modestly makes his *apologia* for his ode. All Christians remember that on the occasion of Christ's birth, the "star-led wizards"—wise men or Magi—came bringing gifts (curiously enough, the Magi and their gifts do not appear in the most familiar and most beautiful account of the Nativity, that in the Gospel according to St. Luke, though they are mentioned by Matthew). A poem by an unknown young poet can bear no comparison with the gold and frankincense and myrrh of the Magi. Milton asks only that he present his poem before they arrive. All this is implied in the fourth stanza, in the phrase, "O run, prevent them with thy humble ode" Milton uses the word *prevent* not in its later sense of "stop" or hinder," but in its Latin sense, "prae venire": to "arrive first or before."

The main part of the poem Milton called the "Hymn," not necessarily implying that it is to be set to music, although it might be more readily set than the introduction. The stanzaic form here was evidently Milton's own invention, aa 3, b 5, cc 3, b 5, d 4, d 6, the last line an alexandrine. Remembering the word "peace" in the introduction, we can see that Milton stresses both word and idea in the first half of the "Hymn," through Stanza XV. The word itself is used in lines 46 and 61. According to old tradition, peace temporarily descended upon the whole world at the time of the birth of Christ: (Stanzas III and IV)

No war or battle's sound
Was heard the world around.

Spear, shield and chariot, symbols of war, temporarily ceased their work of destruction, and "kings sat still with *awful* eye"—that word so reverent in Milton's day, so debased in ours. Over that night in what might have been "winter wild" was the peace of the winter solstice, with hushed winds, seas so still that halcyon birds brooded on the waves. The simple shepherds sat chatting in a row —all things in Nature and among men were as if the Golden Age had returned to earth.

The "Hymn" begins before dawn and ends in early evening when the mother lays her child to sleep. In the first half we are conscious of light. Like Joshua, Milton seems to bid the sun stand still as a "greater Sun" appears. We see the stars, "bending one way their precious influence," in the happiest of all possible astrological conjunctions. As the shepherds watch their flocks by night, we behold a "globe of circular light," far more glorious than the stars, within which we see the "glittering ranks" of Cherubim and Seraphim, and we hear the angelic chorus, "Glory to God in the highest."

The "Hymn" begins with quietness. We are not conscious of sound until Stanza VIII, and then only of a "quiet" sound, the chatting of the shepherds. With them we hear music, such harmony as was heard only once before, "when the morning stars sang together and all the sons of God shouted for joy." (Stanza XII, Job 38, 6-7). We hear the great harmony of the angels, mingling with the music of the spheres. Angelic voices, notes of the planets, strings, organ unite as the "ninefold harmony" of the spheres makes up full concord to the angelic symphony. As in *Lycidas,* Christian and pagan are welded into a whole that is both, yet neither. Like the pagans we welcome the "mighty Pan" with the classical music of the spheres; like the Christians, we welcome Christ with the angelic harmony. In Stanza XIII, our ears may catch yet another echo in the "silver chimes"—Christmas bells ringing from the church steeple most familiar to each of us. During the first half of the poem we linger in a world of peace and music that marked the Age of Gold and momentarily returned to earth at the birth of Christ.

The second part of the "Hymn" is in sharp contrast to the first:

But wisest Fate says No,
This must not yet be so.

(ll. 149-50)

Stanza XVI serves as transition between the two main sections of the "Hymn." In contrast to the peaceful night of the nativity, with its stars and shepherds and angels, we are in a world rather like that of the "first Hell" of *Paradise Lost,* a world of darkness, made only darker by lurid light of smouldering fire. Smoke and earthquake combine in the terror of the Last Judgment. In place of music and harmony, our ears are assailed by dissonance and cacophony: "such a horrid clang," "hideous hum," "hollow shriek," "a voice of weeping heard and loud lament," "cymbals' ring," "lowings loud"—these are only some among the many sounds. As momentarily there was peace on earth when the Christ Child came, so momentarily the false gods were powerless. But both situations were only temporary. The babe who lies in "smiling infancy" must die on the Cross, before any may be saved at the Last Judgment when many shall be destroyed. The power of evil will continue in the world.

Interested in angelology and demonology, Milton had read widely in both before he wrote the great "catalogue" of fallen angels who became devils, which we shall find in Book I of *Paradise Lost*. Even the young Milton of the *Nativity Ode* knew a great deal about the subject, as we find when he calls a little "catalogue" of false gods and false prophets. In part Milton was fascinated by the old lore that he loved to repeat; in part—as we shall see in *Paradise Lost*—he was charmed by exotic names, Biblical, classical, geographical, which he liked to roll over on his tongue. We do not see the gods so much as we hear their names: Greek oracles, Roman Lares, Lemures and Flamens, Phoenician "Peor and Baalim,"— epithets of the sun-god Baal—Osiris, worshiped in Egypt in the shape of Apis, the sacred bull. With two of the false gods we shall later become more familiar: "sullen Moloch," a primitive deity of the Ammonites, worshiped with human sacrifice, particularly of children, will become an important character in *Paradise Lost*. "That twice-battered god of Palestine" (line 199) seems to have had a curious fascination for Milton, to whom he becomes a minor motif. In I Samuel V 1-5 we are told that when the Philistines brought the ark of Jehovah into the temple of Dagon, his followers found Dagon, on two successive mornings, fallen upon his face to the ground before the ark of Jehovah. In the "catalogue" of *Paradise Lost,* Dagon will play a minor part, but in *Samson Agonistes* he plays a major part, even though he does not appear. In his heroic death, Samson triumphs not only over the Philistines but over the false god Dagon, whom they had dared oppose to Jehovah. We shall look back to the "Nativity Ode," also, when we come to the horrible snake pit in the tenth book of *Paradise Lost,* and remember the "Typhon huge ending in snaky twine" (line 226). The "Nativity Ode" is indeed a little *Paradise Lost* in anticipation.

I stop for a moment over a very different interest shown in the
Ode, which looks forward to *Comus.* In Stanza VIII of the poem on
his dead niece, Milton had spoken of Mercy and Truth (personifica-
tions from the Bible) as having been "let down in cloudy throne."
A memory of a masque he had actually seen may well have been
hovering in his mind, since in masques of the period allegorical
characters were frequently lowered from the ceiling by ingenious
mechanical devices. Two stanzas in the *Hymn* suggest to me such
masque contrivances. Stanza III might have been—perhaps was—
adapted from a real masque:

> But he her fears to cease
> Sent down the meek-eyed peace;
>   She crowned with olive green came softly sliding
> Down through the turning sphere,
> His ready harbinger,
>   With turtle wings the amorous clouds dividing,
> And waving wide her myrtle wand,
> She strikes a universal peace through sea and land.

Here is a typical masque-personification: Peace, with her crown of
olives, appears, thanks to the elaborate machinery on which pro-
ducers of masques prided themselves, coming down from the ceil-
ing, through some kind of concentric sphere that turned on its axis
(a device used by producers of masques). At the end of a masque,
which may have celebrated a particular peace, she strikes an atti-
tude with her wand. The second masque-scene, in Stanza XV,
might be the beginning rather than the climax of a masque. Like
the first it involves an elaborate appearance from the ceiling—this
time of three figures, reminiscent of the medieval allegory of the
"four daughters of God," which had its origin in Psalm LXXXV. 10-
11: "Mercy and Truth are met together; righteousness and peace
have kissed each other." The figures were familiar in a number of
morality plays. In the "machine" Milton suggests, three of them are
present, Mercy seated between Truth and Justice. They are gowned
in rainbow colors; like Peace in the earlier stanza, they come down

through clouds which part as they descend. Milton is unconsciously preparing himself to write *Arcades* and *Comus.*

Much of the charm of the *Ode* as of *Comus* lies in its youthfulness. The learning that marks its demonology is still very youthful learning, gleaned from books over which a young scholar had been poring. The conceits upon which all critics comment and over which some shake their heads—Nature and the snow, the sun in bed pillowing his chin upon an orient wave—are part of that "wit" with which we have watched Milton experimenting, but they are more than that. They are youthful conceits, new to us as they were new to the young poet who invented them. The whole poem—with its Christmas scenes mingled with weird idols and animal gods—is a boy's poem, and an English boy's, with its fancy of a semi-tropical rather than a "white" Christmas, a bland climate in which shepherds could sit on Christmas Eve chatting to each other. Each year that I have taught Milton, I have hopefully suggested that a student who could draw and paint—I can do neither —make me a Christmas card designed from the "Nativity Ode." On several occasions students have done so, often delightfully as their youthful imaginations combined with Milton's. Perhaps only Grandma Moses could have reproduced to the full its childlike charm.

Among recent critics, Professor Tillyard seems to me to have best caught the spirit of the "Ode" (*Milton,* pp. 37-38):

The truth is that the conceits cannot be spared from the Ode, for it is partly through them that is created the quality that gives it its unique charm: the clean exuberance of the best primitive art. A fifteenth-century Italian picture of the Nativity gives the simplest comparison. Here the absurdities—the rickety shelter, the far from new-born physique of the child, the cows peering with imbecile faces over a broken wall, and the rest—unite with the simple brilliant colouring to create a most captivating sense of youthfulness and simplicity. The essence of the poem is not stateliness excusing conceit, but homeliness, quaintness, tenderness, extravagance and sublimity, harmonised by a pervading youthful candour, and ordered by a commanding architectonic grasp.

Architectonic it is indeed, as is everything Milton was to write, though the *Nativity Ode* does not have quite the perfection Milton achieved in *L'Allegro* and *Il Penseroso* and in *Lycidas*. But if Milton had written no other poem, the *Ode* might well have found a place in anthologies, far superior as it is to many others that have come down to us from the English Renaissance.

There is already great metrical virtuosity here. There is contrast of light and darkness, of silence and sound. There is tenderness for the smiling Baby and His mother, and sternness of judgment upon false gods. The musical passages, rising to their climax in the full sound of Stanza XIII, would have impressed any reader, whether he knew the author's name or not. And there are phrases and lines that none could have written except a potentially great poet. Over one I stop, because it is, I think, the most "Miltonic" in the poem—and a line curiously neglected by critics who praise or criticize many others. Remembering the prophecy in Revelation that the great Dragon should be cast down, Milton visualized the scene as only a youth not far removed from boyhood would:

> And wroth to see his kingdom fail,
> Swinges the scaly horror of his folded tail.

Milton never saw a dragon, nor did you or I. But all of us who in youth believed in dragons, as we believed in fairies, know that this is just what a dragon would do. In these lines the "Latinate" Milton uses only one Latin word, "horror." For the rest he speaks good Anglo Saxon, and best of all, chooses exactly the right word to describe what a dragon does with his tail. You never heard it before, I suspect, and seldom will again, but you recognize it as inevitable: a dragon *swinges* his tail.

"The Passion" and "The Circumcision"

We shall not linger over these poems as we have over the *Ode* nor would Milton have wished us to do so. His own best critic, he wrote at the end of the eighth stanza of "The Passion": "This subject the author finding to be above the years he had when he wrote it, and nothing satisfied with what was begun left it unfinished."

Since "The Passion" seems to have been written at Eastertime following the Christmas Day of the *Nativity Ode,* it is probable that on another holy day Milton began a poem intended as a companion-piece, in the manner of *L'Allegro* and *Il Penseroso.* It was one thing for a young poet to sing the story of Christ's birth, loved by every Christian child, quite another thing for the same young poet, still untouched by human suffering, to try to retell the story of Christ's agony. When he was blind and old, Milton could sympathetically share the emotions of Samson in his struggle, but, although a good Christian, he could not at this early time really share any part of the passion of the Savior.

In form he intended another ode. The stanzaic form is in rhyme and metre close to that of the introduction to the *Morning of Christ's Nativity.* But from the beginning it is heavy, seldom rising from the ground along which it is laboriously dragged. The "song tuned to sorrow" does not sing. If we had no knowledge of the author or the date of the poem, we might well attribute such a line as, "In pensive trance, and anguish, and ecstatic fit," (line 12) to one of the debased "Longinians" of the eighteenth century. The melancholy of Stanza V is as forced as melancholy was to be among third-rate "Miltonic" poets of that same century. In the sixth book of *Paradise Lost,* when Milton rose majestically with Ezekiel in "the chariot of Paternal Deity," perhaps his memory may have gone back to his failure to accomplish the same feat in "The Passion" when he was twenty-one. But we need not continue to labor the fragment Milton himself acknowledged a failure.

"Upon the Circumcision" is more successful, although it does not rise to greatness. Since he wrote the "Nativity Ode" on Christmas and "The Passion" about Easter, perhaps Milton composed this about January 1, the day in the church calendar sacred to the Feast of Circumcision. Indeed he may have set himself the task of celebrating in verse all the more important days of the calendar. Whatever his plans, Milton was practicing his craft, and particularly experimenting with various metrical patterns and with the possibilities of a new kind of ode. "Upon the Circumcision" is closer to the Pindaric than any Milton had written before. The three-part structure we ordinarily associate with the Pindaric was either not completed or not intended to be, but we find the strophe and the antistrophe, if not the epode. Both strophe and antistrophe of "Upon the Circumcision" are fourteen lines long, each with five rhymes. The line-length is varied, as in *Lycidas,* basically pentameter, but containing trimeter lines (and perhaps a dimeter). If the poem was written in 1633, as the next two certainly were, we may justly surmise that Milton spent that year in developing a semi-Pindaric ode and particularly in experimenting with an irregular stanzaic form and irregular rhyme which he was to bring to perfection in *Lycidas* and again in the choruses of *Samson Agonistes.*

"On Time"

"On Time" is another exercise of this sort and a happier one, perhaps because Milton was not writing a poem in celebration of one of the holy days of the Church. This seems to have been an "occasional" poem in a rather different sense—lines presented perhaps with the gift of a clock or written about a particular clock. It divides itself metrically and thematically into two parts, the first treating Time, the second, Eternity. The clock in question—probably today we would call vaguely a "grandfather's clock"—must have been a dignified and formal time-piece, operated by weights, "heavy plummets," Milton calls them. I suspect that its ticking was slow and deliberate, and that the exact timing of the tick may be echoed in the second and third lines:

> Call on the lazy leaden-stepping hours
> Whose speed is but the heavy plummet's pace.

Deliberately retarded in the first stanza, Time—far from trotting or galloping—almost stands still as the leaden-stepping hours tick their slow-paced way. With the antistrophe (if Milton thought of it in this way) we leave the slow march of Time to soar to Eternity —and this poem soars as "The Passion" failed to do. "Joy . . . overtakes us as a flood." We rise from earth, where life is marked by Time, to Heaven, where there is no Time. We have left the "earthly grossness" of a world in which our hours and days are numbered, and "attired with stars," are among those angels who stand close to the Throne, our eyes turned toward the Beatific Vision. Time has been conquered by Eternity, mortality by immortality. The music soars and we soar with it to that last exultant alexandrine, "Triumphing over Death and Chance, and thee, O Time."

"At a Solemn Music"

This too is an "occasional" poem, though rather in reverse, since there seems little question that it was written on a particular occasion after Milton had been listening to music, perhaps in a church service which dissolved him into ecstasy and brought all Heaven before his eyes. The structure of the poem is extraordinary. Metrically it may be divided, like the other short odes, into two parts, of sixteen and twelve lines respectively, though this division would result in eight separate rhymes in the first part—a larger number than has been used in any previous poem. I think Milton intended it as a three-part Pindaric ode, to be divided into a first part of eight lines with four rhymes, a second also of eight with four, and a third of twelve, with five rhymes. There is one rhyme-device we have not met before, which will occur again in *Lycidas:* in line 9, "jubilee" is a new rhyme, and we do not find its mate until, after four couplets, our ears catch it in line 16, "everlastingly."

There is true stanzaic, metrical and rhythmic virtuosity here. In addition, "At a Solemn Music" is extraordinary in its grammatical structure. It consists of only two sentences, the first twenty-four lines long, but so expertly constructed that we do not realize its length. Indeed, I myself had never noticed it until I read Professor Tillyard's comment. That seems strange, since I have always called the attention of students to a similar *tour de force* in the grammatical structure of Milton's more familiar sonnet on his blindness.

In a way, this group of early poems has anticipated the Heaven of *Paradise Lost,* as did the Nativity Ode in the stanza beginning

That glorious form, that light unsufferable,
And that far-beaming blaze of majesty.

and the "globe of circular light" in which Cherubim and Seraphim, like the morning stars, sang together. In "On Time" we see the "heavenly radiance," the "flaming Powers," and winged "Warriors bright" and the "supreme Throne." "At a Solemn Music" prophesies the epic more than any other early poem—with the possible exception of the Latin verses on the Gunpowder Plot. It is a little epitome of much that Milton will say about the harmony of music that echoes through Heaven, through Earth, and even, pervertedly, through Hell. Indeed, it is a remarkable compression of what the Renaissance made of music, with classical and Christian concepts so inextricably mingled that we have no need and no desire to separate them. Here is the harmony that once moved the universe, echoed in Heaven, where the "undisturbed song of pure content" rises before the Throne as angelic voices sing to harps and trumpets. Such harmony was once on Earth before the Fall, when human sin broke both harmony and proportion. Discord and cacophony now mark the Earth, but in time to come we may hope to join the "celestial consort"—God's company of musicians—when our voices will unite with those of angels in eternal praise.

"An Epitaph on the Death of the Marchioness of Winchester"

How Milton came to write this "Epitaph" we do not know. There is no reason to think that the Miltons had any personal acquaintance with the noble family of Winchester. The fact that the poem sounds entirely impersonal means little, since funerary odes were usually so. Certainly the unfortunate event attracted wide attention, in part because the unusually beautiful and charming Marchioness was so young,

> Summer three times eight save one,
> She had told; alas, too soon . . .

and in part because her death was an ironic accident. Jane Savage, daughter of Earl Rivers, had married John Paulet, fifth Marquis of Winchester, who had succeeded to his father's title in 1628. According to a news-letter quoted by Masson (I.211) the young marchioness "had an imposthume (a boil or blister) upon her cheek lanced; the humour fell down into her throat and quickly despatched her." Apparently she choked to death.

Milton was not alone in commemorating her. Ben Jonson, Poet Laureate and dean of English poets, composed in her memory "An Elegy on the death of Lady Anne (sic) Powlet, Marchioness of Winston." William Drummond was among other poets who wrote elegies or epitaphs. In the eighteenth century, Joseph Warton suggested that Cambridge might have planned a memorial volume, a project that seems to be implied in Milton's epitaph (11. 53-60)

Here, besides the sorrowing,
That thy noble house doth bring.
Here be tears of perfect moan
Wept for thee in Helicon,
And some flowers and some bays,
For thy hearse to strew the ways,
Sent thee from the banks of Cam,
Devoted to thy virtuous name.

The assiduity of David Masson failed to discover such a volume or project, but Warton's suggestion remains a possibility, though, of course, Milton may have merely followed in the steps of the Poet Laureate in composing his elegy.

The poem is in octosyllabic couplets, metrically a forerunner of *L'Allegro* and *Il Penseroso*. As so often, Milton deftly combines paganism and Christianity. Only a short time before the lady's death, her family had celebrated her marriage with a masque, ending, as most wedding-masques did, with Hymen, "the god that sits at marriage feast." Had anyone looked closely, he would have seen that the omens were not auspicious. The torch that should have burned brightly had "a scarce well-lighted flame," and amid the gay garlands Hymen bore a cypress bud, symbolic of mourning. The young Marchioness had borne one child and was expecting another. Calling upon Lucina, goddess of childbirth, she was attended instead by Atropos, the Fate who cut the thread of life, with the result that the young matron and her unborn child died together. In the last fourteen lines, the theme changes from pagan to Christian. Lady Jane has become a saint, welcomed particularly by Rachael, who after bearing Joseph, died in childbirth with a second child. The "new welcome Saint" has been exalted. A Marchioness on earth, she has become a Queen in Heaven.

The poet—still young at twenty-five—has spent the first year of his self-imposed apprenticeship at Horton very well. The body of poetry he produced (or, at least, preserved) is slight in quantity, in comparison with what Keats had written at the same age. He has made mistakes, some of which he has honestly confessed, but he has developed greatly in metrical virtuosity. In spite of the lament in his birthday sonnet, he has left two or three poems, and a number of lines in others, which the world would not willingly let die. If we are to move *L'Allegro* and *Il Penseroso* back to the Cambridge period, or include it in the first year at Horton, Milton had surely reached full poetic maturity not long after he became of age chronologically.

The Minor Poems

L'ALLEGRO AND IL PENSEROSO

Until the publication of E. M. W. Tillyard's essay in 1932 (*The Miltonic Setting: Past and Present*, pp. 1-28) Milton critics and biographers took for granted that the twin poems were written early in the Horton period and reflected the bucolic life of the countryside around Horton. In spite of David Masson's imaginary picture of Milton composing the poems as he sauntered through the countryside, there is nothing specifically suggesting Horton in the landscape. Milton had been in other country places and indeed the country around Horton was not very different from that around Cambridge. Undoubtedly there were "russet lawns and fallows gray" with "nibbling flocks" at Horton, as there were "meadows trim with daisies pied," and "shallow brooks" with a "river wide" not far away, but so there were in the countryside around Cambridge, and so there had been among the classical poets. Masson might have made more than he did of the lines:

> Towers and battlements it sees,
> Bosomed high in tufted trees,

since the towers of Windsor Castle were visible from Horton. But neither at Horton nor at Cambridge had Milton seen

> Mountains on whose barren breast
> The laboring clouds do often rest.

Indeed, before he went to Italy, Milton had never seen a mountain except where these mountains came from—in the pages of books. But Milton had no need for personal observation, whether at Cambridge or Horton, in the landscape of the poems, which is purposely as generalized as such landscape had been in the poems of his many predecessors, English and classical.

Mr. Tillyard's theory is that the twin poems were composed in Milton's Cambridge days, possibly in 1631, shortly after the "Epitaph on the Death of the Marchioness of Winchester," which is also in octosyllabic couplets. His hypothesis is interesting, particularly because he does not pretend to *prove* but merely to suggest. He points out that the poems do not appear in the Trinity Manuscript, as do the other "Minor Poems." This is negative evidence, but of some significance. Much more important is Mr. Tillyard's analysis of the poems against the background of Milton's academic exercises and prolusions. We remember that the First Prolusion was on the topic, "Whether Day or Night is the more excellent." *L'Allegro* and *Il Penseroso,* as any casual reader sees at once, contrast the pleasures of day and of night. Milton's college exercise upheld the pleasures of day, whether because that side of the argument had been set or Milton chose it. Trained in debate as he was, he was capable of defending either side, and aware that the disputant must constantly bear in mind the arguments of his opponent and reply to them, implicitly or explicitly. The First Prolusion, as Mr. Tillyard says, "begins with an elaborate inquiry into the mythical genealogy of Night and Day; goes on to describe the dawning of day, and the glory of the sun; and ends by praising day and abusing night." Even more specifically, in the Prolusion the sun is welcomed first by birds, "who dart upwards as near as they may to the sun"; the birds are followed by the "wakeful cock" who "acclaims the sun's coming," as the lark is followed by the cock in *L'Allegro*. There are other parallels but these are sufficient for the moment.

Most interesting of all is the light thrown by Mr. Tillyard's theory upon the opening ten lines of *L'Allegro* which have often puzzled critics by their complete difference in tone and style from the rest of the poem. What possessed the poet, asks Mr. Tillyard, "that he should write such bombast? If Milton meant to be noble, he failed dreadfully. If, however, he knew what he was doing, he can only have meant to be funny. And if he meant to be funny, to what end?" If Milton wrote the poems at Cambridge, he probably intended them—like the "Vacation Exercise"—for an academic audience which would have recognized, with delighted laughter, just what the young man was doing. The opening lines of the First Prolusion are a deliberate burlesque on classical models which Cambridge undergraduates were required to imitate. Modern students can share the fun Mr. Tillyard evokes as he analyzes the prologue to *L'Allegro:*

> An academic audience would not have found it obscure. . . .
> Every undergraduate would know Ovid with his endless mythology and would be perfectly familiar with the notion of burlesquing it—even without having read *A Midsummer Night's Dream.* Directly they heard of Melancholy being born of Cerberus and blackest Midnight—infamous coupling—they would have a comfortable sense of recognition and begin to grin.

The bombastic prologue, as Mr. Tillyard suggests, is deliberately blown up to contrast as sharply as possible with the simple and joyful swing of the real opening of the poem, as the language is exaggerated to contrast with the homely simplicity of the body of the poem. All readers, as Mr. Tillyard says, appreciate the contrast,

> But an academic audience would have got more of a shock. It must have had its breath fairly taken away by the sudden swing from the familiar, deliberately dismal melodrama to a joyous and serious beauty. Indeed, I have a slight suspicion of a "stunt," a suspicion confirmed by Milton's having treated his audience to things not so very different before.

Much critical ink has been spilt in attempting to answer the question: are L'Allegro and Il Penseroso two persons; are they two sides of a personality in different moods; are they two sides of John

Milton? The question is hardly worth raising; each of us may an-
swer as he will. Both titles, we notice, are Italian, the first suggest-
ing a gay or brisk movement in music. The mood of the *persona* in
the first poem is cheerful, happy, gay. The other speaker is serious
and thoughtful rather than "melancholy" in the sense in which the
word was used of one of the humors, indicating an overbalance of
"black bile." As many critics have pointed out, and as Burton made
abundantly clear in the *Anatomy of Melancholy,* melancholy may
be black or white or in-between. Donne's melancholy in the *Anni-
versary Poems* is black, as is Hamlet's. Milton's is white melan-
choly. Milton knew the *Anatomy of Melancholy* well; indeed one
of the undoubted sources of the poems is the doggerel in Bur-
ton's "Abstract of Malancholy":

> When I go musing all alone,
> Thinking of divers things fore-known, . . .
> When to myself I act and smile,
> With pleasing thoughts the time beguile,
> By a brook side or wood so green,
> Unheard, unsought for, or unseen, . . .
> Methinks I hear, methinks I see,
> Sweet music, wondrous melody. . . .
> All other joys to this are folly;
> None so sweet as Melancholy.

L'Allegro and *Il Penseroso* are companion-poems, a type popu-
lar in a period when people were fond of companion-pictures.
Husband and wife, mother and daughter, brother and sister often
had their portraits drawn in parallel, particularly in miniature, so
that one might carry the other's picture with him. Often the back-
ground is the same in both pictures, and there is repetition of
motif, emphasizing the "companion" idea. I remember many years
ago when I was searching in England for the materials that became
the *Conway Letters,* coming upon companion-portraits of Sir John
Finch and his sister, Lady Anne Conway, in very different places,
and noticing at once that the background was identical—the pillars
of Hampton Court where the Finch family lived—while in the fore-

ground of both pictures was the same dog, a family pet. The other most familiar companion-poems of the seventeenth century are in a very different mood—John Donne's *Anniversary Poems*. Whether sombre and morose, as Donne's, or light and charming as Milton's, there is deliberate repetition in outline and design to which the writer calls attention by various devices. The author of companion-poems uses his ingenuity to set a pattern; he hopes the reader will enjoy the recognition of the pattern as much as he enjoyed setting it. If we stop to analyze Milton's twin poems in close detail, we are —far from spoiling them—doing what Milton wanted us to do, appreciating them. The best way to teach the poems, I have found by long experience, is to take them together, not separately, so that the deft double-structure will appear, and to compare and contrast them as deliberately as Milton wrote them, as a little academic debate between two speakers. Architectonic as Milton was, he was always working from a blueprint.

Both poems follow the same pattern, though in reverse, and many of the parallels are so exact that even a casual reader notices them. Why, then, is *L'Allegro* 152 lines long, and *Il Penseroso* 176 lines? We shall see that the variation is deliberate. Both poems begin with a "dismissal" of ten lines, in which the meter is the same in both poems, iambic pentameter alternating with iambic trimeter, except in the first line, which is tetrameter, with two initial spondees. *L'Allegro* begins in darkness, associated with midnight, with Cerberus, the watcher of Hades, with Styx, the river of Hades. There is a cave and an "uncouth cell," "low browed rocks" and a raven, dark as the night it symbolizes. There is the mythological Cimmerian desert, where night always reigned. The figures are all dark, but they are concrete and defined. Look now at *Il Penseroso,* and notice that there is nothing concrete about the "vain deluding Joys." Vague and formless, they are not associated with specific places or persons but left deliberately formless and vague. They shimmer off in the distance without shape.

In both poems, the "dismissal" is followed by an invocation to a goddess who presides over the poem and sets the mood. The tutelary deity of *L'Allegro* is a classical goddess, Euphrosyne, one of the three Graces, born, some say, by the union of Venus, goddess of love and beauty, and Bacchus, god of wine and love. Or—if you prefer another parentage: Mirth was a child of Zephyr, the west wind, and Aurora, goddess of the dawn, conceived on May Day on arcadian beds of violets and roses, undoubtedly without thorns.

The goddess Melancholy, invoked by Il Penseroso had never been admitted to the Greek or Roman pantheon, though she had a classical parentage, born as she was of Vesta, goddess of the hearth, and Saturn (Cronos) oldest of classical gods, leader of the Titans, father of Zeus. The nuptial couch of the goddess of mirth was a bed of light and flowers. Saturn and Vesta met in "glimmering bowers and glades" and in "secret shades" on Mount Ida. The two invocations conclude with lines that are deliberate parallels, metrically and alliteratively: "Buxom, blithe, and debonair" in the first is balanced by "Sober, steadfast and demure" in the second. In *Il Penseroso* this line is followed by a passage which has no parallel in *L'Allegro*—a description of Melancholy wearing the habit inaugurated by those other daughters of Vesta who called themselves "Vestal Virgins," a costume which descended into Christianity in the dress of many orders of nuns. Robed in black, with the white of "cypress lawn," she moves before us in high dignity, so serene, so dedicated to pensive musing that she seems to become a marble statue.

In both poems, the invocation is followed by a passage telling of the companions of the presiding goddess. Mirth dances across the stage—as in a merry masque—with personified playfellows:

Quips and Cranks and wanton Wiles,
Nods and Becks and wreathed Smiles,

with Sport, and "Laughter holding both his sides." Chief among her companions is "the mountain nymph, sweet liberty." Melancholy, devotee as she is, has as companions, "Spare Fast," Peace, Quiet, Leisure, most of all Contemplation, who is to her what Liberty is to Mirth. Subtly, and almost imperceptibly the poet-speaker

joins the other actors whom so far we have seen at a distance. In
each poem, the transition to the "pleasures" of day or night is by
the song of a bird. In the day-poem we hear the lark, singing just
before sunrise; in the other, the nightingale (a bird loved by clas-
sical poets not only for her song but because of her sad story)
breaks the silence as the moon rises.

In both poems, we follow now the "pleasures of a day," then
the "pleasures of a night." Again we notice the artful parallel lines
that call attention to one important difference between the *per-
sonae:* L'Allegro's "Sometimes walking, not unseen," as he cheer-
ily greets others who like himself are early risers; Il Penseroso's
"And missing thee, I walk unseen," as he wanders alone over field
or in grove in the moonlight. All around him L'Allegro hears the
cheerful shrill sounds of early morning (sounds are intentionally
balanced in the two poems). L'Allegro listens to the shrill crowing
of the cock, the horns of the hunters as they ride to hounds, the
whistling plowman, the milkmaid's blithe song, and, shrillest sound
of all, the whetting of the mower's scythe as he prepares for his
day's work. L'Allegro delights in high-pitched cheerful sounds of
morning. Il Penseroso's are the quiet muted sounds of evening—
the curfew, "Swinging slow with sullen roar" (notice how deliber-
ately the line is retarded), the monotonous chirping of the cricket
on the hearth, the drowsy charm of the bellman's voice as he passes
each door, reiterating monotonously, "Twelve o'clock and all's
well."

From the sounds of early morning, L'Allegro passes to the sights
he sees as he strolls across the countryside. "Straight mine eye hath
caught new pleasures": the placid countryside, with its russet lawns
and trim meadows, in the background a distant mountain and the
towers of a castle,

Where perhaps some beauty lies,
The cynosure of neighboring eyes.

It is still morning and the "beauty" sleeps, but in the foreground
the peasantry is hard at work. Here we see an English cottage,

even though the shepherds have traditional Greek names, Cory-
don, Thyrsis, Phyllis. The midday dinner of the workers leads
L'Allegro on to the afternoon, when he watches the simple amuse-
ments of the English peasantry, youths and maidens dancing to
sounds which are again shrill and cheerful—merry bells and lively
fiddlers—until the sun begins to set. In the early evening, L'Allegro
continues to take part in the simple amusements of the farmers,
over the spicy nut-brown ale. For all their Greek names, the shep-
herds and farmers entertain each other with tales drawn not
from classical mythology but from English legend and superstition
—homely stories of Queen Mab, such as Shakespeare remembered
in *Romeo and Juliet,* superstitions about the will-o'-the-wisp or
goblins who do yeoman's work, all for a bowl of cream. Momen-
tarily in their tales we return to the cock-crow with which we be-
gan. But although their day is over, L'Allegro's is not. When the
peasants go to sleep, L'Allegro perhaps goes to the theatre (we
may read the lines literally if we will, though in Milton's day one
did not "commute" from Horton to London in an evening) or, more
probably, settles down to read. The tales in which he finds pleas-
ure are romances and masques in which knights and barons joust
at tournament, while ladies of high degree watch admiringly,
ready to award the prize to the victor. These are love stories that
end happily, with Hymen, goddess of marriage, appearing, saying
in effect: "And so they were married and lived happily ever after."
From romance he turns to drama, perhaps to Ben Jonson's come-
dies, perhaps to Shakespeare's romantic plays.

L'Allegro would not be a spokesman of Milton if music were
not in the poem—not the music of merry bells and fiddles now,
but vocal music in which the Milton family delighted, verse set to
music, this time an elaborate aria. The theme, as in the romances,
is love, the love-story of Orpheus and Eurydice. With the end of the
aria, the "winding bout of linked sweetness long drawn out," L'Al-
legro's day is over. The poem ends abruptly with a couplet:

These delights if thou canst give,
Mirth, with thee I mean to live.

In the corresponding passage in *Il Penseroso* the poet-speaker describes the pleasures of a night. Alone (Il Penseroso is always alone though never lonely) he burns the midnight oil in study. Two authors most engross him: Hermes Trismegistus, author of the Hermetic books, combining philosophy, magic, astrology, in Milton's time believed to be the work of one author; and Plato, who as he appears in *Il Penseroso* is both more and less than the Plato we know, since his name too, to Milton, combines philosophy, magic and astrology.

Like L'Allegro, Il Penseroso reads drama, but his choices are very different. In L'Allegro mood, one may read the comedy of humors or the romances of Shakespeare. But the more thoughtful man prefers tragedy, particularly Greek tragedy. "Thebes or Pelops line Or the tale of Troy divine," were the three main themes of Greek tragedians. Il Penseroso reads such plays as Aeschylus' *Seven Against Thebes,* Sophocles' treatments of various descendants of Pelops—Agamemnon, Iphigenia, Electra—and the Trojan plays of Euripides, such as *Andromache* and the *Trojan Women.* English drama is mentioned only in the disparaging couplet,

> Or what (though rare) of later age
> Ennobled hath the buskined stage.

One non-dramatic English author is mentioned (ll. 109-115). For a moment the choice of Chaucer seems strange, until we pause to consider that the "tale half told" is the unfinished *Squire's Tale.* In the "virtuous (potent) ring and glass" and "the wondrous horse of brass," Il Penseroso found those elements of magic that attracted him to Hermes Trismegistus. Like L'Allegro, Il Penseroso has a taste for the romance of chivalry, though of a more serious kind. The "great bards" who

> In sage and solemn tunes have sung,
> Of tourneys and of trophies hung,
> Of forests and enchantments drear,
> Where more is meant than meets the ear,

were probably Ariosto and Tasso and certainly Spenser in whose allegory "more is meant than meets the ear." Like L'Allegro, Il Penseroso thinks of music, particularly of Orpheus, though the love story of Orpheus and Eurydice has sadder overtones to him than to L'Allegro.

Il Penseroso has spent the night in reading and study. His poem ends where L'Allegro's began—in early morning. But the morning he prefers is not one of brilliant sunlight. "Hide me from Day's garish eye," he says. His is an early morning of wind and rain

> ushered with a shower still
> When the gust hath blown his fill,
> Ending on the rustling leaves
> With minute drops from off the eaves.

If he must be outdoors in the morning, he prefers to seek the brown shade of a pine or oak grove, where he may fall asleep to the sound of the low buzzing of bees and the murmuring waters of a brook. As he wakes, he asks that "sweet music breathe."

So far the parallels between the poems have been exact, with the exception of the description of Melancholy. One poem is the other in reverse, in time sequence, the succession of light and shadow, of sounds. One is a poem of cheerful, shrill sounds and of light; the other of muted sounds and shadows. Although black is "staid Wisdom's hue," there is nothing funereal about the darkness of *Il Penseroso,* which is not sombre but soothing. The "saintly visage" of Melancholy is too bright for human eyes, as the light of God in *Paradise Lost* is too bright even for the Seraphim who "approach not, but with both wings veil their eyes." The outlines of the two poems have been identical except that, after the first ten lines, each section of *Il Penseroso* is just a little longer than the corresponding section of *L'Allegro,* since the serious man develops his ideas more thoughtfully and at more leisure. For the same reason it is natural that two sections should have been added to *Il Penseroso* for which there is no parallel in the first poem (ll.

155-174). In our lighter moods, we are less likely to think of religion and old age than in our more serious moments. Il Penseroso's mind turns to the studious cloister, the high roof and massy pillars, the storied windows casting a dim religious light and—music again —the pealing organ and the voices of choir and congregation join

> In service high and anthems clear
> As may with sweetness, through mine ear,
> Dissolve me into ecstasies
> And bring all heaven before mine eyes.

The mind of the thoughtful man turns, too, to thoughts of old age. "No young man," said Hazlitt, "believes he shall ever die." L'Allegro is young, Il Penseroso mature (though their chronological ages were probably the same as Milton's) even though there is something very youthful indeed about his picture of himself in "weary age," a hermit, speculating about astrology and increasing in wisdom

> Till old experience do attain
> To something like prophetic strain.

William Vaughn Moody wrote in the introduction to his edition of Milton: "The language of these two little masterpieces has been the despair of poets. It is not that it is so beautiful . . . but that it is, as a French critic has said, so *just* in its beauty. The means are exquisitely proportioned to the end. The speech incarnates the thought as easily, as satisfyingly as the muscles of a Phidian youth incarnates the motor-impulse of his brain. Always fruition is just gently touched. To the connoisseur in language there is a sensation of almost physical soothing in its perfect poise and play." The metrical dexterity is equally remarkable. With the exception of the ten lines of introduction, the metre of both poems is octosyllabic couplets, a metre common enough from Chaucer on. Superficially this is one of the easiest English metres to imitate, so simple that it may easily degenerate into doggerel. Milton's remarkable ability as a metrist is felt by anyone who stops to consider the difference in the feeling-tone of the two poems, giving the reader such opposite sensations. Mirth and her companions dance to the lilting metre:

Come and trip it as you go,
On the light fantastic toe.

Melancholy moves with stately dignity to the same measure:

Come, pensive nun, devout and pure,
Sober, steadfast, and demure . . .

Come, but keep thy wonted state,
With even step and musing gait.

Within the four-stressed lines of the two poems, there is a wealth of metrical diversity. The normal octosyllabic line is an iambic of eight syllables:

To live with her, and live with thee,
In unreproved pleasures free.

(*L'All.* 39-40)

but numerous lines omit the first syllable, so that they begin with a spondee:

Come, and trip it as you go
On the light fantastic toe.

(*L'All.* 33-34)

The addition of a final syllable to such lines may give the impression of trochaic rather than iambic metre:

Straight mine eye hath caught new pleasure,
Whilst the landscape round it measures

(*L'All.* 69-70)

There are many other kinds of variation to the normal metre, which the student interested in prosody will readily detect. By scanning each line, one comes away with high respect for the craft of a young poet who could ring so many changes that he avoided, deftly and dexterously, the dreary monotony or even banality into which a versifier of less craft would have fallen. (Assistance in technicalities will be found in S. Ernest Sprott, *Milton's Art of Poetry;* and Robert Bridges, *Milton's Prosody.*)

With one point made by Mr. Sprott we may return full-circle to the problem of dating the companion-poems with which we began. After discussing the high percentage of seven-syllable lines (catalectic trochaic lines), Mr. Sprott considers Professor Tillyard's theory that the poems had their origin in Milton's academic exercise, and that they were written while he was still at Cambridge, about the time of the "Epitaph on the Marchioness of Winchester." Mr. Sprott points out that the verbal similarities Mr. Tillyard finds between the exercise and the poems are all in the first seventy-eight lines of *L'Allegro* and that, while there are decided metrical similarities with the "Epitaph," they occur in the first one hundred lines of *L'Allegro;* the remainder of that poem shows few, and *Il Penseroso* still fewer. He concludes with an interesting suggestion: "I suggest that the change may have been occasioned by Milton's laying aside the first part and then at a later date taking it up and completing *L'Allegro* and then going on to complete *Il Penseroso.* It is possible that *L'Allegro* was begun about the time of the first prolusion and before the 'Epitaph'; . . . Could it be that *L'Allegro* and *Il Penseroso* were begun at Cambridge, but completed at Horton, perhaps on the same sheet or sheets of paper, and so not preserved in the Cambridge manuscript?"

We may take it as we will—Cambridge or Horton. It makes little difference. The important fact is that in the perfection of the companion-poems Milton has come of full age as a poet.

The Masques

In reading Milton's juvenilia, I have paused on several occasions to point out suggestions of masque figures or scenes: Mercy and Truth "let down in cloudy throne"; Peace descending through an elaborate "turning sphere"; Truth, Justice and Mercy, "with radiant feet the tissued clouds down-steering." In *L'Allegro* the companions of Euphrosyne, from "Jest and youthful Jollity" through "Laughter holding both his sides" dance across the stage in a sort of antimasque reminiscent of Jonson's *Vision of Delight,* in which Delight was accompanied by Grace, Love, Harmony, Revel, Sport and Laughter. (See Enid Welsford, *The Court Masque,* p. 308.) The introduction of Hymen toward the end of the poem is in the masque tradition, as Milton's lines suggest:

> There let Hymen oft appear
> In saffron robe, with taper clear,
> And pomp, and feast, and revelry,
> With masks and antique pageantry.
>
> (ll. 125-28)

Like nearly every poet of his time, Milton was attracted by masques, which contained some of the most charming lyrical poetry of the period. That had been particularly true of the *genre* when Ben Jonson's influence had dominated the form. The masque was designed for private, not public entertainment of the sort for which Shakespeare wrote. It was a form popular, too, with students, particularly at the Inns of Court. Masques were played by amateur rather than professional actors, and nearly always designed for particular occasions—entertainments, banquets, weddings, royal progresses (visits of state). They were presented in and therefore adapted to many different places—courtyards, halls, gardens. The person of chief importance in the production of a masque was not the author but the producer—in the case of Henry Lawes, a musician, in the case of Inigo Jones, a stage-designer and artist. The text and often the music was commissioned by the producer, who would inform the author what kind of script he wanted: how many actors, what kinds of speeches, songs, opportunities for dancing he planned.

How and why Milton, still an unknown young poet, was chosen to write the texts for *Arcades* and *Comus,* we can only surmise. We know that Henry Lawes produced *Comus.* It is entirely possible that he also produced *Arcades.* But how did he happen to select John Milton to write either masque? Possibly his relationship with Milton came about through the Diodatis, a family more closely connected with aristocrats who commissioned masques than the more simple Miltons. Professor Donald Dorian (*The English Diodatis,* pp. 144-49) after a careful study of all members of the two noble families concerned in Milton's masques concludes: "Without exception, every member of the aristocratic family group most immediately concerned in presenting the *Arcades* and *Comus* was connected more or less closely with some patron or patient of Dr. Theodore Diodati." p. 145

The other possible connection—and a very likely one—was, of course, through Milton's father. There is every reason that the professional and the amateur musician should have known each other. Like the elder Milton, Lawes contributed new music for paraphrases of the Psalms. Like the Miltons, Lawes gathered together in his home groups interested in singing and in music in its many phases. In seventeenth-century London, the musical group would not have been large, and there was undoubtedly a good deal of overlapping. Such company was growing by the addition of increasing numbers of Italians who were finding homes in England, many of whom would have been as welcome at the Miltons' home as at Diodati's. If, as some critics believe, Milton's reference in *Comus* (lines 619-628) is a covert allusion to himself as "a certain shepherd lad Of small regard to see to," it would imply that Milton had known Lawes for some time and been charmed by his music:

> He loved me well, and oft would beg me sing;
> Which when I did, he on the tender grass
> Would sit, and hearken even to ecstasy.

ARCADES

Arcades and *Comus* stand at the farthest possible extremes of the literary *genre* to which both belong, and show how broadly the word "masque" could be interpreted. *Comus* comes close to being the longest English masque, *Arcades* among the shortest. Milton's preface indicates that *Arcades* was part of an "entertainment," a term frequently applied to a short masque intended either to greet a guest or to welcome a returning member of a noble family. The Dowager Countess of Derby, the former Lady Alice Spencer, as her title implies, was the widow of the fifth Earl of Derby. Her lustre would have been enhanced in Milton's eyes by the fact that Edmund Spenser (the two families were connected) had dedicated to her *The Tears of the Muses* and alluded to her in *Colin Clouts Come Home Again*. In her own right, as well as through her husband, she was a patroness of letters. Her first husband, a poet himself, had been the patron of the company of actors known first as

Lord Strange's Men, later as Derby's Men, a position which his widow inherited for a time. She married as a second husband the Lord Chancellor Egerton, later Baron Ellesmere and Viscount Brackley, founder of the great Bridgewater Library. Her son by his first marriage married her daughter by her first marriage, so that the lady celebrated in *Arcades* was both mother-in-law and stepmother to John Egerton, for whose inaugural as Lord President of Wales *Comus* was written. The close relationship between the two families suggests a reason that the same poet should have been commissioned to write both masques. The location of the Dowager Countess' estate suggests another possibility. Harefield was only a little more than eight miles from Horton. John Milton was a very personable and cultivated young man, the type to appeal to a Dowager much interested in both poetry and music, who had every reason to pride herself upon her association with Edmund Spenser, whose singing robes Milton was inheriting.

Arcades, as the subtitle suggests, was "part of an entertainment presented to the Countess Dowager of Derby at Harefield by some noble persons of her family, who appear on the scene in pastoral habits." The little masque was evidently given at dusk or in early evening (as line 39 suggests), a preface to "this night's glad solemnity." The Countess Dowager would have been seated in state at the end of the great avenue of elms at Harefield,

> Under the shady roof
> Of branching elm star-proof.

> (ll. 88-89)

Harefield was no stranger to masques. In 1602 another generation of masquers had welcomed Queen Elizabeth as she made her stately way along this same elm-shaded road, to remain for four days of masquing and entertainments at Harefield. Some thirty years later, the younger members of the Dowager's family, dressed as shepherds and nymphs, sang the first song, celebrating her majesty and the "excellent beauty" praised by Spenser long ago, now autumnal beauty. The songs of *Arcades* are all eminently singable and the very kind of lyric in the setting of which Henry Lawes delighted. Since Lawes played the Attendant Spirit in *Comus,* he may have played the Genius of the Wood in *Arcades,* and spoken the lines designed to lead the dancers nearer to the chair of state. The speech would have been peculiarly appropriate for Lawes. It looks forward in a way to the character he assumed in *Comus* of a "faithful swain" who nevertheless had magical powers, "puissant words and murmurs made to bless." The climax of the speech is a tribute to music; as in the *Nativity Ode,* the music of the spheres and the other "heavenly tune" which human ears cannot hear. It is a tribute not only to a beautiful dowager but to the power of music in the hands of an excellent musician.

Arcades looks before and after: Alpheus and Arethusa we shall find again in *Lycidas,* as we shall find the "evening gray." Songs II and III will have echoes in the "printless feet" in Sabrina's song, and in the Epilogue of *Comus.* But it looks back as well—to the light and sound in *L'Allegro* and the drowsy night of *Il Penseroso.* Most of all, it recalls the sonnet of the nightingale and the pure lyricism of Milton's earlier song. Its lyrics have the spontaneity and freshness of "On May Morning."

COMUS

Comus is as complex as *Arcades* is simple—or, rather, modern critics have made it so. I can think of few poems which have been subjected to the overweight of criticism *Comus* has received during the last twenty years. Were it not for its intrinsic vitality, it would have been "pressed" to death, like Desdemona. Reluctantly I shall have to enter into the controversy but I shall not do so until we have read the masque Milton wrote, without benefit or distraction of secondary criticism.

Milton did not call his work *Comus,* but only *A Mask presented at Ludlow Castle.* The occasion is clear enough. John Egerton, first Earl of Bridgewater, of whom we have heard in *Arcades,* had been appointed Lord President of Wales in 1631 but did not take up residence at Ludlow Castle until 1634. For his formal inauguration, which would be attended by local gentry and peasantry, as well as by many dignitaries from as far away as London, he planned an occasion on which a masque would be followed by an evening of dancing. Henry Lawes was to be in charge of the masque. He would commission a text. He himself would compose the music and with whatever assistance he needed, supervise the acting, singing and dancing.

From the beginning Lawes must have made clear to Milton various problems they faced together. The three children of the Earl of Bridgewater must have good parts. Lawes himself intended to have a role, in part because he liked to sing and act, in part, perhaps, because it would be easier to supervise his young charges if he were among them rather than off-stage. He knew the three Egerton children well, since he had been their music-teacher for some years. While the children, like nearly all masque performers, were amateurs, they had already danced in at least two important masques, Ben Jonson's *Chloridia,* three years before, and Carew's *Coelum Britannicum* earlier in the year 1634, when *Comus* was to be given. Lady Alice had also danced, with her older married sister, Lady Penelope, in *Tempe Restored.* Lady Alice was fifteen at the time she played the Lady in *Comus,* the Elder Brother, John, Viscount Brackley, was eleven, and Thomas Egerton, the Second Brother, was nine—young actors indeed for the long roles assigned them (though the speeches in the acting version were somewhat shorter than those we read today). Lady Alice obviously had a pretty voice: hence the "Echo Song." A singing sister, two brothers, an older man—such was the cast of characters with which Milton began. There are two more roles in the *Comus* he produced, Sabrina, and Comus himself. We do not know who played either role, but I shall venture two guesses about Sabrina and one about Comus. Perhaps Lady Alice had a "best friend" whom she wanted to act with her, in which case Milton was clearly instructed that it must be a lesser role, since this was an Egerton occasion. Or—this is my own favorite—what about the older married sister, Lady Penelope, who had had masquing experience, who would certainly be present, and who, as a young matron, would be willing to take a lesser role, leaving her younger sister and brothers to be the stars they were? It would be a charming touch for the older sister to come to the aid of the younger, releasing her from the alabaster chair, and very fitting that the daughter of the new Lord President represent the local Welsh deity, associated with the Severn River, well known to gentry and peasantry alike.

What of Comus? His part was essential, since the basic theme of most masques was the theme of *Comus:* the triumph of Virtue over Vice. There must be a villain, representing Vice in one form or another, with such a "rabble rout" as that of Comus, who could "with goat feet dance the antic hay"—clumsy or humorous dancing, opposed to the courtly elegance of the aristocrats. It is possible that Comus was played by another young member of that large, involved family, though no one person seems to fit exactly. I prefer to think that he was the only professional beside Lawes on the stage at Ludlow Castle that night, brought in by Lawes for his own assistance, for Lawes must have looked forward to a nervous evening keeping his young charges to their lines, their songs and dances.

Since Lawes was stage-manager as well as musician, he would have told Milton what "effects" he wanted, and what "machinery" would be available or could be constructed at Ludlow Castle. Lawes had been a member of the "King's Music" for some time and in that capacity had had much to do with court masques. He had seen a great change since the days when Ben Jonson's power and prestige had dominated most court masques, when poetry and song had been most important in the tradition. Jonson was now

old and ill and after one quarrel too many had been replaced offi-
cially by Inigo Jones, who was primarily interested in stage-
spectacle, of which he was a master. Townshend, Shirley, Carew
and Davenant had taken Jonson's place. Their masques, as a
group, tended to be longer, more episodic, less unified than Jon-
son's, and purposely adapted for spectacle. Whether Lawes ap-
proved or not, he had seen various "machines" used by Inigo
Jones and knew how to produce most of the spectacles. Indeed,
some of the effects in *Comus* deliberately paralleled those in the six
masques Lawes had seen produced by Inigo Jones.

The "spectacles" and "machines" required for *Comus* were less
complicated than several in masques recently produced in London.
Ludlow Castle was in a remote district and while Lawes may have
borrowed "machines" (the Egerton influence would have been
more than sufficient for that), the problem of transportation was
not easy in those days. Let us see from hints in the masque itself
what machinery would have been necessary. The first clue is in the
stage direction: "The Attendant Spirit *descends or enters.*" That
left the decision squarely up to Lawes. If he found it possible to ar-
range for the necessary wires, he could descend from the sky. In
London Lawes had more than once played the part of a spirit,
dressed in a sky-blue robe.

The "transformation" scenes involved in *Comus* were easy.
When the Attendant Spirit changes from his rainbow-hued "sky-
robes, spun out of Iris' woof" (line 83), he needed only remove
his sparkling over-dress, under which he wore the "weeds" of a
swain "that to the service of this house belongs"—whatever garb
the Egerton servitors wore. When he says, "I must be viewless
now," he had only to walk off-stage. Comus' transformation (lines
150-167) from god of revels to "harmless villager" seems more
spectacular but was basically simple. When he said (lines 153-
154)

> Thus I hurl
> My dazzling spells into the spongy air,

he would have thrown into the air fine gold or silver-dust. By the time it had settled, Comus, like the Attendant Spirit, had removed his outer robe and was in the dress of a simple villager.

The lighting effects required by *Comus* would not have taxed Lawes' ingenuity too much. The stage is dark or semi-dark when Comus and his rout appear; part of the "spectacle" was the skillful use of torches in their "light fantastic round," emphasized by the light-dark imagery in Comus' octosyllabic couplets, reminiscent of *L'Allegro* and *Il Penseroso*. The Lady enters on a dark stage, as her lines emphasize, again with light-dark imagery, in which dark predominates. It is she who calls attention to the device by which light begins to appear in the dark heavens:

Was I deceived, or did a sable cloud
Turn forth her silver lining on the night?
I did not err, there does a sable cloud
Turn forth her silver lining on the night.

(ll. 221-24)

Poetically the repetition seems unnecessary and even lame; as a clue to the mechanics the first two lines were essential, and the second two probably coincided with admiring sounds from the audience as sun, moon and stars appeared in the ceiling above them.

The second main scene is in sharp contrast to the first. Instead of darkness or semi-darkness the full blaze of every possible artificial light illuminates the "stately palace, set out with all manner of deliciousness." Comus stands with his charmed glass in his hand. The glass sparkles, probably burning with a flame of lighted brandy or some other alcohol:

And first behold this cordial julep here
That flames and sparkles in his crystal bounds.

(ll. 672-73)

When the Brothers rush in with swords drawn, Comus and his crew disappear from the stage, after a pantomimic battle. But since the Brothers have forgotten to seize Comus' wand, the Lady is still confined by his magic to the alabaster chair. This situation afforded opportunity for the most charming spectacle of all: the invocation to Sabrina, sung by Lawes, and the appearance of Sabrina in her chariot glowing with various colors:

> Thick set with agate, and the azure sheen
> Of turquoise blue, and emerald green.

(ll. 893-94)

Such chariot scenes had been used in masques recently played in London and, with the aid of local carpenters, Lawes should have had little difficulty in adapting one to the scene in Ludlow Castle. The stage directions, "Sabrina rises" and "Sabrina descends," suggest a deep well beneath the room of state, from which the chariot would be hoisted by machinery and into which it would be lowered. The masque ends, as did most masques presented for such occasions of state, with the intermingling of audience and actors: against the painted backdrop showing the town of Ludlow and the castle, local peasantry performed a country dance, then Lawes formally presented the young actors to their parents. This was followed by a certain amount of formal dancing, led by the Earl and Countess, Lawes watching from the stage to interrupt at a propitious moment with the Epilogue, at the end of which he disappeared in the same manner he had entered, since Milton's direction allows him the option of running off or being lifted to the skies by machines: "I can fly, or I can run." The masque is over, but the guests remain to dance and to congratulate the actors and their parents.

Was *Comus* played outdoors or inside Ludlow Castle? Perhaps Lawes himself was not sure when he commissioned Milton and suggested that Milton write in such a way that Lawes might decide after he became more familiar with Ludlow Castle (if he had not actually visited it). Certainly much of *Comus* reads as if it had been designed for outdoor setting, and the lyrics have the freshness that mark *Arcades*. All existing evidence, however, points to indoor performance. Modern guidebooks to Ludlow Castle report the tradition that it was given in the Great Hall on the second floor, a hall that can no longer be seen since only the walls of Ludlow Castle are standing. It would have been charming to sit outdoors and particularly to watch Sabrina appear as if she had actually risen from the Severn River. But the difficulties of artificial lighting and sets—not to mention the problematic British weather—would have been more troublesome outdoors, and the conclusion of the masque seems to imply that actors and audience mingled on the floor of a ballroom prepared for dancing.

We now have the pattern Lawes must have given Milton against which he was to cut his cloth—and cut it very well he did. He has given the three young actors parts excellently adapted to young amateurs, for they had to be only what they actually were: three young people coming to attend their father's inauguration. He develops the character of the Attendant Spirit in such a way that Lawes, too, is what he is, an older man watching over his young pupils. Not all the music Lawes composed for *Comus* is extant, but what there is well warrants Milton's later tribute to Lawes in Sonnet XIII that he was a musician who respected the poetry he set: "thou honorest verse."

Given the pattern of actors, situation, and machines, how did Milton develop his masque? Like a majority of the masque-writers who preceded him, he used the perennial theme of the triumph of Virtue over Vice. Like them, too, he drew his general background from pagan mythology: gods, goddesses or minor deities, nymphs, shepherds, all the stuff of time-honored pastoral tradition. For his Vice, who will try to tempt Virtue, he invented a new pagan deity, for while the name "Comus" had been used earlier—by Ben Jonson among others—there had been no such demigod in the Greek or Roman pantheon. As in *L'Allegro* and *Il Penseroso* Milton gave him a parentage. Comus is the son of Circe, enchantress of the *Odyssey,* and of Bacchus, god of wine and revelry. Like his mother he is a magician, offering travelers his "orient liquor" in a crystal glass. Those human beings who taste ("For most do taste through fond intemperate thirst," sternly warns the young poet-teacher) are changed into the animals they really are. Here Milton, probably at Lawes's suggestion, made a change from the Circe legend. Circe's victims became animals going upon all-fours. Anyone who has directed amateur theatricals knows how awkward such a transformation would prove. When Comus changes human beings, the transformation affects only the heads, "all other parts remaining as they were" so that the "rout of monsters" appear wearing papier-mâché heads, with arms and legs free for dancing.

The newly invented son of Circe has been transplanted to the British Isles, where Comus has arrived after ranging the Celtic and Iberian fields. He now plies his magic in an "ominous wood" in Wales. So Milton neatly brings one of the most familiar classical tales almost to the doors of Ludlow Castle, a situation deftly anticipated in the Prologue by the Attendant Spirit, who also adapts familiar pagan mythology to this specific occasion of celebration. Going back to one of the earliest legends, he reminds his audience that at the beginning of time, the universe was divided among Jove (Zeus, Jupiter), who commanded the heavens, Hades (Dis) god of the underworld, and Neptune (Poseidon), god of the waters, most important of all elements to those who lived on the British Isles. This leads him to pleasant compliments to the "noble Peer," who on this occasion has been installed as governor of "all this tract that fronts the falling sun."

Aware of the dangers that threaten the three young people coming to attend their father's inauguration, we are ready for that "virtuous young lady," the sister. With every good intention, the brothers have left her while they seek berries or cooling fruit to relieve her thirst. Alone in the woods on a dark night, the Lady has every right to be afraid, but the young ethical poet who is writing the masque makes us aware that, in spite of the lovely lines (206-209) about the "thousand fantasies," she is not terrified, assured as she is of the protection of Conscience, Hope, Chastity. The charming Echo song (the young lady was obviously a coloratura soprano) has an effect opposite to what she had hoped: it is heard not by her brothers but by Comus. Comus, to be sure, is the villain of the piece, the Vice, but since he is also an invention of

Milton's, we are not surprised at his response to music (lines 244-64) nor can we feel him too profoundly a villain, if it is true that

> The man that hath no music in himself,
> Nor is not mov'd with concord of sweet sounds,
> Is fit for treasons, stratagems, and spoils . . .
> Let no such man be trusted.

Comus had inherited from his mother Circe other qualities than black magic, for Circe, too, had been a singer—though a more dangerous one than the Lady.

The conversation that follows between the Lady and Comus is in a dramatic form we have not met before, *stichomythia,* dialogue in alternate lines, frequently used by the Greek dramatists. Not unnaturally deceived by Comus's manner and appearance—he seems only the "harmless villager" he pretends to be—the Lady accepts his offer to accompany him to "a low but loyal cottage," making her exit with lines that must have sounded strange (if the audience was really listening to words rather than admiring her beauty and her elocution) spoken by the daughter of an Earl in one of the stately homes of Britain: (321-26)

> Shepherd, I take thy word,
> And trust thy honest-offered courtesy,
> Which oft is sooner found in lowly sheds
> With smoky rafters, than in tapestry halls
> And courts of princes, where it first was named
> And yet is most pretended

> (ll. 321-26)

As always in fairy tales, the Lady leaves just one moment too soon. Hardly is she off-stage with Comus than her brothers enter. Young though they are, their characters are already well defined, particularly that of the Elder Brother. The younger boy is quite naturally alarmed for the safety of his sister but the Elder Brother never swerves for a moment from his calm insistence upon her safety because of her innate virtue:

> Virtue could see to do what Virtue would
> By her own radiant light, though sun and moon
> Were in the flat sea sunk. . . .
> He that hath light within his own clear breast
> May sit in the center, and enjoy bright day.
>
> (ll. 373-382)

That is all very well, protests the more realistic younger brother, but remember that our sister is alone in the woods and that she is a virgin and a beautiful one. (lines 393-403) The Elder Brother, young Stoic as he is, is not concerned with bodies that may be vulnerable. He reads the doubting young Thomas a long and fluent lecture on the theme that it is mind, not body, that really matters. Their sister is safe, because she has a "hidden strength" that will protect her, wherever she is:

> 'Tis chastity, my brother, chastity,
> She that has that is clad in complete steel . . .
>
> (ll. 420 ff.)

John Egerton was still only eleven years old and had not yet had the advantage of a Cambridge education, but his author had, and into John's mouth he put lessons he had learned at the University. It is amusing that the method of development is the characteristic academic one of "appeal to authority," as we see particularly when he comes to the lines beginning:

> Do ye believe me yet, or shall I call
> Antiquity from the old schools of Greece
> To testify the arms of chastity?
>
> (ll. 438 ff.)

The "evidence" is drawn from classical legend: Diana and her dread bow, Minerva and her Gorgon-shield. From classical authority, we rise to Christianity:

> So dear to Heaven is saintly chastity
> That when a soul is found sincerely so,
> A thousand liveried angels lackey her . . .
>
> (ll. 453-55)

The "appeal to authority," pagan and Christian, wins the debate. The lecture of the young potential Cambridge don proves persuasive. The Second Brother momentarily becomes a convert:

> How charming is divine philosophy!
> Not harsh and crabbed, as dull fools suppose,
> But musical as is Apollo's lute.
>
> (ll. 476-78)

The Second Brother is speaking sincerely. There is no trace of irony here, as I am afraid there sometimes is in my voice when I read the lines aloud in class. If I seem to smile, I am smiling not at eleven-year-old John and nine-year-old Thomas Egerton, who did remarkably well when they committed the long passages to memory, but rather at the twenty-six-year-old recent graduate of Cambridge. I smile merely because here and elsewhere *Comus* is so very *youthful*. Milton had learned his lessons in philosophy very well, and—a "pupil teacher"—he is repeating those lessons through an even younger generation.

Fortunately for the audience, the academic debate is interrupted by the Attendant Spirit with the ominous news that their sister has been captured by an enchanter. Young doubting Thomas shifts back to his earlier position, but not the unruffled Elder Brother. He does not take to his heels to save the girl without another little lecture (lines 595-60). At this point, we find another typical fairy-tale device. The Attendant Spirit clearly warns the two young men that they must perform three feats: having forced their way into the magician's hall, they must rush at him with brandished blades, break the glass, and seize the wand. Fairy-tales would not be fairy-tales if the heroes were not always inclined to forget or neglect one of the responsibilities laid upon them, as of course the brothers do. But before we are ready for that scene, we must pause for a moment over the herb given the boys by the Attendant Spirit, who has magic to oppose to Comus'. We shall return to the passage in another connection but for the present we may take it only as it appears on the surface. In the

Odyssey Hermes gave Odysseus a similar root, called *moly,* which had the magic power of safeguarding its owner. In the *Aeneid,* Aeneas returned safely from Hades because he carried a golden bough. The root called Haemony which the Attendant Spirit gives the brothers is specific

> 'Gainst all enchantments, mildew, blast or damp,
> Or ghastly Furies' apparition.
>
> (ll. 640-41)

Haemony is one of the many magic appurtenances in the fairy-tale we are reading. The brothers, armed with it, go off to seek their sister, but in the meantime we, the spectators, anticipate them in finding the Lady in Comus' stately palace. Under the tutelage of our young graduate of Cambridge, we hear still another debate —much better than the one-sided dialogue between the brothers, for the Lady and Comus are more fairly matched disputants than were the two young boys. Milton had not spent all those years on prolusions and argumentation for nothing. He knew that there were two sides to a question and he had been taught that part of the art of writing dialogue or debate consists in giving strong speeches to the opposition. Milton's Lady will win the battle of words, but Comus' speeches are poetically finer and more moving. The subject of the disputation was a time-honored one, "The Appeal to Nature for Standards." Let me tell you in advance that the arguments of both Comus and the Lady, far from being original with them or with Milton, were commonplaces familiar to any educated person in Milton's time. They had already been old when the Roman Stoics were young and they have continued to recur in literature down to our own day. "What does Nature teach?" Man looks up to the heavens at night (as Adam will in Book VIII of *Paradise Lost,* when Milton will return to this argument again), or he looks down into the sea, or he watches flowers or ants or bees; each man may answer the question as he will. Basically the question raised by Comus and the Lady is: "Does Nature teach us to enjoy ourselves, using our bodies and our senses and her gifts to the

full, or is hers a lesson of restraint, moderation, temperance?"
Comus, urging the Lady to enjoy the pleasures of the senses, tries to
tempt her with the liquor in the orient glass, insisting that Nature
intends us to seize the day, to enjoy ourselves. His is the hardy
perennial of a mild and popular Epicureanism, the refrain of
carpe diem, or "eat, drink and be merry" familiar in so much Ren-
aissance poetry. To Comus, Nature is munificent and lavish, pro-
fuse, prolific:

> Wherefore did Nature pour her bounties forth
> With such a full and unwithdrawing hand,
> Covering the earth with odors, fruits and flocks,
> Thronging the seas with spawn innumerable,
> But all to please and sate the curious taste? . . .
>   If all the world
> Should in a pet of temperance feed on pulse,
> Drink the clear stream, and nothing wear but frieze,
> The All-giver would be unthanked, would be unpraised,
> Not half his riches known, and yet despised,
> And we should serve him as a grudging master,
> As a penurious niggard of his wealth,
> And live like Nature's bastards, not her sons.
>
>   (ll. 710-727)

The Lady has not had the benefit of a Cambridge education, but
in Milton's hands she sounds as if she had been "up" with him and
her Elder Brother. Like the latter she is a Stoic. Comus goes fur-
ther, and adds "Cynic." Her concept of Nature is a mild ethical
socialism. Nature is not profligate and wanton:

> Impostor, do not charge most innocent Nature,
> As if she would her children should be riotous
> With her abundance; she, good cateress,
> Means her provision only to the good,
> That live according to her sober laws
> And holy dictate of spare Temperance.
> If every just man that now pines·with want
> Had but a moderate and beseeming share
> Of that which lewdly-pampered luxury

Now heaps upon some few with vast excess,
Nature's full blessings would be well dispensed
In unsuperfluous even proportion,
And she no whit encumbered with her store;
And then the Giver would be better thanked,
His praise due paid.

(ll. 762-776)

If this is Vice tempting Virtue, the Lady's virtue is clearly not temptable. Let me run ahead for a moment to a similar scene in *Paradise Lost* in which Satan is tempting Eve to eat the apple. One circumstance Milton will stress there is that the temptation took place at high noon, after Eve had been working in the garden all morning, that she was naturally both hungry and thirsty, and that the fruit of the tree was a semitropical fruit with luscious odor and full of juice. The Lady in *Comus should* have been hungry and thirsty, after wandering in the woods so long (indeed, the reason the brothers left was to find cooling fruit for her thirst). But in this way the Lady does not seem a human being with human frailties and natural appetites. And it is interesting to notice that the temptation through hunger and thirst is the only one stressed in *Comus*. Decorum, the age of the young actors, the circumstances of a family masque, naturally forbade what might well have been emphasized in a court masque designed for adult actors and audience —trial of the Lady's virginity, implied only in passing when Comus says:

Why should you be so cruel to yourself,
And to those dainty limbs which Nature lent
For gentle usage and soft delicacy?

(ll. 679-81)

The rescuers seemingly arrive just in time, but we, the spectators, feel that the Lady could have withstood Comus indefinitely. With the entrance of the brothers, the fairy-tale proceeds. They have been warned to do three things, but they forget to snatch Comus' wand—fortunately enough for the spectators, for if they had, the masque would have been over without its loveliest scene, the introduction of Sabrina, a "virgin pure" who has become the tutelary goddess of the neighboring river. Invoked by the Attendant Spirit in speech and song, she rises in her chariot and performs the last feat of magic:

> Brightest lady, look on me;
> Thus I sprinkle on thy breast
> Drops that from my fountain pure
> I have kept of precious cure,
> Thrice upon thy finger's tip,
> Thrice upon thy rubied lip;
> Next this marble venomed seat,
> Smeared with gums of glutinous heat,
> I touch with chaste palms moist and cold.
> Now the spell hath lost his hold.

(ll. 910-919)

The fairy-tale is over. All that remains is the formal presentation of the young wanderers to their parents, then the country and the courtly dances, and finally the Epilogue of the Attendant Spirit to which we shall return in another connection.

If I seem to have overstressed *Comus* as a fairy-tale and a story in which magic plays a large part, I have done so deliberately. This is not the interpretation given it in recent years by various critics, a number that has been growing so large that, as Robert Adams amusingly says in *Ikon, Comus* bids fair to become a "major" rather than a "minor" poem. The critical controversalists may be divided into two main groups, one primarily concerned with form and structure, the other with themes and ideas. The beginning of the controversy over form is to be found in Chapter VI of E. M. W. Tillyard's *Milton,* which appeared in 1930, though as Mr. Tillyard's opening remarks indicate, it goes back at least as far as Samuel Johnson, whom Mr. Tillyard quotes: (p. 66)

> As a drama it is deficient. The action is not probable. A Masque, in those parts where supernatural intervention is admitted, must indeed be given up to all the freaks of imagination; but, so far as the action is merely human, it ought to be reasonable, which

can hardly be said of the conduct of the two Brothers. . . . The discourse of the Spirit is too long; an objection that may be made to almost all the following speeches; they have not the sprightliness of a dialogue animated by reciprocal contention, but seem rather declamations deliberately composed, and formally repeated, on a moral question.

Mr. Tillyard's position with regard to the structure of *Comus* is set down in his first sentence: "Readers of *Comus* have usually failed to see that it is an experiment, not entirely unsuccessful, in drama." He goes on to analyze the "mixture of styles" in *Comus:* the Euripidean prologue, the "classicising interlude" of the "most curious stichomythia, that sounds like a very indifferent translation from Greek tragedy"; other passages reminiscent of Elizabethan and post-Elizabethan dramatists; the occasional interpolation of "exquisite circumlocutions of the pastoral,"; the lovely lines of the Lady about "a thousand fantasies," which, he says, "in their self-contained beauty can be detached with no loss of value from their histrionic setting." Mr. Tillyard concludes: (pp. 70-71)

> It is all the more noteworthy that Milton should have tried to be really dramatic in parts, because there was no apparent need for the attempt. He had written a very good masque in *Arcades* and he did not need to alter his style to write another. In fact, had he stuck to the earlier style, the masque, as a masque, would have been better. The inference is that Milton, in writing *Comus* as he did, had motives other than those of supplying a suitable entertainment for the Bridgewater family; and it would seem that he used *Comus* as a private experiment in dramatic style, in preparation for the great tragedy or Morality he at that time intended should be the end or one of the ends of his years of preparation.

Don Cameron Allen is much more drastic in "Milton's *Comus* as a Failure in Artistic Compromise," the title of which indicates the basic contention that *Comus* is a compromise between "the dramatic theme" and "the moral theme," a compromise that failed, since *Comus* is neither masque nor drama. There have been other articles on the subject, but these will serve our purposes.

The controversy over the theme and idea of *Comus* began with an article by A. S. P. Woodhouse, "The Argument of Milton's *Comus,*" a thoughtful and important essay whether one agrees with it or not. Professor Woodhouse takes the "argument" of *Comus* very seriously. He believes that Milton is dealing with two levels of existence, the order of Nature and the order of Grace, which complement each other. Grace has its foundation in Nature, but Nature is perfected by Grace. The basic theme of *Comus* is chastity, which is coupled with temperance and virginity. Temperance belongs to the order of Nature, but virginity, as Mr. Woodhouse believes it is treated by Milton, belongs wholly to Grace. Like Spenser in the *Faerie Queen,* Milton holds that chastity means not merely abstaining from evil but actively pursuing the good. "Chastity" in this sense would have been understood by many pagans, but even the Platonic vision of the Good, the True, the Beautiful fell short of the concept of "virginity" as Milton used it, which is not only a Christian virtue but the highest attainment of the Christian soul—the state of the saints in Revelation whose lives have been without stain and who join in singing the song of the Lamb.

Professor Woodhouse, like some critics who preceded and others who have followed him, makes much of the Epilogue spoken by the Attendant Spirit. Professor J. H. Hanford had earlier said that in the Epilogue Milton was talking of Paradise and the afterlife of the chaste soul. I quote from the shortened version in the *Handbook,* p. 159: "In the Spirit's epilogue Milton introduces in Pagan terms but with a Christian meaning the idea of a mystic marriage of the soul with God, the heavenly compensation for a life of chastity on earth." Professor Woodhouse believed that the Epilogue deals, not with heavenly immortality but with the life which the chaste soul enjoys here on earth—a transfiguration achieved by the soul, that rises from temperance through chastity to virginity.

Some later critics, concerned with the ideas of *Comus,* accept much that Professor Woodhouse says, as do Brooks and Hardy who acknowledge their "heaviest debt" to him (p. 235) even though they do not "minimize the importance of our frequent disagreement with him." They continue: "We do not think, as Mr. Woodhouse seems to think, that Milton's primary intention in the poem is to teach, or to argue, a doctrine. . . . More specifically, we feel that Mr. Woodhouse has all but ignored the evidences of Milton's consciousness in the poem of the possibility of conflict between classical Virtue and Christian Grace." Other critics, notably J. C. Maxwell, and Sears Jayne oppose Mr. Woodhouse sharply. The student should read these essays and make up his own mind.

Before going further, I must clarify one matter about the Epilogue which the reader would not otherwise understand. The text of *Comus* in our modern editions differs in several ways from the one Milton originally wrote for the inauguration of the Lord President of Wales. There are in existence five versions of *Comus:* Milton's original in the Cambridge Manuscript; a somewhat shortened "stage copy," or acting version, presumably used at the time of the production, one of the Bridgewater manuscripts, still in possession of the family. (An edition was published by Lady Alex Egerton in 1910.) There is the edition published by Henry Lawes in 1637 and the one Milton included in his *Poems* of 1645. There is also the one published with his other works in 1673, which does not differ in any important way from the 1645 text. The earliest printed version shows a number of variants from the manuscript copy, one of the most important of which is the insertion in the Epilogue of a number of lines. The passage stressed by modern critics is this:

> (List, mortals, if your ears be true)
> Beds of hyacinths and roses,
> Where young Adonis oft reposes,
> Waxing well of his deep wound
> In slumber soft, and on the ground
> Sadly sits the Assyrian queen;

But far above in spangled sheen
Celestial Cupid, her famed son, advanced
Holds his dear Psyche, sweet entranced
After her wandering labors long,
Till free consent the gods among
Make her his eternal bride,
And from her fair unspotted side
Two blissful twins are to be born,
Youth and Joy; so Jove hath sworn.

(ll. 997-1011)

These lines are adapted in large part from Spenser's account of the Garden of Adonis in the *Faerie Queene* (III.vi). If the main theme of *Comus* is chastity, it is possible, particularly for those inclined to read Milton's poetry autobiographically, to argue that between the manuscript of 1634 and the printed version of 1637, a change came about in the attitude toward chastity of "The Lady of Christ's." Earlier in his life Milton would seem to have equated chastity with celibacy. Has the young man now changed his mind? Had he perhaps fallen in love? Was he considering that it was about time to think of marriage? Personally I doubt that this passage should be read for any autobiographical relevance. *Comus* is not basically about chastity, nor would we think it was except for the long speech of the Elder Brother, who is certainly not Milton's only spokesman, if spokesman at all. The theme of *Comus,* as I have said, is the basic theme of a majority of English masques, the triumph of Virtue over Vice. *Comus,* I insist, was a masque. A masque was what Lawes had commissioned and he would have been the first to know if a masque had not been what he received. Milton himself, remember, did not call it *Comus,* but only *A Mask Presented at Ludlow Castle.* The opposing points of view on this matter are well expressed by Robert Martin Adams in *Ikon,* p. 2:

> Though it is often described loosely as a play and sometimes as a poem, *Comus* is so much a masque that this was its original, and for a long time its only, title. Mr. Don C. Allen has argued

recently that *Comus* is not a masque because "it is much longer than the masque as written by Jonson or Daniel; its cast of speaking characters is much smaller; its locale of action is much less fantastic; its plot, though not exactly more elaborate, is more tense; its theme is more serious; it is totally wanting in humorousness; and its emphasis is more on dramatic crisis than on spectacle, dance, costume, and even singing." . . . But Mr. Allen himself does not use these criteria seriously, or at least consistently; for example, he holds that *Arcades* is a true masque, though it has even fewer speaking characters than *Comus,* lacks humorousness entirely, and is only 109 lines long—far shorter than the masque as written by Jonson and Daniel. Besides, a work of art does not forfeit its position within a genre by differences of this sort; otherwise, one might prove, by comparing *Macbeth* with *Everyman,* that Shakespeare had not written a play.

I can think of a simpler and more practical reason than the modern critics suggest for the addition to the Epilogue of the Cupid-Psyche passage and for Milton's making the whole passage an epilogue rather than leaving some lines (as in the original) in the prologue. Masques, as we know, were written for and adapted to "occasions." But might not a masque be used again for another "occasion"? a young author might hopefully wonder. The addition of those lines would make *Comus* appropriate for a wedding-masque with a far less stereotyped ending than the entrance of Hymen who did so "oft appear."

Obviously I do not agree with the modern critics who find profundity, and somewhat esoteric levels of meaning (some of them concealed from very intelligent readers for three hundred years) in *Comus.* The "ideas" expressed by the Brothers, the Attendant Spirit, and the dialogue between the Lady and Comus, were the veriest commonplaces—most of them clichés taught to young men in the schools and universities. The masque was deftly tailored to three—possibly four or five—young actors, depending on who played Comus and who Sabrina. It was designed for a social gathering in no mood for profundity but probably as responsive as the children to magic and fairy-tale. It was written by a young man, still only twenty-six, and because of his secluded life, young for his age. The greatest single charm of *Comus* is the charm of youth. I hope Milton made the trip to Ludlow Castle to see it and take a bow with Henry Lawes, who had every reason to be proud of the masque he had commissioned from a still unknown young poet.

LYCIDAS

William Vaughan Moody wrote in his edition of Milton's poetry: "His mind was of the kind which delights to draw into one substance the thought-material of all climes and times. Into this magic vessel of the Renaissance pastoral he gathered the mythologies of Greece and Rome, the mongrel divinities of the academic myth-makers, dim old druidical traditions, the miracles of Palestine, the symbolism of the Catholic church, the angelic hierarchies of mediaeval theologians, and the mystical ecstasies of the redeemed in Paradise—all set in the frame-work of English landscape, in the midst of which a Sicilian shepherd sat piping strains of a double meaning. Surely there was never a more strangely compounded thing than *Lycidas*. Surely there was never a more astonishing instance of the wizardry of the imagination than this, where at a compelling word a hundred motley and warring suggestions are swept together and held suspended in airy unity."

Lycidas, most poets and critics have agreed, is the most perfect long short poem in the English language, and one of the greatest poems ever written. But it is so rich in its allusiveness, so pregnant with meaning and implication that readers who lack Milton's background cannot at once realize how beautiful it is. I propose to read it with you—as I have done for many years with my students—twice. The first time I will seem to you to be deliberately taking it apart and analyzing it in close detail, since there is no verse-paragraph but is filled with echoes, no phrase which is not instinct with beauty. If I seem for a time to dissect it, there is method in the "anatomizing"—a word loved by Milton's generation. I promise not to leave it in fragments. The second time, I shall try to reconstruct the parts into the perfect whole which Milton designed.

In form, *Lycidas* is a pastoral elegy. The word "elegy" as Milton and his predecessors used it, was applied broadly to various kinds of lyric poetry (originally, it had denoted certain metres, rather than themes or *genres*) but when we use the term "pastoral elegy," we usually mean a dirge or threnody, a lament for the dead, in which, following the pastoral tradition, a supposed shepherd sings a song mourning the death of another shepherd. The pastoral elegy had not been used by classical Greeks of the Golden Age. It was established in Greek literature by Theocritus, Bion and Moschus, Sicilian poets of the third century B.C., and from them passed particularly to Virgil, who followed and developed their traditions in the *Eclogues* which are the counterpart of their bucolics. These latter treat many themes besides death. The pastoral form was popular throughout the Renaissance in both Italy and England. Milton's most immediate predecessor in the form had been Spenser, particularly in *The Shepherd's Calendar*. Unlike some of the classical forms which Milton inherited, the pastoral elegy did not come to an end in the seventeenth century. Next to *Lycidas* in poetic greatness is Shelley's *Adonais,* his threnody on the death of Keats. Matthew Arnold's *Thyrsis* on the death of Arthur Hugh Clough is in the same tradition, and here the tradition really ends. Tennyson's *In Memoriam* has much in common with *Lycidas* and *Adonais* but Tennyson does not use the pastoral tradition either in structure or style.

With his admiration for the classics, Milton always followed classical models when they existed, as they did for nearly all his poems except the sonnets. When he believed that a pattern had been established, he used the pattern—though he usually transcended it. Before studying *Lycidas,* one should read at least three pastoral elegies written by the Sicilians, to see what patterns they had established: Idyl I of Theocritus, with the lament of the shepherd Thyrsis for his lost companion, Daphnis; Idyl I of Bion, "The Lament for Adonis," the youth beloved by Venus, who had been gored to death by a boar; Idyl III of Moschus, "The Lament for Bion" who had apparently met his death through poison. We notice at once one device used by all three which is not in *Lycidas* but which Milton used in his Latin pastoral elegy on the death of Charles Diodati, *Epitaphium Damonis,:* the refrain, which marks the stanzaic form, usually beginning with a line like, "Begin ye Muses dear, begin the shepherd's song," and changing toward the end to, "Give o'er, ye Muses dear, now cease the shepherd's song." Each of the classical poets begins by indicating the reason for his song—the death of a shepherd. Each suggests what might be called "the lament of Nature" for the dead shepherd. Sometimes the mourning is of animals—wolves, jackals, lions; often it is the lament of trees or flowers, nightingales and swans, or such aspects of Nature as rivers, caves, mountains. Frequently we hear the names of flowers, sometimes in a passage in which they are brought to deck the bier of the dead. Like Nature, the gods come to mourn and praise the shepherd. "Came Hermes first from the hill. . . . Came also Priapus. . . . Yea, and Galatea laments thy song. . . . And the Satyrs mourned thee, and the Priape in sable raiment, and the Panes sorrow for thy song." The lament of Nature, the flower passages, the procession of mourners—these had all been further developed by poets who had followed the tradition which Milton had inherited. We shall find them in *Lycidas* interwoven with other patterns and designs to make a whole which, while purposely derivative, is unique in poetry. Enough for introduction: let us turn to the poem.

Analysis of *Lycidas*

"In this monody the author bewails a learned friend"—we are familiar with the circumstances so that I need not labor the little prose-introduction except to call your attention to the word "monody," to which we shall return. Like the classical writers before him, Milton begins by stating the reason for writing. A shepherd has died, a shepherd who had sung his songs, a young shepherd who had not come to maturity. The shepherd who remains must gather leaves to make the wreaths classical writers associated with funerals, leaves of evergreen plants, laurel, myrtle, ivy. Laurel, we know, was a symbol of triumph, the laurel wreath given to the victor, whether he lived or died. Myrtle, with its darker leaf, is a symbol of mourning. Listen for those two motifs as we go on —triumph and lament. But, because the death was untimely, the plants themselves had not yet ripened. The berries are still harsh and crude, and the fingers of the shepherd are forced to tear them rudely "before the mellowing year." Lycidas is dead, dead ere his prime. What shepherd-poet would refuse to sing a song in memory of the shepherd who was himself a poet? The lines that follow (12-14) echo the belief of our classical ancestors that the spirits of the dead would not rest in peace unless some reverence was paid to the body, a belief deeply embedded in primitive and sophisticated alike, lying behind customs like funerals or memorial services. If you have read the *Antigone* of Sophocles, you will remember that this custom of paying reverence to a dead body lay behind the tragedy of Antigone, torn between the law of the state which had forbidden any kind of burial rites to Polynices and the filial piety of a sister who must do something—even scatter earth or ashes upon the corpse—so that her brother's soul might rest. No reverence could be paid to the body of Edward King who had been drowned at sea but symbolically his brother-shepherds could bring their wreaths of laurel and myrtle (their memorial volume) as their sad service.

Like his classical models, Milton uses an invocation to the Muses: "Begin then, Sisters of the sacred well." The Muses, like many gods, might be invoked at various places. Why did Milton specifically localize them at the Pierian spring? The answer is important, and leads to a reiterated device in *Lycidas*. As you will see, this is a *water-poem,* filled with water-images, peculiarly suitable for a poem on the death of a young man drowned at sea. "Begin, and somewhat loudly sweep the string." If you have a talent, says Milton, and are asked to use it in the service of your friend, do not be coy, do not wait to be teased; do it with all your might and as well as you can. If the situation had been reversed, you would have wanted your friend to sing for you:

> So may some gentle Muse
> With lucky words (words of good auspices) favor my
>   destined urn,
> And as he passes turn,
> And bid fair peace be to my sable shroud.

(ll. 19-22)

So far we have had an introduction or prologue in the classical manner, stating the situation, setting the mood. Now we come to the first of the three main sections into which *Lycidas* is divided. (In spite of identation and punctuation, I prefer to begin Part I with lines 23-24.)

> For we were nursed upon the self-same hill,
> Fed the same flock, by fountain, shade, and rill.

So, indeed, the two shepherds had grown up together on the hill of learning at Cambridge. In those days when the curriculum was prescribed and not elective, two students at Christ's College did many things together.

> Together both, ere the high lawns appeared
> Under the opening eyelids of the morn,
> We drove afield.

(ll. 25-27)

At Cambridge, students began the day at five o'clock with morning prayers and services, went to breakfast at six, and to classes at seven. They were together in the morning, at high noon ("What time the gray-fly winds her sultry horn") throughout the afternoon and into the evening, when Hesperus, the evening star rose. Since King, like Milton, had been an unusually serious student, they had both studied—perhaps together—far later into the night than the regulations required or—indeed—permitted: a serious matter in days when artificial lighting was primitive and, as Milton's case proved, hard on student eyes.

But it had not all been hard work at Cambridge, even for these two young men who studied later and longer than classmates. There had been plenty of extra-curricular activities. As in *L'Allegro* there was singing and dancing ("the rural ditties were not mute"). Then as now there were various kinds of dancers. Students—particularly girls—will catch the sly humor of the "rough Satyrs" and "Fauns with cloven heel," if they know what satyrs and fauns looked like and what they represented. "And old Damoetas loved to hear our song." Many years ago in my salad days, I was sure I knew who "old Damoetas" was, and wrote an article to identify him with Joseph Mede, the great Biblical scholar, one of the most learned men at Cambridge, but also immensely popular with undergraduates to whom he often gave affectionate and teasing nick-names. There have been other claimants since that time. It does not matter: Some "member of the faculty," as we would say, who used to share the evening pleasures of his students.

So far the first part has been happy reminiscence of days and evenings at college, almost as light in mood as *L'Allegro*. Remembering the pleasure of happy times together, we forget for a moment what has happened, until our ears, attuned to the "glad sound" hear a different note:

¹ But Ō the hēavy chañge, now thōu aīt gōne,
Now thōu art gōne, and nēver mūst retūrn!

(ll. 37-38)

Read the words aloud. You should always read Milton aloud and let your ears listen, for he is one of the greatest poets of sound. The spondaic emphasis is the tolling of a bell, cutting across happy memories with the insistent reiteration: "But he is dead." Like the Sicilian poets, Milton phrases his "lament of Nature." The woods and caves are silent, no longer echoing to the young voice that once sang there. The willows and the hazels will never again fan their joyous leaves to the sound of his voice. His death is reflected in the death of many things in Nature. The comparisons are to blights that cause the death of young things. As the disease of canker kills the rose, as the worm kills the young herds and flocks, as frost kills flowers, so ugly death has killed the promise of youth.

Why did God let it happen? (ll. 50-63) It is the rebellious cry of every generation, even though still couched in pagan pastoral language. Edward King was drowned. Where were the nymphs, the guardians of the waves? Either they should have been on the water or, if on land, where they could watch the water. Since King had been drowned in the Irish Channel, Milton calls to the nymphs in places associated with the western coast of the British Isles: Mona (Anglesey), an island off the Welsh coast, hills sacred to the Druids, the river Dee—a water-image—"wizard" because of legends that the motion of the waters of that river prognosticated future events. "If only," as we have all said regretfully, "if only." But we speak in vain. "Ay, me, I fondly (foolishly) dream." If only the nymphs had been there. The mood deepens as the poet remembers another young singer, far more important than this one, who met a sudden death: Orpheus. Here is that recurrent motif we have already found in *L'Allegro* and *Il Penseroso*, but in very different strain. This is not the love story of Orpheus and Eurydice. The founder of music and poetry, who could charm stones and trees and wild animals with his lyre, was killed by enraged Bac-

chantes whose rites he had dared watch, torn to pieces, and his
dismembered body thrown into the Hebrus River—a water-image:

> His gory visage down the stream was sent,
> Down the swift Hebrus to the Lesbian shore.

(ll. 62-63)

Such was the fate of the father of poetry, himself the son of a
Muse, Calliope, who was powerless to save her son.

The mood has deepened and become increasingly sombre, as
Milton's subconscious reflections upon his own life become more
and more involved with the life and death of his subject. The death
of youth is always shocking, and accidental death most unbeara-
ble of all. Milton's mother had died shortly before he wrote this
poem, but she had died in the fullness of years, having lived a good
life. Milton and King had been almost the same age. Like young
people of all times they had felt that "The World was all before
them, where to choose." Suddenly one was dead, by shipwreck.
Milton was about to take ship for Italy. The parallels were very
close between two young men who had devoted themselves to study
and to poetry at Cambridge. "Cui bono?"

> Alas! what boots it with uncessant care,
> To tend the homely slighted shepherd's trade,
> And strictly meditate the thankless Muse?

(ll. 64-66)

Perhaps our classmates were wiser than we, with their easy hedo-
nistic philosophy of "carpe diem." While we studied late at night,
they sported with Amaryllis and Neaera—lovely names for charm-
ing girls. What were we working for, King and I? Was it for fame,
that spur that leads men "to scorn delights and live laborious
days?" (ll. 70-72) The desire for fame may be an infirmity, but
if so, it is the last from which even noble minds free themselves.
(The parenthetical line is almost a direct quotation from Tacitus.)
But what *is* fame? At the very moment that we reach out eager
hands for reward, expecting a blaze of glory

Comes the blind Fury with the abhorréd shears,
And slits the thin-spun life.

(ll. 75-76)

This is an extraordinary figure, so pregnant with meaning that many critics miss its full portent. The shears that cut the thread of life belonged to the Fates; Clotho spun, Lachesis carded, Atropos cut the thread when the time had come. We think of the Fates as some of us have seen them among the Elgin Marbles in the British Museum, much like the presiding spirit of *Il Penseroso* who could forget herself to marble, calm and just, with an immense passivity. What has Milton done? He has deliberately transferred the scissors of the Fates to one of a very different trio—the Furies. They also were three in number, but their function was quite different. Avenging deities, they sought a culprit throughout the world and found him, bringing vengeance upon him. But Milton has done still more with his figure. In pictorial art, the Furies have the brightest and most searching of eyes—which they need to find their prey. Milton has blinded the eyes of the Fury to whom he has given the shears. Life and death—it is all as meaningless as that. We have reached the nadir of Part I.

But across the sombre pessimism, another note strikes on our ears. It begins abruptly in the middle of a line.

"But not the praise,"
Phoebus replied, and touched my trembling ears.

(ll. 76-77)

There is a reminiscence here of a Virgilian eclogue in which Apollo touched the poet's ears, bidding him not be impatient for ambition. The fame of sudden blaze is only Fama, rumor, that flies over the housetops, a false glitter. True fame is not pagan but Christian; God, who alone can pronounce upon each life, says, "Well done, thou good and faithful servant. . . . Enter thou into the joy of thy lord." The first part of *Lycidas* is over. From patterns that

any classical writer might have used, we have imperceptibly risen
from paganism to Christianity*

Part II begins on conventional pastoral strain, again with an in-
troduction:

> O fountain Arethuse, and thou honored flood,
> Smooth-sliding Mincius, crowned with vocal reeds,
> That strain I heard was of a higher mood.
> But now my oat proceeds. . . .

(ll. 85-88)

The two water-images imply the two sources of pastoral elegy.
Arethusa, who to escape Alpheus, was turned into a fountain, was
in Sicily, home of Theocritus, Bion, Moschus. The reedy river Min-
cius was associated with Virgil's Eclogues. Milton is saying in ef-
fect: "Oh, spirit of pastoral poetry, I have risen to the higher
strains of Christianity, but now I return to the pagan conventions
of the pastoral elegy, and again sing my shepherd's song." Yet
there is a subtle change here, which we shall find as Part II de-
velops. In the classical tradition, the "shepherd" was a poet. But
the word "shepherd" had a different connotation to the Christian.
Edward King had written poetry at Cambridge, but primarily he had
been preparing himself for holy orders. To the Christian, Christ
was the Good Shepherd, who gave His life for His sheep. Watch

---

* Here, it will be seen, I disagree with those critics who hold that Part I is
pagan, Part II, Christian. For example, M. H. Abrams says, "Five Types of
Lycidas" (in *Milton's Lycidas: the Tradition and the Poem*), pp. 227-228:
"The immediate comfort is vouchsafed the singer in a thought in which the
highest pagan ethics comes closest to the Christian: the distinction between
mere earthly reputation and the need of true fame awarded by a divine and
infallible judge. The concept is only tangentially Christian, however, for the
deities named in this passage, Phoebus and Jove, are pagan ones." Here I
cannot agree. "Pan" and "Christ," "Jove" and "God" are used interchange-
ably by Milton as by most Renaissance poets. Milton was too good a classi-
cist to give the epithet "all-judging" to the wrong deity. Jove was not the
judge of Hades; Rhadamanthus was. And Milton himself, as Mr. Abrams
notes, indicates that the strain he has just heard was of a "higher mood," just
as in the Prologue to Book IX of *Paradise Lost* and elsewhere, he empha-
sizes the "higher argument" of a Christian epic over a pagan.

and see how imperceptibly we pass from one connotation to the other.

As in Part I, Milton introduced an old convention, the "lament of Nature," so here he uses another, "the procession of mourners." The first lines of Part II might have been written by any of the classical poets. Neptune, god of the sea, sends his herald, who is joined by Hippotades, god of winds, both of whom declare that there was no storm when Edward King's ship went down. Indeed, it was so calm that Panope and her sisters, the fifty daughters of Nereus, were playing on the waves. To the pagan mind, there could have been no explanation other than that the ship had been built during an eclipse, a time when omens were inauspicious, making the bark "fatal" and "rigged with curses dark."

With subtle transition Milton introduces into the conventional pagan procession, Camus—a water-image. The spirit of Cambridge is personified not as *alma mater,* since this is a masculine procession, but as a reverend sire: Cambridge was already old when Milton was young. Milton may have written impatiently to Diodati that Cambridge was no place for poets, but the spell that Cambridge casts over her sons echoes in the lovely lines in which the poet anthropomorphizes the slow little river Cam, so familiar to Cambridge undergraduates of every generation, sedge-grass growing along the banks, shadows in the water, "inwrought with figures dim," and hyacinths along the banks—Greek hyacinths, bearing upon their petals the Greek words "ai, ai" (alas) in memory of the slain youth, Hyacinthus. The spirit of Cambridge speaks only one line, but it is an epitaph any graduate might envy: " 'Ah, who hath reft,' quoth he, 'my *dearest* pledge?' "

Almost imperceptibly we have again risen above the pagan conventions. The "reverend sire" prepares us for a sire more reverend still:

Last came, and last did go
The pilot of the Galilean Lake.

(ll. 108-109)

Among the many associations he might have made with the earlier life of St. Peter, Milton inevitably chooses a water-image, remembering that he was a pilot on the Lake of Galilee. As he stands before us, the climax of the procession, he is the founder of the Church: "Thou art Peter, and upon this rock I will build my church. . . . I will give unto thee the keys of the kingdom of Heaven." Here is another recurrent motif in Milton. The "two massy keys . . . of metals twain," we shall see again in *Paradise Lost*. Upon his head St. Peter wears the Bishop's mitre. Camus had praised Edward King as an outstanding student. St. Peter eulogizes him as the true shepherd-priest who would have devoted his life to his flock. His invective is turned upon the false clergy, "our corrupted clergy, then in their height," as Milton's prose-preface put it.

While reading these lines, every student of Milton should turn to one of the finest explications ever written upon any passage of poetry, Ruskin's first essay in *Sesame and Lilies*. Word by word Ruskin analyzes this passage, showing his audience how to read a piece of poetry close-packed with meaning. The false clergy are those who enter the Church for base motives. They "creep and intrude and climb into the fold." The verbs are chosen carefully, to describe those who creep in underhand ways, those who intrude —thrust themselves—into the fold, those who get to the top by climbing over the shoulders of others. They are in the sheepfold, not to care for the sheep, but only for material gain, for what they can get out of it. They have not bothered to learn their craft. They scarcely know how to hold the instruments they are supposed to use. They eat and drink, and the songs they sing are "lean and flashy." Instead of making music, they "grate on their scrannel pipes of wretched straw." Stop and say that aloud and listen to the cacophony. It is deliberately one of the ugliest lines Milton ever wrote. And meanwhile, what of the flocks? While the shepherds eat and drink, the hungry sheep are not fed. The dread plague of sheeprot spreads among them, a fearful epidemic among sheep that are starving and dirty. Many die in the sheepfold, and for those that live there waits close by the "grim Wolf with privy paw," the Roman Catholic Church, only too ready to eat up sheep neglected by Protestant shepherds.

The bitter invective against "our corrupt clergy" has been summed up in one phrase that falls from the lips of the father of the Church: "Blind mouths." Here is one of the most famous examples of Milton's extraordinary ability to say much in little, to cross-fertilize images until they are so compressed and pregnant with meaning that they become the despair of critics who spend their ingenuity in trying to find still more cryptic meanings. Let us not stop over the many interpretations that have been made of this apparently mixed metaphor. Ruskin was right beyond question, I believe, because he understood better than those who preceded and many who have followed, the way in which Milton's allusive imagination worked.

St. Peter is a bishop. The word *bishop* and the word *Episcopal* are both derived from a Greek word (episkopeo) which means "one who oversees." The function of the Bishop is to watch over his flock. The worst thing that could happen to a bishop is that he should be blind. The word *pastor* is derived from a Latin word meaning "to pasture" or "to feed." Starvation will come upon the flock if the pastor who should feed his sheep becomes a mouth. Here, as in a lightning flash, is the supreme invective of the founder of the Church upon "blind bishops and greedy pastors."

A still more mysterious crux occurs in the last two lines of Part II. Having inveighed against false bishops and pastors, St. Peter prophesies their doom:

'But that two-handed engine at the door
Stands ready to smite once, and smite no more.'

(ll. 130-131)

"Engine" might refer to almost any instrument. "Engines of destruction" was a familiar phrase in Milton's time. I shall make no attempt to summarize the fifty interpretations that have been offered for "that two-handed engine," ranging from a suggestion that it refers to the two Houses of Parliament to a most ingenious theory of a Columbia University student in a Master's essay (published in part by Claude Thompson, " 'That Two-Handed Engine' will Smite") that the "engine" might be the kind of mechanical clock familiar in Milton's day. In the tower of old St. Paul's, for example, was one in which the arm of an angel pointed warningly to the hour that marked the passage of time, ready to strike with two hands the hour of one. If we must visualize the engine of destruction, I think we may best do so as the great sword which the Archangel Michael brought down "with huge two-handed sway" upon Satan in *Paradise Lost* (VI. 251). Personally, I do not think that Milton visualized it, nor did he intend us to. He did not know how judgment was to come upon the corrupt clergy; he was assured only that fearful justice would be meted out to them, prophesied by the voice of doom, saying: "Vengeance is mine, I will repay, saith the Lord." The second part of *Lycidas* is over.

As at the conclusion of Part I, we have again risen from pagan convention to Christianity, though the voice we have heard is that of the Old Testament rather than the New, a "dread voice," as Milton says. We return to the classical tradition and conventions, again through a water-image, the river Alpheus, which takes us back to the "fountain Arethuse" of Part I, since in mythology the hunter-god Alpheus pursued the nymph Arethusa under the sea to Sicily, where Arethusa had become a fountain, whose waters finally mingled with his. Again, the figure implies both Sicily and Italy. Theocritus and Virgil. As in the two previous parts, Milton introduces another convention, this time the passage of flowers, brought to strew "the laureate hearse where Lycid lies." (An interesting interpretation of this and the following passage will be found in Wayne Shumaker, "Flowerets and Sounding Seas," in *Milton's Lycidas: The Tradition and the Poem,* pp. 125-135.) There are reminiscences in Milton's flower-passage of Shakespeare's in *The Winter's Tale,* though Milton naturally emphasizes flowers that seem to mourn: "every flower that sad embroidery wears"; "the rathe primrose that forsaken dies"; "the pansy freaked with jet."

The amaranth sheds its beauty, the cowslips hang their pensive heads, and "daffadillies fill their cups with tears." Again, as in Part I, death in Nature reflects the death of a shepherd.

Across the old convention, as in the tolling of the line in Part I, "But O the heavy change now thou art gone," comes the poignant realization that even the last sad rites of decking the laureate hearse are denied the mourners. The body of Lycidas is lost and will never be found. The water-theme reaches its height in the lines beginning:

> Ay me! whilst thee the shores and sounding seas
> Wash far away, where'er thy bones are hurled.
>
> (ll. 154-155)

The great power of the passage is as overwhelming as the "whelming tide," that relentlessly carries us with it, as it dispassionately and with fearful impersonality, carries the flotsam and jetsam the sea sucks down or casts up—timber of wrecked ships, floating or engulfed bodies of the drowned. "Where'er thy bones are hurled" —our imaginations sweep in a long journey around the British Isles, from the farthest outposts of the "stormy Hebrides," the remote northwestern islands, then to the "bottom of the monstrous world," inhabited only by mysterious sea-monsters, then round the coast, under the Irish Sea, to the southwest corner of England, Land's End, in Roman times called "Bellerium," after the giant Bellerus. Here St. Michael's Mount guards the shore. As in a vision our imaginations are swept again along the southern shore to Spain, "Namancos and Bayona's hold," toward which the Archangel Michael, "the great Vision of the guarded mount" seems to look. Northwest, southwest, south or east—we shall never know on what far-flung journey the lonely body of our dead friend has been carried:

> Look homeward, Angel, now and melt with ruth,
> And O ye dolphins, waft the hapless youth.
>
> (ll. 163-164)

Christian archangel, classical dolphins who in legend carried the living Arion safe to shore, brought to shore, too, the dead body of Palaemon. Pagan and Christian, death and life, the two strains combine in the triumphant conclusion in which they are inextricably conjoined.

> Weep no more, woeful shepherds, weep no more,
> For Lycidas, your sorrow, is not dead.

> (ll. 165-166)

So pagan might have said, so Christian, though they couched the belief in different images. The pagan might use the analogy of the sun setting and rising: at night, the sun seems to disappear into the ocean, but in the morning, with renewed radiance, it "flames in the forehead of the morning sky." The Christian thinks of the Resurrection through Christ. Of the many aspects in which he might have remembered Christ, Milton inevitably chooses a water-image: Christ walking upon the waves that threatened His disciples, "the dear might of him that walked the waves." The pagan shepherd has left this world for the groves and streams and nectar of the Isles of the Blest. The Christian soul has ascended into Heaven, where, as in Revelation, he hears the inexpressible "nuptial song," the marriage supper of the Lamb. As in Dante's *Paradiso,* he enters into the communion of saints,

> In solemn troops and sweet societies
> That sing, and singing in their glory move,
> And wipe the tears forever from his eyes.

> (ll. 179-181)

We hear the echo of Revelation VII. 17, when "the Lamb shall be their shepherd . . . and God shall wipe away every tear from their eyes."

As we began with a pagan convention, so we end, as the shepherds cease their lament. Drowned though he was, their friend has not died in vain. He has become the Genius, the tutelary deity of the shore of the sea that claimed his body but left free his spirit to guide and protect those who come after. Pagan and Christian combine for all of us must "wander in that perilous flood," the dangers of the world each of us must encounter on our journey through life.

The song of the shepherd, with its antiphonal mourning and triumph, is over. Like various of his classical predecessors, Milton adds an epilogue, in which the first person changes to the third: "Thus sang the uncouth swain to the oaks and rills." So an unknown shepherd has sung his pastoral elegy in memory of a dead friend. But the day is over. The sun has stretched out all the hills and dropped into the western bay. It is time to take home the sheep. Life must go on in spite of death. Tomorrow he will lead his flock again, but to another pasture in which there will be fewer memories and echoes of a dead friend. The shepherd's song for Lycidas is over.

Structure of *Lycidas*

I have said that we must read *Lycidas* together twice, once for careful analysis, again for synthesis, and so we shall. But before I turn to synthesis, I must stop over peculiarities of the structure and style of the poem which make it unique in English—or, indeed, any other—poetry. Faithful though it is in many ways to the classical conventions, *Lycidas* is like no preceding classical or Renaissance elegy, as it is unlike the later *Adonais* or *Thyrsis*. It follows no stanzaic pattern known among classical or English poets. Indeed, we usually speak of it as a succession of "verse paragraphs," rather than stanzas. There are eleven of these, in length from ten to thirty-one lines. Some lines rhyme, but in no regular pattern. Ten lines, scattered at irregular intervals, do not rhyme at all. The metre is basically iambic pentameter, but fourteen lines are trimeter, which are always rhymed and always with pentameter lines, not with each other. Only the Epilogue is in a regular form, *ottava rima*. The structure of the whole poem, as I have showed you in my analysis, is tripartite, with an introduction and epilogue, but again there is no regularity in the lengths of the parts. Part I (as I have read it) is sixty-one lines; Part II, forty-six; Part III, fifty-three lines.

Conscious as he always was of models, did Milton have a pattern for his extraordinary non-stanzaic stanza form? Many suggestions have been made, though no two critics tend to agree with one another. Each has his favorite hypothesis, or, indeed, lets his imagination play with several, as I shall let mine. In his juvenilia, we watched Milton experimenting with stanzaic pattern and setting himself metrical exercises. On two occasions, in "On Time" and "At a Solemn Music," we caught ,anticipations of *Lycidas*. I said at that time that Milton might have been attempting a variant upon the Pindaric Ode. If I were to suggest that Part III of *Lycidas* (and to some extent, Part II) consists of strophe (the flower-passage), antistrophe (the "sounding sea") and epode (the apotheosis) I should be using the terms not as Pindar would have used them, to be sure, but hardly more loosely than did many who thought themselves his followers. But I shall not attempt to prove that *Lycidas* is a series of Pindaric odes. Nor shall I develop another hypothesis which sometimes teases me: similarities between *Lycidas* and the *genre* of the "meditation" (what Louis Martz calls "the poetry of meditation") or the kind of devotional literature we find in John Donne's prose-poem *Devotions,* each of which falls into three parts, Meditation, Expostulation, Prayer. (The "fame" passage and that of St. Peter might prove nice examples of "expostulation" and each of the three parts of *Lycidas* rises to religious climax.) But again the passing similarities are too vague to offer any real explanation for the extraordinarily subtle structure of *Lycidas*.

If Milton was following any literary tradition, I incline to that suggested by W. P. Ker and most fully and persuasively developed by F. T. Prince ("The Italian Element in *Lycidas,"* in *Milton's Lycidas: The Tradition and the Poem,* pp. 153-166). Mr. Ker said: "You cannot fully understand Lycidas without going back to Italy and the theory and practice of the *canzone.*" He believed that the "solemn odes" written in England from Spenser's *Epithala-mion* down to the nineteenth century stemmed from Dante's description of the *canzone* in *De Vulgari Eloquentia.* I refer you to Mr. Prince for a much fuller explanation, quoting from him only a few passages which may explain to you what *canzone* implies.

> A *canzone* consisted of a complex, fully rhymed stanza of some length, repeated several times and followed by a shorter concluding stanza, the *commiato.* . . . The stanza of a *canzone* is most commonly built of two sections, which are linked by a key line or *chiave.* Such a stanza was called a *stanza divisa.* . . . The first part of a *stanza divisa* must be linked to the second by a line rhyming with the last line of the first; this line was the *chiave* or key.

In Italy had come about a liberation of lyric verse from such over-rigid stanzaic form, a liberation with which Milton was undoubtedly familiar, particularly in Tasso's *Aminta* and Guarini's *Il Pastor Fido,* marked by irregular lyric and partially rhymed semi-lyrical passages, which are similar in various ways to *Lycidas.* So much for various literary traditions which may or may not lie behind the poem. I have been careful to say, "If Milton was following a literary tradition." But was the model or pattern of *Lycidas* primarily literary, or may he have been deliberately attempting a wedding of two "sister arts," poetry and music?

Lycidas—A Synthesis

When such earlier critics as George Saintsbury, J. H. Hanford, Laurence Binyon and a number of others were writing of *Lycidas,* musical analogies were often on their lips. The effect of the poem was "symphonic," its changing moods were "changing keys"; the pleasure it produces is the pleasure of music. At least as early as 1924, somewhat younger than these elder statesmen, I too was teaching *Lycidas* by musical analogies, and like them using such terms as "symphony" and "sonata." I knew these parallels were

anachronistic, for Milton would not have understood these terms as
we use them in the twentieth century, but I had no musical vo-
cabulary contemporary with Milton's, nor did I know what mu-
sical forms he might have known. It remained for one of my
student-colleagues at Smith College to tell me what I had only
vaguely surmised, that there *were* musical forms familiar to Mil-
ton, resembling closely the structure and style of *Lycidas*. In
Gretchen Finney's "A Musical Background for *Lycidas*" (*Musical
Backgrounds for English Literature,* pp. 194-219), you will find the
vocabulary and the background I lacked, and will learn how close
Lycidas is to certain forms of Italian music contemporary with
Milton. She will explain, too, why Milton wrote in the prose-
preface: "In this monody the author bewails a learned friend."
Monody is a term with both literary and musical connotations. In
literature it is usually associated with a poem of lament sung by
one person for another. It denoted as well a musical style, supposed
to have been used in Greek tragedy. In Italy in Milton's time the
word *monodia,* as Mrs. Finney says, "was used specifically for
music sung by a solo voice in the new recitative style. . . . Mon-
ody was discussed usually in connection with musical drama."
Lycidas is a monody in both the literary and musical senses. Let us
read it again to see how Milton united two arts.

    Lycidas begins with an introduction which is also an overture to
a piece of music, a kind of oratorio, in which Milton sets two dom-
inant motifs, which will echo antiphonally, now in apparent op-
position, now one transcending the other. They are embodied for
me in the "laurel" and the "myrtle" the poet plucks in classical
fashion to symbolize the "melodious tear" shed by the mourner
that the soul of his dead shepherd-friend might find rest. Myrtle
and laurel, sadness and triumph—let your ears listen for them,
and do not forget that the laurel is mentioned first, as it will be
sounded last.

    From the overture, we come to Part I, the first movement of
my anachronistic "sonata-symphony." It begins in pastoral strain,
with the simple music of the shepherd's pipes and a solo voice:

For we were nursed upon the self-same hill,
Fed the same flock by fountain, shade, and rill.

(ll. 23-24)

Simple, quiet, almost prosaic in diction, the lines introduce a passage of conventional pastoral elegy in which the voice of the shepherd tells of long leisurely days spent by two young shepherds on the hill of learning. Rising before daylight, together "ere the high lawns appeared under the opening eyelids of the morn," they "drove afield" until high noon, then into the afternoon and often far into the night, studying while others slept or sported with Amaryllis. But it was not all hard work at Cambridge:

Meanwhile the rural ditties were not mute,
Tempered to the oaten flute,
Rough Satyrs danced and Fauns with cloven heel
From the glad sound would not be absent long.

(ll. 25-32)

There is a change in the music; they dance to the glad sound, the Fauns as light and gay as the dancers in *L'Allegro,* the Satyrs, grotesquely amusing, rather like Comus' rabble rout. The pastoral music of the dance makes us remember only happy days and evenings at Cambridge and forget for a moment that they will not come again.

Across the pastoral fields, as across the dancing music, comes the ominous tolling of the passing bell:

But Ō, the hēavy chānge, nōw thōu art gōne,
Now thōu art gōne, and nēver mūst retūrn!

The mood begins to deepen as the myrtle motif emerges in the lament of Nature for a dead shepherd—canker, taint-worm, frost, ugly names for ugly powers that kill the young in Nature. The myrtle motif deepens still more as the shepherd who is left cries aloud: "Why did the gods—why did God—permit this to happen?" Reflection upon the meaninglessness of life grows more sombre as the poet remembers the death not only of another unknown young poet but of the father of poetry, Orpheus, greatest of them all, torn to pieces by enraged and intoxicated Bacchantes. The music is strident, cacophonous as the furious "rout that made the hideous roar," as the dismembered body of Orpheus was carried by the relentless stream "down the swift Hebrus to the Lesbian shore."

If this is all there is to life, what does anything mean? Why did we labor those long days and nights, Edward King and I? If it was for fame, what then is fame?

> Were it not better done as others use,
> To sport with Amaryllis in the shade,
> Or with the tangles of Neaera's hair?
>
> (ll. 67-69)

Lines which against their somber setting, catch for the moment the Cavalier music of *carpe diem*. Life has not only meaning but tragic irony, for at that moment when we hold out eager hands for the "fair guerdon" and "think to burst out into sudden blaze,"

> Comes the blind Fury with the abhorred shears,
> And slits the thin-spun life.
>
> (ll. 75-76)

Now that you understand the closely-packed figure, you see how horrible it is, a symbol of the blind, perverse meaninglessness of life in which there is no design, no plan, no justice, no God— only blind Fury. This is both the height and the nadir of the myrtle motif.

But across man's questioning of God and the despair that can find no meaning in the universe, abruptly—in the middle of a line —we hear the laurel replying to the myrtle, the beginning of triumph:

> "But not the praise,"
> Phoebus replied, and touched my trembling ears.
>
> (ll. 76-77)

The "fame" you sought was not true fame. Fame is no plant of mortal soil, no guerdon of flashy tinsel, no "sudden blaze" of a moment's adulation from your fellow-men. True fame is in the sight of God. There *is* justice, there *is* meaning, there *is* reward in the "pure eyes And perfect witness of all-judging Jove," who alone can say: "Well done, thou good and faithful servant; enter now into the joy of thy reward." The laurel motif rises to a crescendo as the Divine Voice seems accompanied by a chorus of angels, welcoming the true and faithful shepherd into the joys of Paradise. The first movement of *Lycidas* is over. Instrumental accompaniment, solo voice and choral come to a climax in the "higher mood" as the laurel of Christianity triumphs over the myrtle of lament.

The second movement, like the first, begins with pastoral strain as the shepherd's "oat proceeds," and he introduces the procession of mourners, the Herald of the Sea, Hippotades, Camus. The first movement was secular, devoted to the "shepherd as poet." This is ecclesiastical, a lament for the "shepherd as priest." The spirit of Cambridge, in his one solo line, praises the son he had trained for the priesthood: "Ah, who hath reft," quoth he, "my dearest pledge?" The music deepens as St. Peter (a basso profundo, I feel sure) inveighs against the false clergy who "creep and intrude and climb" into the fold for material gain. The invective rises to a first climax of sound in the passion of that terrible phrase, "Blind mouths!" Deliberate cacophony cuts across the harmony in phrase after phrase of ugly words: "for their bellies's sake"; "how to scramble at the shearers' feast"; "swoln with wind and the rank mist," most of all in the discordant sound as

> lean and flashy songs
> Grate on their scrannel pipes of wretched straw.
>
> (ll. 123-124)

The myrtle motif has remained dominant throughout the second movement. Although the rest of the movement has been recitative, the last two "laurel" lines:

> But that two-handed engine at the door
> Stands ready to smite once, and smite no more
>
> (ll. 130-131)

are—in my ears—choral. Other singers join with the voice of St. Peter as orchestra and the full chorus of "ancestral voices prophesying" rise to a great crescendo. How and when judgment will come, we do not know, but come it will: "Vengeance is mine and recompense." "I will repay," saith the Lord. As in Revelation "there followed silence in Heaven."

The third movement, like the first and second, begins in pastoral strain, with inherited conventions. The "lament of Nature," the "procession of mourners" is paralleled by the "catalogue of flowers," mourning the dead shepherd. This passage might well be choral. The tempo is deliberately slowed in the last line:

To strēw the laūreate heārse where Lȳcid līes (1.151).
Recitative begins in the passage, "Ay me!" but this is the declamatory, the oratorical style. "One is impressed," as Mrs. Finney says, "by its grandiloquence, the loud, open vowels, the prolonged quantity of the words"—all add to that sense of vast distance, remoteness, loneliness as our imaginations are carried with the drowned body from northwest to south, from south across the Channel to Spain, returning again to England with the "great Vision of the guarded mount." We feel the destructive power of impersonal Nature in the "sounding seas" that "wash far away," in the violence of, "where'er thy bones are hurled," the "stormy Hebrides," the "whelming tide," the "bottom of the monstrous world." Across the myrtle of lament not only for death but for the destruction of the body begins to rise the laurel motif, as we hear a Christian promise of Heaven in "Look homeward, Angel," a pagan memory of the salvation of a body by dolphins.

The laurel rises to its climax in the great choral passage in which all voices combine in victorious crescendo:

Weep no more, woeful shepherds, weep no more,
For Lycidas, your sorrow, is not dead.
                                        (ll. 165-166)

The pagan expressed the belief in natural terms—much like those of Ecclesiastes, the Preacher—"The sun also riseth, and the sun

goeth down and hasteth to the place where it riseth." The theme
of the rebirth and renewal in Nature rises with the sun to that glori-
ous line:

> Flames in the forehead of the morning sky.
>
> (l. 171)

So too the Christian strain of the mighty chorus soars as the soul
of the dead shepherd-priest rises to the "solemn troops and sweet
societies" of the saints in Paradise, reaching a climax in the majes-
tic lines:

> That sing, and singing in their glory move,
> And wipe the tears forever from his eyes.
>
> (ll. 180-181)

The rebirth of Nature, the Resurrection of the soul "through the
dear might of him that walked the waves"—for pagan and for
Christian lament and mourning have given way to rejoicing. Life
has triumphed over death. Immortality has overcome mortality.
There *is* meaning, there *is* justice, there *is* reward. A shepherd has
died, a body has been lost at sea, but both body and soul have
risen to immortality. The triumph of laurel over myrtle is com-
plete.

One of the most curious misreadings of a great poem was that
of various critics (largely of the nineteenth century) who spoke of
the "fame" passage in Part I and the "St. Peter passage" in Part II
of *Lycidas* as "digressions." With his mastery of form, his archi-
tectonic sense, how could or would Milton have "digressed" in two
of the longer passages in a poem of less than two hundred lines?
Read as the poem should be read, we know that, far from being
"digressions," these are the musical, the literary, and the religious
climaxes of their movements. There are no digressions in *Lycidas,*
the most perfect long short poem in the English language.

II
THE MIDDLE YEARS

The Making
of a Statesman

The second stage of Milton's life was the "prose period," during which he poured forth hundreds of pages of polemic prose, much of it written to order, and, as he himself said, "with the left hand." If we scan the twenty volumes into which the *Columbia Milton,* still the standard edition, is divided, we see that only four volumes are devoted to poetry, sixteen to prose—an imbalance found in no other great writer who considered himself primarily a poet. Since the subject of this volume is Milton's poetry, I shall treat the prose, not for itself, but only for the light it throws upon Milton's poetic development, in which some of it is of great importance.

The Italian Journey

We left Milton at Horton, composing *Lycidas,* about to set out to "fresh woods and pastures new." His own statement about his travels, written much later in the *Second Defense of the English People,* begins (in translation): "I then became anxious to visit foreign parts, and particularly Italy. My father gave me his permission, and I left home with one servant. On my departure, the celebrated Henry Wotton, who had long been King James's ambassador at Venice, gave me a signal proof of his regard, in an elegant letter which he wrote, breathing not only the warmest friendship, but containing some maxims of conduct which I found very useful in my travels." The Grand Tour (not yet so called) was not as common in Milton's time as it became after the Restoration, but many gentlemen's sons, like Milton, considered such travel the climax of a liberal education.

Of Milton's short stay in Paris, almost no record remains. We know from his own statement that he carried a letter to Thomas Scudamore, ambassador to the King, and that through him he was introduced to Hugo Grotius, ambassador from the Queen of Sweden to the French court. Grotius was not only a diplomat; he was one of the greatest jurists of all time, whose *De Jure Belli et Pacis* (1625) marked a milestone in the history of legal concepts. Perhaps even more important in the mind of the young English Protestant, Grotius at this time was endeavoring to bring about a union of Protestants, among the churches of Sweden, Denmark, Norway and England.

If Milton crossed the Alps on horseback, as most travelers did, he left no comment upon the experience. His own detail begins when he took ship at Nice for Genoa, and found himself at last on the soil which had long been his spiritual home. From Genoa, he proceeded through Leghorn and Pisa to Florence where he settled for about two months, from there to Siena and to Rome for another two months, then south to Naples, where his meeting with John Baptista Manso, marquis of Villa, a poet and the friend of poets particularly of Tasso—marked the literary climax of his journey.

A cultivated young man of good background and attractive personality, who carried letters from such an important personage as Sir Henry Wotton, would have found many doors open to him in Italy. We know from his nephew and others that Milton was welcomed to various "academies" (those originals of our "learned societies," and our academies of arts and letters), that his poetry was praised and that poems of tribute were written to him. In addi-

tion to the formal documents he mentioned, Milton would of
course have had with him more personal letters, particularly from
the Diodatis and probably other foreign families established in
England, which would have opened still other doors. We know
that he came into contact with various musicians. Milton pre-
served three Latin poems, "To Leonora Singing in Rome," written
to Leonora Baroni, whom he probably heard at the Barberini
Palace in the autumn of 1638. Our ears will catch many memories
of Italian music in both *Paradise Lost* and *Samson Agonistes*.

Originally Milton had planned to continue his travels to Sicily
and Greece, but while he was still at Naples, word reached him that
clouds were gathering in England. His own words in the *Second
Defense* are: "When I was preparing to pass over into Sicily and
Greece, the melancholy intelligence which I received of the civil
commotions in England made me alter my purpose; for I thought
it base to be travelling for amusement abroad, while my fellow-
citizens were fighting for liberty at home." He therefore reversed
his steps and made his way back to the north. The return journey
was less carefree than his travels to the south. "While I was on
my way back to Rome," he wrote in the *Second Defense,* "some
merchants informed me that the English Jesuits had formed a
plot against me if I returned to Rome, because I had spoken too
freely on religion." Return to Rome he did, however, where "I
again openly defended, as I had done before, the reformed re-
ligion in the very metropolis of popery." From Rome back to
Florence, with a short excursus to Lucca, the original home of
the Diodatis, then across the Apennines, through Bologna and
Ferrara to Venice. His route then took him across Lake Geneva
to Geneva, where he spent some time with Giovanni Diodati, un-
cle of his friend, distinguished as translator of the Bible into Ital-
ian. And so to France, from which he returned to England in
August 1639.

Milton's Italian journey looks before and after. When he left
England, he undoubtedly felt that this was the climactic chapter in
"The Education of a Poet." But we shall see that during the fif-

ᵗeen months of travel, his imagination was storing up memories other than music which we shall find particularly in *Paradise Lost*. I shall not at this time pause over the Latin poem Milton wrote to Manso, except to say that it shows that he had been deliberating whether his epic (he is still sure that he is "called" to write one) was to be in Latin or English, but that he had now decided that his was to be an English *Arthuriad*.

To what extent Milton's imagination was stimulated by the paintings, murals and statuary he saw in Italy is a question that has not been answered. Some critics feel that the effect was profound and that memories of specific pictures and statues, and particularly of the Sistine Chapel, lie behind Milton's pictures of God and Satan and various scenes in *Paradise Lost*. I shall return later to consider the possibility that Milton drew his graphic picture of the "first Hell" in *Paradise Lost*—the burning lake and burning shores in Book I—from a visit to the strange volcanic district of the Phlegraean Fields near Naples, and that when he constructed his "second Hell" of Pandemonium, his memory returned to St. Peter's in Rome.

There is another problem of a different sort in connection with the Italian journey over which I shall pause at this point. In the *Areopagitica,* written in 1644, Milton said: "There . . . (at Florence) I found and visited the famous Galileo, grown old, a prisoner to the Inquisition, for thinking in astronomy other than the Franciscan and Dominican licensers thought." There seemed no problem here until, some years ago, a Swedish scholar, S. B. Liljegren (a modern counterpart to Alexander More, to whom Milton replied in the *Second Defense*) insisted that Milton lied in this statement and that he never visited Galileo. In my time, I have replied to Liljegren in "Milton and the Telescope." When Milton visited Italy, Galileo was living at Fiesole, near Florence, where his observatory still stands. As letters and other biographical material show, in spite of the fact that he was a prisoner, Galileo received a number of visitors. As I hope I have shown, access to him would have been no real difficulty to a young Englishman, bearing such letters as Milton had, particularly if the visit was made on Milton's trip south, rather than after the Jesuits threatened him.

An actual visit to Galileo is not essential for the point I shall later make of the influence of the Galilean "new astronomy" upon Milton's imagination. Galileo's works were widely known in England both before and after Milton's Italian journey. But the meeting between the two is one of those moments in history that has caught the imagination of many writers and artists. The most familiar English treatment is, of course, Walter Savage Landor's in one of the *Imaginary Conversations*. Another more recent one in poetry is Alfred Noyes', *Watchers of the Sky*. There are a number written in Italian, as well as various pictures, recreating the scene. It is, of course, the irony latent in the meeting that fascinates the sensitive observer. Galileo was old and blind and a prisoner for his scientific opinions; Milton, then in the early prime of life, was to write his greatest work when he was old and blind and for a time a prisoner of another sort of Inquisition, for his political and religious opinons.

Milton's return journey was clouded in another way. Just when he received the sad news that Charles Diodati was dead, he did not say. The one fact that is known is that Charles Diodati was buried in Blackfriars, London, on August 27, 1638, a few months after Milton had left England. Letters traveled slowly in those days though there was regular postal service between England and the continent. Only after his return to England did Milton write his elegy for his friend, the *Epitaphium Damonis,* companion poem to *Lycidas*. It was entirely natural that Milton should have used a more strict classical form of the pastoral elegy and that he wrote in Latin in memory of the dead friend with whom he had so long corresponded in Latin elegies and prose. The poem is the best evidence that news of his friend's death reached Milton late, filled with reminiscences of Milton's feeling that his friend would have joined in the pleasures he had been experiencing in Italy. "Ah, how often would I say, when already dark ashes possessed you, 'Now Damon is singing.' " He had intended to surprise Diodati by bringing him two exquisitely engraved cups Manso had presented to him. As he would have shared his treasured gifts, he would have confided to his friend his new-found assurance that he had been "called" to do for England what Virgil had done for Rome, and write an English epic glorifying English history in the person of King Arthur. But Milton came back to England in August 1639, his travels behind him, to find a very different situation from that he had left in many ways.

John Milton, Schoolmaster

The return to England was—even more than Milton himself was aware—the end of an unusually happy, sheltered and idyllic youth, devoted to "The Making of a Poet." With the exception of a small group of sonnets—"Alas, too few!"—the *Epitaphium Damonis* was the last poetry Milton was to write for many years. Wars and rumors of wars detained him from the *Arthuriad* which he had planned so happily in Italy. But there is still a brief period in his biography which must be considered before discussing the years spent in the service of the Commonwealth. Since I am here concerned with Milton's biography, I shall violate chronology and consider his tractate *Of Education* as if it had been written shortly after Milton's return from Italy rather than in 1644.

Both Milton and his father must have agreed that the time had at last come for Milton to settle down and begin to earn his living. The Church and the law had been dismissed. One profession, however, was open for which Milton had had the necessary preparation. He became a schoolmaster. Instead of returning to Horton, he established himself in London. His nephew, Edward Phillips, one of his two first students, wrote: "Soon after his return and visits paid to his father and other friends, he took him a lodging in St. Bride's Churchyard, at the house of one Russel, a tailor, where he first undertook the education and instruction of his sister's two sons, the younger whereof had been wholly committed to his charge and care." Edward and John Phillips were the sons of Milton's sister, Anne Phillips, and the brother of the "Fair Infant" who had died of a cough before their birth. With them—other boys joined the group later—Milton set into practice the educational theories he had drawn in and reacted against at St. Paul's and Christ's College.

The tractate *Of Education* shows that Milton had done a good deal of thinking on the subject. There is nothing novel or startling about the ideas in the tract, so far as the history of education is concerned. It is a characteristic treatise of Renaissance humanism, written at a period when a great deal of attention was being given to education. Milton dedicated it to Samuel Hartlib, who had apparently suggested that he write it, a man who wrote widely on many subjects, including education, and—more important—a friend of Johann Amos Comenius, (Komensky), a Moravian, one of the greatest educational authorities in Europe, to whom Milton may be referring in the last sentence of the first paragraph. As a result of our study of the "Pigeon of Paules" and "the Lady of Christ's," we can read between the lines and recognize some of the "abuses" Milton had felt in his own education, even at St. Paul's.

Milton shows himself a "modern" rather than an "ancient" in education and also reflects much of the dissatisfaction he had felt at Cambridge, when he inveighs against the "barbarous" methodology which, instead of beginning "with arts most easy . . . such as are most obvious to the sense," schoolmasters and college dons forced down the throats of their young charges, "the most intellective abstractions of logic and metaphysics: so that many of the students 'grow into hatred and contempt of learning,' "—a passage that seems to echo Bacon's invective in *The Advancement of Learning*. Milton was particularly severe upon the time wasted in the learning of Latin and Greek:

> We do amiss to spend seven or eight years merely in scraping together so much miserable Latin and Greek as might be learned

otherwise easily and delightfully in one year, . . . forcing the empty wits of children to compose themes, verses, and orations, which are the acts of ripest judgment, and the final work of a head filled, by long reading and observing with elegant maxims and copious invention. These are not matters to be wrung from young striplings, like blood out of the nose, or the plucking of untimely fruit.

Milton believed in what we call the "direct method" in teaching languages. It may have been possible that in a year or two, youngsters might write and speak Latin as well as "Paules Pigeons" after seven or eight. That Milton's method, whatever it was, "worked" is implied in Edward Phillips' memoir. He mentioned

the many authors both of the Latin and Greek, which through his excellent judgment and way of teaching, far above the pedantry of common public schools (where such authors are scarce ever heard of) were run over within no greater compass of time, than from ten to fifteen or sixteen years of age.

It is an impressive list of ten Latin and eleven Greek authors, both prose and poetry. Milton's students were not limited to the Latin and Greek. Like himself, they learned some Hebrew, and as he suggested most casually in the tractate, "where to it would be no impossibility to add the Chaldee and the Syrian dialect." More than one critic has said ironically that Milton's academy would have been an admirable training ground for students if they had all been young John Miltons. But it is interesting to see that Edward Phillips felt he had profited even by the Chaldee and Syriac. He wrote:

Nor did the time thus studiously employed in conquering the Greek and Latin tongues, hinder the attaining to the chief oriental languages, viz., the Hebrew, Chaldee, and Syriac, so far as to go through the *Pentateuch,* or Five Books of Moses in Hebrew, to make a good entrance in the *Targum,* or Chaldee Para-phrase, and to understand several chapters of St. Matthew in the Syriac Testament.

Characteristically, Milton suggests that in addition to all the scholarly languages, his pupils will easily learn Italian "at any odd hour." One of the most delightful sentences in *Of Education* is that in which Milton tells us how he taught his students to pronounce Latin "as near as can be to the Italian, especially in the vowels. For we Englishmen, being far northerly, do not open our mouths in the cold air wide enough to grace a southern tongue, but are observed by all other nations to speak exceeding close and inward."

There is much more in the tracate over which we might stop if our interest were primarily with Milton's prose. One other sentence must be quoted. No one who reads it can forget Milton's definition, which every teacher should know by heart: "I call therefore a complete and generous education that which fits a man to perform justly, skilfully, and magnanimously all the offices, both private and public, of peace and war." It remains as true for our time as for the Renaissance. No finer definition has been written of the liberal education.

Milton's First Marriage

"About Whisuntide it was, or a little after, that he took a journey into the country; no body about him certainly knowing the reason, or that it was any more than a journey or recreation: after a month's stay, home he returns a married man, that went out a bachelor." So Edward Phillips succinctly summed up the facts of Milton's first marriage, which has torn critics and biographers asunder ever since. When did he wed Mary Powell? How long had he known her? Why did she leave him—as she did for nearly four years? What was the relation between the marriage and Milton's writing the *Divorce Tracts?* Did he actually write the first one while he was on his honeymoon? During the last few years, the "Powell problem" has been made even more acute by William Riley Parker's suggestion that Milton's last sonnet, "Methought I saw my late espoused saint," was written not about the second wife, as we have always believed, but about Mary Powell. ("Milton's Last Sonnet," *RES* 21. [1945], 235-8; see Huckabay Bibl. Nos. 767-768 for replies and a later article by Parker.)

None of the questions has been finally answered and perhaps never will be. But little by little, scholars have thrown light on some of them. There was a time when the romantic notion was widespread that Milton, off on a holiday perhaps, came by chance upon Mary Powell and fell in love at first sight. Milton was not at all incapable of falling in love at sight, as the fifth and seventh elegies suggest; the Italian sonnets suggest that he had been very much in love when he was younger. But his meeting with Mary Powell does not seem to have been as sudden as we used to think. Professor J. Milton French ("The Powell-Milton Bond,") came upon documents proving that the two families had had business associations for some years and that the elder John Milton had made a sizable loan to Mary's father, Richard Powell, a Justice of the Peace in Forresthill, Oxfordshire. The younger Milton may merely have gone to collect the interest from a family he had known for some time.

The problem of the date of the marriage still remains, and that is of particular importance in connection with the *Divorce Tracts*. Edward Phillips dates the marriage in May or June and Mary's return to her family about August first of the same year. But he does not mention the year. He merely indicates that the marriage occurred after Milton moved his school from St. Bride's Churchyard to Aldergate Street. On the basis of the little said by Edward Phillips, Masson and other biographers dated the marriage in May or June 1643, and his wife's return to her family about August 1 of the same year. This seems almost impossible so far as the *Divorce Tracts* are concerned, since the first one was published almost exactly on the date on which his wife supposedly left him. If Milton wrote it on his honeymoon, as a result of marital disillusionment, he must have written with incredible rapidity and the printer must have been far more expeditious than printers usually were or are.

We should remember that Edward Phillips not only did not give the year but that he was writing his memories of his uncle nearly fifty years later and looking back over a period when he himself was just entering his teens. He often kaleidoscoped events; he is sometimes inaccurate; and much of his memory of these early days was undoubtedly colored by family gossip and surmise which he half-heard. Probably his mother or his grandfather was entirely aware of the reason for Milton's journey into the country. We should notice, too, that Phillips himself said that the pamphlets were provoked, not by the wife's leaving but by her refusal to return. When the first tract appeared, Mary Milton would have just left London, with her husband's reluctant consent. It was weeks later that she refused to return. If, however, we date the marriage a full year earlier, as we incline to do nowadays, some problems are resolved. Milton would have been accustomed to his wife's absence. He may well, as some biographers surmise, have wished to marry again, both for normal reasons and because the master of a boarding school, however small, had need of a wife's assistance, particularly because Milton's elderly father had come to live with him, and three generations under one roof involved housekeeping problems almost insuperable for a single man.

Whether or not his wife's desertion was one of the causes for Milton's writing on divorce, it was not the only one. Until the questions of dating have been completely resolved—and even then—it is only just to remember what Milton himself said about the writing and publication of the pamphlets. A decade later in the *Second Defense*, Milton looked back on this period of his life and gave his reason for writing three different groups of works at this particular time. He began by discussing various ideas of liberty with which he and others were concerning themselves at this time:

When, therefore, I perceived that there were three species of liberty which are essential to the happiness of social life—religious, domestic, and civil; and as I had already written concerning the first, and the magistrates were strenuously active in obtaining the third, I determined to turn my attention to the second, or the domestic species. As this seemed to involve three material questions, the conditions of the conjugal tie, the education of the children, and the free publication of the thoughts, I made them objects of distinct consideration.

If we believe what Milton says here, the *Divorce Tracts* began in his mind—however they ended—as an inevitable part of his theory of domestic liberty; this involved freedom in marriage, the education of children, and the freedom of men to publish their own thoughts and read those of other men: the *Divorce Tracts, Of Education,* and *Areopagitica.*

The problem of divorce has always been, and remains, a moot one in England. While divorce was one of the issues on which Henry VIII separated the Anglican from the Roman Church, divorce remained as difficult for the individual Anglican as for the Roman Catholic. Milton was not the only Puritan who believed that the regulations about divorce were far too rigid, though the reception of his tracts by some of his own party, which he reports in the sonnet on *Tetrachordon,* shows that his position was not the prevailing one even among Puritans. No matter what relation the tracts had to his private life, Milton's convictions were always based upon fundamental theories and beliefs. In opposition to all Catholics, and to many of his own party, Milton held that marriage was not a sacrament, which only the Church could dissolve. It was a contract, entered into by two people, which might be voided for sufficient cause. This does not mean that Milton held a low opinion of marriage. Quite the contrary, as we shall see when he interprets the marriage of Adam and Eve in *Paradise Lost.* He believed that marriage involved compatibility on three levels, physical, spiritual and intellectual, and that if it did not, it had not been a true marriage and should be set aside. Whatever his youthful attitude toward male chastity had been, Milton had grown up a very normal man, and as his last sonnet proved, capable of deep love for a wife. His was not the grudging justification of St. Paul, "It is better to marry than to burn," but rather the words of Genesis: "It is not good that man should be alone." Adam is his spokesman in *Paradise Lost* when he asks God for a mate; all other created things had mates; man only was alone:

> But with me
> I see not who partakes. In solitude
> What happiness? Who can enjoy alone? . . .
> Of fellowship I speak
> Such as I seek, fit to participate
> All rational delight.
>
> VIII. 364-66, 389-91

God is all-sufficient. "Not so is man," who asks "collateral love and dearest amity."

Areopagitica

Since Milton himself held that his works on domestic liberty were parts of a whole, we may discuss the *Areopagitica* at this time, rather than when it was published in 1644. It completes the trilogy. As the epigraph for his oration, Milton quoted lines from *The Suppliants* of Euripides, which begin:

> This is true liberty, when free-born men,
> Having to advise the public, may speak free.

Even as early as 1644, Milton was becoming aware that his own party could be as intolerant as those of the monarchy whom they had displaced. Shortly before the Civil War, the Star Chamber had revived and attempted to administer the law of censorship that all publications must be registered with the Stationers' Company, and approved by the Church through the Archbishop of Canterbury, the Bishop of London, or their deputies. In 1643 the Presbyterians, who now held the upper hand in Parliament, again at

tem~ted to enforce censorship. Milton himself had fallen under
the ban, for in the ordinance of Parliament for licensing printing
on June 14, 1623, he was mentioned by name in connection with
the unlicensed publication of the *Doctrine and Discipline of Di-
vorce.* "New Presbyter," as Milton wrote bitterly, "is but old Priest
writ large." From this time on, we shall see that Milton departed
more and more sharply from the extreme right-wing position of
the Presbyterians and felt himself an Independent, though as time
went on, even the Independents seemed to fall short of the ideals of
toleration and freedom of conscience of which he was an ardent
champion.

The *Areopagitica,* as has been said, is the greatest classical ora-
tion in the English language. Milton did not mean actually to de-
liver it, emulating the practice of the Greek orator Isocrates from
whom he borrowed the title and upon whose orations he based the
structure. He was following tradition in seeming to address the
court on the hill of Ares, archetypal symbol of justice, while actu-
ally addressing the British Parliament. His theme is the freedom
of the press, not quite what we mean today when we speak more
loosely about freedom of speech. Surely this is one piece of prose
that Milton did not write with his left hand. In his political tracts,
Milton, like all other pamphleteers, was writing to order, spew-
ing forth invective in answer to diatribe, slinging mud as mud was
slung at him and other members of his party. In *Areopagitica,* how-
ever, as in *Lycidas, Paradise Lost, Samson Agonistes,* he was
roused to the height of his artistic abilities. As in those beautifully
articulated poems, Milton in his oration was following classical
models, and as always transcending them in a "higher mood."
Here, almost alone in his prose, we hear the "organ voice" for
long periods. The *Areopagitica,* even apart from its theme and pur-
pose, is great literature, ranking with the greatest English prose. It
is filled with memorable sentences, particularly about books, many
of which rightly have been carved on library walls throughout the
English-speaking world:

For books are not absolutely dead things, but do contain a potency of life in them to be as active as that soul was whose progeny they are. . . . They are as lively, and as vigorously productive, as those fabulous dragon's teeth; and being sown up and down, may chance to spring up armed men. . . .

As good almost kill a man as kill a good book; who kills a man kills a reasonable creature, God's image; but he who destroys a good book, kills reason itself, kills the image of God, as it were, in the eye.

Many a man lives a burden to the earth; but a good book is the precious life-blood of a master spirit, embalmed and treasured up on purpose to a life beyond life.

There are many sentences over which a teacher finds himself pausing, remembering Milton as a teacher who had thought deeply on the problems of education and the growing-up process:

What advantage is it to be a man over it is to be a boy at school, if we have only escaped the ferula (the schoolmaster's rod) to come under the fescue (teacher's pointer, used for discipline) of an Imprimatur? . . . And how can a man teach with authority, which is the life of teaching, how can he be a doctor in his book, as he ought to be, or else had better be silent, whenas all he teaches, all he delivers, is but under the tuition, under the correction of his patriarchal licenser? . . .

"I hate a pupil teacher, I endure not an instructor that comes to me under the wardship of an overseeing fist."

Not only individual sentences arrest us, but many figures of speech, particularly those recurrent motifs throughout Milton's works of light and darkness—the darkness of superstition, of bigotry, of false belief, the light of truth, of freedom, of reason, reflection in our world of the Fountain of Light. "We boast our light," Milton warns his countrymen, "but if we look not wisely on the sun itself, it smites us into darkness. . . ." These, with other recurrent themes and motifs, come to their climax in the great peroration which should have been spoken, whether in the Areopagus or in the Houses of Parliament. It cries to be read aloud, as does so much of Milton's writing. One feels that even the Presbyterians in the House of Commons, if they were true-born Englishmen, would have been shaken from lethargy and felt their blood stirring, if they had listened to those noble words beginning: "Lords and Commons of England, consider what nation it is whereof ye are, and whereof ye are the governors." "Methinks I see in my mind a noble and puissant nation rousing herself like a strong man after sleep, and shaking her invincible locks." As in *Lycidas,* triumph and warning combine into a whole.

As in all Milton's major works, the theme of *Aeropagitica* is liberty. Censorship has never succeeded, will never succeed, must never succeed, because it deprives man of his inalienable right to learn from books, as from other experience, the lessons he needs in order to maintain his freedom. Milton did not say with easy optimism, "Man is by nature free." *Freedom* and *liberty* were hard words, conditions hard to attain and only too easy to lose.

Controversial Pamplets

Since we are primarily concerned with Milton's poetry, I shall make no attempt to discuss—or even to list—many of the controversial pamphlets that poured from his pen between 1641 and 1660, but shall briefly consider a few that are important in his development toward his major poems. His first entrance into polemical writing was made while he was a schoolmaster in 1641, when he published *Of Reformation in England,* followed in quick succession by two other anti-episcopal tracts. In the comparative leisure of his study, Milton could write as a scholar and an historian, aloof from the pressures of the moment that were later to engage him. The first pamphlet at least reminds the reader of the young poet more than the later polemicist. These were followed during the next year by *The Reason of Church Government* and *An Apology for Smectymnuus,* both written before his marriage and before the actual outbreak of the Civil War on August 22, 1642. During the next three years, his prose was devoted to the *Divorce Tracts, Of Education* and *Areopagitica,* which in many ways look back to the earlier Milton and are still largely the work of the schoolmaster in his study. In 1645 Mary Powell returned to her husband, and to all intents and purposes Milton settled down for a short time to a normal life.

In spite of his close concern with the problems of politics and theology that were tearing his country asunder, the Milton of these years still seems more like the young man who had spent a placid and secluded youth than the later statesman, as we shall see when we read the first sonnet of the middle years, "When the Assault Was Intended to the City." Even in the year following the defeat of the Royalist forces at Naseby, Milton's main efforts were devoted to his teaching and "research," if we may use a modern term. His collected *Poems* were published in 1645, and during the next two or three years he was apparently working on his *History of Britain* and possibly on the *Christian Doctrine,* though the dating of this is extremely hypothetical.

But the apparent placidity of Milton's life was to be rudely interrupted. As we have still better reason to realize in the twentieth century, even those who are not actively drawn into war cannot remain aloof from the consequences of war.

> Yet much remains
> To conquer still; Peace hath her victories
> No less renowned than War, new foes arise. . . .

as Milton wrote in a sonnet to Cromwell. The execution of King Charles, on January 30, 1649, inevitably had a profound effect upon every English mind. In a country which had never known any government except monarchy, and in which one of "the king's two bodies" was revered as almost sacred, no matter what the second body might have been or done, the shock was profound, and the Puritans were forced to spend all their might justifying the regicide. Among the many who came to their aid was Milton, who, a fortnight after the execution, published his *Tenure of Kings and Magistrates*. In March 1649, at the age of forty, Milton received and accepted appointment as Secretary for Foreign Tongues to the Council of State, and entered into full-time political life.

We have no equivalent today for Milton's position. The closest analogue in Great Britain would be a post attached to the Ministry for Foreign Affairs, in the United States to the Secretary of State. One of Milton's chief functions, as the title implies, was correspondence with heads of foreign states or with secretaries in their governments. Latin was still the one international language, although French was beginning to assume some diplomatic importance. Milton's nephew, commenting upon his uncle's importance, said: "He was courted into the service of this new commonwealth, and at last prevailed with . . . to take upon him the office of Latin secretary to the Council of State for all their letters to foreign princes and states; for they stuck to this noble and generous resolution, not to write to any, or receive answers from them, but in a language most proper to maintain a correspondence among the learned of all nations in this part of the world; scorning to carry on their affairs in the wheedling, lisping jargon of the cringing French, especially having a minister of state able to cope with the ablest any prince or state could employ, for the Latin tongue."

In addition Milton was to continue the war of words in pamphlets, some of them obviously written at the order of his superiors in the government. There is no question that Milton was enthusiastic about his appointment and fully aware of the responsibility laid upon him. Belief in those "most valiant deliverers of my native country" rings through the *Defensio pro Populo Anglicano* which he published in March, 1651. He rightly believed that he had the necessary qualifications for the appointment and he intended to use them with all his might. In the *Defensio* he wrote: "and true it is that from my very youth I had been bent extremely upon such sort of studies as inclined me if not to do great things myself at least to celebrate those who did."

We remember that Milton had planned an *Arthuriad,* in which he would have glorified England in its past and have prophesied still higher greatness in the future. By this time, he seems to have decided against it, for reasons that will be discussed later. The heavy duties he had assumed may well have made him feel that he was never to write the epic to which he had long felt "called." If he was not to do great things himself, he would at least celebrate those who did. At this crucial moment in England's history, he sincerely believed that these were the members of his party.

Remembering Milton's definition of a "generous education," we may pause for a moment over a problem which is constantly in the minds of college and university administrators and professors today. What is a "practical" education? One group insists upon the training of students in skills or trades which seem to bear specific relationship to crafts or professions in which the students may earn their living. Another group insists, as in the Renaissance, on a "liberal" education as best fitting men and women for life. Milton's education seems at first glance most "impractical." As a "Pigeon of Paules" and the "Lady of Christ's," he had had an unbalanced education, from the modern point of view. Even he himself had protested the years of drill in ancient languages, the long discipline in logic, in disputation, in rhetoric. Those years of apprenticeship in the "education of a poet" seemed remote from "life"—years in an ivory tower, or the "high lonely tower" of Il Penseroso. But ironically enough, no education could have proved more "practical" for the position to which he was called by the Commonwealth government. "A complete and generous education," he had written, is one "which fits a man to perform justly, skilfully, and magnanimously all the offices, both private and public, of peace and war." Latin was the international language and the new government needed an expert Latinist. In those days when controversy was carried on mainly through the press, and attack demanded counter-attack, the government needed a man who could write rapidly and vehemently in both Latin and English.

Milton was that man. He had already proved himself a dangerous opponent able to write effectively under pressure, to trade

charge for charge. The tone of much seventeenth-century wrang-
ling might lead a modern reader to believe that the tracts were
the production of the vulgar—in all senses. Nothing could be less
true. Milton's anti-episcopal treatises were answers to some of the
most learned bishops of the Anglican Church, such as Bishop Joseph
Hall and Bishop (later Archbishop) Ussher, one of the great schol-
ars of the time. Among many other Puritans who had joined in the
controversy was Milton's early tutor, Thomas Young. In the *Eiko-
noklastes,* the second pamphlet Milton wrote in his new position,
he was on the most perilous ground of all, since he was writing in
reply to the *Eikon Basilike,* a sort of diary supposed to have been
written during the last months or even days by King Charles him-
self. Whatever its authorship and purposeful exaggeration, the
work went far to create in the public mind the portrait of a mar-
tyred saint.

The opponent to whom Milton was called to reply a little later
taxed his powers still more. Castigation of the Puritans who had
put a king to death was not limited to the British Isles. The im-
plications of that sentence were international, of ominous import
in any monarchy. The prestige of the English government sank so
low on the continent that British ambassadors faced insult, humili-
ation, even death. Cromwell's party was in grave peril when the
Defensio Regia pro Carolo I appeared in the autumn of 1649, six
months after Milton's appointment. The author was Salmasius
(Claude Saumaise), a Frenchman living in Holland, recognized ev-
erywhere as one of the greatest scholars in the world. Using all the
wealth of his learning, he published an eloquent tract addressed to
the intellectual leaders of Europe, invoking anathema upon regi-
cides who had dared send to the block the actual body of a king,
and in doing so attempted to destroy kingship.

Here was a situation that tested even Milton's prowess and un-
doubtedly excited him more than any challenge he had ever met.
In spite of the fact that he had long written in the international
language, his audience in the past had been confined either to the
little world of Academe at Cambridge, the still more private world

of Diodati, at most to readers in England. Now he was called to address a European tribunal, far more formidable than the "Lords and Commons of England" to whom he had addressed *Areopagitica*. Milton was well aware of the intellectual stature of Salmasius (whom under other circumstances he would have admired greatly). In the *Defensio pro Populo Anglicano* he was speaking for himself—a scholar replying to a scholar—but he was spokesman even more "for the English people," his party now in precarious ascendancy. He analyzed his emotions as he wrote:

> I imagine myself not in the forum or on the rostra, surrounded by the people of Athens or of Rome, but about to address . . . the whole collective body of people, cities, states, and councils of the wise and eminent, through the wide expanse of an anxious and listening Europe. I seem to survey, as from a towering height, the far extended tracts of sea and land, and innumerable crowds of spectators, betraying in their looks the liveliest interest, and sensations the most congenial with my own.

Germans disdaining servitude, generous and lively French, stately valorous Spaniards—they were all before him as he wrote. There is natural human pride and awareness of his own abilities as he uses his long training in scholarship and debate to the full. He was writing in part for personal "fame," which even though "that last infirmity of noble mind," he had sought and would always seek. But more than that: he was speaking "for the English people," for that courageous group in whose great experiment in government he believed:

> Surrounded by congregated multitudes, I now imagine that, from the columns of Hercules to the Indian Ocean, I behold the nations of the earth recovering that liberty which they so long had lost; and that the people of this island . . . are disseminating the blessings of civilization and freedom among cities, kingdoms, and nations.

We may let his nephew Edward Phillips go on with the story, which he told in spicy, homely language:

> Out comes in public the great kill-cow of Christendom, with his *Defensio Regis contra Populum Anglicanum;* a man so famous and cried up . . . that there could no where have been found a champion that durst lift up the pen against so formidable an adversary, had not our little English David had the courage to attempt the great French Goliath, to whom he gave such a hit in the forehead, that he presently staggered, and soon after fell.

Phillips' account of the effect of Milton's reply upon the prestige of Salmasius may have been slightly exaggerated, so far as Salmasius' death is concerned, but basically it is not far from the truth:

> Immediately upon the coming out of the answer . . . he that till then had been chief minister and superintendent in the court of the learned Christina, Queen of Sweden, dwindled in esteem to that degree, that he at last vouchsafed to speak to the meanest servant. In short, he was dismissed with so cold and slighting an adieu, that after a faint dying reply, he was glad to have recourse to death, the remedy of evils and ender of controversies.

Milton's pamphlet did not actually win the war for his party; Cromwell's victories in Ireland and at Dunbar were doing that by the time the *Defensio* appeared—but he did win the Battle of the Books, and he won it at great cost. If Milton had been a soldier, he might well have given his life for his party. As it was, he gave what was almost as precious—his sight. Although his eyes had been failing for some time—he had already lost the sight of one— there is no question that his total blindness was hastened and indeed caused by his refusal to stop his intensive work on the reply to Salmasius.

> When my medical attendants clearly announced, that if I did engage in the work, it [the remaining eye] would be irreparably lost, their premonitions caused no hesitation and inspired no dismay. . . . My resolution was unshaken, though the alternative was either the loss of my sight, or the desertion of my duty. . . . I resolved therefore to make the short interval of sight which was left me to enjoy, as beneficial as possible to the public interest.

The medical problems of Milton's blindness have engaged the attention of various modern writers—some of them physicians. His adversaries not unnaturally proclaimed that his blindness was a retribution of God for everything from his daring to reply to the King to his attack on Salmasius. But blindness had been coming upon Milton for several years. All the medical evidence was brought together a few years ago by Eleanor Brown in *Milton's Blindness* (pp. 16-48), a book of unusual interest in the study of Milton because it was written by a blind woman, who could understand some aspects of Milton's work we might not. Without entering into modern theories or vocabulary, we know how Milton's own physicians characterized it from a phrase in the Prologue to Light in Book III of *Paradise Lost:*

> but Thou
> Revisitest not these eyes, that roll in vain
> To find Thy piercing ray, and find no dawn:
> So thick a drop serene hath quenched their orbs,
> Or dim suffusion veiled.

The "dim suffusion" might suggest cataract, but we know from Milton's own remarks and those of his contemporaries that his eyes were not clouded in any way but remained as they had been, unusually bright. His physicians could classify it only by the phrase "drop serene," a translation of the medical term, "gutta serena," which as Miss Brown explains, was the medical term for "all blindness in which the eye retains a normal appearance."

The period immediately following his entrance into the political arena was undoubtedly the most difficult in Milton's life, as we can tell from a few remarks and many more implications in the tone of both his prose and his sonnets. In addition to his rapidly failing sight, Milton was laboring under serious ill health when he wrote the first *Defence,* "forced," as he says, "to write by piecemeal and break off every hour." In addition his domestic problems were made acute by the death of Mary Powell Milton in childbed in June 1652, a little over a year after his total blindness occurred.

She left three daughters, Anne, Mary and Deborah. We shall return to Mary Powell when we come to consider Milton's last sonnet. Milton continued to perform his duties as Secretary—with some assistance beginning in 1652—until he was relieved of his chief duties in 1655. It is still another indication of the value of a "generous education" that the successor chosen was another great poet in both English and Latin, Andrew Marvell.

During the intervening years Milton not only carried on the work for the state "to foreign princes and states," but continued to write in support of his party. The most important publication of these years is one of the greatest of Milton's prose works—second only to *Areopagitica* stylistically and surpassing the oration in some ways in mood: the *Defensio Secunda* or *Second Defence of the English People,* another chapter in the Salmasius controversy. Though embedded in earlier prose works we find passages on his life, his education, his political aspirations, adding up to what may be called his "Biographia Literaria," those in the *Second Defence* are the longest and most personal of all his biographical digressions. In style Milton rises to heights he never reached in the first *Defence.* He could be wickedly and saltily amusing. He could be simple and straightforward, plain, clear, but immensely moving, as in the account of his life. He could throw volleys of invective; he could write in the grand oratorical style, as in the panegyric on Cromwell. But as E. M. W. Tillyard points out in his excellent stylistic analysis of the *Second Defence (Milton,* pp. 198 ff.), the effects are particularly felt only when one reads the Latin; they are lost (or at least muted) in most English translations. Mr. Tillyard says:

> By writing in a foreign tongue Milton has of necessity sacrificed the homeliness and freshness that enlivened the style of his English prose. We are remote from the language of everyday speech and frankly in the realms of rhetoric. But granted the rhetorical setting, the way Milton makes the Latin language obey him, rousing it to eloquence, subduing it to plainness, hushing it to a poetical solemnity, or goading it to the brutalities of his satire,

is astonishing. He seems perfectly at ease in the sonorities of Latin and puts them, regally, to whatever use he desires.

The great English prose of *Areopagitica,* as well as some of its themes, in a way looked back to *Comus* and *Lycidas. The Second Defence,* in its mastery of styles and in its moods, looks forward to *Paradise Lost.* As I reread the *Second Defence* recently, I found myself wondering whether the effects that total blindness was to have upon the organ voice and the basic attitudes we feel in the three major poems had not already begun. Certainly we find them in the change from the early sonnets to those he wrote after he lost his sight.

There is little more that need detain us in the middle years. In November 1656, four and one-half years after the death of Mary Powell, Milton married Katherine Woodcock, a young woman of twenty-eight. She lived only fifteen months, dying as the result of the birth of a child who also died. In September of that year occurred the death of the Lord Protector, Oliver Cromwell. Less than two years later, the experiment of the Commonwealth ended and on May 29, 1660, Charles II was welcomed to London. During the following summer, Milton who had continued his pamphleteering in spite of his blindness, was hiding in a friend's house. Orders had been issued for his arrest, as an enemy of the state. For a time he was under arrest, but since he was not named in the Act of Indemnity—the act of oblivion, as his nephew called it—he was released and free to take up his life again, though two of his pamphlets were burned by the public hangman, as a symbol of his guilt against the monarchy. On that occasion, when Milton's work joined the long roster of "banned and burned books," we may hope that others than he remembered his own words "For books are not absolutely dead things, but do contain a potency of life in them to be as active as that soul was whose progeny they are; nay, they do preserve as in a vial the purest efficacy and extraction of that living intellect that bred them."

The Sonnets

During the twenty years between 1640, when he wrote the *Epitaphium Damonis,* and 1660, the year of King Charles' Restoration, Milton published no poetry, with the exception of the 1645 edition of his early poems. He had been thirty-one when he wrote his lament for Diodati; he was fifty-one when he went into hiding after the Restoration of His Majesty. While he may have been working on *Paradise Lost,* the only poetry that can definitely be assigned to these middle years is the small group of sonnets. Some of the early ones had been published in the *Poems* of 1645. Nearly all the others remained unpublished until 1673, the year before Milton's death, while three or four, for obvious political reasons, did not appear until 1694, long after the author's death. The most important evidence for the order in which Milton wrote them and for their dating comes from the manuscript in which Milton preserved them, the Trinity or Cambridge Manuscript, in the library of Trinity College, Cambridge.

We know that Milton had written Italian sonnets when he was very young, well before his journey to Italy. Some of these may be among the most personal of his poems if they are really to a young Italian woman with whom Milton had fallen in love, although it is equally possible that they merely represent Italian traditions Milton was following. One Italian sonnet was addressed to Diodati to

whom Milton seems to confess that he, who had once scoffed, had
fallen in the snare. His love, he says, is not an English girl "of
golden locks, or damask cheek":

>   More rare,
> The heartfelt beauties of my foreign fair,
> A mien majestic, with dark brows that show
> The tranquil lustre of a lofty mind;
> Words exquisite, of idiom more than one,
> And song.

Sonnet IV (Cowper translation)

We have paused momentarily over the English sonnet, written for
his birthday, when he felt that his "late spring no bud or blossom
showeth." One other early English sonnet remains, Sonnet I on the
nightingale, conventional and imitative enough of the Italians,
which, some critics suggest, may have been intended as an in-
troduction to the five Italian sonnets and a canzone, which combine
to form a short love-sequence of a kind familiar among both Ital-
ian and English sonneteers. These early verses I shall not consider
further, but, after a brief discussion of the sonnet-tradition, pass on
to the sonnets we know were written early or late in the middle
years.

THE SONNET TRADITION

"Scorn not the sonnet," Wordsworth warned his generation, re-
minding both critics and poets of their goodly heritage:

> Scorn not the Sonnet; Critic, you have frowned,
> Mindless of its just honours; with this key
> Shakespeare unlocked his heart; the melody

Of this small lute gave ease to Petrarch's wound;
A thousand times this pipe did Tasso sound;
With it Camöens soothed an exile's grief;
The Sonnet glittered a gay myrtle leaf
Amid the cypress with which Dante crowned
His visionary brow: a glow-worm lamp,
It cheered mild Spenser, call'd from Faery-land
To struggle through dark ways; and when a damp
Fell round the path of Milton, in his hand
The thing became a trumpet; whence he blew
Soul-animating strains—alas, too few!

The sonnet is one of the few forms he used for which Milton had no classical precedent or model though it is possible that Milton, like some modern critics, thought of it as a variant upon the classical epigram which it resembles in succinctness and compression. Even if we were not familiar with its history, Wordsworth's brief catalogue would tell us one reason for its inevitable appeal to Milton. It was an Italian form, the greatest practitioners of which had been Dante, Petrarch and Tasso. In England it had been adapted by many but the two English poets he mentioned would have been "authority" enough for Milton, had he needed it—"sweetest Shakespeare, Fancy's child" and "our sage and serious Spenser."

In addition to its long history in the hands of poets he admired, Milton would have been attracted to the sonnet by the limitations the form imposed upon any poet who uses it. It is one of the few English forms (Italian has many more) in which the poet's craft is taxed to the full to keep within boundaries and limitations, yet challenged to transcend those limitations by adaptation of materials to the metrical rules. The form requires the terseness Milton admired in Greek poetry, the opportunity and the challenge to say much in little. Many English poets who used the poem have suggested by analogies the restraint it implies. "What is a sonnet?" asked Richard Watson Gilder, and replied,

> 't is the pearly shell
> That murmurs of the far-off murmuring sea;

A precious jewel carved most curiously;
It is a little picture painted well.

Dante Gabriel Rossetti also developed the traditional themes of the sonnet:

> A sonnet is a coin: its face reveals
> The soul,—its converse to what power 't is due:—
> Whether for tribute to the august appeals
> Of Life, or dower in Love's high retinue,
> It serve; or, 'mid the dark wharf's cavernous breath
> In Charon's palm it pay the toll to Death.

"Nuns fret not at their narrow convent room" as Wordsworth wrote in still another sonnet upon sonnets; the very limitations of the convent room symbolize the values they sought in the life they have deliberately chosen. So poets have felt for generations about the limitations imposed by the sonnet.

As Milton inherited the sonnet, he was free to choose among several forms, some Italian, some English, each having the authority of great poets. Most English students think of the Italian sonnet as being divided between an octave and a sestet, though the practice of various Italian poets seems to indicate that they were really writing two quatrains and two tercets. Since, however, there was almost universal agreement that the two quatrains must be constructed by the use of only two rhymes, we may legitimately consider the first eight lines an octave. Dante and other early and modern poets sometimes used alternate rhymes, *abab;* Petrarch did so infrequently. The octave of the Italian sonnet adopted by most English followers is *abba, abba.* The tercet offered more variety. Sometimes it too was limited to two rhymes, often arranged *cdc, cdc* or *cdc, dcd.* Not infrequently a third rhyme was added, *cde, cde; cde, dce* and other combinations were possible. Occasionally a final couplet appears, though it is far from common. The "Petrarchan sonnet," to Milton as to most of us, consists of an octave with enclosed, not alternate lines, and a sestet with three rhymes, arranged in various ways.

In England two simpler forms developed among those who did not follow the Petrarchan model. The simplest, used by Surrey and most famous in Shakespeare, consists of three quatrains, each with its own alternate rhyme, and a couplet, introducing still another rhyme: *abad, cdcd, efef, gg.* Spenser experimented with a form basically like the Surrey-Shakespeare sonnet, except that a rhyme was carried over from one quatrain to the next: *abab bcbc, cdcd, ee.* In spite of Milton's admiration for both Shakespeare and Spenser, it was natural that with his love of Italian poetry and his tendency toward the "classical" model, if there was one, he should have followed Petrarch and adapted the tighter and more difficult of the various rhyme schemes. His octave is always *abba, abba,* his sestet often limited to two rhymes, although he uses combinations of *cde* in five English sonnets. Only in one—the sonnet to Cromwell —does he use a final couplet. "On the New Forcers of Conscience," Milton's one "tailed sonnet," concludes with a triple rhyme in the first coda, a couplet in the second.

As the sonnet grew in Milton's "right hand"—a poetic release from the "left-hand" prose—it became a form characteristically Miltonic, not only in its becoming a "trumpet," as Wordsworth said, but in its rhythmic dexterity and virtuosity. As we have seen in *Lycidas,* the paragraph rather than the sentence seems to have been Milton's unit and we find ourselves thinking of his best sonnets as beautifully articulated paragraphs rather than as a series of couplets, quatrains, tercets. Unlike various earlier and later poets, Milton did not feel a necessary separation between octave and sestet. More and more, he tends to enjambment—carrying over the sense from either the eighth or the ninth line. In some of his finest sonnets, for example the two on his blindness, the one on Cromwell and the sonnet on the massacre of the Piedmontese, we notice that a new sentence, introducing the theme of the sestet, begins in the middle of either the eighth or ninth line, sometimes implying a dramatic change in mood.

In considering Milton's sonnets, I shall divide them into three groups, which I call conventional, personal, and political, although there is some inevitable overlapping between the first two. Sonnet XVII to Sir Henry Vane is really a conventional sonnet of tribute, but because of the political references I shall put it into the third group. In the numbering of the sonnets I follow, as do most modern editors, the numbering of John S. Smart, which is based, so far as possible, upon the order in which they were preserved in Milton's manuscript.

CONVENTIONAL SONNETS

The conventional sonnets follow time-honored traditions though in Milton's case the themes are not those most frequent in Italian and English sonnets—love. They are largely tributes to a particular man or woman, except for Sonnet XX which is in the classical tradition of "inviting a friend to supper."

Sonnet IX, "Lady that in the Prime"

"Lady that in the prime," has been called in some editions "To a Virtuous Young Lady." Since this was one of the sonnets included in the *Poems* of 1645, we can date it merely as being earlier than that year. The subject has not been identified, though various suggestions have been made. In spite of the generic word, "Lady," this sonnet is addressed to a young girl, probably the daughter of a family friend who may have confided to Milton that the girl had been criticized by her young friends for what seemed to them priggishness (lines 6-7). Particularly if she was just entering her teens, she may have seemed to other youngsters a creature much too bright and good for human nature's daily food. In his words of comfort and encouragement, Milton uses more Biblical allusions than in any other sonnet—Biblical allusions were hardly sonnet conventions. He reminds her of other virtuous young women, recalling the story of Ruth and Naomi in the Old Testament (Ruth I. 14), of Mary, the sister of Martha (Luke X. 42) who chose the better part. The sestet develops the parable of the wise and foolish virgins (Matthew XXV. 1-13), the foolish who wasted the oil for their lamps, the wise who saved it. Even the opening quatrain suggests the Bible, since Milton combines an old classical *topos* of "Hill Difficulty" with various Christian analogues, particularly Matthew VII. 13-14: "Strait is the gate and narrow is the way that leadeth unto life, and few there be that find it." (Notice the rhyme of "Ruth . . . ruth" in lines 5 and 8, one of the very rare examples of identical rhyme in Milton.)

Sonnet X, To the Lady Margaret Ley

This was also published in the *Poems* of 1645. The sonnet is a tribute to a lady, but even more to her illustrious father. Both are readily identified. Lady Margaret Ley and her husband, Captain John Hobson, were Milton's neighbors when the two families lived in Aldersgate Street. Edward Phillips said, "This lady, being a woman of great wit and ingenuity, had a particular honour for him, and took much delight in his company, as likewise Captain Hobson, her husband, a very accomplished gentleman." Lady Margaret, as the sonnet says, was "daughter to that good Earl," the Earl of Marlborough, who had had a distinguished career as lawyer, judge, statesman. As Lord Chief Justice, he had presided over the bribery trial of Francis Bacon, Lord Chancellor, in 1622 and pronounced sentence. Under Charles I he held the offices of Lord High Treasurer and Lord President of the Council, retiring from the latter in 1628, shortly before his death. As Milton's sonnet suggests, his last days were bitterly unhappy because of the "sad breaking of that Parliament,"—the forcible dissolution of the Parliament in 1629—which marked the sharp break between Charles and the Parliamentary leaders, and was really the beginning of the end, so far as monarchy and arbitrary government were concerned. There is no other evidence than Milton's words that the political crisis hastened Marlborough's death, although Lady Margaret may have told Milton so. In the tribute to Marlborough (line 3) that he lived "unstained with gold or fee," we may perhaps find a covert allusion to the Bacon trial. In lines 6-8 Milton's allusive mind goes back to Greek history for an analogue to Marlborough's death. When Philip of Macedon defeated Thebes and Athens in the Battle of Chaeronea in 338 B.C., Milton implies that it was a "dishonest," that is, a "shameful," victory since it marked the end of freedom in the Greek city states. He compares Marlborough's death (I. 8) with that of the great Greek orator, Isocrates, who was reported to have starved himself to death after what he felt was the disaster of Chaeronea. The sonnet ends with a tribute to the daughter in whom the moral virtues of the father are "living yet."

Sonnet XIII. Mr. Henry Lawes

This sonnet, written in 1646, was, with the exception of those early enough for the *Poems* of 1645, the only poem published during Milton's middle years. It appeared, with other tributes, in the volume of Lawes' *Choice Psalms* in 1648. Milton's admiration for Lawes, which we remember from the *Comus* period, had not diminished because Lawes remained an ardent Royalist. His brother William, also a musician, had been killed in the battle at Chester. Milton rightly praises Lawes' setting of lyrics to music. Unlike some composers of that period and much later, he adapted the music to the words, rather than forcing the accent of the words to music (a process that many of us often notice in familiar hymns). Lawes, says Milton, scanned as a poet should scan, not as Midas might have done. (According to Ovid, Midas' ears were transformed to those of an ass because he preferred the piping of Pan to the music of Apollo.) Lawes was never guilty of "committing" —that is, setting in conflict—short and long stresses. On the manuscript Milton wrote "misjoining" as a possible alternative to "committing." The allusion to a "story" (1. 11) might have remained unknown had not this line been annotated by Milton himself in the only marginal note he ever appended to a poem. In the edition of the *Choice Psalms* Milton explained: "The story of Ariadne set by him in music," calling attention to the fact that Lawes had set to music William Cartwright's *The Complaint of Ariadne.* In the last three lines of the sonnet, Milton's memory goes back to a scene in the *Purgatorio* (II.76-117) in which Dante met the spirit of Casella, a Florentine musician, who had set some of Dante's canzoni to music. Milton implies that his friend Lawes would deserve an even higher place on the progress to Paradise.

Sonnet XIV. Mrs. Catharine Thomason

Many students of literature and history who have never heard of Mrs. Catharine Thomason will recognize the last name because her husband, George Thomason collected the "Thomason Tracts," more than 22,000 pamphlets published between 1642 and 1661, now deposited in the British Museum. Thomason's original collection included *Areopagitica* and various others of Milton's tracts, all of them gifts of the author. The fact that this sonnet, like the one to the virtuous young lady, is phrased in basically Christian terms led John Smart to suggest that the girl may have been Mrs. Thomason's daughter, in which case she would have been a child not older than twelve when the sonnet was addressed to her.

Sonnet XX. Lawrence of Virtuous Father . . .

Edward Phillips noted in his memoir of his uncle that one friend who often visited Milton was "young Lawrence, the son of him that was President of Oliver's Council, to whom there is a sonnet among the rest in his printed poems." Henry Lawrence, the "virtuous father," had two sons, Edward and Henry. Earlier biographers were inclined to think that the subject of the sonnet was Henry, who outlived his father, but evidence presented by John Smart makes it much more probable that the young man, who often came to Milton's house, was the older son Edward, far more serious and intellectual than his brother. This remarkable young man was elected to Parliament in 1656—the year of Milton's sonnet—when he was only twenty-three. Unfortunately he died the following year at the age of twenty-four. In theme and detail, this sonnet follows closely the form of "invitation to a friend," particularly the pattern established by Horace in *Epistles* I. ix. The form was a popular one among English poets. The student may compare Milton's use of the convention with Ben Jonson's "Inviting a Friend to Supper." Whether because of the sonnet's limitation of length or because of Milton's more ascetic way of life, we find no such table as Jonson's, loaded with "olives, capers or some better salad" serving as *hors d'oeuvres* to meats in profusion; mutton, perhaps a hare, fowl of various sorts from "a short-legged hen" through larks to partridge, pheasant, or woodcock, not to mention "digestive cheese" which the gargantuan guest must have needed by the time he reached it in his menu. At both Milton's and Jonson's tables wine was served but obviously in greater quantity and variety at Jonson's than at Milton's. Jonson's guest would have heard Virgil, Tacitus or Livy read aloud. Milton's friend Lawrence listened to, perhaps joined in, music. It is interesting, even in this classically conventional sonnet, to catch the Biblical strain in "the lily and rose, that neither sowed nor spun." Like Jonson and many others in the tradition, Milton ends with a bit of mild moralizing, the "lesson" of which depends upon the meaning of "spare" (1. 13) which Milton uses in a sense now lost in English. Smart would make Milton more austere than he probably was by interpreting it, "forbear." More recent commentators interpret it as "afford." Mild moralizing indeed in the Horation vein; but similar enough to what we shall find in the next sonnet, written to a young man who had been one of Milton's students, to make us wonder whether Lawrence, the "virtuous son," had once also been a pupil of Milton's.

Sonnet XXI. "Cyriack, whose Grandsire . . ."

This is one of two sonnets addressed to the same person, the other of which will be considered among the "Personal Sonnets." It bears a slight resemblance to the sonnet to Lady Margaret Ley in that a parent or grandparent is also praised. Otherwise the Horatian vein more closely resembles the sonnet to Lawrence we have just read in that the poet is writing to a much younger friend, this time one we know to have been *in statu pupillari*. The "grandsire" was Sir Edward Coke, Chief Justice of the King's Bench, one of the great jurists of England, and (another passing reminiscence to the Ley sonnet) the arch enemy of Sir Francis Bacon, in whose political downfall he was undoubtedly involved. Cyriack Skinner had been one of the first pupils in Milton's school, and affection between teacher and pupil continued as long as Milton lived. We know that he served Milton as amanuensis, and William Riley Parker believes that he was the author of the "anonymous" life of Milton, which Miss Helen Darbishire attributed to Milton's other nephew, John Phillips. In the light moralizing of this, as in the previous sonnet, we catch the tone of a friendly schoolmaster delivering a little lecture to the young, and if we interpret the "spare" of the preceding sonnet as "afford," we find the "lesson" much the same.

The line, "Let Euclid rest and Archimedes pause," may be a laughing reference to the interest Skinner had showed in mathematics when he was at Milton's school, and the next line, "And what the Swede intend, and what the French," to Skinner's mature interest in international affairs. In spite of the fact that in 1655, the date of this sonnet, Sweden was campaigning against the Poles and many things were happening in France under Cardinal Mazarin, the lines probably were not intended to refer to anything specific. Milton is following the Horatian pattern of admonition to the young, particularly *Ode*s II. xi, in which Horace bids Quintus Hirpinus forget the warlike Cantabrians and the Scythians and remember that he is young and youth is fleeting. Any student educated in Milton's school would have caught the echo.

PERSONAL SONNETS

Again my division is arbitrary since, of course, some of the political sonnets are personal, dealing as they do with Milton's own works or with his highly personal opinions. I group them as I do in part because the political sonnets lead us into problems of political or religious history so that they can best be treated together, and in part because these "personal" sonnets are a small group of *private* reflections on Milton's part concerning either his blindness or his dead wife.

Three sonnets, the Prologues in *Paradise Lost,* some choruses and speeches in *Samson Agonistes,* and the long passage in the *Second Defence,* already discussed, give us our chief knowledge of Milton's blindness and his attitudes toward it. Recent editors date both sonnets on his blindness 1655, but I am of the group who still feel that the first sonnet may have been written around 1652, in spite of its place in the manuscript and other evidence that has been offered for 1655. The mood reflected in this most familiar of his sonnets must have been one he often experienced when he was facing the calamity for the first time. He must have believed, indeed, that the great work for which he had been "called" would never be written.

Sonnet XIX. "When I Consider . . ."

In structure, this is one of the three most masterly of Milton's sonnets, reminding us of the architectonic expertness of *Lycidas*. I have said that Milton's basic principle in structure is the paragraph rather than the sentence, but in this case I find a remarkable example of a sentence that is a verse-paragraph or a verse-paragraph that is a sentence. I hope that the reader will forgive a personal digression, because I think that my youthful pleasure in my "discovery" of the structure of this sonnet may be shared by others. When I was still in grammar school, we were required to analyze and parse in the old-fashioned way, a fashion long outmoded but to my mind, like many other "antiques," extremely valuable. On "exhibition days," when parents and friends came to visit, each of us was told off to perform some task in public, and since I—who could not sew or draw or do anything really useful—*could* analyze and parse, I was told that I might quietly diagram on the blackboard the longest sentence I could find. Among the many books on my father's shelves, over which I pored for days, was this sonnet, fortunately for my theory in an old-fashioned text. If you will make a simple substitution, you will read the sonnet as I first read it: instead of periods, use semicolons, and reduce the capital letters to lower case. Then you will find that the sonnet really is what my old-fashioned editor and I thought it was—one magnificent compound-complex sentence. It took me the whole afternoon and the largest blackboard in the classroom to prove it but prove it I did to my complete satisfaction as I excitedly but carefully drew one of those intricate trees we used to create in diagramming, with the vertical line indicating subject, predicate and object, and all those fascinating angle lines growing as the modifiers grew—a tree as intricate as Ygdrasil (of which I had never then heard), the tree whose roots and branches bind together heaven, earth and hell. In my compound-complex diagram the basic structure on the vertical line is: "I ask; Patience replies." All the rest will fall into place, sprung from one father and mother, these two simple phrases. Enough of personal digression except to say that this was my very youthful introduction to the art and craft of a great poet, which has increased over all these years.

The metaphor around which the sonnet is developed is the parable of the talents in Matthew XXV. 14-30, in which the unprofitable servant, who buried in the earth the money his master had given him, was cast out into darkness. "That one talent which is death to hide," implies, of course, the double meaning of a *talent* as a piece of money and the other connotation of *talent* as the gift of genius, which Milton believed God had given him. As Smart points out (*Milton's Sonnets,* p. 108) the parable of the talents was in Milton's mind when he wrote that early sonnet on his birthday, since a letter of Milton's to a friend, with which he enclosed it, referred to "the terrible seizing of him that hid the talent" with Christ's command that all men should labor while it is light. That early sonnet ended on a note of resignation to the will of God:

> All is, if I have grace to use it so
> As ever in my great Task-Master's eye.

The sonnet on his blindness proceeds from grief through questioning to final resignation, but both mood and meaning are far more profound than they had been in the youthful reflections on his birthday. Milton had labored with all his might while it was still light, but darkness of a different sort had fallen before the working-day was over—before half his working-days should have been over. Was the laborer still responsible for increasing the talent which he could no longer see? We must remember that blindness was a far greater impediment to Milton than it might have been to a poet of another "school" to whom poetry might literally have been the spontaneous overflow of powerful feeling. Milton was not only a "classical" poet; he believed that one who would write a poem "doctrinal to a nation" must be a "learned" poet. For his great poem he needed to turn to books, as does a scholar, who is far more dependent on his eyes than is a novelist or lyric poet. When total darkness descended, he must have believed there was no possibility of his continuing with the great work he had laid aside at the call of his party. For a time he could only submit, saying with Job, "The Lord gave and the Lord hath taken away. Blessed be the name of the Lord." In the reply of Patience in the sonnet, Milton expresses his resignation to God's will in terms of the hierarchy of angels we shall find in *Paradise Lost*. Some angels

> in God's presence, nearest to His throne,
> Stand ready at command, and are His eyes
> That run through all the Heavens or down to the Earth
> Bear His swift errands over moist and dry,
> O'er sea and land.

(P.L. III. 649-653)

But in the Heaven of *Paradise Lost,* as we shall see, are other angels, sometimes, but not always, Seraphim and Cherubim, who are angels not of action but of contemplation. As among angels, so among men who serve God on earth, there must be those who, no longer able to be God's "eyes," serve in some other way: "They also serve who only stand and wait." Here, as so often, we find a double meaning, for in addition to the connotation that we read into the word, Milton is remembering the meaning of "wait on" as used so often in the Bible: "Wait on the Lord; be of good courage and He shall strengthen thy heart. . . . Wait, I say, on the Lord." (Psalm XXVII. 14.)

Sonnet XXII. To Cyriack Skinner

The second sonnet on his blindness was apparently written on the anniversary of the day on which Milton had been forced to realize that his blindness was total, three years earlier. Addressed to his former student, the lines are in a very different vein from the other sonnet inscribed to Skinner in the same year. Here, as in the passage in *Paradise Lost* on the "drop serene," Milton tells us that, whatever the cause of his blindness, his eyes remained clear to outward view. As we shall see in some of the Prologues to *Paradise Lost* and some lines in *Samson Agonistes,* he laments first the loss of light—of sun or moon or star—and then, as in his sonnet to his wife, his inability to see the faces of men and women around him. The mood of this sonnet is quite different from that of the preceding one. This is not quiet, almost passive, resignation to the will of God. This is the "true warfaring Christian" who will fight on, the mood in which he had imperiously replied in the preceding year in the *Second Defence* to enemies who had taunted him that his blindness was the judgment of God upon him:

> I considered that many had purchased a less good by a greater evil . . . that though I am blind, I might still discharge the most honorable duties, the performance of which, as it is some.. thing more durable than glory, ought to be an object of superior admiration and esteem. . . . I have been enabled to do the will of God.
>
> (p. 180)

"What supports me?" He answers, not as Patience had once replied to him, but proudly, in full consciousness of his service to his people and to God in the deliberate sacrifice of his eyes:

> The conscience, friend, to have lost them overplied
> In Liberty's defence, my noble task,
> Of which all Europe talks from side to side.

Milton was not exaggerating. He had humbled and abased the great Salmasius, toppling the intellectual giant of Europe from his proud place, and his fame in Europe was even greater than in his own country.

Milton's is not a personal and vainglorious boasting. He is exulting that it was he who had been chosen for a great mission, and that he had performed it to his fullest ability. The most striking difference between the two sonnets lies right here: the first in language and mood echoes the New Testament; the second is the temper of many passages in the Old Testament. It is the mood in which he wrote the first *Defence,* when he was speaking as David had spoken to the Philistine Goliath, enemy of his people and of his God: "Thou comest to me with a sword and with a spear, and with a javelin; but I come to thee in the name of Jehovah of hosts, the God of the armies of Israel, whom thou hast defied. This day will Jehovah deliver thee into my hand. . . . that all the earth may know that there is a God in Israel."

Here is the sense of triumph and exultation of one who has fought the good fight, who has kept the faith. If he has not finished the whole course, he has not given his eyes in vain. If he has not been called to be a great poet, he has been called to avenge the adversaries of his party, who in his mind were the antagonists of God. In the two sonnets on his blindness we feel the same difference Professor Tillyard feels between the two *Defences,* and our minds, like his, go forward to *Samson Agonistes,* in which both moods appear. For a time Samson, like Job, suffers despondency and discouragement, from which he rises to a period of submission and patience, first passive, then active. As his strength returns, so does his courage and a rising optimism he cannot fully explain:

> Be of good courage, I begin to feel
> Some rousing motions in me which dispose
> To something extraordinary my thoughts.
>
>   (*S.A.* 1381-83)

The sestet of the sonnet marks a rising line in Milton, as in Job's, "Though He slay me, yet will I trust in Him." Milton had fulfilled one calling; perhaps he was still to fulfill the other.

Sonnet XXIII. Methought I saw . . .

I have said that Milton's conventional sonnets did not follow the convention most common among sonneteers—that of love—and that he wrote no love-sonnets in English. Yet in a different way, this is a love-sonnet, the tenderest, the most private of all his personal sonnets, and the most poignant of the sonnets on his blindness. Before considering its structure and mood, it is necessary to enter into the controversy I have mentioned, which was caused by William Riley Parker's suggestion that the subject was not, as we had always supposed, Milton's second wife, Katherine Woodcock whom he married after he was blind, but Mary Powell. Professor Parker will forgive me, I hope, if I over-simplify his argument for our present purposes. His contention is based chiefly upon the lines:

Mine, as whom washed from spot of child-bed taint,
Purification in the Old Law did save.

Milton's reference here is to Leviticus XII, 2-5, in which were laid down laws concerning women after childbirth, some of which were carried over into Christianity in what is called "The Churching of Women." According to Professor Parker, the phrase, "washed from child-bed taint" could apply only to Mary Powell who died three days after her child was born, and not to Katherine Woodcock, who lived three months after the birth of her child. Professor Parker, and others who follow him, quite naturally read lines 7-8

And such as *yet once more* I trust to have
Full sight of her in Heaven without restraint,

as implying that Milton is referring to a wife he had seen, not to one he married after he became blind.

Mary Powell, we remember, had returned to her husband in the summer of 1645. She died in May, 1652, three months after Milton's blindness was total. During these years she had borne three daughters who survived her, a son who had died at the age of two, and the child who had died with her. Milton remained a widower for four and a half years before marrying Katherine Woodcock, who lived only a year and a half, dying in February 1658. The sonnet to his dead wife was written in that year, though we do not know the month. (Her daughter, christened October 19, 1657, was buried March 20, 1658.) It is difficult to imagine Milton or any other man writing his most personal and moving sonnet to a first wife a few weeks or months after the death of the second. If, as Parker and others suggest, the reconciliation with Mary Powell had been such that Milton deeply treasured her memory, it seems more likely that he would have written the sonnet shortly after her death when he was suffering the first shock of blindness. The theory of happy reconciliation between husband and wife is hardly borne out by the legal documents filed after Milton's death in connection with his will, in which he left his estate to his third and surviving wife, after these words, as reported by his lawyer-brother Christopher:

> The portion due to me from Mr. Powell, my former wife's father, I leave to the unkind children I had by her, having received no part of it: but my meaning is, they shall have no other benefit of my estate than the said portion, and what I have besides done for them; they having been very undutiful to me.

Two final points may be made in connection with the "washed from spot of child-bed taint." Whatever the Church or the doctors may have found concerning Katherine's death, Edward Phillips considered that both women had died from the same cause. He said, 'In this House his first Wife dying in Childbed, he Married a

Second, who after a Year's time died in Childbed also." Phillps was undoubtedly speaking as any layman of his age would have spoken, using the same phrase for the wife who had died almost immediately after bearing a child, and the one whose death was unquestionably a remote result of childbirth. The Puritan Milton, with his attitude toward various sacraments of the Roman or Established Church, would hardly have been seriously concerned whether one wife or the other had been "churched," but since the reference in the sonnet is to the Old Law, we should remember that Leviticus laid down a period of thirty-three days of purification after the birth of a son, sixty-six after the birth of a daughter. Katherine Woodcock had lived beyond sixty-six days, and may even have been "churched."

At the opposite extreme to Parker is Leo Spitzer (*Hopkins Review*, IV [1951] 20-22), who thinks that the sonnet is not about any real woman. Milton was merely following conventions of Dante's and Petrarch's use of the *donna angelica*, the ideal of a poet in a heavenly vision. But enough of controversy. I shall continue, with others, to read the sonnet, as I believe it was written, as a tribute to Katherine Woodcock shortly after her death. The basic figure of the first four and last six lines is drawn from the legend of Alcestis, particularly as the story was treated in Euripides' play of that name. Alcestis, wife of Admetus, had given her life in place of her husband's. Hercules fought for her and brought her back, stipulating that Admetus agree to marry this apparently strange woman without putting back her veil until after the ceremony. In Milton's poem the "late espoused saint" appeared to him veiled. Blind students whom I have been privileged to teach have told me that it is a frequent experience for those who have lost their sight in adulthood to dream of people they have never seen with faces veiled or clouded in one way or another. Mr. Parker and others of his school read the "late" of "late espoused saint" in the general sense in which we use it of speaking of the dead: "My late wife," for example. But "late" was frequently used as an adverb, so that "late espoused" can equally well mean "the wife I had lately married." Milton had never seen Katherine Woodcock in reality, but he had apparently recently seen her in a dream, in which her face was clouded. He trusts that he will have "full sight of her in Heaven" "once more" when the mists have been cleared from his eyes. Admetus had been more fortunate than Milton; his wife though "pale and faint," had been saved from death, but Katherine Woodcock, "pale and faint" had slipped away, not to return in this life. Both husbands saw their wives with veiled faces, but when Milton in his dream eagerly put out his hand to remove the veil, he experienced the tragedy felt each morning by the recently blind. In the Prologue to Book III of *Paradise Lost,* after suggesting that during the night he had been with the Muse, he seems to recall much the same situation as in the sonnet:

> but not to me returns
> Day, or the sweet approach of even or morn,
> Or sight of vernal bloom or summer's rose
> Or flocks or herds *or human face divine.*

In the sonnet he suggests that this was the first time he had dreamed of his dead wife. Like Admetus, he would gladly have put forth his hand to see the "love, sweetness, goodness" he had felt during their short married life. At that eager moment he woke to the daily tragic realization of the blind, expressed in the poignant last lines:

> But oh as to embrace me she inclined,
> I waked, she fled, and day brought back my night.

In the masterly interweaving of classical and Christian themes and material, the last sonnet takes us back to *Lycidas,* in which pagan and Christian are inextricably intertwined. Basically the dominant figure is classical legend. The lines on the Old Law take us back to the Bible. Milton's "saint" is in a Christian heaven, but while her costume recalls Alcestis, it does so with overtones of the vision of Revelation VII. 13-14:

Those that are arrayed in the white robes, who are they, and whence come they? . . . These are they that come out of great tribulation and they washed their robes and made them white in the blood of the lamb.

POLITICAL SONNETS

Sonnet VIII. "Captain or Colonel, or Knight in Arms"

Nothing can better remind us of Milton's cloistered youth than the tone of this sonnet against its background. We remember that Milton said that he had changed his plans for further travel when the "melancholy intelligence" reached him of growing unrest in England. But for a time he remained as aloof from the practical problems of the state as he had always been. True, the year before the sonnet was written he had entered the war of words with his anti-episcopal tracts. But on August 22, 1643 Civil War became an actuality. According to the manuscript Milton originally considered as a title, "On his door when the city expected an attack," replaced by "When the assault was intended to the city," neither of which was used when the sonnet was published in the *Poems* of 1645. It is true that there was little chance for success on the part of Charles' forces. "When the assault was intended to the city," they found themselves facing a hastily assembled but well drilled militia of over 20,000. Neither side attacked, and in a short time the King withdrew. Nevertheless, although there proved no real danger, there was natural alarm and suspense in London. I suspect that the tone of the sonnet was less a result of Milton's "inflexible composure," to which Smart pays tribute, (*Milton's Sonnets,* p. 57) than the fact that he was still spiritually dwelling in his impregnable ivory tower with *Il Penseroso.*

Scansion of the first line shows that Milton, like many others, pronounced "Colonel" in three syllables. Derived through French, this spelling was used alternatively with "Coronel," from which we have our modern pronunciation. Milton is saying: If the commanding officer, whoever he may be, will spare this house of a poet, he will be rewarded, since the poet has power through his art to perpetuate the memory of his benefactor. When his city was in peril, "the education of a poet" sent Milton's memory back to classical analogues. At the time of the sack of Thebes in 336 B.C., the "great Emathian conqueror," Alexander the Great,—so legend if not history tells—spared only one house, that of the poet Pindar. And, according to Plutarch, when Athens was captured by the Spartans in 404 B.C., the conquerors were about to raze the city and turn the district into a sheep-pasture until "a man of Phocis" began to sing the first chorus in Euripides' *Electra:*

Electra, Agammemnon's child, I come
Unto thy desert home.

At which, according to Plutarch, "they were all melted with compassion," remembering the glorious past of the city.

It is fitting that the sonnet should first have appeared in the *Poems* of 1645 that hark back to Milton's cloistered youth. One can hardly imagine Milton, the statesman, whose life became so inextricably involved with that of his country, publishing it for the first time in 1673.

Sonnet XI. "A Book was writ . . ."

We are already familiar with the situation that provoked this sonnet and the next one—Milton's publication of the *Divorce Tracts,* one of which he called *Tetrachordon.* The word, a technical musical term, meant a combination of four notes into a chord. In the tract Milton had analyzed the four chief passages in Scripture, which were interpreted by Roman Catholics and Anglicans as interdicting divorce, in such as a way as to prove to his own satisfaction that they did no such thing. To Milton, with his knowledge of Greek and music, the word was a familiar one; but many of his contemporaries had found it as unintelligible as it seems to most modern readers. As you read the sonnet, notice that its irony is deliberately enhanced by some of the rhymes. Inveighing against what seemed to him illiterates, Milton cuts his pattern to fit their shoddy cloth, and with the word "Tetrachordon" rhymes "pored on," "word on," "Gordon." In addition he makes rhymes for "style," not only by using the internal rhyme, "while," but by deliberately dividing between two lines "Mile-End Green," a familiar word to any Londoner. These are tricks of Samuel Butler, of W. S. Gilbert, in our time of Ogden Nash.

The setting of the sonnet is among bookstalls where passers-by did much of their casual browsing, if not their buying. It is an impatient rejoinder on Milton's part to some of the bewildered readers he may actually have seen puzzling over the title without bothering to read the book. In his tracts Milton had been dealing with a fairly new and certainly provocative subject—justification of divorce. He had gone to pains over both form and style; the tract was as compact as he could make it, "woven close." Clearly, it had not proved a "best seller." For a time it had found a small audience among intellects that could appreciate it, but now, as if it had been "remaindered"—as we might say—it is tossed on the rubbish heap of a stall, where an ignoramus may turn it over, getting no farther than the title: "Bless us! what a word on A title-page is this." He is followed by other stupid oafs who have no intention of buying, but "spelling false"—misread it, and, stupid as they are, take almost as much time spelling out the title as it would require a walk to Mile-End Green, the outward limit of London. Into the faces of those to whom "Tetrachordon" seemed a hard word, Milton throws a group of Scottish proper names of a kind that were more and more infiltrating into London from the barbarous North. Some were names of real people, though "Galasp" is unknown as a proper name. Possibly it was a mutilated form of "Gillespie," though I rather suspect it was merely a satiric invention of Milton's as another rhyme for "asp" and "grasp." Imagine, says Milton, how these Scottish names would have sounded to Quintilian, great orator and authority upon usage, who had particularly warned against the use of proper names of foreign origin, "uncouth" in both the seventeenth-century and the modern usage. Milton is saying in effect what Matthew Arnold said in *The Function of Criticism* about "the growth of such hideous names as Higginbottom, Stiggins, Bugg . . . by the Ilissus there was no Wragg, poor thing!" Byron put it more succinctly: "Oh, Amos Cottle—Phoebus, what a name!"

Milton's little peroration is addressed to the soul of Sir John Cheek, the great English humanist of the preceding century, first Professor of Greek at Cambridge, and tutor to King Edward VI. The compression of the penultimate lines is puzzling enough that such authorities as John Smart and J. H. Hanford interpret the last three lines in opposite ways. Mr. Hanford reads: "Thy age did not, as ours does, hate learning." Mr. Smart quotes at some length to emphasize the fact that "the introduction of the New Learning into England was accompanied by much prejudice and hostility," and mentions a statement of Cheek's, "The Greek language was hateful to many, and is so now. . . . The good men of the present age abhor the scholarly mind." Smart's reading of the line is: *"They hated not learning worse than toad or asp*—but as much as they hated either." Two of my ingenious students have suggested a slight change in typesetting, one of which will bear out Hanford's, the other, Smart's reading. For Hanford, let the printer set: "Hated not-learning worse than toad or asp"; for Smart, "Hated not learning—worse than toad or asp." Milton, writing in ironic mood as he was, might well have approved one or the other.

Sonnet XII. On the Same

The previous sonnet dealt specifically with one tract. In this one, Milton is thinking of the series as a whole. More deeply serious than the first one, the mood of which is irony and irritation, it has yet some of the same quality of invective against a generation of barbarians, which we feel particularly in the cacophonous medley of animal-noises in line 4, and in the deliberate use of such words as "hogs" and "bawl." We know that Milton had every reason to be both startled and deeply disturbed by the reception of his tracts among members of his own party. Milton was not only mentioned by name in the order of Parliament for licensing the press, but he was held up to public censure by Herbert Palmer, a spokesman for the Puritan party, in a sermon preached to both Houses of Parliament. The State was urged to allow no toleration of the new theory of divorce, "of which a wicked book is abroad and uncensured, though deserving to be burnt." Already disillusioned by the attitude of the Presbyterians, Milton shows himself in this sonnet and the next turning further and further from the right wing of the Puritan party. The theme of his *Divorce Tracts,* as well as *Areopagitica* and *Of Education,* he had said, was *liberty.* What he had hoped for his country was the liberty for which he once believed his party was ready to fight and die. Instead of the applause he had expected for his frank statement of opinion, he heard a hiss of ugly sounds, "Of owls and cuckoos, asses, apes, and dogs," all with ugly voices, and each one traditionally a symbol: the owl of ignorance, the cuckoo of ingratitude and vanity, the ass, of stupidity and obstinacy, the ape of empty mockery, and the dog of quarrelsomeness. To carry out the animal imagery, Milton goes back to classical legend and recalls a story of Ovid, that Jove, father of Diana (moon goddess) and Apollo (sun god) turned into frogs a group of peasants who refused to help them and their mother,

Latona. Such was the thanks of his party. This, Milton reflects, is what one gets for casting pearls before swine. They have bawled for freedom, but they have no idea what freedom really implies. In the lines that follow Milton makes one of his famous distinctions, echoing, as so often when he speaks of liberty, the words of Christ in the Gospel according to John: "Ye shall know the truth, and the truth shall make you free." The freedom they wish is not freedom but the abuse of it, the licence for every man to do exactly what he wants to do. True liberty is a hard thing, to be attained only by those who are wise and good.

"On the New Forcers of Conscience under the Long Parliament"

This sonnet bears no number, probably because it is the one sonnet written by Milton which is not in the conventional form of fourteen lines. In many modern editions it is printed after Sonnet XII, the place it holds in the Trinity Manuscript. The form is that of the *Sonetto Caudato,* a sonnet with a coda or tail. Practitioners of the form did not limit themselves to one tail; Milton has two (lines 15-17, 18-20). He might have added others if he had wished to do so. Among the Italians it was largely a humorous form, or as in Milton, satiric. Continuing the theme of *liberty* in the preceding sonnet, Milton is here particularly attacking the Presbyterians in the Westminister Assembly, from whom he is departing further and further.

In 1643, the Long Parliament, after abolishing episcopacy—the government of the Church by Archbishops and Bishops—proposed to establish another form which Milton satirizes as "a Classic Hierarchy" (*Presbytery* and *Classis* could be used interchangeably), in which the governors would be a group of Presbyters, or elders. Sharp opposition arose from a group of Independents (with whom

Milton was in accord at this time) not only on the form of Church-government but even more on the question whether Independent congregations would be permitted to exist outside the national Church, and to what extent freedom of belief would be tolerated. The Presbyterians refused freedom of dissent and demanded conformity to the Established Church, while the Independents continued to fight for freedom of conscience.

As in *Areopagitica,* so in his tailed sonnet, Milton stresses the irony of the fact that Presbyterians who had battled to throw off the yoke of episcopacy were now coming to practice the very abuses against which they had fought. For example, "Plurality" (or "Pluralism," the practice of holding two or more benefices at once) had been one of the Anglican abuses against which Presbyterians had rebelled. Now they are doing it themselves, says Milton, and it becomes clear that they really did not detest the practice but rather "envied" this easy way of increasing their incomes. In the lines that follow, Milton states the position of the Independents against the Presbyterians who sought to confine all men within the straitjackets of conformity and refused to permit the liberty of conscience demanded by the Independents. They would force our consciences that Christ set free; again our ears catch the echo of the Gospel according to John.

In the lines introducing proper names (8-12) Milton attacks a group of the most reactionary Presbyterians: Adam Stuart, a Scot, one of whose pamphlets was signed only with his initials ("mere A.S."); Samuel Rutherford, Professor of Divinity at St. Andrews, whose pamphlets threatened drastic persecution of nonconformists; (a later anti-toleration tract was directed chiefly against Roger Williams and Jeremy Taylor); Thomas Edwards ("shallow Edwards"), Puritan preacher and pamphleteer; and "Scotch What-d'ye-call," Robert Baillie, another Scottish tractarian. During the recent skirmish, these had been the most vocal and most rigid of the Presbyterian foes of toleration. Against these he opposes, by implication, a group of his own more liberal Independents,

Men whose life, learning, faith, and pure intent
Would have been held in high esteem with Paul.

He is referring in particular to a group of Independent clergymen
(William Bridge, Jeremiah Burroughs, Thomas Goodwin, Philip
Nye, Sidrach Simpson) who had recently published a joint mani-
festo, the *Apologetical Narration,* sharply opposing the regulations
proposed by the Presbyterians and demanding toleration and free-
dom of conscience.

The *Sonetto Caudato* concludes with a sharp warning to the
Presbyterians. The Independents will discover all the tricks and
plots of these men. The Parliament may stop short of ("baulk")
cutting off their ears, as William Prynne's had been cut off, but
(here Milton goes back first to the Old Testament, then to the
New) the sharp shears of Parliament will "clip your phylacteries."
These had originally been small boxes containing passages from
Mosaic Law, worn on forehead and arm by pious Jews, but to Chris-
tians they had become, as Jesus Christ implied (Matthew XXIII.
5) symbols of hypocrisy among men who pretended to be spiritual
leaders but who actually, according to Jesus, "love the chief places
of feasts, and the chief seats in the synagogue." As in *Lycidas,*
Milton is accusing the corrupt clergy of creeping, intruding and
climbing into the fold "for their bellies' sake." He succeeded mag-
nificently in *Lycidas* but failed here. With the exception of the last
coda, this is far inferior to most of his other sonnets. However it
may have impressed contemporaries who would have understood
at first hearing the many covert allusions and double meanings, it
is too "occasional" to live long after the period of controversy that
provoked it. In this way it is like those tractates of Milton's which
are now read only by the historians, not like the great prose of the
Second Defence and the *Areopagitica* which transcend the alterca-
tion of an age and remain "doctrinal to a nation." Embroiled in
controversy Milton slaps back at his adversaries with name-calling,
vituperation, personal invective, never rising to the heights of
which he is elsewhere so capable, like the great prophets of doom.

Only in the last line do we momentarily feel the power of words of which he was usually master:

When they shall read this clearly in your charge:
New Presbyter is but old Priest writ large.

The "tailed sonnet," like the scorpion, carries its sting in its tail. Even a schoolboy in Milton's day would have recognized the double-play here. The English forms, *Presbyter* and *Priest* are both derived from the same Greek word, *presbuteros,* "elder," the former keeping the Greek form, *priest* coming from Latin through French. Those "elders" of the Presbyterian Church who had thrown off their Prelate Lord have in their turn become as bigoted and intolerant as the tyrants they once opposed. The sentence is intellectually brilliant, but we are not moved as we were in *Lycidas.*

Sonnet XV. To the Lord General Fairfax at the Siege of Colchester

This and the next are two of the sonnets Milton omitted from the edition of 1673 for obvious political reasons; they were not published until 1694. Sir Thomas Fairfax had proved himself a great military leader in various engagements throughout the Civil War, particularly at the Battles of Marston Moor and Naseby. Always in the thick of battle, he had impressed his men by his indomitable vigor and complete disregard for his personal safety. Peace, following the rout of the Royalists, had continued for two years when in 1648, the year of this sonnet, "new rebellions" raised their "Hydra heads," calling, as had the appearance of the legendary nine-headed monsters, for another Hercules. There were uprisings of Royalist troops in Wales and Kent, and at about the same time, the "false North," the Scots, invaded England in violation of the Solemn League and Covenant they had made with Parliament. Cromwell, after quelling the Welsh insurrection,

moved north and defeated the Scots at the Battle of Preston. Fair-
fax took Maidstone and, when the Royalists strongly entrenched
themselves in the walled town of Colchester, blockaded and be-
sieged it until the Royalists were literally starved out and sur-
rendered on August 27, 1648. Like all members of his party, Mil-
ton had reason to praise Fairfax's "firm unshaken virtue," a word
used in both its moral sense and its more literal meaning of "manly
strength." In this sonnet, unlike many of the others, Milton makes
a sharp division between octave, devoted to praise of Fairfax's
valor, and sestet, in which he turns from what Fairfax has already
accomplished on the field, to warning of tasks that lie before him
in the period of reconstruction that inevitably follows war. The
sestet is unconsciously ironic, so far as Fairfax is concerned, since
after his great triumph at Colchester, he passed into political ob-
scurity. Although he continued to bear the title, Commander-in-
Chief, military power passed imperceptibly from him to Crom-
well. A year after his victory he retired from his military duties,
and at no time took upon him duties of the State.

Milton was quite right in feeling that the situation of his party
in England would be a parlous one, not to be finally settled by any
amount of fighting on battle fields. "For what can war but endless
war still breed"—Milton's generation had had no such drastic ex-
perience as has ours of the twentieth century, but it had learned, as
must every generation torn by war,

> In vain doth valor bleed
> While avarice and rapine share the land.

Estates of Royalists had been confiscated, exorbitant financial
penalties laid upon them, taxes were sharply rising, bribery, cor-
ruption and fraud were everywhere. The abuses were not limited
to Royalists. The party in power was responsible for many of the
burdens under which Puritans, too, were suffering almost as much
as the enemy they had conquered. "O for that warning voice,"
Milton wrote in *Paradise Lost*. His function—and he felt it
deeply in those days when his party was boasting of its triumph in

battle—was to warn them that the real struggle lay ahead. No one can doubt the sincerity that rings through this sonnet and the next, which have much in common.

Sonnet XVI. To the Lord General Cromwell

This sonnet, as the long subtitle indicates, was written at a particular time for a specific purpose: "On the proposals of certain ministers at the Committee for Propagation of the Gospel." Such a committee had been appointed by Parliament in the spring of 1652 to consider the extent of toleration to be permitted in religious teaching outside the clergy. The members were specifically faced by a proposal of fifteen ministers, headed by John Owen who had been chaplain to Cromwell. From Milton's point of view, their proposals implied serious restrictions upon freedom of conscience, restrictions which he was right in thinking would involve still greater prohibitions as their authors continued to lay down limitations. Cromwell had so far opposed such measures, but Milton was aware that Cromwell might either not be willing or not be able to go as far in toleration as Milton wished him to go.

Unlike the tailed sonnet, this one would live even if we knew nothing of the particular circumstances that provoked it. It reflects Milton's reiterated warning to his party in *Areopagitica* and in some of the preceding sonnets, that the professed champions of liberty were in danger of imposing the very kind of bondage against which they had fought, and that "new Presbyter" was indeed likely to prove "old Priest writ large." As in the sonnet to Fairfax, the octave is devoted to praise, the sestet to warning and admonition, though octave and sestet are not arbitrarily divided here. In the octave Milton praises Cromwell, as he had praised Fairfax, for his past achievements. With "matchless fortitude" Cromwell, our "chief of men" had triumphantly led his country through war. All were aware of his great victories at the Battle of Preston on the banks of "Darwen stream," at Dunbar and at Worcester. Through every adversity he had plowed his way to peace and truth (l. 4). (Professor Merritt Hughes has called attention to an interesting double meaning in this line. The figures of Truth and Peace appeared upon a coin issued by Parliament in honor of Cromwell's victories at Preston, Dunbar and Worcester.) But across the well-justified praise, we hear again the note of admonition and warning: "yet much remains to conquer still." We have won the war, but will we win the peace? There are enemies who threaten our souls, as dangerous as any of those who on the field of battle threatened our bodies. The new foes will attempt to bind our souls with secular chains. Milton cries out to Cromwell to help England save the free conscience of true religion from the wolves —the figure recalls the one in *Lycidas* and will appear again in *Paradise Lost*—who threaten the sheep. The final couplet is used deliberately, as is the simple but intentionally ugly rhyme, "paw" and "maw"—mean words for base objects.

Sonnet XVII. To Sir Henry Vane the Younger

Sir Henry Vane (usually spoken of as "Young Sir Henry," because his father, "Old Sir Henry" was alive) was an important member of the Council and of Parliament, concerned with foreign affairs and the administration of the Navy. The duties of his office had become acute by the declaration of war between England and Holland. Milton sent a copy of this sonnet to Vane on July 3, 1652, three days after the Dutch ambassadors were dismissed from England. In the octave Milton is writing about these recent political developments and, as usual, thinking in terms of classical analogues. In his tribute to the statesman, he reminds him of the righteous firmness of the Roman Senate, which, even more than the valor of soldiers, defeated Pyrrhus, King of Epirus, "the fierce Epirot," and Hannibal, "the African bold." He feels sure that Vane will be capable of equal firmness, whether peace is declared or war continued with the "hollow states." Here Milton is punning upon the "hollow"—deceitful—character of the Dutch, and the "hollowness" of Holland, much of which lies below sea-level. In the sestet, beginning in the middle of a line, as so often, Milton passes from the immediate political issues, to what was always of paramount importance in his mind: the basic problems of liberty of conscience. Both Milton and Vane were among the Independents who insisted on the distinction between civil and ecclesiastical authority, making a sharp division between "the bounds of either sword." He is assured that Sir Henry Vane's firm hand will guide the state and will uphold the true religion.

Sonnet XVIII. On the Late Massacre in Piedmont

The outrage of the slaughter of the Piedmontese, by order of the Duke of Savoy on April 24, 1653, had shocked all Protestants. In their eyes, the Vaudois, or Waldensians, living quietly apart in an isolated section of the Alps, were true primitive Christians who for hundreds of years had kept alive the spirit of the teaching of Christ. Without warning they were set upon and slaughtered with every kind of barbarity. It is estimated that 1712 men, women and children were killed. The few fugitives who escaped over the wild and desolate snow-covered mountains carried word of the massacre to Paris, begging the protection of Protestants.

In his capacity as Latin Secretary, Milton, acting for Cromwell, wrote an official protest to the Duke of Savoy, followed by letters of state to the kings of Denmark, Sweden, to the Dutch Republic and the Swiss Protestant cantons, urging them to join the British Commonwealth in protest. Similar appeals were sent to Cardinal Mazarin and to the King of France. Cromwell also sent a special ambassador to Savoy to protest the persecution and to indicate that Cromwell was willing to go to war if necessary. From his state papers which, though firm and outspoken, nevertheless had to be restrained within the limits of international diplomacy, Milton turned to poetry for release of his profound emotion. In structure, style and intensity of feeling, this is Milton's greatest "trumpet."

Even Milton never so surpassed himself in keeping within the limitations of a form yet in releasing that form from the narrow restrictions it might have imposed. There is no line, with the possible exception of the second, at the end of which we pause as we read the sonnet aloud. Inevitably we are carried on through the first quatrain to find the governing verb, "Forget not." We cannot be sure whether the sestet begins in the eighth line with "Their moans" or in the tenth, with "Their martyred blood and ashes," nor does it matter, since octave and sestet are magnificently welded into one masterly whole.

In *Lycidas* alone has Milton so far achieved such majestic control over sound, meaning and structure. Here again we hear the smiting of that two-handed engine at the door—the prophecy of doom. The sheep in *Lycidas* died of sheep-rot, while their crass shepherds made raucous music, but the situation here is even more drastic. The Piedmontese had been the original sheep of the Good Shepherd; they had followed His gospel while our rude ancestors were still worshipping stocks and stones. As from the dragon's teeth once sprang up armed men, so from the martyred blood and ashes strewn over the fields of Italy will come retribution upon the "triple Tyrant." We cannot break this sonnet into artificial distinction of two themes, one in octave, another in sestet. It is all one great invective, calling for vengeance, from "Avenge, O Lord" to "Babylonian woe," the destruction foretold in the Apocalypse. In its compelling resonance (the sonnet must be read aloud) Milton continues the "dread voice" of the Old Testament, "Vengeance is mine" with the "loud voice" of Revelation, at the opening of the fifth seal, "How long, O Lord, holy and true, dost thou not judge and avenge our blood on them that dwell on the earth."

III
THE MAJOR POEMS

Paradise Lost

DEVELOPMENT

In "The Education of a Poet" we have found some indications that the youthful Milton aspired to write an epic. Indeed, during his second year at Cambridge, he tried his hand at a "little epic" in a Latin poem, "In Quintum Novembris." As the title implies, the poem was written for November 5, "Guy Fawkes' Day." Fawkes and eight other conspirators had plotted to blow up Parliament House on November 5, 1605, when James was present for the opening of Parliament. The plot was detected just in time. By order of Parliament, the day was to be forever memorialized by England. The universities always held formal exercises which, at Cambridge, had produced such poems as Milton attempted, written in part under the influence of the "Spenserians," Giles and Phineas Fletcher, Cambridge dons, who had set the fashion. Milton's Latin exercise vaguely foreshadows *Paradise Lost,* in that its main character is Satan. Satan, jealous of the blessings he finds in England, speeds to Italy to urge the Pope to action against English heretics, then calls a council of devils in Hell to make his own plans—presumably to instigate the Gunpowder Plot. At the end of the poem, God, looking down from Heaven, laughs—as on three occasions God laughs in *Paradise Lost*—foreknowing how frustrate these diabolic plans will be. Two years later, however, in the "Vacation Exercise," Milton indicated that he intended to write his epic not in Latin but in his native language. The references in the Exercise and in the Sixth Elegy, naturally vague, suggest that his chief model was to be the *Odyssey,* but do not indicate any particular epic theme.

During the Horton years Milton must have given a good deal of thought to the project, while he was training himself in many different kinds of English verse. His ideas seem to have crystallized during his Italian travels, perhaps because his acquaintance with Manso seemed to bring him closer to Tasso, the Italian poet of epic in the vernacular, whose theory and practise were very influential on Milton. In the Latin verses he addressed to Manso, Milton, after paying high tribute to Italian literature, patriotically declares that the English, too, are votaries of Phoebus Apollo, and suggests that he himself has in mind an English epic. That the plan is still only tentative is implied in the Latin construction with which he introduces it: "si quando": "If ever I shall summon back our native kings into our songs, and Arthur, waging his wars beneath the earth, or if ever I shall proclaim the magnanimous heroes of the table . . ." Milton had apparently begun to think of an epic based upon King Arthur and the knights of the Round Table.

Milton's statement in the *Epitaphium Damonis* suggests that he had gone farther with his plans and was only waiting to discuss them with Diodati: "I, for my part, am resolved to tell the story of the Trojan ships in the Rutupian sea and of the ancient kingdom of Inogene." The *Iliad* and the *Aeneid* were to come home to British shores. Milton apparently intended to begin his epic with the coming of the Trojan fleet to England under Brutus, who married Inogene. Homer, Virgil and Spenser come together, since Spenser, too, had treated some of the themes Milton suggests. This would have been Milton's *Arthuriad,* in which, as Virgil had glorified Rome, Milton would sing the great past of Britain and her still greater future.

The plan was still in his mind when Milton set down about one hundred possible subjects for a major work in the Trinity or Cambridge manuscript. Among the thirty-three subjects from British history, Arthurian materials are mentioned. All the subjects in the Trinity manuscript are for dramas, but it is probable that Milton made another list for epics, which has not been preserved. That he continued his plans for an *Arthuriad* until at least 1642 is shown in his prose works. In the *Apology for Smectymnuus,* Milton speaks of stages in his early reading and interests: after "grave orators and historians," "the smooth elegiac poets," and "the two famous renowners of Beatrice and Laura," he mentions as another path "whither my younger feet wandered," "those lofty fables and romances, which recount in solemn cantos the deed of knighthood founded by our victorious kings." In another passage, often quoted from the *Reason of Church Government,* Milton describes the task he had set himself for writing three major works. One is in "that epic form whereof the two poems of Homer and those other two of Virgil and Tasso, are a diffuse, and the book of Job a brief, model." His mind is still on an English epic, since he adds: "and lastly, what king or knight before the conquest might be chosen in whom to lay the pattern of a Christian hero."

Just when and why Milton gave up the idea of an *Arthuriad* remains a matter of surmise. The subjects in the Trinity manuscript suggest that he had been reading British history. A little later he began to devote his spare time to his *History of Britain.* Certainly by that time he had come to question the authenticity of the Arthurian story, since he raises the question whether any such person as Arthur ever reigned in England. Such a doubt would have been sufficient grounds for Milton to discard the idea of an *Arthuriad,* since basic to his conception of the function of a poet was the fact that the poet must deal with *truth.* Something of this growing doubt is implied in the Prologue to Book IX of *Paradise Lost,* where he mentioned among materials he had dismissed, "fabled knights, In battles feigned," and other trappings of chivalry, which, he says with some contempt, are "not that which justly gives heroic name To person or to poem."

Even if Milton had not given up the idea of an *Arthuriad* fairly early in his middle years, it seems inevitable that he would have done so as his political career developed, not so much for lack of time as for his changing attitude to the party he had once believed would bring about a glorious England. He had reached a point in his study of history when he could no longer believe in the authenticity of Arthur and England's reputed great past. He had reached a point, too, when he could hardly have prophesied the great future he had once envisioned for his country.

When, then, did he begin to write *Paradise Lost* as an epic? That question too can be answered only by surmise. We know that he had planned a drama on the Fall of Man well before he changed to an epic. For this we have the evidence both of the Trinity manuscript and of Milton's nephew, Edward Phillips, who said in his *Life* of his uncle: "This subject was first designed a tragedy, and in the fourth book of the poem there are six verses, which several years before the poem was begun, were shown to me and some others, as designed for the very beginning of the said tragedy." Phillips then quoted Satan's address to the sun (IV. 32-41). Phillips does not date his reminiscence, which Hanford and others give as "circa 1642." A legend has grown up that Phillips heard his uncle read the lines when he was still a schoolboy under his direction, but there is no evidence for this in Phillips' own words. He merely says, "Several years before the poem was begun." The passage that follows implies that Milton began the actual writing of *Paradise Lost* as an epic after he became blind. Phillips seems to have acted as a sort of editor-in-chief for his uncle. He says that he "had the perusal of it from the very beginning," and that for some years he read "parcels" of it—ten, twenty, thirty lines at a time—"which being written by whatever hand came next" often needed correction "as to the orthography and pointing"— that is, spelling and punctuation. This sounds as if Milton had been dependent from the beginning on a succession of amanuenses.

A majority of the subjects in the Trinity manuscript are Biblical. Of all the subjects, Milton seemed most interested in the Fall of Man. Four drafts appear in the manuscript, the first two listing only the characters, the third including a prologue, with a brief outline of speakers and speeches, in five acts. The fourth, "Adam Un-paradised," is a fairly complete scenario of the action, again in five acts. Each draft includes a chorus. In the first three drafts we notice more allegorial than real figures: Wisdom, Justice, Mercy, Conscience, Sickness, Death and others, suggest the kind of masque-figures in which Milton showed interest in his early poems. Perhaps some vestiges of these early plans still remain in *Paradise Lost* in the allegory of Sin and Death, and the suggestion of dumb-show and pantomime of Death and Sickness in Michael's prophecies in Book XI.

Let us assume that Milton actually wrote "Adam Unparadised," in part or in entirety as a drama. He might have done so in the early 1640's while he still had comparative leisure, good health and sight. When he returned to the theme, presumably in blind-ness, after he had been relieved of the heavier duties of his Secre-taryship, why did he develop the materials into an epic? More in-teresting still, what sections of the original drama may still be found in the epic?

The second question may be answered more easily than the first. The scenario of "Adam Unparadised" opens with a prologue in which the Angel Gabriel describes Paradise. The Chorus com-ments on his coming to keep watch because of Lucifer's rebellion. Gabriel tells of the creation of Adam and Eve, their love and mar-riage. Some such conversations occur in *Paradise Lost,* although the speakers are changed. In Book V Raphael, rather than Mi-chael, comes down to Eden (of which there are various descrip-tions in Book IV and elsewhere), tells Adam of Satan's rebellion and of the Creation. Adam in turn describes his memories of his own creation and of that of Eve.

In the third division of the scenario, Lucifer appears, "bemoans himself; seeks revenge upon Man." The Chorus sings of the vic-tory in Heaven, and also a hymn of the Creation. We find the sec-tion mentioned by Phillips in Satan's soliloquy in Book IV, the warfare in Heaven in Book VI and the angelic hymn on Creation in Book VII.

In the next act of the drama, Adam and Eve appear after the Fall, accusing each other. These speeches may well have been incorporated into the scene at the end of Book XI. At the end of the scene, the Chorus bewails Adam's Fall, as the angels mourn it in Book XI. In the last act of the scenario, Adam and Eve continue to accuse each other—as in Book XI—until Justice and the Chorus both admonish Adam. The Angel is sent to banish them from Paradise, "but, before, causes to pass before his eyes, in shapes, a masque of all the evils of this life and world." Here may be part of Book XI in which Michael shows a pageant of the future which begins with dumb-show before it becomes a series of scenes from Biblical history. It is entirely possible, then, that a series of "parcels," as Phillips called them, might have been picked up without much change from the drama and may now lie embedded in the epic.

But the most magnificent parts of *Paradise Lost* were not in the drama at all. Satan and his fallen legions in Hell, the great Council Scene in Pandemonium, Satan's voyage through space were not in the dramatic version. The scenes in Heaven in Book III are not there, nor do God or Christ appear as actors in "Adam Unparadised." The earlier Adam and Eve of Book IV do not appear, though their marriage is described, and the Chorus might conceivably have sung the Epithalamion, "Hail, wedded love!" Since Adam and Eve appear in the drama only after the Fall, the tenderest of their scenes together, as well as their long conversation with Raphael, are lacking. Let us put it this way: most of the scenes and speeches that make *Paradise Lost* memorable to us could not have been contained within the confines of a classical tragedy. We begin to have a clue to the answer to the first question: why did Milton write or rewrite his Fall of Man in epic form?

Milton would inevitably have found the unity of time impossible for full depiction of his characters and theme. Unless Adam and Eve fell on the very day of their creation (there is exegetical authority for such interpretation), nothing earlier than the Fall itself could have been depicted. There was little possibility of explaining why Adam and Eve fell, or why Satan rebelled and degenerated, within the limitation of a drama. The unity of time adds to the greatness of the Biblical drama upon which Milton finally decided. The last day of Samson's life proved the climax of his whole career, ethically, artistically, dramatically. But Adam and Eve, and particularly Satan, as Milton came to imagine them, could be restricted within no such limitation. As we read *Paradise Lost* and watch the art with which Milton traces Satan's degeneration and as we come to know Adam and Eve before and after the Fall, we shall better understand why Milton freed himself from the unity of time.

Was there any advantage Milton might have had in "Adam Unparadised" that he lost by making the Fall of Man epic rather than drama? Various critics of *Paradise Lost* will say, *yes*. In the drama God and Christ did not appear as characters, and many critics feel that Milton would have been wiser not to make them actors in *Paradise Lost*. These are problems which we may consider further as we read the version of "Adam Unparadised" that became *Paradise Lost*.

BOOK I

The Prologue

There are four prologues in *Paradise Lost*—to Books I, III, VII, IX. Perhaps Satan's address to the sun in Book IV is another, but if so, it is deliberately in reverse to the plan of the others, all of which follow a pattern established in the general prologue. Fol-

lowing classical example, Milton took for granted that the epic poet
would at once state the theme of his work and invoke a Muse.
Homer began the *Iliad* (in Pope's translation)

> Achilles' wrath, to Greece the direful spring
> Of woes unnumbered, Heavenly Goddess, sing!

The Muse of the Odyssey was asked to sing of the wanderings of
long-tried Odysseus. Virgil opened the *Aeneid,* with the words,
"Arma virumque cano" (Arms and the man I sing). Milton states
the subject of *Paradise Lost* as "man's first disobedience." Notice
that the emphasis is upon *Man,* not upon Satan, who is not men-
tioned in the Prologue and not referred to until line 34. Milton is
following his classical ancestors not only in the immediate intro-
duction of his chief subject but in the grammatical structure, which
is highly Latinate. We do not know the construction of the first
phrase until line 6, when we find it in, "Sing, Heavenly Muse."

The prologue shows clearly that the subject matter will be taken
from the first chapters of Genesis: the disobedience of Man in eat-
ing the fruit of the tree of the knowledge of good and evil, and his
Fall as a consequence, bringing death into the world, and all the
woes from which Man has continued to suffer. But we should no-
tice that, although the story begins with the man who fell, it also
mentions the "greater Man" Who will redeem us. The significance
of this, we shall understand later in *Paradise Lost.*

The invocation to a Muse is a classical device, and in later pro-
logues, Milton will give his Muse a classical name, Urania, goddess
of astronomy, a fitting choice for a poem leading to Heaven. Here,
however, she is called "Heavenly Muse," and is localized not, as
she might have been by Homer or Virgil, upon Mount Olympus or
Mount Helicon, but "on the secret top" of Horeb, Sinai, sacred in
Hebraic belief, associated here particularly with Moses,

> That shepherd who first taught the chosen seed
> In the beginning how the Heavens and earth
> Rose out of Chaos.

Since a Muse was invoked by a classical poet to aid him in what he was attempting to write, Milton asks his Muse to lead him higher than the "Aonian mount" of the classical poets, since the subject of his epic is "higher" than theirs. Here our memories may go back to *Lycidas* where on two occasions we heard a strain of a "higher mood," as Christianity rose above the pagan tradition. The prologues in *Paradise Lost* begin as classical invocations, but, with one exception, they rise to Christian prayers to the Holy Spirit, read by Christians into the second verse of Genesis: "and the Spirit of God moved upon the face of the waters."

> Thou from the first
> Wast present, and with mighty wings outspread,
> Dove-like satst brooding on the vast Abyss
> And madst it pregnant.

Milton's prologues are the more poignant in that, in addition to the problems implied by every poet who invoked his Muse for aid, Milton was always conscious of his greatest limitation—his blindness. In other prologues he will refer to it more specifically. Here it is suggested only in, "What in me is dark, Illumine:"

> That to the height of this great argument
> I may assert Eternal Providence,
> And justify the ways of God to men.

In twenty-six lines, we have learned the theme of *Paradise Lost,* "man's first disobedience"; we know that the materials are to be drawn chiefly from Genesis, that Milton is writing a classical epic, but that he intends, with the aid of the "Heavenly Muse" to transcend the classical, and in a poem both Hebrew and Christian, deal with the most profound of all problems, "to justify the ways of God to men." In twenty-six lines Milton has fused three great civilizations, the main sources of Renaissance religious poetry: classical, Hebrew, Christian. (I suggest that the student read at this point the first section of Gilbert Murray, *The Classical Tradition in Poetry:* in which Mr. Murray analyzes in close detail these twenty-six lines, showing how they reflect the classical tradition.)

The Degeneration of Satan

With Blake, Shelley, Byron, the "Satanic School" of Milton criticism began to develop. Milton, said Blake, was of the devil's party, whether he knew it or not; Satan is the hero of *Paradise Lost*. The idea had been suggested as early as Dryden, though not so vividly expressed as by the later writers. It is easy to understand why such an interpretation would appeal to Romanticists, rebels in various ways, who sympathized with the fact that Milton, too, had been a rebel, allying himself with the party that put a king to death. It is probably true that Milton's position in regard to the authority of kingship made him more capable of understanding the First Great Rebel than a Cavalier might have been, but we must constantly be on guard against over-reading any author's biography or personal character into his works. Whether Shakespeare was Hamlet or not, he was certainly not always and not only Hamlet. The "Satanists" did not prove Satan the hero of *Paradise Lost*. They could not. When I discover tendencies to "Satanism" among my students (many of whom do not know that there ever was such a school) I usually find that they have read no farther than Books I and II of *Paradise Lost,* the books usually excerpted in anthologies. Had Blake and Shelley and Byron, I wonder, read Book X?

The character of Satan is one of the greatest creations in any language. The greatness lies not only—indeed, not primarily—in the depiction of the majestic character of Books I and II, but in the slow and steady degeneration of an angel who once stood next to God Himself in Heaven. As we read *Paradise Lost* we watch the subtlety of Milton's art as the character gradually diminishes from grandeur and magnificence to baseness and final degradation, so that we are inevitably alienated from admiration. In following the degeneration of Satan, we must realize that Milton is, as always in *Paradise Lost,* writing on two levels, a literal and a moral. On the lit-

THE MAJOR POEMS 🌿 187

eral level, Satan is a character, a person, about whom a story is woven. Milton's basic technique is a subtle change in figures of speech, mutation of the images to which Satan is compared. Let me sketch this technique in general so that you may have the pleasure of watching it for yourself as you accustom yourself to noticing carefully each comparison Milton makes.

The first physical attribute of Satan as he emerges from the burning lake and made toward the shore is his tremendous size. As he moves toward shore, we are still more conscious of physical size. Following classical tradition, Milton does not describe him in detail but emphasizes two objects he carries. His shield, Milton compares (I. 284-291) to the largest round object human eyes had ever seen, the moon seen through Galileo's telescope. His spear (I. 292-294) is so gigantic that the tallest pine tree, used for the mast of a flagship, seems only a wand in comparison. On the basis of that shield and spear, our imaginations begin to frame the gigantic stature of this Titan. After the commander-in-chief has brought order out of the chaos into which his army had fallen, Satan stands reviewing them. Now he is like a proud tower, then like the sun (I. 591, 594). In the sun-figure, we see what Milton's technique will be. Satan has not yet lost all the original brightness of an angel in heaven, for he still may be compared with the sun and moon. But some of the glory has been lost, for he is like the sun seen through morning mist, or like moon in eclipse. The sun through a mist, the moon in eclipse, but still the sun and moon. So Satan continues for some time, majestic, grand, yet always a little more flawed. After his extraordinary voyage in Book II, when he "holds gladly the port," he is compared with a ship with "shrouds and tackle torn." (II. 1043-44) One of the last occasions that Milton uses a grand comparison for Satan is the scene at the end of Book IV in which the angelic squadrons begin to hem Satan round and he turns upon them with all the courage he still possesses:

On the other side Satan, alarmed,
Collecting all his might, dilated stood,

Like Teneriffe or Atlas, unremoved:
His stature reached the sky, and on his crest
Sat Horror plumed.

(IV. 985-989)

Earlier in the same book, we have had evidence that the figures
of speech are changing. When Satan is seeking entrance to the
Garden of Eden, he disdains the gate and leaps over the wall. As in
Lycidas, Milton thinks of Satan as "a prowling wolf" leaping over
the fence into the sheepfold, as a thief, forcing his way through sub-
stantial doors for plunder. "So clomb this first grand Thief into
God's fold."

In Book IV the analogues are largely animal-imagery. After
Satan has entered Eden, he chooses as his vantage point a tree on
which he "sat like a cormorant." (IV. 196) Later in that book, he
is like a "proud steed reined," "champing his iron curb." (IV. 857-
59) When Satan begins the temptation of Eve through her dream, he
is "squat like a toad," a grotesque and almost comic figure. His po-
tential greatness is still there, however, for as Ithuriel touches him
with his spear:

   Up he starts,
Discovered and surprised. As, when a spark
Lights on a heap of nitrous powder, laid
Fit for the tun, some magazine to store
Against a rumored war, the smutty grain,
With sudden blaze diffused, inflames the air,
So started up, in his own shape, the Fiend.

(IV. 813-19)

The momentary blaze of glory does not obscure the danger of
Satan, the spark that ignites gunpowder stored for war.

When the comparisons are with birds, they are with the cor-
morant or the vulture, which far off seem both grand and mag-
nificent, but which are carrion birds of prey. More and more the
analogues are with low things. In his search of the serpent

> through each thicket dank or dry,
> Like a black mist, low-creeping, he held on
> His midnight search.

(IX. 179-181)

Subconsciously we are prepared for that climactic scene in Book X in which he becomes the snake he has permitted himself to be.

In the meantime, we watch a degeneration in Satan's moral character parallel to the changes in his physical appearance. I shall not anticipate the pleasure the reader will have in studying this for himself, except by giving one clue and explaining one key-word, whose meaning might not at first be clear. The moral degeneration of Satan is suggested in part by Milton's subtle changes in figures of light and darkness. When he was an angel in Heaven, Satan, like God and the other angels, had been clothed in light. Even in the early scenes in which he is still majestic, he is losing some of his original brightness. Watch this in the scene in which, having aroused his followers, the great commander brings his fallen army to order, and reviews them, as a general his troops. (I. 587-619). We never feel the contrast between what he was and what he is permitting himself to become more than in this poignant scene. In the later books, as Satan deliberately continues to choose evil rather than good, light gives way more and more to darkness.

The first dangerous quality of Satan emphasized by Milton is "obdurate Pride" (I. 58), which proves his besetting sin. The word is repeated again and again. To modern readers Pride often seems an admirable quality, but we must understand the word as did Milton and his contemporaries. From their classical ancestors, they had inherited a conception of Hybris (the Greek word for Pride) as a dangerous quality. Many of the most familiar stories of classical mythology were based upon the belief that Hybris was the sin most frequently punished by the gods. The idea is a reiterated motif in classical tragedy, as well as in legend. In addition to this was the Christian emphasis upon meekness and humility, according to which Pride was the most deadly of the Seven Deadly Sins. Later in our study, when we come to consider the idea of "hierarchy," as Milton and his contemporaries understood it, we shall find the belief that, as all things were created in the universe, they were established in "degree" and "order" in a scale or ladder of Nature, a great chain of being (there were many different phrases in which the idea was expressed). In that scale, ladder or chain, men and angels all had ranks or degrees. As they were created, so they should be content to remain. Classical and Christian teachers combined in their warning to man to be content, not to aspire for a higher place, not to permit himself to fall to a lower rank. Pope put the time-honored ethical belief into couplets in the *Essay on Man,* among them these:

In Pride, in reas'ning Pride our error lies;
All quit their spheres, and rush into the skies.
Pride still is aiming at the blest abodes,
Men would be angels, angels would be gods.
Aspiring to be gods, if angels fell,
Aspiring to be angels, men rebel.

(*Essay on Man,* I. 123-28)

Pope said, again, as Raphael will warn Adam in Book VIII of *Paradise Lost:*

The bliss of man (could Pride the blessing find)
Is not to think or act beyond mankind.

(I. 189-90)

"Know thy own point" is the lesson of the *Essay on Man,* echoing centuries of the teaching of such ethics. Do not break the chain of being: "Whatever link you strike, Tenth or tenth thousandth, breaks the chain alike." Satan, we shall learn, deliberately broke the chain of being. Listen for the word "Pride," frequently reiterated, watch the increasing obduracy of Satan, his persistent refusal to choose right, his deliberate choice of evil, with his accompanying physical and moral degeneration.

Epic Figures of Speech

A favorite figure, inherited by Renaissance poets from their classical ancestors, was the "Homeric simile." If we stop over an example in Book I, the student will easily learn to recognize such figures and analyze them for himself. Let us take the first extended description of Satan (I. 192-210), emphasizing his gigantic size. We see Satan still lying on the lava-lake, his head "uplift above the wave," the rest of his body

Prone on the flood extended, long and huge
Lay floating many a rood.

Briefly he is compared first to the legendary Titans, then at much more length to the Leviathan of Psalm CIV. 26, "which God of all His works Created hugest." In a Homeric simile we start with a comparison between A (Satan) and B (Leviathan) but the second member grows until it eclipses the first. Milton develops old mariners' "fish stories" of a sea-creature larger even than the whale, which had been often mistaken by pilots for an island against which they tried to moor their boats. Only after eight lines of such detail do we return to A: "So stretched out, huge in length, the Arch-Fiend lay."

Milton is a master of similes, Homeric and others. We find one of the finest sequences in Book I, showing how deftly the artist chose his comparisons to produce his effects. After Satan and Beelzebub have roused from stunned unconsciousness and reached the shore, the other fallen angels still lie stupefied upon the burning lake. Only at the sound of the clarion-voice of their commander do they begin to rouse from lethargy. Watch carefully each of Milton's similes in the long passage (ll. 301-360). All the comparisons have one thing in common: the fallen angels are innumerable. The Bible had said that "a third part" of the angels fell with Lucifer, but neither Satan nor Milton knew how many angels had originally been in Heaven.

In the first simile two aspects are emphasized: the *vast number* and the *confusion*. Milton's mind went back to his Italian journey for the first comparison. The angels lay, "Thick as autumnal leaves that strew the brooks in Vallombrosa." Anyone who has scuffed through autumn leaves knows how numberless they seem, but in Vallombrosa ("shady valley"), famous district of woods and forests near Florence, they were even more impressive than in England. In the second figure Milton's imagination goes back to one of the most familiar stories in the Old Testament, the passage of the Israelites through the Red Sea, pursued by Pharaoh, whose chariots and horsemen were destroyed and lay floating confusedly in the waves that closed behind the chosen people. Again we have the sense of confusion and an uncounted number of carcasses and chariots. And notice (as in *Lycidas*) the underlying water-imagery of brooks in Vallambrosa and the Red Sea, appropriate because the fallen angels are still lying on the lake.

At Satan's call, "Awake, arise; or be forever fallen" the legions begin to rouse from stupor. Again there are two comparisons, one brief, one more Homeric. The first, appropriate for fallen soldiers, is to sentinels asleep on duty. Then Milton goes back again to the Bible in the more expanded comparison of the fallen angels to the plague of locusts called up by Moses, that "o'er the realm of impious Pharaoh hung Like night, and darkened all the land of Nile." Again the angels are numberless (1.344) and again the comparison is with an unnumbered throng of flying pests that descended upon the land. First stupefied on the lake, then flying upon their wings, the legions of Satan reach the shore. In the third series of figures, an ordered army begins to emerge from chaos, (I. 347ff.) but not before Milton introduces one more figure emphasizing untold numbers and the sense of confusion among the fallen angels, whose swarming down to earth is like the descent of the barbarians upon Rome:

A multitude like which the populous North
Poured never from her frozen loins, to pass
Rhine or the Danube, when her barbarous sons
Came like a deluge on the South.

(I. 351-54)

Notice one other matter of craft in this masterly passage of figures
of speech. With the exception of the autumn leaves and the senti-
nels, the comparisons—like those in the degeneration of Satan
—have been with things dangerous and destructive—the carcasses
and chariots in the Red Sea, symbols of destroyers who were de-
stroyed, the pitchy cloud of locusts that blotted out the sun from
the earth, the barbarians from the north who strove to destroy
the grandeur that was Rome.

Milton's Hells

It is a misnomer to talk about "Milton's Hell." There are at least
three distinct physical Hells in *Paradise Lost* in addition to the eth-
ical or moral Hell that gives unity to all of them. Basically the first
Hell is a place of darkness which the lurid flickering light of fire
serves only to make more dark. (ll. 62 ff.) Geologically, it is a vol-
canic region, "fed With ever-burning sulphur unconsumed." Satan
and his followers have fallen into a "fiery gulf," a lake that burns
continually with "liquid fire." The beach of that "inflamed sea"
marks the beginning of a "dreary plain, forlorn and wild." When
Satan "rears from off the pool His mighty stature," he flies to what
seems dry land

if it were land that ever burned
With solid, as the lake with liquid fire.

(I. 228-229)

The land proves to be "firm brimstone," but the heat is as intense
as was that of the boiling pool, with the result that Satan walks

delicately with "uneasy steps Over the burning marl." Heat is everywhere in "the torrid clime . . . vaulted with fire." In the background, we learn, is a volcanic mountain:

> There stood a hill not far, whose grisly top
> Belched fire and rolling smoke; the rest entire
> Shone with a glossy scurf—undoubted sign
> That in his womb was hid metallic ore,
> The work of sulphur.

(I. 670-674)

While there are both classical and medieval analogues to other aspects of Milton's first Hell, those I have been emphasizing are different from the traditional and familiar elements, and lead me to believe that Milton was drawing upon visual memory as well as upon imagination and combining actual sense impressions with literary reminiscence. In his blindness, I think that his memory went back to an occasion during his Italian journey when he had visited the Phlegraean Fields, lying close to Naples, near which the Puteoli villa of Manso was situated. This extraordinary volcanic district was usually a part of the traveller's tour and particularly impressed English visitors who had nothing in their own country to correspond to the strange sight. While Milton did not specifically refer to a visit to the Phlegraean Fields, it would have been almost inconceivable that he should not have visited a place with so many legendary and literary associations. For centuries this district had been considered the locale of the early battles between the gods and giants. It was also said to be the dwelling place of Homer's "sunless Cimmerians" who lived in perpetual darkness around the Lake of Avernus, across which no bird might safely fly. Its great crater was the entrance to Hades, through which Aeneas and others descended to the infernal regions. Apart from legend, it had many literary associations. It was said that Virgil's spirit often appeared there, hovering about his sepulchral urn near the Grotto Vecchia, close by his villa on the Pausilypon. Cicero's villa was not

THE MAJOR POEMS 🌸 195

far from Avernus, and at Puteoli St. Paul had spent seven days on
his journey to Rome.

The topographical similarities between the Phlegraean Fields
and Milton's first Hell are striking even today. The Solfatara—
called in ancient times the Forum Vulcani—is the crater of a half-
extinct volcano, destitute of vegetation; on the right, there is still a
pool of hot water; other pools have formed and disappeared. The
"dreary plain" around the lake is still as hot as when Satan and his
companions walked with uneasy steps over the burning marl. But
a volcanic district is not static. Hills are thrown up, depressions and
pools change their places. The most spectacular change in the
Phlegraean Fields occurred in 1538 when a mountain—Monte
Nuovo—appeared almost overnight.

Fortunately—for my theory at least—we have a first-hand ac-
count of the appearance of the district in 1638, the year of Milton's
visit to Naples, by one of the greatest living experts of that day
on volcanoes and earthquakes, Athanasius Kircher, a Jesuit priest
of wide scientific interests. Kircher described the entrance through
a dark grotto into "a Plain altogether formidable and full of hor-
ror." The soil, he said, "sounds and rattles like a Drum . . . and
you may feel boiling waters under your feet." Most of all, the boil-
ing lake amazed him. "Yet an huge Laky-ditch in the same Plain
did wonderfully affect me. For it is found full of boiling waters,
and ready to fright one with their blackness." Kircher's conclusion
to his long and detailed account in the *Mundus Subterraneus* is
significant of the impression made by the district on an observer
more travelled and much more familiar with volcanic districts than
the young Milton had been: "You would think yourself almost in
the midst of Hell; where all things appear horrid, sad and lamenta-
ble, with a most formidable face of things." *

* In my article on this subject, "Milton's Hell and the Phlegraean Fields
(*U.T.Q.* VII [1938] 500-513), I included two contemporary pictures, one
from Kircher's account, and one from George Sandys, *Relation of a Journey*
with some of the descriptions given by Sandys, whose book seems to have
been a sort of "Baedeker" for the region.

Milton's Second Hell

At the end of Book I (ll. 670-798) we watch the building of Pandemonium, the second Hell. The word "Pandemonium" in Book I, implies simply that it is a place of "all devils or demons." Not until Book X does it take on the connotation of "confusion" with which we associate it today. Although I have suggested, in the article referred to above, passing similarities with the accounts of Kircher and Sandys, these are not very significant, and certainly far less important than two other sources. On the one hand, the building of Pandemonium is the work of human—or angelic—hands. The architect, we learn (ll. 732-750) was a fallen angel who in times to come would become the architect Mulciber (Greek, *Hephaestus,* Roman, *Vulcan*). The work was performed under the direction of Mammon by artisans and craftsmen who like "bands Of pioneers, with spade and pick axe armed. . . . Rifled the bowels of their mother earth For treasures better hid." (ll. 678-688) But in addition to the art and craft of fallen angels, magic is implied in

> Anon out of the earth a fabric huge
> Rose like an exhalation, with the sound
> Of dulcet symphonies and voices sweet.

> (I. 710-712)

Here the ears of some modern critics catch echoes of a masque presented at court on Sunday after Twelfth Night in 1637 (three years after the production of *Comus*), in which the "spectacle" was of the opening of the earth and the rising of a "richly adorned pallace, seeming all of goldsmith's work." Details of vaulted porticos, pilasters and "capitels of gold" are very similar to the details of Pandemonium. (For more complete details see Merritt Hughes' note on this passage, p. 229).

Even more striking are parallels between Pandemonium and St.

Peter's Cathedral in Rome, which persuade me that here, as in the
first Hell, Milton's visual memory merged with literary traditions.
No English traveller of the seventeenth century, no matter what
his religion, could fail to be impressed by St. Peter's, the largest and
most magnificent building he had ever seen. While St. Peter's was
still unfinished when Milton visited Rome, all the details men-
tioned in the description of Pandemonium were there. Many years
ago one of my students at the University of Chicago studied all the
pictures and plates she could find by contemporary architects and
engravers and pointed out the striking similarities between the
architecture of St. Peter's and that of Pandemonium. (Rebecca W.
Smith, "The Source of Milton's Pandemonium.") A more recent
student, Mrs. Margaret Byard, added still more details in an un-
published seminar paper at Columbia University. The pilasters,
architrave, cornices, sculptures, pillars were all there, though the
pillars of St. Peter's are Corinthian, not Doric, as in Pandemonium.
Both the cathedral and Pandemonium were lighted by "starry
lamps and blazing cressets." One of the things that most impressed
visitors to St. Peter's was the immense size of the doors, in com-
parison with which human beings seem to shrink into insignifi-
cance. So Milton suggests when his fallen angels—giants though
they are—are compared first with bees swarming about a hive,
then with other puny and tiny creatures:

> So thick the airy crowd
> Swarmed and were straitened; till, the signal given,
> Behold a wonder! they but now who seemed
> In bigness to surpass Earth's giant sons,
> Now less than smallest dwarfs, in narrow room
> Throng numberless, like that Pygmean race
> Beyond the Indian mount, or fairy elves. . . .
> Thus incorporeal spirits to smallest forms
> Reduced their shapes immense, and were at large,
> Though without number still, amidst the hall
> Of that infernal court.
>
> (I. 775-792)

Most striking of all the similarities between Pandemonium and St. Peter's is the fact that there is evidently another building close by Pandemonium. While the hosts of lesser angels throng into the temple, Satan, Beelzebub and the other more important angels enter a council chamber apparently attached to but somehow separate from the Cathedral. This is obviously the Vatican, the library of which we know Milton visited when he was in Rome. The closing lines of Book I and the first part of Book II must be read on two levels of meaning. In addition to the literal story on the surface, another level begins to be implied in these lines:

> But far within,
> And in their own dimensions, like themselves,
> The great Seraphic Lords and Cherubim
> In close recess and secret conclave sat—
> A thousand demi-gods on golden seats,
> Frequent and full. After short silence, then,
> And summons read, the great consult began.
>
> (I. 792-99)

"Close recess" and "secret conclave" were phrases Protestants liked to throw at Roman Catholics. Book II opens with a description of the throne, which is not only the throne usurped by Satan, but the papal throne in the Vatican. It is interesting to know, in connection with the figure of the bees Milton used, that bees were the emblems of the Barberini Pope Urban VIII, who dedicated St. Peter's, and that his followers were frequently called "bees." The Council scene in Book II, in addition to its many classical reminiscences, is on the other level of meaning, Milton's Protestant parody of the election of a Pope by the College of Cardinals in "close recess and secret conclave."

Milton's Third Hell

The two Hells discussed so far are very different. In spite of the fact that, during the council, some of the speakers refer to the discomforts of the Hell into which they have fallen, it is clear that Pandemonium is not only magnificent but very comfortable indeed— the Belial party is quite willing to stay there indefinitely—and that the fallen angels seem to forget the smoke and stench and fire they first encountered. Perhaps the unnamed architect of Pandemonium was the father of modern air-conditioning! But the first two hells are alike in that they occupy a limited area. In the passage beginning in II. 750, however, we are given a quite different conception of the size of Hell. After the council has disbanded, some of the angels take part in Olympic games of celebration. One group of angels, inquiring Renaissance spirits as they are, set out to explore their new domain and find that Hell is not a limited part of a world, but a world in itself. Parts of it are very hot, as the angels had already discovered, but parts are as intensely cold. There is "a frozen continent" with perpetual storms, with hail that never melts. But Hell is much more than a continent: it is a world, topographically much like our own world, with rivers and seas, with mountains and valleys, with a "gulf profound" into which whole armies might have sunk:

> Thus roving on
> In confused march forlorn, the adventurous bands
> With shuddering horror pale, and eyes aghast,
> Viewed first their lamentable lot, and found
> No rest. Through many a dark and dreary vale
> They passed, and many a region dolorous,
> O'er many a frozen, many a fiery Alp,
> Rockes, caves, lakes, fens, bogs, dens and shades of death.
> (II. 614-621)

In addition to many other sources that went to the making of this passage, I have suggested (*Science and Imagination,* pp. 78-9) the possibility that Milton may be reflecting here the picture of the new world in the moon drawn by Johann Kepler in his *Somnium,* a description so graphic that, once read, it cannot be forgotten. There is something of the combined grandeur and grotesqueness of Kepler's picture here. Milton's third Hell, like Kepler's moon, is a place of "fierce extremes, extremes by change more fierce." Its cold is colder than anything on earth, its heat more torrid. As Milton says, "the parching air Burns frore, and cold performs the effect of fire." Milton's frozen world in Hell is much like Kepler's. Kepler's lunar mountains, too, tower to vast heights, and his caverns and fissures on the moon are as profound as Milton's Serbonian bog. But I shall not labor these comparisons, which I do not attempt to prove but merely to suggest. The important thing is not the source of the third Hell, but the fact that Milton's Hell is no such limited and constricted place as Satan and his fallen angels first believed when they roused from their stupor on the burning lake.

The Catalogue of Fallen Angels

We remember that, as early as the *Nativity Ode,* Milton had shown a great deal of interest in demonology, and had called a lesser roll of demons, stressing the fact that many of them were worshiped under various titles by Phoenicians and Assyrians, appearing with more familiar names in Greece and Rome. In Book I of *Paradise Lost* (ll. 376-521) Milton summons before us a much more extensive band of demons. He was following here a familiar pattern of epic poets that began in the *Iliad* with the "catalogue" of ships and commanders engaged in the Trojan War. Formidable as the many unknown names may seem, the student need not be disturbed because he recognizes so few. While more of them would have been familiar to Milton's contemporaries, even they would

THE MAJOR POEMS 🌿 201

have been impressed with the "learning" lying behind this passage. Some of Milton's sources have been suggested by Grant McColley in "The Epic Catalogue of *Paradise Lost,*" (*ELH,* IV (1937) 180-91) but apart from specific sources to which the blind poet must have referred his amanuensis, Milton here as elsewhere loved long passages of proper names, both for their sound and for their evocation of legend and lore.

For our purposes, it will be enough to stop over a very few of the fallen angels, either those of whom we have heard before or those we shall meet again. Notice the point Milton makes before he begins to recite the "catalogue." These names were not the names the angels had borne in Heaven. Those we shall never know,

> Though of their names in Heavenly records now
> Be no memorial, blotted out and razed
> By their rebellion from the Books of Life.
>
> (I. 361-63)

Nor had some of the former angels as yet taken on various names by which they were to be known among "the sons of Eve"—false gods, idols, worshiped by men in place of the true God.

About half-way through the catalogue, Milton introduces one false god of whom we have already heard in the *Nativity Ode*— Dagon, the "twice battered god of Palestine." In lines 457-466 Milton repeats the story that the "captive ark Maimed his brute image. . . . Where he fell flat, and shamed his worshipers." But the two most important characters in the catalogue are those to whom Milton gives the prominence of the first and last place, Moloch and Belial. We shall understand why they hold these places better after we see and hear them in the Council Scene in Book II.

> First Moloch, horrid king, besmeared with blood
> Of human sacrifice, and parents' tears.

Moloch was a primitive deity, worshiped by primitive peoples. His worship was accompanied by blood-sacrifice, particularly of children, whose cries were concealed by the roll of drums and the loud clash of timbrels. Essentially a simple deity, he was associated with violence, savagery, cruelty and noise. At the opposite extreme is the last fallen angel mentioned in the catalogue (ll. 490-505)

> Belial came last, than whom a spirit more lewd
> Fell not from Heaven, or more gross to love
> Vice for himself.

Moloch appeared early, Belial late in human history. Belial is a god of highly sophisticated men living in periods of decadence. He is not worshiped in a particular temple or at a smoky altar. When he is found at an altar, indeed, it is not in his own shape but "when the priest Turns atheist." His followers are in courts, in palaces, in luxurious cities—the Sodoms and Gomorrahs of any period of sophisticated degeneracy—degenerate and decadent men, often with unnatural vices. Moloch had a real history as a demon-god, since he had been worshiped by the Ammonites, and, under the name of Chemosh, by the Moabites. He was mentioned in the Old Testament (II Kings XXIII. 10) in connection with child-sacrifice. Belial, on the other hand, was never a real character but a personification. The word meaning "worthlesssess" was used in the Old Testament to imply evil, particularly lust. Before Milton made him a living character, he had occasionally appeared in medieval literature as a type of sensuality.

In the meantime we should add one other "speaking character" who will appear in the Council Scene, whom Milton did not mention in the catalogue since he had reason to introduce him in another way. Mammon is the leader of the band of "pioneers" who dug into the sulphuric earth for gold and other metals from which to build Pandemonium:

> Mammon led them on:
> Mammon, the least erected Spirit that fell
> From Heaven, for even in Heaven his looks and thoughts
> Were always downward bent, admiring more
> The riches of Heaven's pavement—trodden gold—
> Than aught divine or holy else enjoyed

In vision beatific. By him first
Men also—and by his suggestion taught—
Ransacked the center, and with impious hands
Rifled the bowels of their mother Earth
For treasures better hid.

(I. 678-88)

Like Belial, Mammon was a personification rather than a legend-
ary or historical devil. The word meant "wealth" in Syriac, and be-
came familiar in the New Testament, particularly through Mat-
thew's use of it (VI. 24): "Thou canst not serve both God and
mammon." (Cf. Luke XVI. 9, 11, 13): Milton's Mammon is a
thoroughgoing materialist. We shall come to know each of these
fallen angels more intimately in the Council Scene, and hear of some
of them again in connection with the battle in Heaven.

BOOK II

The Council Scene

In Book II we sit comfortably within the walls of Pandemonium,
hardly conscious of the "darkness visible," the smoke and stench,
the physical discomforts of the first Hell. While the great majority of
the fallen angels remain within the "temple" of St. Peter's, a
smaller group—though even they number one thousand—met in
conference in the adjoining building to take part (like their an-
cestors in the *Iliad* or the *Aeneid*) in a council to determine plans
of strategy. This, too, is a magnificent hall, accommodating "a
thousand demigods on golden seats" with Satan as their center:

High on a throne of royal state, which far
Outshone the wealth of Ormus or of Ind,
Or where the gorgeous East with richest hand
Showers on her kings barbaric pearl and gold,
Satan exalted sat.

(II. 1-5)

As chairman, Satan opens the meeting. Notice that—as nearly always—he addresses his compatriots by their former titles, "Powers and Dominions, Deities of Heaven." As commander-in-chief it is essential for Satan to make his followers feel that, though they have lost a battle, they have not lost the war. "I give not Heaven for lost," he declares. We will return "to claim our just inheritance." This council has been called for deliberation:

by what best way,
Whether of open war or covert guile,
We now debate. Who can advise may speak.

(II. 40-42)

We must read the Council Scene on various levels. The anti-Catholic satire of the "secret conclave" of the College of Cardinals in the Vatican, is not stressed, except in a few passing phrases. There are reminiscences, as I have suggested, of council scenes in classical epics. But one matter we must bear constantly in mind. Milton had lived through a period of war and the inevitable aftermath of war and reconstruction. As a servant of the State, he had been present at various councils and intimately familiar with others, both within and without the Houses of Parliament. The Council scene has a "political level" which can be paralleled again and again in later periods, particularly in our own troubled century, in London, Paris, Rome, Washington, in Geneva or the United Nations. From his first-hand knowledge, as well as his wide reading, Milton knew that whenever a council was called to consider such emergencies as those faced by Satan and the fallen angels, certain positions or "platforms" would be expressed and upheld by certain types of men. Expert rhetorician as he was, Milton adapts the speech of each one to his own particular nature. Each speech is a masterpiece of the oratory in which Milton had had long training. It would not surprise me to discover that each of them (like the *Areopagitica*) was based upon a real model among classical orators or historians. The speakers rise in an order which is far from fortuitous, involved as it is in the psychology of each speaker.

As Moloch had been the first to appear in the procession of demons, so he is the first on his feet when Satan declares the meeting open. We have heard that he was a primitive deity, worshiped by primitive people with blood-sacrifice. Milton now introduces him as "the strongest and the fiercest Spirit That fought in Heaven, now fiercer by despair." Somewhat like Shakespeare's Hotspur, Moloch, "rather than be less Cared not to be at all." His rhetoric is entirely consistent with his character. He does not address the chair or his colleagues. He plunges abruptly into his speech and gives his position in the first six words, "My sentence is for open war." If there was a table before him in the council chamber, I am sure he pounded on it. For wiles and guile he has as little inclination as for parliamentary procedure or subtle flattering of his colleagues. Let us *do* something and *do it now*. To the Molochs of this world, the answer is a simple one: "Let's fight." Moloch sees no problem in getting back to heaven in order to fight again. The natural motion of angels, he reminds the Council, is *up* (lines 75-82). Only by force were they pushed down to Hell. (Moloch might have pointed out, as we learn later, that God was quite aware that even fallen angels retained their natural "proper motion," since He caused a roof to be placed over Hell, presumably to keep the angels down.) Getting back to Heaven, then, is no problem to simple-minded Moloch. Once there, they will fight. Either they will be victorious or the Torturer (notice that Moloch and the other fallen angels refuse to say "God" and use various circumlocutions to avoid the word) will destroy them, so that they will be "quite abolished, and expire"—a fate far preferable to Moloch to the forced inactivity and ignominy of remaining vanquished in Hell.

Moloch concludes as abruptly as he began: "Which if not victory is yet revenge."

Hardly is Moloch seated than Belial rises, though not in apparent haste. A greater contrast could not be imagined between two speakers. Moloch "ended frowning," again undoubtedly pounding that hypothetical table or striking his prize-fighter hands together. Belial is dignified, suave, "graceful and humane." "A fairer person lost not Heaven." As an orator he is superb, as a disputant so adept that he can confuse any antagonist by apparent logic that is really sophistry:

> his tongue
> Dropped manna and could make the worse appear
> The better reason, to perplex and dash
> Maturest counsels.
>
> (II. 112-115)

His speech is almost twice as long as Moloch's and a marvel of casuistry. He is as conscious of parliamentary procedure, of "audience psychology" and of oratorical art as Moloch was impervious to all three. Belial has a most important reason for rising just when he does. He gives the audience no opportunity to respond to Moloch's program of action and fighting. The last thing decadent Belials want is activity and hardship. As an orator should, he addresses his peers. To those who may share Moloch's desire for action and revenge, he is careful to say that he, too, desires vengeance, that he is "not behind in hate." He would be the first to move for war, were it not. . . . And then comes a series of, "buts"—questions, quibbles, logical hair-splittings by means of which Belial, the subtle disputant, confuses all the issues, and reduces to nonsense the whole platform proposed by simple Moloch. He makes the audience aware of the insuperable difficulties involved in a proposal of war. It would be no such simple process as Moloch implied for the fallen angels to get back to Heaven (129 ff.). Angelic sentries and scouts are everywhere on guard. And even could they force their way back, what then? Here Belial enters into the kind of

philosophical and theological questions that would never occur to
a Moloch: the nature of deity (137-142) which

> would soon expel
> Her mischief, and purge off the baser fire.

What then? "Our final hope Is flat despair." The possibility of to-
tal annihilation was one thing to Moloch; it is quite another matter
to the highly intellectual Belial:

> Sad cure! for who would lose
> Though full of pain, this intellectual being,
> Those thoughts that wander through eternity,
> To perish rather, swallowed up and lost
> In the wide womb of uncreated Night,
> Devoid of sense and motion?
>
> (II. 146-151)

As Moloch reminds me of Hotspur, I wonder whether there are
overtones of Hamlet in Belial? Critics have suggested parallels be-
tween these lines and some of Claudio's in *Measure for Measure,*
but *Hamlet* was in Milton's conscious memory later in Belial's
speech, when in line 185 he paraphrased Shakespeare's "un-
houseled, disappointed, unanealed" with three other negatives,
"unrespited, unpitied, unreprieved." In lines 151-158 Belial re-
turns again to the philosophical question of the nature of deity,
suggesting an argument of scholastic logic over which I will not
pause at present, since I shall discuss it in a more important context
in Adam's soliloquy in Book X. All this philosophy and theology
must have confused Moloch so much that, as Belial intended, he
would never have ventured a rebuttal. Is this really the worst fate
that could befall us? asks Belial (lines 163-186)? Here in this mag-
nificent building, he implies, are we not physically far better off
than when we were struck by the thunder of Heaven, when we lay
chained on the burning lake? The tortures we have already ex-
perienced may prove as nothing in comparison with those with
which the Victor might "arm again His red right hand to plague
us." No, let us not talk of further war; for the present let us be glad

to remain where we are. (Belial is very comfortable in Pande-
monium and physical comfort is the first desideratum of Belials.)
His program is largely negative—what not to do, rather than what
to do. In so far as he proposes a more positive one, it is curiously
reminiscent of a phrase my generation remembers well from the
First World War—"watchful waiting." (ll. 208-225) Let us wait
and watch and see what happens, and in the meantime do nothing
but enjoy ourselves as much as we can.

> Thus Belial, with words clothed in reason's garb,
> Counselled ignoble ease and peaceful sloth,
> Not peace.
>
> (II. 226-228)

Mammon rises next. Belial has prepared the way for him, for the
Mammons and the Belials have much in common. The Mammons
want war only for the material gain it may bring them, not for ardu-
ous labor and physical suffering. Indeed the Mammons have always
proved most successful "draft dodgers," pleading their great value
behind the scenes. Mammon does not want war, nor does he wish
to return to Heaven for indefinite eons of "warbled hymns" and
"forced hallalujahs." "How wearisome Eternity so spent." In this
way, he is at one with Belial (lines 229-49). But he has a more
specific plan to propose than had Belial. Instead of talking further
about the possibility of storming Heaven, let us

> rather seek
> Our own good from ourselves, and from our own
> Live to ourselves though in this vast recess,
> Free, and to none accountable, preferring
> Hard liberty before the easy yoke
> Of servile pomp.
>
> (II. 252-57)

Expressed thus, Mammon's position momentarily sounds lofty,
even noble in its contrast between the servility of Heaven and the
"hard liberty" of Hell, particularly when he goes on to urge the
fallen angels to work together in such a way that they will "thrive

under evil and work ease out of pain Through labor and en-
durance." Almost he persuades us of his high-mindedness—al-
most, but not quite, when we come to the specific plan he proposes:

> This desert soil
> Wants not her hidden luster, gems and gold;
> Nor want we skill or art from whence to raise
> Magnificence, and what can Heaven show more?
>
> (II. 270-73)

To Mammon Heaven is only a *place*—a place with golden pave-
ments, handsome buildings encrusted with more precious jewels than
even those in Aaron's ephod. During the short time they have been
in Hell, the "pioneers" under his direction have built Pandemo-
nium, rivalling in magnificence any edifice in Heaven. Mammon's
eyes seem to sparkle like those precious gems as he anticipates the
building of another metropolis, far more splendid than the City of
Heaven. It has not taken him long to estimate cannily the natural
resources of the new world into which he has fallen.

Mammon's platform sounds even more reminiscent than Belial's
to some of our modern ears. He says in effect: we have all the nat-
ural resources; let us seek our own good from ourselves. Was there
not a period in fairly recent American history when some men
urged a platform of "self-sufficiency?" "Free and to none accounta-
ble"—did we once hear about "no entangling alliances?"

> Nor want we art and skill from whence to raise
> Magnificence; and what can Heaven show more?

For "Heaven," read "Europe"; transfer the locale, and we may
possibly have a platform once called "America first."

Milton has not told us of the audience-reaction to either Moloch
or Belial. There is no question of the applause received by Mam-
mon:

> He scarce had finished when such murmur filled
> The assembly, as when hollow rocks retain
> The sounds of blustering winds . . .

> such applause was heard
> As Mammon ended, and his sentence pleased . . .
>
> (II. 284-91)

Not only do most of the fallen angels dread another war, but, venal as they are and nationalists at heart, they have no less desire than Belial

> To found this nether empire which might rise
> By policy and long process of time
> In emulation opposite to Heaven.
>
> (II. 295-97)

Satan has undoubtedly been following all the speeches with the closest interest. The enthusiastic reception of Mammon's platform is momentarily disturbing, since Satan has a very different platform of his own which he intends shall be carried. Beelzebub, his spokesman, has been watching the meeting as carefully and knows that the time has come to divert the attention of the council from Mammon. Next to Satan in Heaven, Beelzebub is the vice-regent in Hell, a Prime Minister to the monarch, a statesman *par excellence,* in appearance, manner and oratory fully worthy his exalted position:

> with grave
> Aspect he rose, and in his rising seemed
> A pillar of state: deep on his front engraven
> Deliberation sat, and public care;
> And princely counsel in his face yet shone,
> Majestic through in ruin. Sage he stood,
> With Atlantean shoulders fit to bear
> The weight of mightiest monarchies; his look
> Drew audience and attention still as night
> Or summer's noontide air, while thus he spake.
>
> (II. 300-309)

Like Satan he addresses his colleagues by the titles they had borne in Heaven, then ironically warns them that, if they continue as they seem to be going, they will change those honored titles for "Princes of Hell." In the first part of his speech, he replies in effect to the three previous speakers: Moloch's simple, "I want war"; Belial's, "I want to stay here in peaceful sloth"; Mammon's, "I want to build a rival kingdom." All would prove equally unrealistic in the eyes of the King of Heaven (notice again the circumlocution). Clearly no one can win against omnipotence and any attempt on our part to rival His kingdom will meet with an "iron scepter" that has replaced the golden one with which he ruled over us in Heaven, "custody severe And stripes and arbitrary punishment." There is no weak spot in the armor of such a King. But in a very different way we may achieve the revenge we all desire. Beelzebub goes on to tell the fallen angels of something most of them did not know: in place of the third part of angels who fell, the heavenly Conqueror intends to create another world and a "new race called Man," to love Him, to serve Him, and in time to replace in Heaven the angels who rebelled. Far greater revenge than any so far proposed will be ours if we can find this new world, and either drive out the inhabitants as we were driven out, or, better still,

> Seduce them to our party, that their God
> May prove their Foe, and with repenting hand
> Abolish his own works. This would surpass
> Common revenge and interrupt His joy
> In our confusion, and our joy upraise
> In His disturbance: when his darling sons,
> Hurled headlong to partake with us, shall curse
> Their frail original, and faded bliss—
> Faded so soon.

(II. 368-76)

Beelzebub's—actually Satan's plan is eminently practicable and involves the only kind of revenge possible against an omnipotent deity who can never be defeated by physical strength—the seduction by force or guile of the new race God has created to serve and love Him and in time to replace the rebel angels.

> The bold design
> Pleased highly those infernal States, and joy

Sparkled in all their eyes; with full accord
They vote.

(II. 386-89)

Beelzebub has interrupted himself only momentarily. He rises
again with the deliberate intention of building up in the imagina-
tons of his listeners the almost incredible difficulties that will be
encountered by anyone—and this is a one-man mission—who un-
dertakes to find the new world and the new race. All this, ob-
viously, so that Satan's volunteering, which Beelzebub knows is
coming, will seem as courageous and dramatic as it needs to be.
Let us give the devil his due; the mission is really as perilous and
hazardous as Beelzebub makes it seem. When we begin to follow
Satan on his cosmic voyage, let us remember the passage in which
Beelzebub for the first time suggests the new sense of vastness and
space that was being felt in the seventeenth century:

> But, first, whom shall we send
> In search of this new world? whom shall we find
> Sufficient? who shall tempt with wandering feet
> The dark unbottomed infinite Abyss,
> And through the palpable obscure first find out
> His uncouth way, or spread his airy flight,
> Upborne with indefatigable wings
> Over the vast abrupt ere he arrive
> The happy isle? What strength, what art can then
> Suffice, or what evasion bear him safe
> Through the strict sentries and stations thick
> Of angels watching round? Here he had need
> All circumspection, and we now no less
> Choice in our suffrage—for on whom we send
> The weight of all, and our last hope, relies.

(II. 402-416)

The stage is set. The breathless audience, appalled at the dangers,
"sat mute." Satan rises to the dramatic moment which he has so
consciously prepared through Beelzebub. He too stresses the
dangers and difficulties of the mission, beginning with a paraphrase

of the Virgilian words familiar to every reader of the *Aeneid:*
"Easy is the descent to Hell; but to retrace one's steps, this is the
labor, this the task." "Long is the way and hard," Satan paraphrases,
"that out of Hell leads up to light." But he would "ill become this
throne" if he were to leave to others the carrying out of the most
important mission of all, the only one that may free them from the
bondage into which they have fallen. Go, then, says Satan, go
"mighty Powers, Terrors of Heaven,"—titles again—go on with
your plans for rendering Hell more tolerable, while I set out on my
mission to an unknown world, over uncharted ways. Valorous,
gallant, indomitable—Satan is all these and more, but he is also a
crafty exhibitionist:

> Thus saying rose
> The Monarch, and prevented all reply:
> Prudent, lest from his resolution raised
> Others among the chiefs might offer now.
>
> (II. 466-69)

The Council is followed by scenes of celebration, modeled by
Milton in part upon the funeral games for Patroclus in the *Iliad*
and those for Anchises in the *Aeneid.* Some of the fallen angels en-
gage in Olympic games, chariot races, feats of strength. Not all the
angels were athletes, however. Both the Olympic and the Pythian
games had had a place for music and for oratory. So in Milton's
Hell

> Others more mild.
> Retreated in a silent valley, sang
> With notes angelical to many a harp.
>
> (II. 546-48)

and another group sat apart on a hill, engaged "in discourse more
sweet," arguing philosophical and theological problems:

> Of providence, foreknowledge, will and fate,
> Fixed fate, free will, foreknowledge absolute,
> And found no end in wandering mazes lost.
>
> (II. 559-61)

Still another more adventurous band of explorers set forth to map
and chart the new world into which they had fallen, Milton's third
Hell, which we have already discussed. Meanwhile we follow Satan
as he sets out on his great adventure.

Sin and Death

At last appear
Hell-bounds, high reaching to the horrid roof,
And thrice threefold the gates; three folds were brass,
Three iron, three of adamantine rock
Impenetrable, impaled with circling fire,
Yet unconsumed.

(II. 643-48)

At the entrance to Hell, we meet two more of the "speaking charac-
ters" in *Paradise Lost,* Sin and Death. Basically, this episode is
allegory—showing to some extent the influence of Spenser—in
which classical and Biblical elements are interwoven. Milton's
point of departure was a Biblical verse (James I.15) "Then the lust
when it hath conceived, beareth Sin; the Sin, when it is full grown,
bringeth forth Death." At first the two ugly creatures are as strange
to Satan as to us. Death he has not seen before, and Sin has changed
so greatly that he does not recognize her. Only after Sin reminds him
of their earlier relationship does he realize who she is. In her
speech (II. 747-767) Milton allegorizes the first part of the Bibli-
cal verse: "Then the lust, when it hath conceived, beareth Sin." On
the occasion (of which we shall hear more later) when Satan, hear-
ing of the exaltation of Christ to be next to God, became jealous,
sin for the first time entered into his mind. Here Milton adapts to
his own use the old classical legend that Wisdom (Athena, Mi-
nerva) sprang full-grown from the brain of Zeus (Jupiter, Jove).
So Milton:

All on a sudden miserable pain

Surprised thee, dim thine eyes, and dizzy, swum
In darkness, while thy head flames thick and fast
Threw forth till, on the left side opening wide,
Likest to thee, in shape and countenance bright,
Then shining heavenly fair, a goddess armed,
Out of thy head I sprung.

(II. 752-58)

The first reaction of Satan and his fellow-angels had been astonishment and fear at what seemed an evil omen, but as time went on

> familiar grown
> I pleased, and with attractive graces won
> The most adverse—thee chiefly, who full oft,
> Thyself in me thy perfect image viewing,
> Became enamored, and such joy thou tookest
> With me in secret that my womb conceived
> A growing burden.

(II. 761-67)

These lines Alexander Pope deftly paraphrased when he wrote

Vice is a monster of so frightful mien,
As to be hated, needs but to be seen.
But seen too oft, familiar with her face,
We first endure, then pity, then embrace.

(*Essay on Man,* II. 219-220)

Satan now remembers the situation very well, although he had not known of the birth of his son, but the change in Sin (another indication of the physical degeneration suffered by all the former inhabitants of Heaven) is such that he had not recognized her, for now she

> seemed woman to the waist, and fair,
> But ended foul in many a scaly fold
> Voluminous and vast; a serpent armed
> With mortal sting. About her middle round
> A cry of Hell-hounds never ceasing barked
> With wide Cerberean mouths full loud, and rung

A hideous peal; yet when they list, would creep
If aught disturbed their noise, into her womb,
And kennel there; yet there still barked and howled
Within unseen.

(II. 650-59)

Again both Spenser and classical mythology echo in Milton's mind. Spenser's Error in the *Faerie Queene* (I. 1.14) was half-woman and half-serpent. The ugly addition of the Hell-hounds Milton drew from Ovid's account of Circe's transformation of the once-beautiful nymph, Scylla, into a monster whose lower body was a mass of barking dogs. Scylla and Charybdis, other transformed women, as any schoolboy knew, were identified geographically with the two points in the Straits of Messina most dangerous to mariners: Scylla, a reef of rocks on the Italian side, Charybdis, a whirlpool on the Sicilian side, so that the phrase, "between Scylla and Charybdis" implies "between two evils or dangers, either one of which could be avoided only by exposure to the other."

Sin is ugly enough, but she is at least comprehensible and may be visualized, since she can be compared with objects familiar to man. Death is far more horrible:

The other shape,
If shape it might be called that shape had none
Distinguishable in member, joint, or limb;
Or substance might be called that shadow seemed:
For each seemed either—black it stood as Night,
Fierce as ten Furies, terrible as Hell,
And shook a dreadful dart; what *seemed* his head
The likeness of a kingly crown had on.

(II. 666-73)

Many men know sin, but no man has seen death, until he can no longer tell us what it looks like. Milton's technique here is like that of writers of "horror stories" (for example, Ambrose Bierce, *The Damned Thing,* or some parts of *Dracula*) where horror becomes the more intense because we never see the creature of horror. The climax of Milton's fearful incomprehensible creature is in the last phrase: *"What seemed his head,* The likeness of a kingly crown had on."

One of the ugliest details in the allegory of Sin and Death is Milton's addition to the Biblical original of lust and death. Not only was Death born of the lust of Satan and Sin, but immediately following his violent birth occurred a scene of incest:

> I fled, but he pursued (though more, it seems,
> Inflamed with lust than rage) and, swifter far,
> Me overtook, his mother, all dismayed,
> And, in embraces forcible and foul
> Engendering with me, of that rape begot
> These yelling monsters that with ceaseless cry
> Surround me.
>
> (II. 790-96)

In spite of the shock of this revelation, Satan is always an opportunist who realizes at once that, thanks to his mistress, he may solve his most immediate problem, how to escape from Hell through the ninefold gates. As soon as he explains his mission, he can count upon complete cooperation, for he can offer both Sin and Death a much vaster scope for their energies, a new race of living creatures upon whom they may prey:

> He ceased, for both seemed highly pleased, and Death
> Grinned horrible a ghastly smile, to hear
> His famine should be filled.
>
> (II. 845-47)

Again we hear the motif of the keys of Heaven and Hell, which echoed in both *Comus* and *Lycidas,* "The golden opes, the iron shuts amain." Sin, the wardress of Hell-gates, looking forward to the time when she will sit at Satan's "right hand, voluptuous," is more than willing to open the adamantine doors:

> Thus saying, from her side the fatal keys—
> Sad instrument of all our woes,—she took,
> And toward the gate rolling her bestial train,
> Forthwith the huge portcullis high up-drew.
>
> (II. 871-74)

Notice in the passage that follows the emphasis upon the harsh sounds of the opening of Hell-gates, which Milton will contrast with the "harmonious sound" of the opening of the golden gates of Heaven as Christ goes forth to create new worlds (VII. 205-209). In Book II we are conscious of "impetuous recoil and jarring sound," of hinges grating like harsh thunder, of the seismic shaking of Hell as those great doors slowly open. Once they are opened, Sin cannot shut them. And so the gates of Hell stand forever open, thanks to the perversity of the perverted Sin, Death and Satan. With them we look out upon a terrifying sight.

Satan's Voyage

Particularly when it is read in its seventeenth-century context, Satan's voyage,—which begins here and is continued in Book III —is one of the most graphic episodes in *Paradise Lost*. The "New Philosophy" of the seventeenth century, springing from Copernicus, Galileo and Bruno, had discovered the vastness of a new space, stretching indefinitely, possibly even infinitely, had discovered also the existence of a plurality or infinity of worlds. Today we are space-conscious but no more so than our ancestors. As Satan stands with Sin at the gates of Hell, even his intrepid soul is momentarily appalled:

> Before their eyes in sudden view appear
> The secrets of the hoary Deep, a dark
> Illimitable ocean, without bound,
> Without dimension, where length, breadth, and height
> And time and place are lost. . . .
>   Into this wild Abyss—
> The womb of Nature, and perhaps her grave:
> Of neither sea, nor shore, nor air, nor fire,
> But all these in their pregnant causes mixed
> Confusedly, and which thus must ever fight,

Unless the Almighty Maker them ordain
His dark materials to create new worlds—
Into this wild Abyss, the wary Fiend
Stood on the brink of Hell and looked a while.

(II. 890-917)

There was as yet no vocabulary to describe the new space, and
there can be no positive vocabulary for any description of Chaos.
Milton produces his effect by negatives: illimitable, *without* bound
or dimension, where there is *no* length or breadth, *no* time or place,
neither earth, air, fire, water.

But Satan would not be the indomitable character he is if his
hesitation had been more than momentary:

At last his sail-board vans
He spreads for flight, and in the surging smoke
Uplifted spurns the ground.

(II. 927-29)

The journey through chaos requires all the courage and strength
even of Satan. He finds himself for a time falling through what was
later to be called an "air pocket," only to be carried aloft again by
a "tumultous cloud." (932-38) His ears are assailed on all sides by
a "universal hubbub wild" of stunning noises. He has no idea what
direction to take until he finds the throne of Chaos (951-1010)—
the least successful scene in the journey in my mind, since the per-
sonification here does not bring Chaos to life, as Sin and Death were
brought, and Satan's chance meeting with him detracts from the
sense of loneliness that marks the rest of the journey. The immense
strength and courage required for his mission, together with the
unknown dangers he constantly faces, is well suggested in the lines
in which the Fiend

O'er bog, or steep, through strait, rough, dense, or rare,
With head, hands, wings or feet pursues his way,
And swims, or sinks, or wades, or creeps, or flies,

in which the long succession of spondees drives home to us the in-
credible difficulties of Satan's slow progress through chaos.

In my *Voyages to the Moon,* I have suggested that Satan's voyage belongs to the literary genre "the cosmic voyage," which, while founded in early times by Lucian's two moon-voyages, took on new form and meaning after 1610, when Galileo's telescope proved that the moon was a little world, much like our world in topography, with mountains and valleys and—Galileo at first believed—seas. Seriously, satirically, fancifully, seventeenth-century imaginations vied with each other in suggesting ingenious ways by which man might reach the moon or even the planets—artificial wings, the harnessing of birds, "flying chariots." In Books II and III Milton adds still another "cosmic voyage" in which we follow Satan through chaos to the outposts of the newly created universe, then travel with him to the sun and back again to our own world. At the end of Book II we reach the point at which light begins to dawn through darkness, and Satan looks first up to Heaven, his former home, then discovers what he has not seen before:

And, fast by, hanging in a golden chain
This pendant World.

(II. 1051-52)

BOOK III

The Prologue to Light

All Milton's prologues, in a way, are invocations to light but this one is so much so that it is often called "The Prologue to Light." It is easy to see why Milton introduces a prologue here. Throughout Books I and II we have been in the "darkness visible" of Hell, and we have just accompanied Satan on his voyage through chaos, in which the "sacred influence of light" appears only at the end. As in *L'Allegro* and *Il Penseroso*—though on a grander and more cosmic scale—Milton uses the light-darkness contrast throughout *Paradise Lost*. "God is Light," dwelling in such brightness

> that highest Seraphim
> Approach not, but with both wings veil their eyes.
>
> (III. 381-82)

So many sources and analogies for the invocation have been suggested that even to list them would result in a dull and tedious catalogue. (For a very competent brief summary of the more important, see Headnote 56 in Merritt Hughes' edition.) There may well be memories here of Dante in the *Paradiso* and of Spenser in the *Hymne of Heavenly Beautie*. There certainly are echoes of the Gospel according to St. John (1.5). Most of all the invocation echoes Genesis I.3, "And God said, Let there be light, and there was light." Was light the first creation of Deity, Milton asks in the opening lines, or was it coeternal with Deity, since God is light? We know from Genesis that light existed "before the sun, Before the Heavens." Sun and moon were not created until the fourth day, while light was there on the first day.

This is the most personal of Milton's invocations and the most beautiful. It is personal, in part, because of the very specific references to his blindness, and even more because it expresses the theory of poetry we have seen developing throughout Milton's early work, his profound belief in the function of the poet, the classical but even more Christian feeling that the great poet must have illumination from above. Milton makes us acutely conscious of the limitations imposed by blindness upon a poet attempting such a classical and learned epic as *Paradise Lost:*

> for the book of knowledge fair,
> Presented with a universal blank

Of Nature's works, to me expunged and razed,
And wisdom at one entrance quite shut out.

(III. 47-50)

As a poet striving to write a great epic upon classical models, he
may feel some solace in thoughts of great classical predecessors:

Those other two equalled with me in fate
So were I equalled with them in renown,
Blind Thamyris and blind Maeonides,
And Tiresias and Phineus, prophets old.

(III. 33-36)

Here are Homer (Maeonides was his patronymic) and an even
more ancient Thracian poet, whom Homer had mentioned, deprived
of his sight by the Muses whom he challenged to a contest in po-
etry. And, because Milton believed that the great poet was also a
prophet, here are two blind classical prophets, Phineus, a Thracian
king who chose long life and blindness rather than a short happy
life, and Tiresias, Theban prophet, celebrated in Greek literature,
most of all in Sophocles' *Oedipus Rex* and *Antigone*. We are even
more poignantly aware than before of that recurrent tragedy of the
blind, waking each morning to darkness:

but Thou
Revisitest not these eyes, that roll in vain
To find thy piercing ray, and find no dawn.

(III. 22-24)

As in his last sonnet, we feel the loneliness of those who become
blind in maturity, "from the cheerful ways of men Cut off," de-
prived of the sight of the most familiar and loved objects:

Thus with the years
Seasons return, but not to me returns
Day, or the sweet approach of even or morn,
Or sight of vernal bloom or summer's rose.
Of flocks, or herds, or human face divine.

(III. 40-44)

As the prologue begins with light, so it ends, rising to a Christian prayer by a blind poet to the God who is Light:

> So much the rather Thou, celestial Light,
> Shine inward, and the mind through all her powers
> Irradiate, there plant eyes; all mist from thence
> Purge and disperse, that I may see and tell
> Of things invisible to mortal sight.
>
> (III. 51-55)

Milton's God

The most serious problem Milton faced when he transformed "Adam Unparadised" into *Paradise Lost* lay in the character of God. What he gained through leisure and detail in the degeneration of Satan, he lost in his depiction of God, since—other problems aside—God can neither degenerate nor develop but must remain static. Of all the characters in the epic God has been most seriously attacked. During recent years, particularly, batteries of both heavy and light artillery have been turned upon Him by such commentators as F. R. Leavis, A. J. A. Waldock, John Peter, William Empson. (See Bibliography.)

To be sure Milton's basic problem here was not peculiar to him, but has been shared by every artist who has attempted to draw God as a character in literature, sculpture, painting, though the depiction in the plastic arts has been more often satisfying than in literary works in which God appears as a speaking character. If God is truly "ineffable," He should neither speak nor be spoken to. If He is, as the angels hymn Him in Book III (372 ff.) "omnipotent, immutable, immortal, infinite, eternal," how can Infinity be expressed in finite terms, Spirit clothed in body and localized— even on a Throne in Heaven? Milton is inconsistent with himself. Our introduction to God and Heaven has come through the Pro-

logue, in which God is Light and dwells in "unapproached Light."
We are told again by the angelic chorus that God is the

> Fountain of Light, Thyself invisible,
> Amidst the glorious brightness where Thou sitst,
> Throned inaccessible but when Thou shadest
> The full blaze of Thy beams, and through a cloud
> Drawn round about Thee like a radiant shrine,
> Dark with excessive bright Thy skirts appear,
> Yet dazzle Heaven that brightest Seraphim
> Approach not, but with both wings veil their eyes.
>
> (III. 375-82)

Although Milton's God is more often Hebraic than Christian, we
feel little of the awe (of which terror is a compound) of the Israel-
ites, when, warned by Moses to expect His coming on the third day,
they felt Him in the thunders, lightnings and thick clouds, in "the
voice of a trumpet exceeding loud. . . . And Mount Sinai, the
whole of it, smoked because Jehovah descended on it in fire."
(Exodus XIX. 16-18) Great poet of light and sound as Milton was,
could he not have made his God an awesome Presence, unmoved
and unmoving, whom we feel, but whom our eyes—weaker
than those of the Seraphim—cannot and should not see? Samson's
destruction of the temple remains far more vivid than it would be
in a modern moving-picture in which we see the detail. In *Samson
Agonistes,* we do not see but only imagine it, our ears still ringing
with the "hideous shout," the "universal groan" as if the whole
inhabitation perished. Milton's angels could have reported to us
God's theological justification of the ways of God to men (as Moses
reported the Law to the children of Israel), as indeed, God's fiats,
injunctions, admonitions were made clear to Adam by Raphael,
by Michael, by Christ.

There is more than a suggestion of the technique which might
have been used regularly in Book VI, when the faithful Abdiel re-
turns from opposing Satan, and is led by the angels to the Seat
Supreme:

                    whence a Voice
From midst a golden cloud thus mild was heard:
'Servant of God, well done!'. . . .

                                        (VI. 27-29)

When the accolade has been bestowed, the mood changes to that
of Exodus:

So spoke the sovereign Voice; and clouds began
To darken all the hill, and smoke to roll
In dusky wreaths, reluctant flames, the sign
Of wrath awaked; nor with less dread, the loud
Ethereal trumpet from on high 'gan blow.

                                        (VI. 56-60)

It is not enough to say, as C. S. Lewis does (*A Preface to Para-
dise Lost*, p. 126): "Many of those who say they dislike Milton's
God only mean they dislike God,"—though this is part of the prob-
lem, to be sure, since even those who "acknowledge God" do so
under many aspects: Hebraic, Roman Catholic, Anglican, Lu-
theran, Calvinist, and a myriad other far-flung faiths and sects. A
modern reader of Book III feels rebuffed and repelled when he
first meets Milton's God. If he does not "believe in God," he
might have been appreciative enough of literature to have risen
with Beatrice and Dante to the great light in the center of the rose,
but it is not likely that Milton's God would have converted him
from unbelief to belief. If he "believes in God," he has even more
difficulty, since he starts off with specific prejudices *pro* and *con* the
positions God goes out of His way to expound.

    Milton's God denies Milton's own premises, since, in spite of
the fact that we are told that we cannot see Him, Milton gives us no
alternative to visualizing Him, as He "bent down His eye" to view
His works, particularly to chart the course of Satan's voyage. Not
only must we see Him, but we must listen to those long speeches,
which show a startling attitude to newly created Man. Even Satan
had believed the "rumor" in Heaven that God intended to create
another race to love and serve Him, and in time to replace the

fallen angels in Heaven. But what does the Creator say about His creation?

> Man will hearken to his glozing lies. . . .
> So will fall
> He and his faithless progeny. Whose fault?
> Whose but his own? Ingrate, he had of Me
> All he could have.

> (III. 93-98)

No matter what our logical or theological position in regard to free-will and predestination, God's first speeches are shocking to our sensibilities. He suddenly emerges to come down to our own level, speaking not with the voice of trumpet or thunder but with that of a somewhat querulous schoolmaster at a glorified desk, or an academic don debating on a Cambridge dais. It is this kind of shock that is reflected by various recent commentators. John Peter says (*A Critique of Paradise Lost*, pp. 15-16):

> One of the most obvious defects in the God of *Paradise Lost* is that he is a heterogeneous complex of ingredients, part man, part spirit, part attested biblical Presence and part dogma. . . . Here and elsewhere in the poem, two distinct images are being crudely superimposed: the figure of an irritable, very occasionally friendly uncle or stepfather, and the figure of an awesome divinity.

And, as Mr. Peter implies, the attitude of the reader has to adjust itself to Milton's technique, with the result that (p. 19) "in what relates to God, he begins to read like a book-reviewer: conceding as little as possible, deliberately misunderstanding in order to disagree, querying propositions which in their context are unexceptionable." William Empson goes further, interpreting God's speech to the Son (III. 80 ff.) as "the first of God's grisly jokes." He continues (*Milton's God,* pp. 119-120):

> Nobody says that it is a joke . . . but there is no opportunity, because what God goes on to say is so lengthy and appalling. His settled plan for punishment comes steadily out, and the

verse rhythm becomes totally unlike the thrilling energy of this
first sentence. In his first reply to the Son, we find him talking
in rocking-horse couplets. . . . This is also where we get the
stage-villain, 'Die he or Justice must.'

Even so sympathetic and judicious a critic as Douglas Bush (*English Literature in the Earlier Seventeenth Century,* p. 381) can
say: "If at times He seems to resemble an almighty cat watching a
human mouse, the trouble lies in the somewhat legal character of
Christian theology itself, and in the inevitable effects of dramatization. God suffers, paradoxically, through being the mouthpiece for
the very doctrines which clear Him of arbitrary cruelty and justify
the ways of God to men."

No one can deny for a moment that in a poem devoted to the
justification of God's ways to men, it was essential for Milton to
make abundantly clear the attitudes of God on basic issues of
theology, particularly on those which in his own time tore families
asunder, lay at the basis of much sectarianism, lay indeed behind
the Civil War. It was essential that Milton emphasize the freedom
of the will, the fact that, although God foreknows He does not foreordain (one of the most difficult of all theological paradoxes).
Always a fair disputant, he must make clear not only that Satan
had free will, but that he knew he had, then drive home the same
truth in regard to Man. Satan and Adam both acknowledge that
they are aware of their freedom and of the responsibilities it entails.
In fairness to all the disputants in his "great argument," Milton
seemed to feel that we must hear God's position from His own lips.
We would have been quite willing to believe it from the lips of
Christ, or Raphael, or Michael, had God remained the awful unspeaking Presence we could wish Him to have been. As it is, as
J. B. Broadbent says (*Some Graver Subject,* p. 144), "The Father
speaks as judge, counsel, and plaintiff in one." Milton's God is at
His greatest only when we are free to imagine him as the angels
hymn Him, an Idea, eternal, infinite, immutable, invisible "amidst
the glorious brightness."

Milton's Christ

Even the very recent commentators, who seem to have gone out of their way to pick all possible flaws in Milton's technique, show surprising respect and even affection for his Christ. Some seem almost tempted to make Christ a "friend to man, foe to God." (John Peter, *A Critique of Paradise Lost,* p. 21.) Mr. Empson seems quite willing to forgive the passages in which Christ echoes "God's grisly jokes," saying more than once: "Even if we call the Son simple minded here, we don't feel that it is to his discredit. . . . The Son regularly talks like a young medieval aristocrat eager to win his spurs." (*Milton's God,* pp. 97, 108.) Mr. Peter says on another occasion (*Idem,* p. 21): "It is something of a puzzle to see why an Arian like Milton should have given such dignity and refinement in comparison with the Father to the Son."

Our interpretation of Christ depends in part on whether we read *Paradise Lost* as it was read for a century and a half after it was published or whether we approach it (as do most modern commentators) in the light—or darkness—cast upon it by Milton's prose work, *De Doctrina Christiana* (*Of Christian Doctrine*), which remained unknown until the manuscript was discovered in the Public Record Office in 1823. Published with a translation in 1825, it at once attracted wide attention. Macaulay's famous essay on Milton appeared as a review of the book. Clergymen debated it *pro* and *con* from the pulpit. Milton was condemned as a heretic by Trinitarians and "kidnapped" by Unitarians. We do not know when or why Milton wrote the treatise. In his preface he said that he began his reading for such a work in his youth. His nephew spoke of his "returning" to it in 1655. The fact that the manuscript is in the hand of amanuenses indicates that it was dictated after Milton became blind. One theory about its purpose is that Milton (long interested in the problem) was attempting to establish a broader and more liberal basis for Protestantism than any offered by the warring sects of his time. The theory that has been generally accepted by literary students is that developed by Maurice Kelley, *Milton's De Doctrina Christiana as a Gloss upon Paradise Lost,* the title of which indicates the thesis: that Milton was building up his background for the theological positions to be treated in *Paradise Lost.* If we accept that interpretation, we will naturally read the heresies of the *De Doctrina* into *Paradise Lost* and start out with a conviction that the poem is anti-Trinitarian, since in the prose work Milton specifically denies the co-eternity and co-equality of the Three Persons, Father, Son and Holy Ghost.* It is well to remember, however, that no such heresy was found in *Paradise Lost* during the century and a half that it had been accepted as almost a holy book by Anglicans and Protestants alike.

Without entering further into the *De Doctrina* at this time, let us see what the text of Book III says about Christ. His appearance as a speaking character comes as no such shock to our sensibilities as did that of God, for whether or not we "accept Christ" as part of the Godhead, we are familiar with the Jesus Christ who lived as a man among men. Let us see the Idea of Christ Milton presented. God says:

> Son of my bosom, son who art alone
> My Word, my Wisdom, and effectual Might.
>
> (III. 168-69)

* Although nearly all modern commentators who follow Mr. Kelley say—as does Mr. Peter above—"an Arian like Milton," Milton's heresy in the *De Doctrina* was not Arianism. This has been established by Ruth Montgomery Kivette, *Milton on the Trinity* (Columbia University doctoral dissertation, published on microfilm, 1960). Mrs. Kivette shows by careful comparison of relevant texts that it is "impossible to identify Milton's anti-trinitarianism with Sabellianism or modalism . . . Arianism . . . or Socinianism." There is no question that Milton denies Trinitarianism in the *De Doctrina,* but his position is peculiarly his own. Mrs. Kivette says in a personal letter to me: "His position is, I think, more properly termed 'subordinationist.'"

We hear the echo here of Matthew III. 17, at the time of the Baptism in the Jordan: "And lo, a voice out of the heavens saying, This is my beloved Son, in whom I am well pleased." We hear, too, the familiar words of the Gospel according to John: "In the beginning was the Word, and the Word was with God, and the Word was God." Most students are familiar at least in passing with the term *Logos* (the Greek term may be translated both as *word* and as *wisdom*) and realize that John was here combining the Christian idea of the Second Person of the Trinity with the Platonic conception of the Logos, as intermediary between the One and the Many. If they do not at once understand why Milton calls Christ the "effectual Might" of God, they will find the idea several times in *Paradise Lost*. According to Genesis, the world was created by God; in Book VII of *Paradise Lost* we shall see that it was created by Christ. So too in Genesis it was God who descended to the Garden of Eden to pass judgment upon Adam and Eve. In *Paradise Lost,* it is Christ, the "effective Might" of God. Such an interpretation was in no way original with Milton ànd far from heretical, widely accepted for centuries in Christianity.

In the hymn of adoration sung by the angels (III. 372-415), the Idea of Christ is quite consistent (as the Idea of God was not) with Milton's introduction of Christ as a character:

> Thee next they sung, of all creation first,
> Begotten Son, divine Similitude,
> In whose conspicuous countenance, without cloud
> Made visible, the Almighty Father shines
> Whom else no creature can behold.
>
> (III. 383-87)

One aspect of Milton's Godhead is an Old Testament God of Justice, sometimes of Wrath; the other is a New Testament God of Mercy and Love. Love is emphasized in all the passages of interpolation between speeches: "His meek aspect . . . breathed immortal love to mortal men." (III. 266-71) He is the aspect of God "in whom the fulness dwells of love divine." (III. 325-26) In His face

Divine compassion visibly appeared,
Love without end, and without measure grace.

(III. 138-42)

One of the chief functions of Christ as a character in *Paradise Lost* is as the antagonist of Satan, as He will prove in the warfare in Heaven and at the end of the epic, with its prophecy that in the future He will conquer Satan forever. It is hardly necessary to point out the close parallel and contrast Milton intends in Book III to the scene in Book II. Satan's offer to undertake the mission of finding the new World and seducing Man, had been followed by the "Black Mass" of acclamation by the fallen angels. Christ's offer to sacrifice Himself for the salvation of Man is followed by a corresponding scene of jubilee and hosanna:

> Lowly reverent
> Towards either throne they bow, and to the ground
> With solemn adoration down they cast their crowns.

(III. 349-51)

Satan's Voyage Through Limbo

Through the eyes of God, we realize that Satan is still on his voyage of discovery of the new world and the new race of beings,

> Coasting the wall of Heaven on this side Night,
> In the dun air sublime, and ready now
> To stoop with wearied wings and willing feet
> On the bare outside of this World.

(III. 71-74)

Later, Milton will again direct our attention to Satan who has alighted "upon the firm opacous globe." He finds the World far different from the one he had seen at a distance, which had seemed in bigness as a star of smallest magnitude. Milton's description here is curiously similar to that of the world Galileo's telescope had discovered and Kepler's imagination had envisioned in the *Somnium*—the new world in the moon:

> A Globe far off
> It seemed: now seems a boundless continent,
> Dark, waste and wild, under the frown of Night
> Starless exposed, and ever-threat'ning storms
> Of Chaos blustering round, inclement sky—
> Save on that side which from the wall of Heaven
> Though distant far some small reflection gains
> Of glimmering air less vexed with tempest loud.
>
> (III. 422-429)

Like a vulture Satan descends, seeking his prey. But before Milton goes further with Satan's quest, he interrupts the story to introduce another allegorical passage, this one on Limbo, or the Paradise of Fools. It appears before our eyes (not Satan's, for this is a vision of the future) like a mirage. With many readers, from Addison down, I feel that Milton's Limbo adds little to *Paradise Lost*. It is difficult to see why Milton introduced it at this particular point. There was no source or analogue in Homer or Virgil, as will be the case with another passage to which I shall take exception. Milton's literary memory went back here rather to the Italian epic writers. Dante described a Limbo of Vanity in the *Inferno* (IV. 138) in which he too placed Empedocles, but Dante's Limbo was a circle of Hell which included philosophers, poets, heroes. In the *Orlando Furioso,* Ariosto had also introduced a Limbo, where his Astolfo lost his wits. Some critics have justified the inclusion of Milton's Limbo here (see F. L. Huntley, "A Justification of Milton's Paradise of Fools,") on the ground that the shadowy characters symbolize some of the many types of pride, error, arrogance that Satan, with Sin and Death, introduced into the world. Here in the future will be gathered together many who through arrogance strove to bring about confusion, like the builders of the Tower of Babel (III. 466-68), such philosophers as Empedocles and Cleombrotus who committed suicide. The longest single passage (III. 476-95) takes us back momentarily to the anti-Catholic satire of the end of Book I, for here Milton satirizes the Catholic orders of "Friars white, black and gray, with all their trumpery," Carmelites, Dominicans, Franciscans, all of whom attempted to do "vain" things. If the passage belongs in *Paradise Lost* at all, I think Milton would have found a better place for it in Books XI-XII, in which Michael shows Adam a vision of the future, with all the evils his sin has brought into the world. Introduced where it is, the passage does little more than distract our attention from the journey of Satan.

After waiting for some time on the dark globe, Satan—as at the verge of chaos—begins to see light. Looking up he beholds a "structure high" (III. 503-540) a magnificent stair connecting the new world to Heaven. "Each stair mysteriously was meant," that is, had a secret meaning. Here is Jacob's ladder, which Jacob in his vision (Genesis XXVIII. 12) saw reaching to Heaven, and on which angels descended and ascended. Standing on the lowest stair, Satan first looks up, then

> Looks down with wonder at the sudden view
> Of all this World at once.
>
> (III. 542-43)

With Satan we share the first of the grand scenes of "cosmic perspective" which I believe Milton drew from the sense of the "new space" discovered by the telescope, influenced also by such philosophers as Bruno. The world-scheme of *Paradise Lost,* so far as it may be charted, is Ptolemaic, but space so dominates the whole as to make the canvas of *Paradise Lost* the most extensive any poetic imagination (with the possible exception of Lucretius) ever conceived. We feel it as Satan feels it as he looks up and down:

> Round he surveys (and well might, where he stood
> So high above the circling canopy
> Of Night's extended shade) from eastern point
> Of Libra to the fleecy star that bears
> Andromeda far off the Atlantic seas

Beyond the horizon; then from pole to pole
He views in breadth, and, without longer pause
Down right into the World's first region throws
His flight precipitant, and winds with ease
Through the pure marble air his oblique way,
Amongst innumerable stars that shone,
Stars distant, but night-hand seemed other worlds . . .

                                            (III. 555-66)

For a moment Milton's imagination plays with an idea that en-
thralled his generation and continues to enthrall ours: the possibil-
ity that other planets or stars may be inhabited, an hypothesis to
which Galileo's telescopic discoveries had added new possibilities.
At the moment, intent as he is on his mission, Satan does not pause
to discover "who dwelt happy there." Satan's cosmic voyage, like
that of Cyrano de Bergerac, includes a visit to the sun (III. 572-
622). Milton's mind again goes back to one of the discoveries of
Galileo, who through his telescope found that both the moon and
the sun had spots. With wry humor he suggests:

There lands the Fiend, a spot like which perhaps
Astronomer in the sun's lucent orb
Through his glazed optic tube yet never saw.

                                            (III. 587-89)

Like St. John in Revelation (XIX. 17) Satan "saw an angel stand-
ing in the sun," and recognizes the archangel Uriel,

                    one of the seven
Who in God's presence, nearest to His throne,
Stand ready to command, and are His eyes
That run through all the Heavens, or down to the Earth
Bear his swift errands over moist and dry,
O'er sea and land.

                                            (III. 648-53)

Uriel, who once knew him well in Heaven, does not recognize
Satan. He might not have known him under any circumstances,
since Satan has not faced the extent of his physical degeneration,
but to make assurance even more sure, Satan has transformed him-

self into a "stripling Cherub," appearing as one of the younger lesser angels. (III. 636-44) Satan's deliberate dissembling leads Milton to stress, as he will on other occasions, the fact that hypocrisy is one of Satan's many sins, "Hypocrisy—the only evil that walks Invisible, except to God alone." (III. 683-84) Uriel has no reason to be surprised that one of the lesser angels is eager to see the new world. He himself had been present at the creation, which he describes in brief. (III. 708-20) Quite willingly, he shows his supposed fellow-angel the particular orb which has been created for man. Ironically, one of God's most trusted servants gives Satan the final direction which enables the Tempter to speed to earth on his fatal mission,

> To wreak on innocent frail Man his loss
> Of that first battle, and his flight to Hell.

> (IV. 11-12)

BOOK IV

Satan's Soliloquy

"Oh, for that warning voice." So Milton opens Book IV, which begins, not with a prologue in the usual sense, but with Satan's debasement of the Invocation to Light. As the fallen angels paid Satan the obeisance they had denied to God, so Satan invokes Light in tones that are blasphemous. This invocation, we recall, is the section of *Paradise Lost* that Milton's nephew remembered his uncle's reading long before he actually wrote the epic.

Milton uses the soliloquy as Shakespeare and other Elizabethan dramatists had used it, particularly, here and elsewhere, to permit us to listen to Satan at a time when he can speak frankly with himself, and also let us determine to what extent he is aware of his own motives. This soliloquy marks a definite step downward in Satan's degeneration. "Inflamed with rage" as true angels never are, he boils with passion. He is not as certain of his final success as he has pretended to his followers:

> Horror and doubt distract
> His troubled thoughts, and from the bottom stir
> The Hell within him—for within him Hell
> He brings, and round about him, nor from Hell
> One step, no more than from himself, can fly
> By change of place. . . .
> Which way I fly is Hell, myself am Hell.

(IV. 18-23, 75)

Here is Milton's fourth Hell, not a place but a state of mind.

But Satan's degeneration is not yet total. He is still able to feel the prick of conscience, and poignantly capable of contrasting "what he was, what is, and what must be Worse." (IV. 23-26) Alone with himself, he can acknowledge that the fault was not God's but his own. Lifted up so high, he thought one more step would set him highest. His followers have not realized that Satan has wavered more than once about the possibility of a return to Heaven. He knows that repentance is still possible, but it would involve submission—"and that word Disdain forbids me and my dread of shame." (IV. 82-83) The overweening Pride that had caused his rebellion is there, in still greater degree. Deliberately, knowing fully what he is doing, he chooses wrong, refusing to submit, refusing to repent, again expressing that platform he had adopted in Hell: if God's purpose is to bring forth good out of evil, his, as Antagonist, will continue: "Evil, be thou my good." (IV. 110) Further changes in his physical appearance reflect the moral descent. "Thrice changed [his face] with pale, ire, envy, and despair."

Coming to the thicket of trees that surrounds the Garden of Eden,

Due entrance he disdained, and in contempt
At one slight bound high overleaped all bound
Of hill or highest wall, and sheer within
Lights on his feet.

(IV. 180-83)

Satan chooses as his perch from which to spy out the terrain before him the highest tree in Paradise, ironically, the Tree of Life, on which, like a cormorant, he "sat devising death." With him we have our first glimpse of the Garden of Eden.

The Garden of Eden

Milton's Garden of Eden ("Eden" literally means "pleasure") had so many sources and analogues in earlier literature that it would be impossible even to list them in brief space. Classical and Christian writers alike had pictured the "hortus conclusus," the garden withdrawn from the world to which contemplation might retire. Church Fathers, Hebrew and Christian, had argued about the location and the size of the original Paradise, one group holding that it was comparatively small and limited to the Garden of Eden, the other that Paradise originally covered a large part of the Earth. Some, indeed, held that Paradise was not on Earth but in the "middle regions of the air." Milton's Garden is clearly a circumscribed portion of the earth, geographically located within limits which he defines in lines 208-215. The Garden is surrounded by a thick forest of trees and shrubs—reminiscences perhaps of the forests around Dante's Earthly Paradise in the *Purgatorio* and Spenser's Garden of Adonis in the *Faerie Queene*.

Apart from its relation to earlier literature and theology, Milton's Garden had an important place in the history of landscape gardening and architecture. In the seventeenth century, England was becoming increasingly interested in a question that became of major importance to landscape architects in the eighteenth century; should gardens be "regular" or "irregular"? Basically this involved that age-long "appeal to Nature for standards" which we have met in *Comus,* though the problem here is aesthetic rather than ethical. Should flowers and trees grow as Nature lets them grow, or should Art improve upon Nature, by laying out gardens geometrically and clipping shrubs and even trees into geometrical figures?

"God Almighty first planted a garden," said Bacon in one of the great opening sentences in his essays. But what kind of garden did God plant? Here Milton's Garden took on great significance, particularly in the eighteenth and nineteenth centuries when *Paradise Lost* was often read as religiously as if Milton had actually been present at the Creation. If we notice carefully all that Milton says about the Garden, we will see that unconsciously he gave ammunition to both sides. His Garden is, of course, tropical or semi-tropical, located in a climate in which Nature is luxuriant and all things grow in great variety. (IV. 246-63) It is the most beautiful Garden ever known, as Milton shows by comparisons with gardens in legend and story. (IV. 269-85) On the first occasion that Milton mentions the Nature-Art controversy in connection with Eden, he says:

Flowers worthy of Paradise, which *not nice Art,*
In beds and *curious knots,* but *Nature boon*
Poured forth profuse on hill and dale and plain.

(IV. 241-43)

In another such passage in Book V (291-97) we shall find such phrases as: "Nature . . . *wantoned.* . . . *played* at will. . . . pouring forth . . . *wild above rule or art enormous bliss.*" But in the meantime we should notice that Adam and Eve consider their chief duty the curbing of a too-luxuriant Nature of which Comus would undoubtedly have approved. In Book IV (lines 624-32), Adam tells Eve that their function is to "reform" the arbors, to clear away the overgrown branches, that need more hands than theirs "to lop their wanton growth." When in Book IX Eve pleads to work apart from Adam (IX. 205-212), she does so on the ground that the Garden is getting beyond them. What they laboriously prune or prop or bind in a day, "One night or two with wanton growth derides." The duty of man is to impose order upon a Nature that went to "wanton" extremes.

Adam and Eve

In the earlier books of *Paradise Lost,* Milton deliberately stresses the idyllic and generic qualities of Man and Woman before the Fall, very different from the man and woman we shall find later when they are reduced to our own level. The first Adam and Eve are prototypes of what Man might have been, as far removed from us in their perfection as they seem in time and place. Beautiful moving and speaking statues, they are like the angels who did not fall, models of a great impassivity:

> Two of far nobler shape, erect and tall,
> Godlike erect, with native honor clad
> In naked majesty, seemed lords of all,
> And worthy seemed, for in their looks divine
> The image of their glorious Maker shone—
> Truth, wisdom, sanctitude severe and pure.
>
> (IV. 288-93)

Some modern women, heiresses of an age of militant suffragism, take umbrage at the distinction between the sexes Milton immediately implies:

> though both
> Nor equal, as their sex not equal seemed:

For contemplation he, and valor formed,
For softness she, and sweet attractive grace:
He for God only, she for God in him.

(IV. 295-99)

It would have been impossible for Milton to feel differently. Apart from the fact that this was basic teaching of Hebrew and Christian —indeed, of pagan—religion, and that of law, stemming from Roman Law, it was also a basic concept of the "hierarchy" or "order" of the universe, almost universally accepted in Milton's time, of which we shall learn more. Differentiation of the sexes into "higher" and "lower" was inevitable in the nature of things. If his position gave Adam precedence in some ways, it also made his responsibilities heavier, as we shall see when we come to the Temptation.

The physical appearances of Adam and Eve emphasize the distinction, as does the symbolism of the hair implied in the following passage. Paul had written (I Corinthians XI. 14-15) "Does not nature itself teach you that for a man to wear long hair is degrading to him, but if a woman has long hair, it is her pride?" Adam's "hyacinthine" (dark) locks hung "clustering, but not beneath his shoulders broad." Eve's golden curls hung like a veil to her slender waist. Adam is the stalwart tree on which the vine depends.

Life in Eden is idyllic, as are all things. After only toil enough to make "wholesome thirst and appetite More grateful," Adam and Eve sit down to their evening meal. (IV. 327-31) Eve faces none of the housekeeping problems of later young brides: fruits grow ready to her hand; the rind serves for cups and glasses; their drink is from the running stream. There is no want of entertainment, since around them are the animals all friendly, lion dandling the kid. Like children of all ages, our simple "Grand Parents" take particular pleasure in "the unwieldy elephant" who to amuse them, "wreathed his lithe proboscis." (IV. 345-47) The scene of simple innocence and love has its psychological effect upon Satan, watching from his high perch. He has still enough angelic conscience to feel some compunction for what he plans to do, yet his "fixed mind" is ever more fixed. Casuistical as he had become, he justifies his action by "public reason," political expediency, leading Milton to brief "double talk" of a Puritan about "necessity," the tyrant's plea. (IV. 393-94) Capable as he is of metamorphising himself into other shapes than his own, Satan approaches closer and closer to his prey, first as a lion, then as a tiger, so that he overhears their intimate conversation, and particularly learns from Adam about the one prohibition given them by God: that they may not taste the fruit of the tree of knowledge of good and evil. (IV. 419-36) This information gives Satan exactly what he needs for a plan of action, as his later soliloquy makes clear. (IV. 512-27) If Satan's still latent angelic qualities might have wavered before, there is no possibility of his doing so after the still more intimate scene, in which Eve recalls her Creation and her first sight of herself, into which some modern critics read psychoanalytical overtones, and in which others find the "original flaw" in Eve's nature. The newly created Eve had seen her reflection in a still pool of water:

> As I bent down to look, just opposite
> A shape within the watery gleam appeared
> Bending to look on me. I started back;
> It started back; but pleased I soon returned;
> Pleased it returned as soon with answering looks
> Of sympathy and live. There I had fixed
> Mine eyes till now, and pined with vain desire. . . .
>
> (IV. 460-66)

In modern parlance, this is "narcissism." (The word comes from the mythological tale of Narcissus, a handsome youth who fell in love with his own image in the water.) Eve's "flaw" is vanity, which will lead her to the fatal step she took. "Narcissism" is defined by modern dictionaries as "erotic gratification derived from admiration of one's own physical or mental attributes; a normal condition at the infantile level of personality development." I do not dispute the contemporary reading on the ground that psychoanalytical interpretation of seventeenth-century writers is in any way anachronistic. We need no better guide than Robert Burton to remind us that "psychoanalysis" did not wait for Freud or Jung. It is merely difficult for me to understand how Milton could have believed that Eve, as created by God, had an "original flaw." It seems entirely possible to explain Eve's supposed "narcissism" by saying that Eve was still an infant—just now created—and her experience was that of any child for the first time noticing its reflection in mirror or water, as childlike as that described by Thomas Traherne in "Shadows in the Water."

There is no question, however, of the effect of this scene and the next one on Satan. As he watches the "conjugal attraction" between Adam and Eve (IV. 494-97) both jealousy and lust are aroused. In Heaven Satan had had a mistress whom he had recently seen. Even in her debased condition she was capable of arousing lust. The love-scene between Adam and Eve becomes a "Sight hateful, sight tormenting . . . these two Imparadised in one another's arms," while Satan has been thrust to Hell

Where neither joy nor love, but fierce desire—
Among our other torments not the least—
Still unfulfilled, with pain of longing pine.

(IV. 509-511)

There is no question now that Satan will proceed with his plan as soon as he can find the tree, and find it he will, even though at this moment Gabriel, warned by Uriel, who has recognized Satan too late, sounds the alarm.

There follows one of the most idyllic scenes in the earlier books of *Paradise Lost,* Eve's decking of her nuptial couch with flowers of Eden. The bower of bliss blooms with flowers, "iris all hues, roses and jessamine . . . the violet, crocus and hyacinth." Before entering the bower, our original parents "turned, and under the sky adored, The God that made both sky, air, Earth and Heaven." Here, as earlier, are paraphrases of the Psalms, such as were worthy their great original, this time (IV. 724-35) verses of Psalm LXXIV, "Thine is the day, Thine also the night," and of Psalm CXXVII, "for he giveth his beloved sleep." Milton's "Hail,

Wedded Love" is his Epithalamium, praising the marriage relation of which he had written in the *Divorce Tracts,* a marriage of bodies, minds and souls. Here too is his conception of "married chastity":

> Founded in Reason, loyal, just and pure. . . .
> Perpetual fountain of domestic sweets,
> Whose bed is undefiled and chaste pronounced. . . .
> There, lulled by nightingales, embracing slept,
> And on their naked limbs the flowery roof
> Showered roses, which the morn repaired. Sleep on,
> Blest pair.
>
> (IV. 756-74)

But almost at its beginning, the idyll is approaching its end. As Eve sleeps, Satan begins his temptation by whispering in her ear a "prophetic dream." "Squat like a toad" at her ear, he reaches "the organs of her fancy"—a process we shall better understand in Book V. At this point we know only that he inspired a dream, not what Eve dreamt.

Discovered just too late by Ithuriel and Zephon, he starts up, resuming his own grand stature, proud, arrogant, disdainful of minor angels who fail to recognize one who was long their superior. The figures of speech, from grand to base, follow each other in rapid succession. The former good and the increasing evil in Satan are inextricably mingled here. For a moment he stands abashed before the severe purity of the youthful angels, feeling "how awful goodness is" and "virtue in her shape how lovely." His indomitable Pride wins over momentary regret and remembrance of times lost. Like a proud steed he goes "haughty on," even though the steed is reined and champing his curb. So too in the scenes with Gabriel, who had been among his most mighty antagonists in the battle in Heaven. One of the last majestic similes we shall find for Satan occurs here, as the angelic squadron sharpened its phalanx and began to hem him round:

> On the other hand, Satan alarmed (aroused)
> Collecting all his might, dilated stood,

Like Teneriffe or Atlas, unremoved;
His stature reached the sky, and on his crest
Sat Horror plumed.

(IV. 985-89)

So majestic, so unconquerable does Satan seem at this moment that we feel that even with the phalanxes of Gabriel surrounding him, he might have proved invincible.

At this last moment of Satan's grandeur and power, Milton's ending of Book IV seems to me his least artistic denouement— and basically unfair to the great Adversary of God and Man. Milton takes refuge in a device of old "epic machinery." It had been artistic enough as Homer had used it twice in the *Iliad,* when Zeus weighed the destinies of the Greeks against the Trojans, and of Hector against Achilles. It still seemed fitting when Virgil imitated it in the use of scales to weigh the fates of Aeneas and Turnus. But although Milton attempts to make the scales less literal and more cosmic by interpreting the balances of God as the constellation Libra (the Scales) in the heavens, the pagan device has no artistic justification when used by Milton's Hebraic-Christian God to decide an issue in what might have proved a battle grander and more dangerous than that in Heaven. If Milton felt it essential to use the scale-motif at all, he might better have justified it by making the dominant overtones not those of Homer and Virgil, but Daniel's warning to Belshazzar: (Daniel V. 27) "Thou are weighed in the balances and found wanting." The scene fails ethically as well as artistically. Until this moment, the various steps in Satan's downfall have seemed just, right and inevitable, because he has taken each step of his own deliberate choice. This time his author has unfairly imposed the sudden ignominy upon him by a "deus ex machina." Even Homer nodded, to be sure, but Milton, fair antagonist and great architect as he was, so seldom does that I can only continue to wish that when his amauensis read this passage aloud to him, he had shaken his head, and said: "Strike out that ending."

BOOK V

Eve's Dream

When Adam and Eve wake, we know the nature of the dream Satan has sent into her mind. A "prophetic dream," indeed, anticipating in detail the actual Temptation. She has seen the Tree, beside which stood an angel who had eaten the fruit, which he found "able to make gods of men," and the eating of which would make Eve a goddess. She remembers the "pleasant savory smell" that quickened appetite, with the sense of "high exaltation" she had experienced after eating. (IV. 30-93)

Adam is as much disturbed as she by "this uncouth dream, of evil sprung, I fear." Neither one, of course, has any idea of the origin of the dream, but it is clearly Adam's duty as the "head" to explain how evil could come into the mind of a person in whom there was no knowledge of evil. This leads Adam to a little lecture on "dream psychology," as his generation understood it. Basic to what he says is again the fundamental concept of "order" or "gradation," which Milton will elaborate more fully later in Book V. I shall reserve fuller discussion of the general concept until then, and consider only one aspect here. Adam's explanation to Eve (V. 100-16) is a brief explication of what was called "faculty psychology." The human personality (the "soul") consists of various "faculties," (powers or abilities) of which Milton here mentions only three: Reason, Fancy, Imagination. He might have added others that will be implied in later scenes, such as the Passions and the Senses. To Milton, as to most thinkers before Locke, such "faculties" were innate, given man at birth. They existed—like Man and Woman—in a hierarchy of higher and lower. To Milton, here and throughout *Paradise Lost,* the highest faculty is Reason; all others should be subordinate to "Reason as chief." God's supreme gift to man, whom He made in His own image, was Reason, as we shall see in the Creation scene, when man is created with "sanctity of Reason." It is man's duty to keep Reason always in the ascendant. So long as he does so, he will be able to know and to do what is right. Notice from this time on the recurrence of that word "Reason," and watch the connotations of the word on each occasion.

The two other faculties mentioned in the dream-passage are Fancy and Imagination:

> Among these Fancy next
> Her office holds: of all external things,
> Which the five watchful senses represent,
> She forms imaginations, airy shapes,
> Which Reason, joining or disjoining, frames
> All what we affirm or what deny, and call
> Our knowledge or opinion.

(V. 102-108)

There was little or no distinction in Milton's time between Fancy and Imagination. Indeed, as late as Addison's essays on *The Pleasures of the Imagination* in the 1712 *Spectator,* the words were used interchangably. Later in the eighteenth century we begin to find the exaltation of Imagination familiar in the Romantic period. Insofar as Milton makes a distinction, he uses the words in a reverse order to that familiar to us: Fancy is a higher faculty, "imaginations" (we would say, "fancies") are whimsical and capricious. Clearly Imagination-Fancy is not a shaping faculty nor the creative faculty it was to become to the Romanticists. That function belonged rather to Reason. If Reason is not on the alert, as in sleep, "mimic Fancy" imitates her, "misjoining shapes," "ill matching words and deeds." Thus in dreams our minds may make irrational combinations, bringing together events of different periods of our lives, people we have known who have never known each other. To some extent, Adam feels, Eve's dream was a result of their conversation of the preceding evening, when he had reminded her of the injunction laid down by God about the Tree of Knowledge, "but with addition strange," the work of Fancy. "Yet be not sad," he concludes:

Evil into the Mind of God or Man
May come or go, so unapproved, and leave
No spot or blame behind.

(V. 116-118)

For a moment we may be startled at the idea that evil may come into the Mind of God, but there is no reason for astonishment. Since God is omniscient, He knows all, and all ideas are in His mind. The important thing, says Adam, is that evil, coming into the mind from whatever source, should not be "approved." We have seen the occasion on which evil came into Satan's mind and the extent to which—unfortunately for mortal men—he "approved" his Sin.

Comforted though she is, Eve is still disturbed over her dream, and the first human tears fall in Eden. (V. 130-34) As in the evening, so in the morning Adam and Eve lift their voices up to God in another great paraphrase of the Psalms. Memories of his youth, when his Puritan family sang together such paraphrases, must often have been in Milton's mind when he described the unaccompanied songs of Adam and Eve:

such prompt eloquence
Flowed from their lips, in prose or numerous verse
More tuneable than needed lute or harp
To add more sweetness.

(IV. 150-52)

Basically this paraphrase is of Psalm CXLVIII; see the opening verse: "Praise ye Jehovah from the heavens: Praise Him in the heights: . . . Praise Him, sun and moon; Praise Him, all ye stars of light." There are other overtones, as Milton expands the Psalm to include "all created things," which will be mentioned in the account of Creation. Here, in a way, is the hierarchy of created Nature: Angels, sun and moon, stars and planets, the waters above and the waters upon the earth; winds, fountains; birds, animals. Through Adam and Eve all Nature lifts its voice to praise the Creator.

The Visit of Raphael

God—knowing, as Adam and Eve do not—why Eve has dreamed a dream of evil, sends Raphael, "the sociable angel" from Heaven to converse with men. Raphael is instructed to tell Adam all he may wish to know:

> such discourse bring on
> As may advise him of his happy state;
> Happiness in his power left free to will—
> Left to his own free will, his will though free
> Yet mutable.
>
> (V. 233-37)

In Raphael's descent we see another scene of "cosmic perspective" (with another passing reference to Galileo's telescope) as the magnificent angel leaves the gates of Heaven and speeds down to earth:

> Down thither prone in flight
> He speeds, and through the vast ethereal sky
> Sails between worlds and worlds.
>
> (V. 247-93)

A "glorious shape," indeed, this magnificent angel with his six great wings of "colors dipt in Heaven." The scene that follows is one of the most charming in the epic, still stressing the idyll of life in Eden before the Fall, yet involving some very human touches as the newly wedded Adam and Eve prepare to entertain their first guest. Adam goes forth to meet him in true Puritan fashion:

                    without more train
Accompanied than with his own complete
Perfections; in himself was all his state—
More solemn than the tedious pomp that waits
On princes when their rich retinue long
Of horses led and grooms besmeared with gold
Dazzles the crowd and sets them all agape.
Nearer his presence Adam, though not awed,
Yet with submiss approach, and reverence meet
As to a superior nature, bowing low. . . .
                                        (V. 351-60)

In the meantime, Eve is preparing a luncheon much more sumptuous than she and Adam would have had alone, proud of her well-stocked larder. (V. 321-400) The fruits of spring, summer, autumn are all at her hand. By the time the angelic guest joins them, the young housekeeper, proud of her table, must have felt a momentary shock when Adam raised the question whether angels eat, and if so, whether they can eat human food. (V. 401-402) But her fears are at once over when she learns that angels not only can eat human food but enjoy it.

Milton's school of angelology makes his angels much more attractive to us, as well as to Adam and Eve, than they might have been. Angels of some theological factions would have proved immensely difficult guests, incorporeal as they would have been, sharing no human qualities, certainly feeling neither hunger nor thirst. Raphael, on the other hand, sets to with a very good appetite:

                    nor seemingly
The Angel, nor in mist—the common gloss
Of theologians—but with keen dispatch
Of real hunger.
                                        (V. 434-37)

Angel, like man, eats food, concocts, digests, assimilates and "corporeal to incorporeal turns." The passage is an interesting—to modern readers, an amusing—combination of Christian angelology and the Platonic idea of the elements passing one into another in an unbroken circle. From his analogy of all created matter to the tree, Raphael discusses the hierarchy in human psychology which Adam had tried to explain to Eve, but carries it a step further:

> flowers and their fruit,
> Man's nourishment, by gradual scale sublimed,
> To vital spirits aspire, to animal,
> To intellectual, give both life and sense,
> Fancy and understanding, whence the soul
> Reason receives, and Reason is her being,
> Discursive or intuitive; discourse
> Is oftest yours, the latter most is ours,
> Differing but in degree, of kind the same.
>
> (V. 482-98)

Here is the hierarchy of the faculties we met before, with the addition of Understanding. All other faculties should be subservient to Reason, the "being" of the soul. Angels and men both possess Reason, differing not in kind but in degree. The distinction Raphael makes between angelic and human Reason was a very old one: the "discursive Reason" of man is logical Reason, by means of which he works things out intellectually. Angelic Reason is intuitive. Angels have no need to intellectualize; they know instinctively and immediately.

Hierarchy, Degree, Order

Raphael's explanation of the angelic nature leads him—and Milton—to the first of two major passages in which Adam and Eve learn of the hierarchy everywhere in the universe, governing both Heaven and Earth.

There is "order" among angels, as we have seen more than once, "higher" and "lower" as among human beings. The angels are "spiritual" and "intelligential;" man is "rational," not yet so high in the order of Nature as angels, though he may in time become so. Raphael's explanation of the fact that angels eat and drink leads him still further:

> For know, whatever was created needs
> To be sustained and fed. Of elements
> The grosser feeds the purer: earth the sea;
> Earth and the sea feed air; the air those fires
> Ethereal.
>
> (V. 414-18)

Here are the four elements—earth, water, air, fire—of which both Nature and man are composed, which exist in order from the lowest and grossest, earth, to the highest and most spiritual, fire. (The reader who wishes to see how universal this idea was in the earlier seventeenth century will find additional material in E. M. W. Tillyard, *The Elizabethan World Picture,* and Marjorie Nicolson, *The Breaking of the Circle,* Chapter I.) Raphael's speech (V. 468-505) is Milton's fullest discussion of the order in Nature. The basic analogy used by Raphael (it is interesting that on this occasion Milton gives him the title, "winged Hierarch") is that of a tree or plant, in which we find in order the root (earth), the green stalk with sap (water), the leaves "more airy" (air), the bright flower breathing odorous spirit (fire). All things in the universe came from God and all aspire to return to Him:

> O Adam, one Almighty is, from whom
> All things proceed, and up to Him return.
>
> (V. 469-70)

Among the elements, earth aspires upward through water, air, to fire; in the plant, the root aspires through stalk, leaves, flowers, to fruit, "man's nourishment." So man should aspire to "turn all to spirit" and ascend to God in Heaven.

Why does Raphael go into this detail about order, degree, hierarchy, and why has he paused over the "faculty psychology" which shows the same order and interrelations in the faculties of man's soul? Milton is laying the basis for the Temptation, in which the subordination of lesser faculties to Reason will be of the utmost importance. Adam has learned—and the Angel has driven home to him—that Reason must be paramount. As God gave man Reason, it is man's duty to follow it. At the moment Adam wonders at Raphael's reiteration: "If ye be found obedient," since, in spite of Eve's dream, it never occurs to him that he could prove anything but obedient.

The Beginning of the Warfare in Heaven

Adam's question to the Angel serves as prelude to all the central portion of *Paradise Lost*. Since Milton was writing in the tradition of the classical epic, he began his story, not at the beginning but in *medias res*. Now that he is approaching the middle of the epic, he must go back, as Homer did in the *Odyssey* and Virgil in the *Aeneid*, and give his reader the antecedent action. Raphael proceeds to do so through the rest of Book V, and all of Books VI, VII, VIII, nearly one-third of the whole poem. We should notice a warning he gives Adam, that because of human limitations, man cannot fully understand Heaven or angelic nature, and therefore

> what surmounts the reach
> Of human sense, I shall delineate so,
> *By likening spiritual to corporeal forms*
> As may express them best.
>
> (V. 571-74)

Indeed, Raphael encounters difficulty at once, when he speaks of the "day" on which trouble began in Heaven, for in Heaven there is no "time" in our human sense. Using the term as we use it, Raphael tells of the occasion on which insurrection began in Heaven. Calling the angels before Him "in orbs of circuit inexpressive . . . orb within orb," (V. 582-600) God speaks:

> This day I have begot, whom I declare
> My only Son, and on this holy hill
> Him have anointed, whom ye now behold
> At my right hand. Your Head I Him appoint,
> And by myself have sworn to Him shall bow
> All knees in Heaven and shall confess Him Lord.
>
> (V. 603-608)

One group of modern critics has made this—usually called "the begot passage"—the most moot problem in *Paradise Lost*. If the word *begot* is taken in any of the senses familiar in modern dictionaries, it certainly indicates that on a particular occasion, well after the creation of many other angels, God "created" or "generated" His Son. So interpreted, these lines alone would be proof that the Christ of *Paradise Lost* is non-Trinitarian, since the Son was not coeval with the Father.

The passage does not seem to have troubled any commentator on *Paradise Lost* until after the publication of the *De Doctrina,* since the word "begot" can be interpreted in another way. It may be considered Milton's adaptation of Psalm II. 6-9:

> Yet I have set my king
> Upon my holy hill of Zion.
> I will tell of the decree:
> This day I have begotten thee.
> Ask of me, and I will give thee the nations for thine inheritance.

In the *Christian Doctrine* Milton quoted this Psalm which was one he had included in his Psalm-paraphrases in 1653. His version reads:

> but I saith hee
> Annointed have my King (though ye rebell)
> On Sion, my holi-hill. A firm decree
> I will declare: the Lord to me hath say'd
> Thou art my Son I have begotten thee
> This day: ask of me, and the grant is made;
> As thy possession I on thee bestow

Th' Heathen, and as thy conquest to be sway'd
Earth's utmost bounds.

Notice that in his paraphrase Milton used both "anointed" and
"begotten." "Anointed" and "exalted" are the words generally
used by translators of this Psalm. Christ was not "created" or
"generated" on that particular occasion, but "elevated" to His new
position as the "Head" of the angels. This was, in effect, His coro-
nation.

Satan's Rebellion

We have already heard part of this episode from Sin and Satan.
At God's announcement all the angels seemed pleased "but were
not all." Satan, "of the first if not the first Archangel,"

> could not bear
> Through pride, that sight, and thought himself impaired
> (i.e. demoted)
> Deep malice thence conceiving and disdain.
>
> (V. 664-66)

At midnight Satan wakened Beelzebub and bade him summon
"those myriads whom we lead." So complete was the confidence in
Satan that Beelzebub and others did not question his plan. Here is
another Council Scene, chronologically earlier than that in Book
II, Satan opening the meeting with an address in which he tries to
rouse in others the jealousy he himself feels at demotion under a
new administration. So persuasive is he, and so trusted, that he
meets opposition from only one of his followers. Abdiel "than
whom none with more zeal adores the Deity" opposes him on every
count:

> Among the faithless, faithful only he;
> Among innumerable false unmoved,

Unshaked, unseduced, unterrified,
His loyalty he kept, his love, his zeal.

(V. 896-900)

BOOK VI

The Warfare in Heaven

Book VI requires much less explication than the five that have preceded it. It is largely straightforward narration, involving almost no philosophical or theological problems. From the point of view of artistry, it has been frequently criticised, some think by Milton himself, when in the Prologue to Book IX he described himself as

Not sedulous by nature to indite
Wars, hitherto the only argument
Heroic deemed.

(IX. 27-29)

In the classical epic tradition, wars had been an inevitable part of the narrative pattern. Since Milton was dealing with only two human beings, he had no such opportunity as either Homer or Virgil to describe "heroes half divine" who could engage in single combat or warfare between opposing armies. His one possibility for introducing war lay in the rebellion of Satan and the fallen angels.

One problem Milton immediately encountered was really insuperable. Angels are indestructible and cannot possibly be killed. This at once removes any possibility of the suspense felt by readers of the *Iliad* or the *Odyssey* in the fate of the heroes, and reduces the drama of those scenes in which Satan is attacked in single combat. His first adversary is the faithful Abdiel, who brings down "a noble stroke" on "the proud crest" of Satan (VI. 189-97). More surprised than injured, Satan recoils ten steps, thrust down on bended knee. The second attack by Michael is more drastic (VI. 320-53). His great sword cut Satan in half, then entered ais right side:

> Then Satan first knew pain,
> And writhed him to and fro convolved—so sore
> The griding sword with discontinuous wound
> Passed through him.
>
> (VI. 327-30)

Blood—in the case of angels or gods, "nectareous humor" or "celestial ichor"—spurts forth, but even such a wound is of no lasting consequence:

> Yet soon he healed; for Spirits that live throughout
> Vital in every part—not, as frail man,
> In entrails, heart or head, liver or reins,
> Cannot but by annihilating die;
> Nor in their liquid texture mortal wound
> Receive.
>
> (VI. 344-49)

This scene Pope deftly and properly parodied in *The Rape of the Lock* when Sir Plume's scissors, snipping the lock of Belinda's hair, cut through the body of the little guardian Sylph. But do not be concerned, Pope implies with a shrug: "Celestial substance soon knits up again!" At the most, Satan and his antagonists in single combat prove little more than glorified prize fighters or adversaries in a fencing match.

Another criticism that has been brought against these scenes is the basic unfairness of the fact that the Supreme Commander, God, is both omniscient and omnipotent. The outcome is never in doubt. There may be suspense among Satan's troops but there should be none among God's. Not only does He know the end from the beginning, but, omnipotent as He is, His victory is certain. To be sure, Greek and Roman deities often matched their strength and craft behind their chosen warriors, but not even the pagan King of the Gods was omnipotent and omniscient as was Milton's Hebraic-Christian deity. From the beginning, Satan and the rebel angels are doomed to defeat.

This does not mean that there are not great passages in Book VI, none more majestic than the climactic scene in which Christ, at the bidding of God, goes forth in the "chariot of Paternal Deity," a still more glorious Ezekiel's chariot (VI. 748-73). This is a masterpiece of color and light, sound and darkness, coming to its artistic climax in the great line, "He on the wings of Seraph rode sublime." But the greatness of the passage comes not from Milton's narrative art but from his poetic genius. For the most part, the battles in Heaven seem fought by glorified tin soldiers.

The Cannon in Heaven

The device most frequently censured is Milton's introduction of cannon into the warfare in Heaven (VI. 465-630). Not only is the use of gunpowder anachronistic, critics say, but it is grotesque to have angels in Heaven shooting each other with modern cannons. To be sure, the unexpected weapons prove more effective than others, and give Satan's army a moment of victory, for at the first volley against the unsuspecting angels:

> down they fell
> By thousands. Angel or Archangel rolled
> The sooner for their arms. . . .
> Foul dissipation followed, and forced rout.
>
> (VI. 593-98)

Logically, Milton could as readily justify the discovery of gunpowder in Heaven as the finding jewels and precious stones in Hell. Satan, in response to Nisroch, pointed out that the originals of all

things are in Heaven (of which we have heard that Earth was a
little copy). There grow, he said,

> Deep under ground materials dark and crude,
> Of spirituous and fiery spume. . . .
> These in their dark nativity the deep
> Shall yield them, pregnant with internal flame.

(VI. 477-83)

Milton not only deliberately introduced cannon, but he had ob-
viously prepared himself for some of the technical details in the
scene by reading carefully military textbooks of his own period
which permitted him to describe the "engines" with a good deal of
verisimilitude:

> Which to our eyes discovered new and strange,
> A triple mounted row of pillars laid
> On wheels, for like to pillars most they seemed,
> Or hollowed bodies made of oak and fir,
> (With branches lopped, in woods or mountains felled),
> Brass, iron, stony mold, had not their mouths
> With hideous orifice gaped on us wide,
> Portending hollow truce. At each, behind,
> A Seraph stood, and in his hand a reed
> Stood waving, tipped with fire.

(VI. 571-80)

Only a few lines later, Milton went to the other extreme of warfare
and described the faithful angels tearing up the hills with all their
load of rocks, waters, wood, and—giants as they were—bearing
them aloft to cast at their enemies. At this moment, we almost feel
suspense, believing that the piling of Pelion on Ossa will win, where
modern cannons have not, until—again unfairly—the Supreme
Commander interferes in what almost proved a first-rate fight (VI.
663-75).

Why did Milton introduce such disparate scenes, unconvincing
and inartistic to modern readers? Many years ago Professor J. H.
Hanford made a suggestion which still has validity. ("Milton and
the Art of War," *M.P.* XVIII [1921] 232-66.) Milton is delib-

erately depicting every kind of warfare known in his time, from the earliest mythological legend of Titans and Giants who piled mountains on each other, down to the most "modern" warfare of his own day, when his contemporaries in the Civil War had fought with gunpowder and cannon. In between he pictured the single combat of swords and other weapons used by Homeric heroes, then by knights in medieval romance. In Book VI we have an epitome of the whole history of war. Back of it lies the lesson Milton implied in his sonnet: "For what can war but endless war still breed?"—the ineffectuality of all kinds of war for settling human differences. Professor Hanford said: (I quote not from his original article but from a shortened version in the *Milton Handbook,* p. 206)

> He intends to suggest that the last end of war is like its beginning—bestial, anarchic, inconclusive. The utmost refinements of human slaughter are but a mask of chaos and can only end in a disruption of the orderly civilization of which they are the products. The significance of the account is definitely indicated at the close of the book (lines 695 ff.) when the Almighty, beholding the confusion, declares that

> War wearied hath performed what war can do,
> And to disordered rage let loose the reins,
> With mountains as with weapons armed; which makes
> Wild work in Heaven and dangerous to the main.

I shall add a reminiscence from my own experience, since it taught me a lesson about Book VI of *Paradise Lost.* Shortly after the end of the First World War I was teaching a class of what we called "War Specials" at the University of Minnesota. There was no "G.I. Bill" after that War to draw to universities the influx of veterans who swarmed to educational institutions after World War II, but certain relaxations of regulations governing admission attracted a number. My survey course included *Paradise Lost.* When I made the usual criticisms of Book VI, I was surprised and pleased to receive an unsolicited "term paper" from one of the "War Specials," in which he took sharp exception to what I had said and reported his own reactions on first reading *Paradise Lost,* after he had returned from active service in Europe. The First World War, we must remember, was very different from the Second, fought, not in the air, but on sea and land. My student said that he had read widely in the contemporary war-literature that was pouring from the press, trying to find some expression in prose or poetry for what he had felt, but found nothing until he came to Book VI of *Paradise Lost.* There he found scenes which recalled those he had experienced and others he had imagined at night in his dugout, warfare on a vast scale, with two great armies drawn up on opposing fields, each wondering but never sure what Satanic new engine of destruction might be used against them the next day. So far as the cannon were concerned, he felt them as justified as the mountains of the Titans or the swords of Abdiel and Michael: in war, any means of destruction, old or new, might be used indiscriminately. And he made another point I have not forgotten: Milton was a great poet of sound, and in my veteran's ears, the sound of Satan's cannon reverberated as had the deadly sound of German artillery.

With no personal experience of warfare during either World War I or II I cannot judge my veteran's response to Book VI, but I have never forgotten it, and I report for another generation, which has known a very different kind of war, the defense of my "War Special" for Milton's description of the war in Heaven.

BOOK VII

With the exception of a very few passages, Book VII, like the preceding one, requires little explication. Particularly from lines 235 ff., it is largely an amplification of the Creation in Genesis, which Milton follows reverently, introducing every detail given in the Bible, yet letting his imagination and his wide reading in Scriptural exegesis add to the brief original details, even contemporary allusions to his own time.

The Prologue

In addition to the general prologue in Book I, we have found the Prologue to Light at the beginning of Book III, when Milton turned from Hell to Heaven, and the Satanic Prologue to Light in reverse in Book IV, in which we were led to Earth. There we have remained, since we did not witness the war in Heaven but merely heard it from Raphael's lips, as we shall hear of the Creation. Milton has two reasons for using a Prologue in Book VII: he calls upon Urania to descend from Heaven, where the Creation begins, to Earth, which is about to be created. A still more obvious use for the Prologue Milton himself mentions in line 21: "Half yet remains unsung." We are at midpoint of the epic, which in the later edition Milton divided into twelve instead of the original ten books. Milton addresses a classical Muse, but as always in the prologues, the Christian transcends the pagan. "The meaning, not the name, I call," he says (line 507). His invocation was not actually to one of "the Muses nine"; his guardian spirit did not dwell on Olympus but was "Heavenly born":

> Before the hills appeared or fountains flowed
> Thou with eternal Wisdom didst converse,
> Wisdom thy sister, and with her didst play
> In presence of the Almighty Father, pleased
> With thy celestial song.
>
> (VII. 7-12)

"Standing on earth, not rapt above the pole," the poet feels that "more safe I sing, with mortal voice," since his chief subject is now Man, rather than God, his locale, Earth. As usual in the prologues, Milton introduces a personal *apologia,* showing his awareness of the difficulty he faces in attempting to write a great Christian epic. There is only passing allusion to his blindness, in the word "darkness." Primarily he is concerned with the question whether an age as degenerate as the one in which he is living can understand or appreciate a Christian epic. These lines, we know, were written after the Restoration when Milton and his party found themselves in a parlous state:

> though fallen on evil days,
> On evil days though fallen, and evil tongues;
> In darkness and with dangers compassed round
> And solitude.
>
> (VII. 25-28)

The temper of the times had changed since Milton began to write *Paradise Lost.* The Cavaliers had other interests than religious epic poetry. Theirs, in Milton's ears, was "the barbarous dissonance of Bacchus and his revellers." As so often in the past, Milton remembers the recurrent motif of Orpheus, father of poetry, and his tragic death at the hands of the bacchantes, "nor could the Muse herself defend her son." Yet in spite of blindness, in spite of ignominy, Milton will finish the work on which his mind has been set so long, the work he had felt himself "called" to write in youth. The most he can hope in this dissolute Restoration period—to Milton an age of Belial—is that the work may find "fit audience, though few."

The Creation

In answer to a question from Adam, Raphael goes on to describe the creation of a new World, beginning with the speech in which God announced to the angels his intention of creating

> Another World, out of one man, a race
> Of men innumerable, there to dwell,
> Not here, till by degrees of merit raised
> They open to themselves at length the way
> Up hither, under long obedience tried,
> And Earth be changed to Heaven, and Heaven to Earth.
>
> (VII. 155-60)

You will notice at once that it is not, as in Genesis, God who creates the world, but Christ. I do not intend to enter into the controversy over lines 168-73, precipitated by Denis Saurat's *Milton: Man and Thinker,* in which the so-called "retraction" of God became the central passage in *Paradise Lost.* (An advanced student should read Saurat's theory, together with some of the commentators, *pro* and *con,* discussed by Robert Adams in *Ikon.* The most recent reply is by R. J. Zwi Werblowski, *Journal of the Warburg and Courtauld Institute* XVIII [1935] 90-113.) For our present purposes, it is sufficient to see that the First Person remains on His throne, while Christ, the "efficient Might," goes forth on the mission of Creation, as in Book X, it is Christ, not God, who descends to the Garden of Eden to pass judgment upon Adam and Eve.

As we read the magnificent scene (VII. 192-209) in which Christ sets out in his chariot to create a World, surrounded by Cherubim, Seraphim, Potentates, Thrones and Virtues, our memories may well go back to the parallel scene in Book II in which Satan set out on his lonely voyage to destroy a World. We remember the jarring sounds of the gates of Hell, grating harsh thunder, and feel the contrast as

> Heaven opened wide
> Her everlasting gates, harmonious sound
> On golden hinges moving, to let forth
> The King of Glory, in His powerful Word
> And Spirit, coming to create new worlds.
>
> (VII. 205-209)

Like Satan, but from a very different vantage point, Christ and the angels look out upon the vast reaches of Chaos:

> On Heavenly ground they stood, and from the shore
> They viewed the vast immeasurable abyss,
> Outrageous as a sea, dark, wasteful, wild,
> Up from the bottom turned by furious winds
> And surging waves.
>
> (VII. 210-214)

Satan made confusion worse confounded. Christ brings order out of Chaos. For the actual process of Creation, Milton uses the figure of the golden compasses. Much has been written of the interest in the compass-figure during the seventeenth century, largely because of Donne's "Valediction: Forbidding Mourning," in which the two legs of the compass, the fixed foot and the moving, reflect the two lovers. Since the circle was the most universal figure in this period, the compass which described the circle could be used symbolically. The figure was much older than Donne's use of it. Milton was not thinking of its literary history when he used it to describe the Creation but rather of the same chapter of Proverbs that was in his mind in the Prologue—the words of Wisdom:

> When he established the heavens, I was there,
> When he set a circle upon the face of the deep,
> When he made firm the skies above. . . ,
> Then I was by him.

So Milton's Christ, as the angels stayed the "fervid wheels" of the chariot at the brink of Chaos:

> In His hand
> [Christ] took the golden compasses, prepared
> In God's eternal store, to circumscribe
> This universe of all created things.
> One foot he centered and the other turned
> Round through the dark profundity obscure,
> And said: 'Thus far extend, thus far thy bounds,
> This be thy just circumference, O World!'
>
> (VII. 224-31)

Milton's Expansion of Genesis

The account of each day's work opens with the Scriptural words, largely following the King James' Version, quoted as closely as metrical demands permitted. There is hardly a phrase in Genesis I. 1-31 which is not used in Milton's account. Beginning with the Third Day, however, Milton's description begins to be much longer than the original, as his imagination adds details to the austerely limited account in Genesis. Without attempting to analyze each section, I will suggest three different kinds of amplification Milton used, with an example or two of each:

The first kind of development appears in the World of the Third Day. Genesis had said merely: "And God said, Let the waters under the heaven be gathered together unto one place, and let the dry land appear: and it was so." Milton has added specific details:

> Immediately the mountains huge appear
> Emergent, and their broad bare backs upheave
> Into the clouds; their tops ascend the sky.
>
> (VII. 284-86)

Here Milton reflects a theological position about which Church Fathers were divided for many years: were mountains original with earth, or did they appear later in history, primarily as a result of the Flood? Mountains are not mentioned in the Bible until Noah's ark rested upon Mount Ararat. I shall not labor the passage to attempt to prove that Milton was taking a conscious part in a matter of theological disputation, since the lines closely parallel a similar scene in *The Divine Weekes and Workes* of Du Bartas, as translated by Joshua Sylvester, one of Milton's undoubted sources.

In the same passage, Milton expresses an opinion upon another issue which, while never as moot as the problem of the origin of mountains, also had had a long history:

> So high as heaved the tumid hills, so low
> Down sunk a hollow bottom broad and deep,
> Capacious bed of waters.

> (VII. 288-90)

Many men had believed, as Milton's contemporary, Godfrey Goodman, put it, "that the highest mountains upon earth, carrie some kind of proportion to the lowest bottome at Sea . . . that God might observe some kind of proportion." Here is the persistent idea that the Great Geometer laid out the World with line and measure, with proportion, symmetry, correspondence in all the parts. (The background of these passages is discussed in Marjorie Nicolson, *Mountain Gloom and Mountain Glory,* Chapter II.) Whatever the theological position suggested, Milton did not hesitate to add to Genesis details long discussed by classical and Christian writers.

A second kind of addition to the Biblical original is found in the Work of the Fourth Day. After God said, "Let there be Light," follows the account of the creation of sun and moon. Milton expands the original by many lines, adding a number of details about sun and moon, notably sections drawn from discoveries of Galileo, as in this passage:

> Hither, as to their fountains, other stars
> Repairing in their golden urns draw light,
> And hence the morning planet gilds her horns.

> (VII. 364-66)

This is Galileo's discovery of the phases of Venus. A few lines later we find another Galilean observation; that the moon shines not by its own light, but by light borrowed from the sun:

> less bright the moon,
> But opposite in levelled west, was set,
> His mirror, with full face borrowing her light
> From him; for other light she needed none.
>
> (VII. 375-78)

Milton's most beautiful adaptation of Galilean astronomy occurs toward the end of the Creation scene. When Christ returns to Heaven after creating the World, He and the angels return in triumph over Galileo's Milky Way:

> He through Heaven,
> That opened wide her blazing portals, led
> To God's eternal house direct the way—
> A broad and ample road whose dust is gold
> And pavement stars, as stars to thee appear
> Seen in the galaxy, that Milky Way
> Which nightly as a circling zone thou seest,
> Powdered with stars.
>
> (VII. 574-81)

The third type of expansion is more subtle and leads us back to that "order" and "degree" found everywhere in the universe, then involves another basic attitude that has not been discussed. On the First Day one element is paramount: light. In the account of the Third, Fourth and Fifth Days, we are conscious of the four elements. On the Third Day, our attention is called to Earth and Water, as these two elements are separated, then specifically to Earth, as it brought forth grass, then herbs and trees, then again to the interaction of Earth and Water, as the dewy mist rises from Earth to Water. On the Fifth Day we are most conscious of Air, as the birds in caves and fens and shores begin to hatch their eggs, and as bird after bird rises, "soaring the air sublime."

The concept of degree and the great chain of being is charm-

ingly developed through the successive scenes, so that we seem
again and again to rise from lower to higher. On the Third Day, our
imaginations rise from "tender grass" through "herbs of every
leaf," through "clustering vine" and shrubs, until we reach the
"stately trees" and the high woods. On the Fifth Day we begin with
life in the sea, where "fry innumerable swarms and shoals of fish,"
rise from smaller fish through seals and dolphins to "Leviathan,
hugest of living creatures." In the same way, our imaginations soar
from birds hatching in caves to birds on the wing, from smaller birds
to the eagle. On the Sixth Day we hear of the creation of animals,
from the "innumerable living creatures" in the fertile womb of
earth, to larger and larger beasts, to Behemoth, which is to ani-
mals as Leviathan to swimming creatures.

The climax of "order" in Creation occurs on the Sixth Day, with
the creation of Man. We have risen in the scale of being, from the
emergence of earth, through various degrees of life—vegetable,
animal, but

> There wanted yet the master-work, the end
> Of all yet done—a creature who, not prone
> And brute as other creatures, but endued
> With sanctity of Reason, might erect
> His stature and upright with front serene
> Govern the rest, self-knowing and from thence
> Magnanimous, to correspond with Heaven.
>
> (VII. 505-11)

Man is created last of all God's works on Earth, only a little lower
than the angels which, in the great Hierarchy, stand next to God
Himself in Heaven.

Still more subtle and beautiful is the impression given by Book
VII that Milton felt these scenes in which the World appears as a
great cosmic dance. There is motion everywhere, and a pervasive
sense of the happiness and gladness of all parts of Nature as they
emerge from Chaos.

The waters "hasted with glad percipitance," wave rolls after
wave, rivers and streams find their places, all following their ap-

pointed motions. The tender grass covers the earth with pleasant green, the spring flowers "make gay," the bosom of earth:

> last
> Rose, as in dance, the stately trees, and spread
> Their branches hung with copious fruit, or gemmed
> Their blossoms . . .

(VII. 232-35)

As the sun is created, "the Pleiades before him danced."

Throughout the scene of creation of life in the ocean, movement is incessant, as the fish glide under the waters, graze the sea-weed, stray through groves of coral, while the seals and the dolphins play on the surface of the water. Leviathan, sleeping or swimming, "seems a moving land." Then birds are everywhere, walking, wading, rising, soaring, flying. Animals first "half appear," then rise: the "tawny lion pawing to get free"; "the swift stag bore up his branching head": Behemoth "upheaved his vastness." The motion of all other living creatures comes to a climax the moment before the creation of man:

> Now Heaven in all her glory shone and rolled
> Her motions as the great First Mover's hand
> First wheeled their course: Earth, in her rich attire
> Consummate, lovely smiled; air, water, earth,
> By fowl, fish, beast was flown, was swum, was walked.

(VII. 499-503)

Implied in the Creation scenes is a great cosmic dance of the sort described by Sir John Davies in *Orchestra*. All is in motion, yet all is ordered by the harmony of the universe, in which each living thing—indeed, inanimate Nature as well—has its own part, its own step to make the pattern of the universal dance. All is the harmony which pervaded Nature before the Fall, rising to its climax in the music Adam heard as he emerged into life:

> the sound
> Symphonious of ten thousand harps that tuned
> Angelic harmonies: the earth, the air

Resounded (thou rememberest, for thou heardest);
The Heavens and all the constellations rung:
The planets in their studious listening stood,
While the great pomp ascended jubilant.
"Open, ye Heavens, your living doors! Let in
The great Creator, from His work returned
Magnificent, His Six Days' Work, a World!"

(VII. 557-68)

On the Seventh Day angels and created Nature unite, accompanied by harp, dulcimer, pipe, "all organs of sweet stop," intermixed with "voice, choral or unison" (VII. 594-98). This great Hallelujah-chorus is Milton's most magnificent Psalm-paraphrase. He has not limited himself to one Psalm, but combines phrases from many with others from Revelation. Our ears have already caught echoes of Psalm XXIV, "Lift up your heads, O ye gates." We remember the Psalm of David, XIV, "The Heavens declare the glory of God," and other Psalms of thanksgiving, such as Psalm IX, "I will show forth all thy marvellous works," and the great scene in Revelation, IV. 6, the "clear Hyaline, the glassy sea" before the throne of God. We hear the angels sing of the exalted position of Man in Psalm VIII: "Thou hast made him but a little lower than God," with the climactic verse, "O Jehovah, our Lord, how excellent is thy name in all the earth!"

So sung they, and the empyrean rang
With hallelujahs: thus was Sabbath kept.

BOOK VIII

The Dialogue on Astronomy

We have seen on various occasions that Milton's imagination, like that of nearly all intelligent men in the seventeenth century, had been stirred by the "new Philosophy" that had "called all in doubt" to John Donne in 1611, the year after Galileo announced his first celestial observations in the *Sidereus Nuncius*. Milton was still an infant at that time. Men of his generation never experienced the shock Donne felt as a new philosophy seemed to destroy the old established nature of the universe. Milton grew up with a generation intellectually aware of the discoveries of such men as Galileo and Kepler, and of the philosophical theories of Bruno, whether they accepted them or not. The Ptolemaic world-scheme still remained the most familiar and describable one. The world-scheme of Milton's universe, in so far as it can be mapped and charted, is Ptolemaic, yet we have found various references to Galileo, none more interesting than the introduction of his observations into the scenes of Creation. We have also become aware of the extent to which a new conception of indefinite space in *Paradise Lost* often shatters the boundaries of a finite Ptolemaic universe.

For this, his longest passage on astronomy, Milton used certain specific sources. (See Grant McColley, "Milton's Dialogue on Astronomy," *P.M.L.A.* LII [1937] 728-63). Undoubtedly in part because the materials he was treating led into technicalities, and in his blindness he needed some check for his memory; in part because he wished to present opposed points of view as they were actually presented in his time, Adam's speeches in the dialogue are largely based upon works of John Wilkins, a scientist and popularizer of science, a member of a group at Oxford which assisted in the development of the Royal Society. Wilkins was a "modern," a proponent of the "new philosophy." Raphael's part in the dialogue (though with some variations) follows Alexander Ross, a crusted diehard "tawny port" conservative, who devoted most of his life to opposing the "new" and "modern" in various fields of thought. In astronomy Ross was an adherent of Ptolemy, Wilkins of Copernicus and Galileo.

The dialogue on astronomy takes us back in memory to the debate between Comus and the Lady: "the appeal to Nature for standards." We remember the general problem: What does Nature teach? Is Nature superabundant, prolific, pouring her bounties forth with lavish hand, as Comus said, or is she a model of temperance, restraint, proportion, as she was to the Lady? The argument of Book VIII is basically the same, though the evidence is different. Comus had drawn his illustrations from the spawn in the sea, the profusion of gems and ore in Nature's loins; there was only a passing reference to the stars and none to astronomy as such. The "new Philosophy" had not caught young Milton's imagination as it was to do in more mature years. Looking up at night to the heavens, Adam's mind has been stirred by the vast expanses, the profusion of "stars that seem to roll Spaces incomprehensible." (VIII. 19-20) How could Nature, "wise and frugal," have committed such disproportion; why did her "superfluous hand" create so many heavenly bodies? If the stars were only to give light to man, was such profusion necessary? (VIII. 25-29) There is a certain ironic charm in the fact that the Angel gives Adam so much astronomical information—indeed, introducing ideas hardly necessary for his argument, developing basic attitudes of Copernican-Galilean astronomy, even if only to refute it, or at least deny its ultimate importance. He finds no fault with Adam's interest in the subject:

> To ask or search I blame thee not; for Heaven
> Is as the Book of God before thee set

Wherein to read His wondrous works.

(VIII. 66-69)

"The Book of God's Words"—the Bible—and "The Book of God's Works"—created Nature—these were persistently reiterated phrases in the seventeenth century, familiar in such different mouths as those of Francis Bacon and Sir Thomas Browne, who agreed that there was and should be no conflict between the teaching of the two Books. Knowledge of one should enhance knowledge of the other. The tree, the fruit of which Adam and Eve had been forbidden to eat, was not the "tree of knowledge" *per se,* but the "knowledge of good and evil,"—a quite different matter. Yet although Raphael makes clear that man should desire knowledge, he stresses "knowledge within bounds." Man need not rack his brains in attempts to determine the truth or falsity of the Copernican hypothesis. Whether Heaven or Earth moves is not of importance for man. One of the most amusing aspects of the dialogue is that Raphael, even though he is an Angel, is not quite sure of himself when it comes to astronomical hypotheses, introducing certain parts of the theory with the phrase, "What if?" What if the sun is center to the universe, what if the moon does not shine by its own light—what if? (VIII. 132-35; 140-44.) Raphael's final lesson on the matter is clear:

> Solicit not thy thoughts with matters hid:
> Leave them to God. Him serve and fear. . . .
> Be lowly wise;
> Think only what concerns thee and thy being.
> Dream not of other worlds . . .

(VIII. 167-75)

"Dream not of other worlds," indeed—and here is part of the ironic charm of the passage. One of the most fascinating of all possibilities raised by the "new astronomy" in seventeenth-century minds—as in our own—was that of the inhabitability of the moon or planets. Milton had briefly mentioned the idea during the voyage of Satan. Raphael develops the idea in more detail (VIII.

144-52). There was no reason that Adam should have known any-
thing about such a possibility. If in the future he "dreamed" of in-
terplanetary flight, it would have been entirely the fault of Raphael
for putting such a conception into his mind.

One passage I have omitted has a different kind of charm. For
the first time since the arrival of the Angel, Eve left the gentlemen
alone and went to look at her flowers. She remained with Raphael
and Adam throughout the long accounts of Books V, VI, VII, not
speaking, to be sure, and just a little apart, "where she sat retired
in sight." Now, seeing Adam "in studious thoughts abstruse," she
withdraws. Is this another reminder that she was Adam's inferior?
To some extent, of course, though Milton is also sending Eve off-
stage before he tells Raphael of his great love for her, as he could
hardly have done in her presence. Let the modern feminist—or
anti-feminist—notice carefully just what Milton said:

> Yet went she not as not with such discourse
> Delighted, or not capable her ear
> Of what was high.
>
> (VIII. 48-50)

After all, there was very little to talk about in Eden, particularly by
two people who were together constantly. Eve realized that Adam
would have great pleasure in telling her what the Angel had said,
and also that he would make these astronomical technicalities just
a little easier—but let Milton speak:

>   such pleasure she reserved,
> Adam relating, she sole auditress,
> Her husband the relater she preferred
> Before the Angel, and of him to ask
> Chose rather; he, she knew, would intermix
> Grateful digressions and solve high dispute
> With conjugal caresses—from his lip
> Not words alone pleased her.
>
> (VIII. 51-57)

Eve was a good wife—and a very womanly woman.

Adam's Memory of His Creation

So far the Angel has been the chief speaker, ever since his arrival in Eden. In the remainder of the book, Adam is able to tell Raphael about some matters he has not known at firsthand, since Raphael had been on a mission for God during the period of the Creation. (VIII. 227-48) We have already heard Eve's recollection of her emergence into life; now we have Adam's. Like Sin, though with very different connotation, Adam came into the world full-grown. "As new-waked from soundest sleep," he had found himself on flowering herbs and grass, gazing upward at the sky. From a prone position, he sprang upright—again Milton emphasizes the idea that man, alone among animals, is erect. We feel the pleasure of watching a child in the scene in which Adam discovers his body, now walking, now running, in the sheer joy of using his limbs. He discovers the gift of reason and his ability to recognize and name the animals. In this passage Milton uses the same technique as in the scenes of Creation in Book VII, expanding three passages in Genesis by adding various details, using such devices as Adam's dream (VIII. 287-309), then of the Heavenly Guide (VIII. 295 ff). It is interesting that in this scene Milton does not expressly indicate which Person of the Trinity it was that appeared to Adam. In the creation and Judgment scenes, it is Christ as the "effective Might" of God, but in the dialogue in which Adam asks for a helpmate, at least one speech, as we shall see, should refer not to the Second but to the First Person of the Trinity.

Modern critics frequently compare Milton's Adam in his Garden with another possible Adam in "The Garden" of Andrew Marvell, Milton's contemporary in poetry, his associate and successor in the post of Latin Secretary. If Marvell's is a Garden of Eden, and if his character who speaks in the first person is Adam, the two poets stand at opposite poles in theological interpretation on one

point. Marvell's "Adam" is more than content with his solitary life
in the garden. Indeed, some interpreters go so far as to say that
Marvell's Adam is androgynous—that is, combining within himself
both male and female. Milton follows the much more customary
interpretation of Genesis, when his Adam not long after his own
creation, asks God to make him a mate. Milton may be implying
the lonely state of Adam as early as the line, "Pensive I sat me
down," (VIII. 287) but begins to develop it after the scene in
which Adam names the animals, who came before him "two by
two." Among them, "I found not what methought I wanted still,"
even though Adam is not sure just what he wanted. In the later
dialogue with his Heavenly Guide, he has clarified his thinking, so
that the "want" emerges clearly:

> Thou hast provided all things. But with me
> I see not who partakes. In solitude
> What happiness? Who can enjoy alone,
> Or, all enjoying, what contentment find?
>
> (VIII. 363-66)

In this scene, as so often in Milton, two debaters engage in logical
disputation. The Almighty tries out his new pupil to find how able
he is in argument:

> What think'st thou then of me, and this my state?
> Seem I to thee sufficiently possessed
> Of happiness, or not, who am alone
> From all eternity; for none I know
> Second to me or like, equal much less?
>
> (VIII. 403-407)

Here are lines which might well give pause to a Trinitarian, but
let us add a passage from Adam's reply:

> Thou in Thyself art perfect, and in Thee
> Is no deficience found . . . No need that Thou
> Shouldst propagate, already infinite,
> And through all numbers absolute, though one.
>
> (VIII. 415-21)

Whatever Trinitarians or non-Trinitarians wish to make of the lines, it is no irreverence to say that Milton has suddenly shifted Gods, and that Adam, without knowing it, is replying not to an Hebraic or a Christian deity but to Aristotle. These two speeches are almost a paraphrase of a passage is the *Eudemian Ethics* of Aristotle: (VII. 1244b-1245b).

> One who is self-sufficient can have no need of the services of others, nor of their affection, nor of social life, since he is capable of living alone. This is especially evident in the case of God. Clearly, since he is in need of nothing, God cannot have need of friends, nor will he have any.

(For further discussion of Milton's passage and the Aristotelian original, see Arthur O. Lovejoy, *The Great Chain of Being,* Chapter II.) The chief dramatic function of the discussion between the Almighty and Adam is to emphasize a basic distinction between Infinite God and finite man—man's need for companionship and for fulfilling the command laid upon him: "Be fruitful and multiply and replenish the earth." It leads Milton to an account of the creation of Eve.

The Creation of Eve

The latter section of Book VIII offers the finest expression of Milton's conception of "wedded love." Adam's loneliness in Paradise has been augmented by the procession of living creatures that pass before him in pairs to be named. As they were created, all these, beasts, birds, fish, are his inferiors; among them he can find no companionship:

> Among unequals what society
> Can sort, what harmony or true delight,
> Which must be mutual, in proportion due,
> Given or received? . . .

> Of fellowship I speak
> Such as I seek, fit to participate
> All rational delight, wherein the brute
> Cannot be human consort.

(VIII. 383-91)

Mutual harmony, fellowship, "collateral love and dearest amity," —these are the essentials of true marriage. The Almighty, well satisfied by Adam's argument, agrees with his desire for "fit help; thy other self," (VIII. 450), phrases in which Milton combines the Biblical term for wife, "helpmeet" with the classical for an ideal friend, "alter ego."

Adam remembers the creation of Eve, since although the Creator had closed his eyes, He "open left the cell of Fancy, my internal sight." (VIII. 460-61) In a trance, Adam watches Eve's creation from his rib, and sees her as she first appears:

> Man-like but different sex, so lovely fair
> That what seemed fair in all the world seemed now
> Mean, or in her summed up, in her contained. . . .
> She disappeared and left me dark; I waked
> To find her, or for ever to deplore
> Her loss.

(VIII. 470-80)

In the last lines we catch echoes of Milton's sonnet to his dead wife.

There are more lyrical love-poems but there are few higher tributes to woman in English poetry than Adam's to Raphael, attempting to describe his feelings toward Eve:

> Yet when I approach
> Her loveliness, so absolute she seems
> And in herself complete, so high to know
> Her own, that what she wills to do or say
> Seems wisest, virtuousest, discreetest, best.
> All higher knowledge in her presence falls
> Degraded; wisdom in discourse with her
> Loses discountenanced, and like folly shows;
> Authority and reason on her wait,

As one intended first, not after made
Occasionally; and, to consummate all,
Greatness of mind and nobleness their seat
Build in her loveliest and create an awe
About her, as a guard angelic placed.

(VIII. 546-59)

Adam has gone so far in his adulation that Raphael warns him against going too far. Milton is carefully preparing the way for the Temptation scene. Adam must remember, Raphael warns, his two-fold responsibility for Eve and for himself; he must learn the difference between true love and passion: "In loving thou dost well, in passion not." The Angel concludes his warning with lines in which Milton adapts the Neoplatonic scale of love, rising from profane to sacred, a conception used by many Renaissance poets from Dante to Spenser:

Love refines
The thoughts, and heart enlarges—hath his seat
In Reason, and is judicious—is the scale
By which to Heavenly Love thou mayst ascend.

(VIII. 589-72)

As the long account of Raphael began with Adam's question whether angels could eat and drink so it ends with another question of Adam's about the corporeity of angels: whether the heavenly spirits love, in the sense in which man uses that word, and how they express their love:

To whom the Angel, with a smile that glowed
Celestial rosy-red, Love's proper hue
Answered: "Let it suffice thee that thou knowest
Us happy, and without love no happiness.
Whatever pure thou in the body enjoyest
(And pure thou wert created) we enjoy
In eminence, and obstacle find none
Of membrane, joint or limb—exclusive bars.
Easier than air with air, if Spirits embrace

Total they mix, union of pure with pure
Desiring. . . .

(VIII. 618-628)

Milton's angelology was, indeed, far removed from that of the more austere Fathers. Adam's last question—which literally brought blushes to an Angel's cheek—was not the reason for Raphael's departure—though he might well have wondered what else that innocent child of Nature might ask! Raphael leaves with one final admonition, pointing forward to the Temptation scene:

Be strong, live happy, and love—but first of all
Him whom to love is to obey, and keep
His great command; take heed lest passion sway
Thy judgment to do aught which else free-will
Would not admit; thine and of all thy sons
The weal or woe in thee is placed: beware.

(VIII. 633-38)

BOOK IX

Prologue

This Prologue differs from the earlier ones in several ways. It is not an invocation to a Muse (though the Celestial Patroness is mentioned in lines 20-24 and 46-47). It does not become a prayer to the Holy Spirit, nor does Milton refer to his blindness, though he suggests other limitations. The primary function of the Prologue is to change the tone from that of the leisurely books in which Adam and the "sociable Angel" talked so easily together in the idyllic days before sin entered the Garden of Eden to the mood of the four final books. "I now must change Those notes to tragic." In addition, the Prologue serves as Milton's defense for the kind of poetry he is attempting: a *Christian* epic, "not less but more heroic," he insists, than the three great classical epics (IX. 13-19). His account of his "long choosing and beginning late" and his *apologia* for not being "sedulous by Nature to indite wars" or to deal with the trappings of chivalric romance has been analyzed earlier in "The Development of Paradise Lost," and in the discussion of the warfare in Heaven, and need not detain us here.

The Return of Satan

Except for the account of the earlier warfare in Heaven, we have heard nothing of Satan since we saw him "squat like a toad" at Eve's ear, then springing up to face Gabriel and the other angels. Having learned a lesson about the angelic guards who now surround Eden, he has ventured out only at night. "The space of seven continued nights he rode with darkness" (IX. 63-64) considering closely all the animals, trying to decide which one would suit his purposes, settling finally upon the serpent. Again, as in Book IV, we are alone with him as he reveals himself in soliloquy. There is momentary regret for the Heaven he has lost, a faint flickering of the former angelic conscience at the idea of destroying the Paradise on earth. But the "fixed will" and "obdurate Pride" have hardened still more. Wherever Satan is, *there* is Hell:

> the more I see
> Pleasures about me, so much more I feel
> Torment within me, as from the hateful siege
> Of contraries; all good to me becomes
> Bane, and in Heaven much worse would be my state.
>
> (IX. 118-23)

Through Satan's lips, Milton utters the theory of tragedy he shared with his classical predecessors and Elizabethan near-contemporaries, the tragic irony of a degeneration such as Satan's:

> O, foul descent! that I who erst contended
> With gods to sit the highest, am now constrained
> Into a beast, and mixed with bestial slime,
> This essence to incarnate and imbrute
> That to the height of deity aspired!
> But what will not ambition and revenge
> Descend to? who aspires must down as low
> As high he soared.
>
> (IX. 163-70)

Descent from his once grand nature and stature to the baseness he has deliberately chosen is emphasized by the figures of speech in the passage. "Wrapped in mist" he has glided obscure, and pried in bush and brake to find the serpent. As the soliloquy ends, Milton comments:

> Like a black mist low-creeping, he held on
> His midnight search.
>
> (IX. 180-81)

At last, finding the serpent sleeping, "in at his mouth The Devil entered."

The Separation of Adam and Eve

The next step, in preparation for the Temptation, comes in the morning when Eve suggests to Adam that they divide their labors, and work in different parts of the Garden. She justifies her proposal on the ground that the luxuriant Garden is growing beyond them. On the surface, her suggestion is reasonable enough, but those commentators who read sin into Eve even before the Fall, find here both subtlety and slyness, and also call attention to the fact that in her next speech she openly acknowledges that she overheard (perhaps by deliberate eavesdropping) the parting words of Raphael to Adam. (IX. 275-78) Adam demurs, although he does not do so strongly. Later he will look back and realize that at this moment he should have taken a firmer stand. Eve's feelings are hurt at his suggestion that she may not be strong enough to stand alone, "as one who loves and some unkindness meets." Critics who find her over-subtle read her reply to Adam (IX. 273-89) as in part the kind of casuistry Satan will use in her Temptation, the result of Eve's arrogance and self-assuredness.

It is all very well for us, with celestial hindsight, to say what Adam should have done at this point. Commentators who find his chief fault in the Temptation "uxuriousness" do not seem to see that in this scene Adam is dealing less with a wife than with a somewhat rebellious adolescent daughter. His is an experience only too familiar to every parent and teacher. Eve is experiencing "growing-up pains." Like most young people, she resents the suggestion that she needs protection, that she is not capable of standing on her own feet, of doing what she should. "And what is faith, love, virtue, unassayed alone?" It is the persistent cry of adolescence: "How can I ever grow up if you won't let me?" Adam is entirely wrong in yielding to her insistence, but he is doing and saying what parents and teachers have said for generations:

> Go; for thy stay, not free, absents thee more.
> Go in thy native innocence, rely
> On what thou hast of virtue; summon all,
> For God toward thee hath done His part; do thine."
> (IX. 372-75)

Before leaving the scene, however, let us read with care the words in which Adam, remembering the lessons of the Angel, returns again to the "faculty psychology," since this is a passage we should remember when we come to the actual Temptation":

> Within himself
> The danger lies, yet lies within his power:

Against his Will he can receive no harm.
But God left free the Will, for what obeys
Reason is free, and Reason He made right,
But bid her well beware, and still erect,
Lest by some fair-appearing good surprised,
She dictate false and misinform the Will
To do what God expressly hath forbid.

(IX. 348-56)

Here, in little, is the "psychology" of one part of the Temptation.

The Temptation of Eve

As Eve leaves her husband, we can see that Milton is deliberately stressing the idyllic qualities of both Eve (IX. 385-96; 424-33) and the Garden (IX. 434-54) because the idyl is almost over. Eve was never lovelier than when we see her for the last time in her innocence.

Compared to Adam's, Eve's Temptation and Fall are so complex that we must watch each step closely. Satan realizes that he has been fortunate to find her alone, without Adam, who would have proved a "foe not informidable." He appears before Eve in all the splendor a prelapsarian serpent might have possessed, not prone on the ground, but rising in towering folds; with burnished neck and eyes like carbuncles, "pleasing was his shape and lovely." Eve, of course, has no reason to fear any of the animals. She is amazed but not frightened to find that this particular animal has the power of speech, but has no reason to doubt his circumstantial account of eating fruit which conferred on him the power of reason and of speech.

The first step in Satan's temptation of Eve is flattery. He calls her by titles, "sovereign Mistress"; "Empress of this fair world, resplendent Eve," a lofty language unfamiliar to her. He assures her that all living things "adore" her celestial beauty, and gaze at her "with ravishment" from afar. (IX. 539-41) Such beauty, he flatters, deserves universal admiration; it should not be wasted, as it is, upon beasts and the one man who alone is privileged to see her. The second step is hypocrisy, a sin over which Milton has paused more than once, a kind of hypocrisy which the innocent Eve, with her limited experience, could not possibly have detected. Interested and curious, Eve is quite willing to allow the serpent to lead her to the tree, the fruit of which has caused such a transformation. When she realizes that it is the forbidden tree, Eve's first reaction is that of an entirely good and innocent person; it is impossible that she should touch the fruit. This is the moment at which Satan must use his best strategy. Calling upon all the art of which he is master (notice Milton's analogy with a great orator, lines 670-74) he proceeds as a most subtle disputant to use every kind of casuistry in order to confuse Eve's mind. Eve knows that it is her duty to follow Reason, but subtly and deftly, step by crafty step, Satan confuses her Reason by apparently irrefutable logic, the fallacies of which she is incapable of detecting—quite unlike that early Lady who was more than a match for Comus. Satan's technique is very similar to Belial's when he suavely reduced Moloch's proposal to ashes by logical hair-splitting. Eve grows more and more confused as Satan seems to show the logical weaknesses of God's prohibition, particularly since he does so hypocritically "With show of zeal and love To man and indignation at his wrong." A much more acute disputant than Eve might well have been deceived, particularly because the experience of the serpent seems proof-positive that eating the fruit of the tree was not mortal, but had caused the serpent to rise in the chain of being and become in part man:

> Ye shall not die.
> How should you? By the fruit? It gives you life
> To knowledge. By the Threatener? Look on me,
> Me who have touched and tasted, yet both live
> And life more perfect have attained than fate
> Meant me, by venturing higher than my lot.
>   (IX. 685-90)

We of a post-Romantic era, to whom Pride seems a lofty virtue, should sympathize with Milton's Eve more than his own generation perhaps could. From one point of view, it may be a sin to wish to rise higher than one is; from another, it seems not only a natural human desire but an enviable one.

First flattery, than hypocrisy, then confusion of Eve's Reason by specious though seemingly convincing logic about the nature of man and the nature of God, step by step the temptation mounts. It is possible that Eve might still have withstood had the temptation occurred at any other time of day. As it is,

> Meanwhile the hour of noon drew on, and waked
> An eager appetite, raised by the smell
> So savory of that fruit.
>
> (IX. 739-41)

No one has ever known, or rather no two interpreters have agreed, what kind of fruit grew on the forbidden tree, though dozens of identifications have been suggested in literature, in Biblical exegesis and in plastic art. Obviously it was tropical or semi-tropical, luscious, filled with juice and with a very savory odor. The commentators who have spent so much discussion on Eve's character, her weaknesses, her vanity, often forget the simplest and most human reason for her Fall. The mature Milton has come a long way from that temptation in *Comus,* in which a young Lady, who had every reason to be hungry and thirsty, remained untouched by human appetite. Eve was a normal human being who was hungry and thirsty, in addition to being confused by specious logic which she thought she understood—her pattering of Satan's arguments shows that—but did not understand at all:

> So saying, her rash hand in evil hour
> Forth reaching to the fruit, she picked, she eat.
>
> (IX. 780-81)

The effect is instantaneous. Not only does she eat but, as never before, to excess. Momentarily she fancies that she really feels the

effect the serpent has promised, "expectation high of knowledge."
Watch the vocabulary that follows:

> *Greedily* she *engorged* without restraint
> And knew not eating death. *Satiate* at length,
> And *heightened* as with wine, *jocund* and *boon,*
> Thus to herself she pleasingly began.
>
> (IX. 791-94)

The italicized words were all used in Milton's time to describe
physical excess in eating and drinking. Eve is more than a little
drunk, and like many intoxicated persons, experiences euphoria.
She believes herself not only in complete control of the situation
but entirely justified in all she has done and plans to do. She has sud-
denly become crafty and sly, like the serpent who tempted her.
Ambition and aspiration have done their work. One most impor-
tant question remains: shall she share her discovery with Adam or
keep it to herself?

> . . . But keep the odds of knowledge in my power
> Without copartner? so to add what wants
> In female sex, the more to draw his love
> And render me more equal and perhaps—
> A thing not undesirable—sometimes
> Superior?
>
> (IX. 819-25)

Here speaks the First Feminist, who has evidently subconsciously
rankled under the pronouncement: "He for God only, she for
God in him."

Eve's first instinct, to keep the knowledge to herself, almost im-
mediately gives way to another. Suppose it is true, as God said, that
if you eat of the fruit you shall surely die?

> Then I shall be no more!
> And Adam, wedded to another Eve,
> Shall live with her enjoying, I extinct!
> A death to think! Confirmed then I resolve

Adam shall share with me in bliss or woe.
So dear I love him that with him all deaths
I could endure, without him live no life.

(IX. 827-33)

Whatever it had been before the Fall, Eve's love for Adam at this
moment is purely selfish. Not for a moment does she think of him.
She for Eve only, he for Eve in her. So far has she descended from
the Eve who had lifted up her voice with Adam's to praise her
Creator, that, before she leaves the tree, she genuflects before it,
as in Book II the fallen angels bowed with "awful reverence prone"
before Satan, as they had refused to bow before God. Eve thinks
she has risen in the chain of being; she has fallen.

The Fall of Adam

The idyl of Eden is nearly over. The last moments are spent by
Adam, as he waits for Eve's return, weaving a chaplet of flowers to
put on her hair. The end of Arcadia is symbolized by his uncon-
scious gesture when he sees his wife:

From his slack hand the garland wreathed for Eve
Down dropped, and all the faded roses shed.

(IX. 892-93)

Still intoxicated—"in her cheek distemper flushing glowed"—Eve
pours out her story breathlessly, excitedly, insisting that he share
her experience of "eyes more open," "dilated spirits, ampler heart,
And growing up to godhead." (IX. 875-77)

Eve's temptation was complex; Adam's is simple. His Reason is
not clouded for a moment. His mind is entirely clear. He under-
stands perfectly what has happened. But he also knows exactly
what he intends to do:

I feel
The link of Nature draw me. Flesh of flesh

> Bone of my bone thou art, and from thy state
> Mine never shall be parted, bliss or woe. . . .
> So forcible within my heart I feel
> The bond of Nature draw me to my own. . . .
>   we are one,
> One flesh: to lose thee were to lose myself.
>
>   (IX. 913-16; 955-59)

The emphasis is upon physical not spiritual love, love of flesh for flesh. Deliberately Adam permits Passion to triumph over Reason:

>   He scrupled not to eat,
> Against his better knowledge, not deceived,
> But fondly overcome with female charm.
>
>   (IX. 996-99)

As with Eve, the effect of the fruit is instantaneous. Again the vocabulary changes. The words Milton chose to describe the effect of the fruit on Eve were words of excess in eating and drinking. The vocabulary now combines intoxication and gluttony with excess in sexual indulgence:

> As with new wine intoxicated both
> They *swim in mirth.* . . .
>   But that false fruit
> Far other operation first displayed,
> *Carnal desire inflaming.* He on Eve
> Began to cast *lascivious eyes;* she him
> As *wantonly repaid. In lust they burn:*
> Till Adam thus 'gan Eve to *dalliance move.*
>
>   (IX. 1008-1016)

The scene that follows is at the opposite pole from the earlier nuptial bower and the hymn to wedded love. Eve "inflames" Adam's sense "with ardor to enjoy." He "forbore not glance or toy Of amorous intent." Eve's "eye darted contagious fire." They took "their fill of love and love's disport"; they sealed "their naked guilt" with "amorous play." (IX. 1031-45) When they wake from "grosser sleep," innocence is gone. Their naked bodies now seem shameful—"how unlike to that first naked glory!" They go out to make themselves loincloths of fig-leaves. Not only have self-consciousness and shame come upon them, but "tears rained at their eyes," tears happy man had not known except for those two idyllic ones Adam had kissed away from Eve's eyes after her dream. Anger, hate, distrust, suspicion, discord enter into Eden. We listen to the first quarrel of man and woman—no longer Man and Woman. They fling recriminations at one another as some of their descendants were to fling pots and pans. It was all your fault! Why didn't you do what I told you to? Why didn't you stop me? It was all *your* fault. Back and forth, back and forth, the perennial seesaw of two human beings who once loved and now hate each other. In "mutual accusation" they "spent the fruitless hours, *but neither self-convincing.*" Our First Parents, those great impassive statues, prototypes of what Man might have been, have suddenly come alive, stepping down from their pedestals to a level only too familiar to their descendants. Shrew, fishwife, virago, Xantippe—it is easy to find terms of abuse for Eve. Our language seems to have fewer for the weak uxorious Adam, who sounded like the noblest of men when he justified his physical passion for Eve, but to whom Christ said in the Judgment: "Thou didst resign thy manhood." (X. 148) Milton chose the best of the figures:

> So rose the Danite strong,
> Herculean Samson, from the harlot-lap
> Of Philistian Dalilah, and waked
> Shorn of his strength.

(IX. 1059-63)

Each commentator and critic has his own vocabulary with which to suggest the particular sins of Adam and of Eve in the Fall. Those of our own time are "psychological" or "psychoanalytical." Milton too explained it on "psychological" grounds, even though he did not know the word. His explanation remains the only convincing one to me:

> For Understanding ruled not, and the Will
> Heard not her lore; both in subjection now

To sensual Appetite, who from beneath
Usurping over sovereign Reason claimed
Superior sway.

(IX. 1127-31)

BOOK X

The structure of Book X is different from that of any preceding
book of *Paradise Lost,* consisting of a series of episodes in from six
to nine scenes, depending upon whether we divide those of Sin
and Death and those in which Satan appears as chief character. Mil-
ton's technique here is rather like that of Dickens toward the end
of a novel: the artist is gathering into his final pattern strands he
has woven separately. All the characters appear in all the places
we have visited.

The action begins in Heaven as "the angelic guards ascend, mute
and sad." (X. 18) From the cloud the Voice of God exonerates
them from blame. Man had free will to stand or fall; like Satan he
has fallen. Judgment will be passed upon him. Again it is Christ,
the "effectual Might," who goes forth from Heaven. He leaves alone
with little of the splendor that accompanied Him at the time of
Creation. We should notice from the beginning the dual motifs
implied in the Judgment, since this is an important clue to the mood
of the ending of *Paradise Lost*. Christ says to God:

Yet shall I temper so
Justice with Mercy as may illustrate most
Them fully satisfied, and Thee appease.

(X. 77-79)

292 OF JOHN MILTON

The reception of the Heavenly Visitant by Adam and Eve is very different from their attitude when Raphael came down to man. "Love was not in their looks, either to God Or to each other." Their guilt and shame are apparent (X. 111-114). In answer to Christ's question whether they have eaten the fruit, each of them throws the blame elsewhere, Adam at some length (X. 124-43) developing the Biblical words: "The woman gave me of the tree, and I did eat." Eve, abashed before her Judge, is more succinct: "The Serpent me beguiled and I did eat." In the Judgment Milton follows Genesis closely, making no attempt to develop or embroider the Scriptural account. The Judgment is tripartite: first, upon the serpent which has permitted itself to be used for other purposes than those for which it was created, "vitiated in nature." Forever it will be accursed, grovelling upon its belly. As long as man lives, there will be enmity between the snake and the descendants of Eve. Eve's sentence is a brief paraphase of Genesis III. 16: In pain and travail she shall bring forth her children, and she shall remain subservient to her husband. Adam will learn, "cursed is the ground for thy sake; in sorrow shalt thou eat of it all the days of thy life; thorns and thistles shall it bring forth to thee. . . . In the sweat of thy face shalt thou eat bread, till thou return unto the ground, . . . for dust thou art, and unto dust thou shalt return."

Although Milton follows the text of Genesis as closely as metrical paraphrase would permit, there are two passages in the Judgment Scene that show him allying himself with one side or another in long arguments among Biblical interpreters. In the Judgment upon Satan, the lines about enmity between the serpent and the seed of woman (X. 179-81) are a close paraphrase, but there is no parallel in Genesis to a passage Milton added in lines 182-91, indicating that this was a prophecy which would be "verified"

When Jesus, Son of Mary, second Eve,
Saw Satan fall like lightning down from Heaven,

Here Milton's Christian imagination went forward to a passage in Luke X. 18: "I beheld Satan as lightning fall from Heaven." As Arnold Williams has pointed out (*The Common Expositor,* p. 128) this interpretation is different from that of many Protestants, notably Calvin, and closer to the Roman Catholic position in its reference to "Jesus, Son of Mary, second Eve." We shall see the significance of this later in connection with "The Paradox of the Fortunate Fall."

The other passage is the judgment upon Adam, in which Milton has scrupulously followed the translation of the King James Version: "Cursed is the ground for thy sake." For centuries, Church Fathers had disputed about this passage, many of them following a mistranslation of Jerome in the Vulgate, which implied that the whole earth (terra) was cursed in the curse of man, others insisting that the curse had been limited to the *ground* or *soil* (humus). The adoption of one reading or another implied more than a semantic dispute. The basic problem was: Did the curse of God apply to the whole earth (world) or was it limited to the ground? With this passage in mind, I shall turn to a later section of Book X before considering the episodes of Sin, Death and Satan. (The reader interested in the long theological controversy about the curse on "Nature" will find a discussion of it in Marjorie Nicolson, *Mountain Gloom and Mountain Glory,* Chapter II).

The Effect of the Fall Upon Nature

With the exception of the brief passage about thorns and thistles and Adam's earning his bread in the sweat of his brow, Genesis says nothing about changes in external Nature caused by the Fall of Man. For centuries, however, both Jewish and Christian exe-

getes pondered the problem whether Nature had reflected the sin
of man. Basic to much thinking on the subject had been the idea
of the Decay of Nature shared by various classical, Jewish, Chris-
tian thinkers. Milton first expressed himself on the problem in Book
IX. When Eve ate the fruit:

> Earth felt the wound, and Nature from her seat
> Sighing, through all her works gave signs of woe.
>
> (IX. 782-83)

When Adam ate:

> Earth trembled with her entrails, as again
> In pangs, and Nature gave a second groan.
>
> (IX. 1000-1001)

At that time the skies darkened, thunder was heard and rain fell
for the first time. In Book X Milton devotes a much longer passage
to the matter (X. 651-714). Without entering into the technicali-
ties involved (explained in Merritt Hughes' notes) we may see in
general changes God commanded the angels to bring about in Na-
ture. The position of the sun was changed in such a way as to
cause "cold and heat Scarce tolerable." The aspects of the moon
and planets were altered so that their influence would be malign
rather than benign. Winds rose, the thunder rolled with greater ter-
ror. The position of the earth with relation to the sun was changed
also. Here Milton offers alternative theories, each one beginning,
"Some say." Whatever theory is followed, the result is the same:
extremes of cold and heat. The inclemency of seasons was accom-
panied by another alteration in animal life: "fierce antipathy" be-
tween beasts and man (X. 706-14). All these have one thing in
common—man's life is to be made infinitely more difficult, the
soil from which he must earn his living, more intractable, living
things dangerous as never in the past. The idyl of Eden is indeed
over.

Sin and Death

From the Judgment Scene on earth, we return briefly to Hell where Sin and Death still remain at the gates that will never be closed. Restive at inactivity, Sin proposes (X. 235-63) that they set forth to the new world, and, in case Satan is experiencing difficulty in his return, that they build a causeway between Hell and Earth. Sin's complete assurance that Satan has accomplished his mission and that he will raise her to be his darling at his right hand is expressed in terms that parallel closely the vocabulary of Eve when Satan tempted her to rise in the scale of being:

> Methinks I feel new strength within me rise.
> Wings growing, and dominion given me large
> Beyond this deep.
>
> (X. 243-45)

Milton turned to Herodotus, Xenophon, Caesar for the technical language in which he described the building of a bridge over Chaos, "by wondrous art Pontifical (bridge-building)." Again we have a momentary impression of the vastness of the new space which Satan had traversed with so much toil (X. 300-306). Again, too, the final line, "Smooth, easy, inoffensive, down to Hell," echoes the Virgilian words: "Easy is the descent to Hell." As the last pins of adamant are driven home and Earth is forever linked to Hell, as formerly to Heaven, by chains, Sin and Death meet Satan who has been skulking in Eden by night to make sure of the results of his temptation, fleeing only when he sees the descent of the Son of God.

They part, Satan to return to his followers in Hell, Sin and Death to spread their evil influence through the new world. They first infect the heavenly bodies (X. 410-14): stars turn pale, eclipses occur. Arrived on Earth, they seek their prey (X. 585-613), Death

2

5 JOHN MILTON

trying to glut his insatiable hunger first on herbs, then on fish, fowl, beast, to all of which he brings death. Sin casts about to find ways in which man will sin further.

The Fall of Satan

Satan descends to Hell with every reason to anticipate a scene of acclamation even more stirring than the "Black Mass" in which his followers had celebrated his courageous offer to undertake the perilous and lonely mission to the new world. By this time it is clear to all readers that the scenes in Hell are blasphemous parodies of their greater parallels in Heaven. Satan's return proves a bitter travesty of his departure in ways he had not anticipated. In order to make his appearance even more dramatically spectacular, he passes through the lesser fallen angels, waiting outside the council hall, in the disguise of a "plebeian Angel militant Of lowest order" (X. 441-42) and reascends his throne, still invisible. Down he sat, and looked about him, himself unseen. Little by little occurs the spectacular appearance of whatever glory still remains of Satan's original brightness:

> At last as from a cloud, his fulgent head
> And shape, star-bright appeared, or brighter, clad
> With what permissive glory since his fall
> Was left him, or false glitter.

(X. 449-52)

The grand spectacle of the exhibitionist becomes falsely theatrical, a parody, even a cartoon, the reverse-technique of Lewis Carroll when the Cheshire Cat fades out, leaving only a grin. The theatricality is as false as Satan himself. The anticipated acclaim begins, but Satan stills it with a gesture as he rises to deliver his oration. For the last time, he rolls out the grand titles of the Princes of Hell: "Thrones, Dominations, Princedoms, Virtues, Powers." The oration is Satan's glorification of Satan—his courage, his strength, his guile and subtlety, his triumph over Man, his revenge upon God, who is deliberately debased to a comic character, an ineffectual coward:

> [Man] by fraud I have seduced
> From his Creator, and, the more to increase
> Your wonder, with an apple! He, thereat
> Offended—worth your laughter—hath given up
> Both his beloved Man and all His World
> To Sin and Death a prey, and so to us
> Without our hazard, labor, or alarm. . . .
>
> (X. 485-501)

Anticipating a Hallelujah Chorus, he stands proudly before them waiting his greatest moment. The sound he hears is shockingly different from that he expected:

> he hears
> On all sides from innumerable tongues,
> A dismal universal hiss, the sound
> Of public scorn.
>
> (X. 506-509)

Now we witness the complete degeneration of a grand and majestic Archangel, who once stood next to God in Heaven, a scene that would be unbearable if it had not been so completely motivated, artistically and ethically, in the steady descent of Satan. The moment has come when he no longer has the power of choice. "Punished in the shape he sinned," he becomes the serpent he had permitted himself to be when he tempted Man:

> He wondered, but not long
> Had leisure, wondering at himself now more.
> His visage drawn he felt to sharp and spare,
> His arms clung to his ribs, his legs entwining
> Each other, till, supplanted, down he fell,
> A monstrous serpent on his belly prone,
> Reluctant, but in vain.
>
> (X. 509-15)

Read aloud the sentence, "His visage drawn he felt to sharp and spare," and *feel* what it does to your mouth: your lips are tight-pursed, contracted, constricted by a styptic or astringent, as if you had alum in your mouth. So, too, Satan's body is constricted, arms clinging to ribs, legs entwining each other. We share the physical discomfort by empathy, by motor mimicry. Satan's reward is not a scene of acclaim, but one from which all order, dignity, grandeur, are banished. "Pandemonium" has taken on the connotation it earned at this moment and has continued to bear ever since. It is a place of uproar and confusion:

> Dreadful was the din
> Of hissing through the hall, thick-swarming now
> With complicated monsters, head and tail . . .
>
> (X. 521-23)

We are in a snake-pit. We share the horror of those "plebian Angels" outside the council hall, still waiting for their Chief, as the doors open and "a crowd of ugly serpents" swarm forth. "Horror on them fell." They too at first feel empathy, "horrid sympathy," but as if by contagion, they too are changed to serpents. Scalded by thirst, famished by hunger, all seek to allay hunger and thirst, as Satan had tempted Eve to do, by the luscious fruit of a tree. Like Eve "greedily they plucked the fruitage fair to sight," only to find that instead of fruit they chewed bitter ashes, "which the offended taste With spattering noise rejected." (X. 547-70)

It is the ugliest scene in *Paradise Lost,* one of the most horrible scenes in literature. Through the wild confusion and terror of the writhing snake-pit, echoes persistently the sound of those explosive sibilants. Milton calls a catalogue of serpents, as he had once called a catalogue of the fallen angels: *s*corpion, a*s*p, amphis-baena, cera*s*pe*s,* hydru*s,* dip*sas:*

> Thus was the applause they meant
> Turned to exploding hiss, triumph to shame
> Cast on themselves from their own mouths,
>
> (X. 545-47)

Adam's Soliloquy

Adam's soliloquy (X. 720-844) is one of the most difficult passages in *Paradise Lost,* based as it is upon theological and philosophical ideas, many of them strange to modern readers. It is impossible here to analyze every sentence in it, since to do so would lead into speculations and debates of scholastic logic, much more familiar in Milton's time than in ours. If I agreed with some modern commentators that the soliloquy marks the crisis of *Paradise Lost,* I should attempt fuller line-by-line analysis than I shall give it. I do not think it marks a crisis, even in Adam's attempt to justify the ways of God to men, certainly not in Milton's.

The Biblical sources and analogues are many and various. Parallels with the Book of Job are clear in several phrases of the soliloquy, as is the general situation. When Job's friends come to comfort him, they find Job lying upon the ground and arguing aloud, now with God, now with himself. So too in *Samson Agonistes* the Chorus of friends will find Samson lying on the ground and hear him arguing with himself and to some extent with God. Parallels have been drawn, too, between this scene and that of Jesus in Gethsemane (Matthew XXVI. 26-46). As we see Adam lying on the cold ground cursing his creation, our memories may go back to our first sight of Satan, lying on the lake of fire, and remembering the Heaven he has lost as he realizes the Hell he has found. As Satan in Book IV curses the light of the sun, Adam wishes to hide himself from the light of God in which he once gloried, and bitterly contrasts the present with the past (X. 720-25). Adam has been shocked to realize that the punishment for his sin will not be limited to himself and Eve but that their descendants will share the inherited curse. (X. 726-41) God had bidden him "increase and multiply," but what can he multiply but curses on his head? Like sons of many succeeding generations, Adam throws back to his Maker the perennial protest of youth: "I did not ask to be born." (X. 743-45) Milton's memory here echoes Isaiah XLV. 10: "Woe unto him that saith unto his father, 'Why begettest thou?' " As God made him without any solicitation on his part, God has the right to destroy him (X. 746-52). But why has God added "the sense of endless woes?" "Inexplicable thy Justice seems." God and Adam had entered into a contract, which Adam had accepted upon God's terms. At that time they had seemed easy enough.

> Yet to say truth, too late
> I thus contest; then should have been refused
> Those terms whatever, when they were proposed.
> Thou didst accept them: wilt thou enjoy the good,
> Then cavil the conditions?
>
> (X. 751-59)

Ralph Waldo Emerson used to quote a Spanish proverb he paraphrased as: "What wilt thou have? quoth God. Take it and pay for it." Adam had easily accepted God's offer; he found the payment far more drastic than he had known.

Adam's mind returns to his own complaint to God, "I did not ask to be born," but sees it now from another angle:

> What if thy son
> Prove disobedient, and, reproved, retort:
> "Wherefore didst thou beget me? I sought it not!"
> Wouldst thou admit for his contempt of thee
> That proud excuse?
>
> (X. 760-64)

The sentence following: "Yet him not thy election, But natural necessity begot," is one which could lead to long discussion about the phrase "natural necessity." I shall not enter into that but merely paraphrase it: It is not solely the choice of the parent that lies behind the birth of a child; there are many who wish children and cannot have them. There are laws of Nature, as well as acts of parents, that determine birth.

Adam has proceeded so far as to grant the apparent justice of a

Deity who arbitrarily gives life and as arbitrarily puts an end to it. "The Lord gave and the Lord hath taken away." Indeed at this moment he would welcome death (X. 769-71). Why does God delay to execute his sentence? Adam would gladly "lay me down As in my mother's lap." Adam has been thinking of death as complete extinction when he should return to the dust of which he was made, and be as before his creation, no longer suffering, as now, from guilty conscience and conviction of sin. But a horrid possibility enters his mind:

> Yet one doubt
> Pursues me still, lest *all* I cannot die.
>
> (X. 782-83)

The dozen lines that follow lead into another theological problem, familiar in Milton's time, forgotten today by all but historical scholars, the question whether both body and soul are extinguished at the time of death. "Mortalism," as it was called, was a heresy to Roman and Anglican Catholics and to a majority of Protestants, who held that the body alone died, the soul was immortal. In the *Christian Doctrine* Milton raised the question and suggested his belief that both soul and body died, though he did not consider it a very important problem but what he called "indifferent." "Mortalism," while not widespread, was familiar among a number of seventeenth-century writers, the one best known to literary students being Sir Thomas Browne who in the *Religio Medici* said that in his youth he had been "addicted" to several heresies, among them this one. In the soliloquy it serves chiefly to lead Adam's tortured mind still further to despair, as again he faces the possibility that the death for which he longs may not put an end to conscience and realization of sin (X. 808-10). Our memories may go back to Belial's speech in the Council scene in which he implied another attitude:

> And that must end us—that must be our curse:
> To be no more. Sad cure! for who would lose
> Though full of pain, this intellectual being,

Those thoughts that wander through eternity,
To perish rather?

(II. 142-49)

We may be reminded even more of Hamlet's soliloquy: "In that
sleep of death what dreams may come?"

Philosophically and theologically the most difficult section of
Adam's soliloquy is the passage (lines 769-808) in which Milton's
mind goes back to a long-protracted disputation among scholastic
philosophers:

Can He make deathless death? That were to make
Strange contradiction, which to God Himself
Impossible is held, as argument
Of weakness, not of power?

(X. 798-801)

I shall over-simplify the arguments of the followers of Duns Scotus,
on the one hand, and of Thomas Aquinas on the other by using
the scholastic question most likely to be familiar to modern stu-
dents: "Can God make a square a circle?" One group would have
replied, Yes, because God *can* do whatever God wills to do. God
is omnipotent; His Will is supreme. The other group would have
said: No, God cannot make a square a circle, because to do so
would involve contradictions and cause confusion in the nature of
things. A square would no longer be a square nor a circle a circle.
God is Reason; His Will is restrained by Reason. We have already
heard enough about the importance of Reason. To create con-
tradictions in the nature of things would make God less, not
greater ("as argument of weakness, not of power.")*

The conclusion reached by Adam as a result of his tortured and
tortuous soliloquy is acknowledgment that the fault and the re-
sponsibility for the Fall were his, not God's:

---

* I am purposely not entering into the still more difficult lines (X. 804-
808) about "Nature's law," since to do so would require a disproportionate
amount of time and space, so far as the actual soliloquy is concerned.

> Him after all disputes
> Forced I absolve. All my evasions vain
> And reasonings, though through mazes, lead me still
> But to my own conviction: first and last
> On me, me only, as the source and spring
> Of all corruption, all the blame lights due.
>
> (X. 828-33)

Intellectually, Adam has justified the ways of God to Adam. He has done so by argument and debate with himself, by entering into subtleties of philosophy and theology, which were to tear asunder many of his "sons," particularly during the Middle Ages. But—this is the important point—so far as the soliloquy is concerned, it has been only an *intellectual* justification of God's ways to men. Adam has been rationalizing, intellectualizing with his "discursive Reason." He acknowledges God's justice with his mind, but he does not *feel* it in his heart. Indeed his despair is even more profound at the end of the speech than it was when he began by saying, "O miserable of happy!" His last sentence is significant of the fact that he has found no comfort:

> O Conscience! into what abyss of fears
> And horrors hast thou driven me, out of which
> I find no way, from deep to deeper plunged!
>
> (X. 842-44)

In the *Christian Doctrine* (I. xix) Milton outlined four steps in the process of Regeneration: "Conviction of sin, contrition, confession, departure from evil and conversion to good." Adam has taken the first step: he has convicted himself of evil. How will the others come about, if they are to occur?

Contrition and Confession

Certainly Adam's long ratiocination has not carried him far on the road to contrition. The second step toward regeneration begins not with Adam, but with Eve, who has been experiencing an emotional change. Sitting apart, "desolate," she has watched Adam suffering. That he is still unregenerate so far as she is concerned, is shown by the violence of his vocabulary as she tries to approach him: (X. 867-908) "Out of my sight, thou serpent!" It is as violent and insolent as Samson's, "Out, out Hyena!" when Dalilah tries to come close to him. Eve is still false and hateful in his sight. Adam would have "persisted happy," had it not been for her pride and vanity. She, whom he had idealized as wise, constant and mature, has proved a rib indeed, "but a rib Crooked by nature." Conveniently forgetting that he had begged God to create a helpmate, he inveighs against her creation, bitterly regretting that God had not created only men upon the new Earth. Eve has not spent the intervening hours in intellectualizing about the ways of God to men, but in *feeling* more and more poignantly her own sin, against God, to be sure, but even more against Adam. With tears "and tresses all disordered" she falls as a suppliant before him, embracing his feet. Adam still continues to say bitterly, "It was all your fault." Far from retaliating, as she had during their first quarrel, Eve now takes upon herself the complete responsibility for both, and, even more, wishes to bear the punishment for both, praying that the sentence

> may light
> On me, sole cause to thee of all this woe,
> Me, me only, just object of His ire.

(X. 934-36)

The second step of regeneration has been taken by Eve; through her it is shared by Adam. The sincerity of her repentance "wrought commiseration." "His heart relented"; "his anger all he lost"; "with peaceful words" he raised her from the ground. Each of them has felt the loneliness of separation and withdrawal. Henceforth they will contend no more, but strive "in offices of love" to lighten each other's burdens. It is Eve rather than Adam who makes two specific proposals for averting the fearful punishment which will descend for generations upon their progeny. It lies within Adam's power to prevent the birth of that "unblest race" that must suffer for the sins of their ancestors (X. 979-91). There is another alternative: rather than linger indefinitely through the "long day's dying," let Adam and Eve enter into a suicide pact.

Touched though he is by Eve's "contempt of life and pleasure," Adam realizes that they cannot and should not seek to circumvent the Judgment that has been passed on them. After all, he says, now that they can begin to consider it more calmly, is their penalty very severe? Eve will bring forth her children in labor, but "soon recompensed with joy." (X. 1052) Adam will earn his bread in the sweat of his brow. "What harm? Idleness had been worse." (X. 1055) Most of all, says Adam, let us remember those words in the Judgment: "Thy seed shall bruise the Serpent's head." This is the beginning of a rising line in the mood of our postlapsarian Parents, reminiscent of the structure of the Book of Job. Black despair has given place first to resignation; now hope begins to dawn. Notice from this time forward the persistent reiteration of the word "Seed" which sounds the note of hope: the bruising of the serpent's head, the final triumph of Good over Evil. Led by Eve, Adam has taken the second step in Regeneration: contrition. At the end of Book X, we hear of the third step, taken together:

> They forthwith to the place
> Repairing where He judged them, prostrate fell
> Before Him reverent, and *both confessed*
> *Humbly their faults,* and pardon begged, with tears
> Watering the ground, and with their sighs the air
> Frequenting, sent from hearts contrite, in sign
> Of sorrow unfeigned and humiliation meek.
>
> (X. 1098-1104)

BOOK XI

The action returns to Heaven, as the prayers of Adam and Eve fly up to the Intercessor. God sends Michael to banish Adam and Eve from the Paradise which Man has lost. Justice and Mercy—God and Christ—are balanced in the instructions given to the Angel. The sentence must be executed, "but, lest they faint At the sad sentence" rigorously executed

> all terror hide. . . .
> Dismiss them not disconsolate; reveal
> To Adam what shall come in future days,
> As I shall thee enlighten; intermix
> My covenant in the Woman's seed renewed,
> So send them forth, though sorrowing, yet in peace.
>   (XI. 108-117)

The arrival of Michael in the Garden of Eden is in sharp contrast to that of Raphael. Prelapsarian Adam had felt neither surprise nor fear as he watched the approach of the earlier Angel to the Garden which was in its greatest beauty when the first Angel arrived. Now the air is darkened, and because "carnal fear that day dimmed Adam's eyes," he felt the Visitant not "sociably mild," as Raphael had been, but "solemn and sublime." Michael arrives, ironically enough, just at the moment that Adam and Eve feel peace returning to their hearts, and look forward to continued life together in the Garden, still very familiar in spite of the changes it has suffered. The first speech of the Angel strikes consternation to their hearts: "to remove thee I am come And send thee from the Garden forth." (XI. 259-61) Adam stood speechless, "heartstruck, with chilling grip of sorrow." Eve's reaction is very moving;

Must I thus leave thee, Paradise? thus leave
Thee, native soil, these happy walks and shades,
Fit haunt of Gods? where I had hope to spend,
Quiet though sad, the respite of that day
That must be mortal to us both. O flowers,
That never will in any other climate grow,
My early visitation, and my last
At even, which I bred up with tender hand
From the first opening bud, and gave ye names,
Who now shall rear ye?

(XI. 269-78)

Adam had named the animals but Eve had named the flowers which were peculiarly her own. She is a symbol of the true-born Englishwoman to whom her garden is her spiritual home. Adam's most poignant regret is less for the garden, in Eve's sense, than for his birthplace, to which his sons would have returned to hear the patriarch tell them that here their father had walked and talked with God (XI. 317-33). Raphael reminds him that Paradise has been lost by Adam himself, and that God is not only in Heaven or the Garden of Eden; He is everywhere (XI. 335-54).

When Michael informs Adam that he has come to tell him what will happen in the future, we hear again the dual motif:

Good with bad
Expect to hear, supernal grace contending
With sinfulness of men—thereby to learn
True patience and to temper joy with fear
And pious sorrow.

(XI. 358-63)

The Vision of the Future

The scenes in Books XI and XII follow the epic tradition established by Virgil, in Book VI of the *Aeneid* when the future of Rome is foretold. To Adam, this is prophecy; to us, it is Biblical

history. Having drenched Eve's eyes in sleep, Michael leads Adam
to the top of the highest hill in Paradise, where they look out upon
an extensive scene (XI. 377-441) foreshadowing much the same
kind of setting in *Paradise Regained*. As in a vision, the future
passes before Adam's eyes, which Michael has prepared to see
them. (XI. 411-20) The technique of Books VI and XII differs.
In Book XI Adam actually sees the visions, while in Book XII Mi-
chael relates the various chapters of history. There is another vari-
ation in technique in Book XI which makes the first two visions dif-
ferent from those that follow. The first scene, the slaying of Abel by
Cain, (XI. 429-47) is a sort of dumb-show or pantomime between
actors who are not identified until they have disappeared. The sec-
ond, the lazar-house of loathsome illnesses (XI. 477-85) is also
pantomimic, reaching its climax as triumphant Death shakes his
dart. It is generic rather than specific. The two scenes are separate,
yet parts of a whole: they constitute Adam's first real knowledge
of that "death" of which he had been warned and which he had
thought himself ready to face. The first death is the result of hu-
man sin, the malice and violence of fratricide. The other deaths,
even uglier, because more lingering and painful, are also the result
of sin—the sin of gluttony:

> "Their Maker's image," answered Michael, "then
> Forsook them when they vilified
> To serve ungoverned appetite, and took
> His image whom they served—a brutish vice
> Inductive mainly to the sin of Eve."

> (XI. 515-19)

(It is interesting to notice that when an Angel comments on the sin
of Eve, he stresses not her "levity," "frivolity," or "conceit," as do
many modern commentators, but her "ungoverned appetite.")

When, appalled by the sight of death either by violence or suf-
fering, Adam asks if there is no less painful way to death, Mi-
chael's answer paints a sombre picture of old age even at its best
(XI. 530-46). If life is lived temperately, man may "like ripe fruit
. . . drop into thy mother's lap." But even then, he must outlive

youth, strength, beauty; he must feel his senses becoming obtuse, his blood "a melancholy damp of cold and dry." A far cry this from Browning's

> Grow old along with me,
> The best is yet to be,
> The last of life for which the first was made.

Milton's picture of old age is closer to Swift's Struldbrugs or Tennyson's Tithonus, without their immortality.

The later visions are drawn specifically from Genesis. In the first (XI. 556-627) Adam sees "on a spacious plain" the sons of Lamech (Genesis IV. 20-22) who were often interpreted as having established three important steps in the history of civilization: Jabal, "the father of all such as dwell in tents and have cattle"; Jubal, "the father of all such as handle the harp and pipe"; "Tubal-Cain, "an instructor of every artifice in brass and iron." Milton would not have been the poet-musician we have known so long had he not inserted into the passage about the Biblical father of instrumental music the intricate lines (XI. 561-63):

> his volant touch
> Instinct through all proportions, low and high,
> Fled and pursued transverse and resonant fugue,

the rhythm of which, as James Whaler has shown (*Counterpoint and Symbol,* p. 74) exactly corresponds to a fugal effect. When the descendants of the inventors of arts and crafts are joined by "a bevy of fair women," who sing and dance together and invoke the god of marriage, while the tents resound "with feast and music," Adam thinks the scene a happy one, until he is warned by the Angel that all this is on the surface only. These men are descendants of Cain who, although they were "inventors rare," and "studious of arts," have forgotten their Maker. The women, baser daughters of Eve, are tempters of men.

In the next scene (XI. 638-710) Adam sees what war will make of the once fair and innocent world. Cities have taken the place of tents. As in the warfare in Heaven, war is seen in various guises:

horse and foot; single combat and armies drawn up in array; raiders descending upon herds of cattle and sheep; a city besieged and assaulted by "battery, scale and mine." Each effort toward peace meets with "factious opposition," until one great statesman, Enoch, makes a final attempt to dissuade his rebellious generation:

> till at last
> Of middle age one rising, eminent
> In wise deport, spake much of right and wrong,
> Of justice, of religion, truth and peace,
> And judgment from above.

(XI. 664-68)

The lawless crew would have laid violent hands upon him had not God sent down a cloud that translated Enoch to Heaven, where again he would walk with God.

These scene changes, it seems at first, much for the better, since "the brazen throat of war had ceased to roar" and all was changed "to jollity and game." (XI. 713-14) Appearance is deceptive. This is a decadent generation, worthy Belial himself, men who love "luxury and riot, feast and dance . . . rape and adultery." Again a "reverend sire" rises among them, warning them of their ways, urging "conversion and repentance," but his words fall upon deaf ears. This is Noah, who, like Enoch, has walked with God. Despairing of saving men who will not save themselves, Noah "removed his tents far off," and set himself to building the ark. The last part of Book XI (728-901) is devoted to an account of the Flood, with interpolations and questions by Adam and explanations by Michael. The book ends with the return of the dove, the safe arrival of Noah and his family on Ararat and the appearance of the rainbow, "betokening peace from God and covenant new."

Since the Creation of the world was dated by Biblical scholars as approximately 4000 B.C. and the Flood as 2000 B.C., the timescope of Book XI is the first two thousand years of human history. Michael had warned Adam that he would hear of good mingled with bad, the grace of God contending with the sinfulness of man, and so indeed he has, though the sinfulness of man has seemed in the ascendant throughout. What is Milton's philosophy of history? Certainly it is not the "cyclical theory," most pervasive in Greece and Rome, shared by many other civilizations. At first reading, it sounds as if Milton were rather a follower of the "degenerative" theory, implied to some extent in the classical Four Ages and frequently read into Genesis, a pessimistic theory often very acute among Reformation teachers. The visions Adam has seen are sombre pictures of generation after generation which deliberately chose to follow wrong rather than right. To be sure, he has had an occasional vision of "one just man" who in a period of sin strove to save his people and did save himself. But Adam has wept, almost fainted, as he realized the depravity of his descendants. The greatest consolation he can find he expresses:

> I revive
> At this last sight, assured that man shall live
> With all the creatures and their seed preserve.
> Far less I now lament for one whole World
> Of wicked men destroyed than I rejoice
> For one man found so perfect and so just
> That God vouchsafes to raise another World
> From him and all His anger to forget.
>
> (XI. 871-78)

Before we conclude that Milton's was a pessimistic theory of history, we must add to Book XI the final interpretation of Book XII.

BOOK XII

The time-scope of the last book is the same as that of Book XI—two thousand years, from the Flood to the birth of Christ. With the Angel we pause, as the book begins, "Betwixt the World destroyed and World restored." The Biblical sources for Book XII are somewhat more extensive than for the preceding book, although, until the introduction of Joshua and David, the episodes are drawn chiefly from Genesis and Exodus. The technique, as has been said, changes from vision to narrative, as Michael perceives Adam's "mortal sight to fail."

The Lesson of Nimrod and Babel

For a time after the Flood, Michael tells Adam, men will live in peace "with some regard to what is just and right," (XII. 16) but then, as in the past, trouble will begin anew:

> One shall rise
> Of proud, ambitious heart, who not content
> With fair equality, fraternal state,
> With arrogate dominion undeserved
> Over his brethren, and quite dispossess
> Concord and Law of Nature from the Earth.
>
> (XII. 24-29)

This is Nimrod, "the mighty hunter before the Lord" (Genesis X. 8-9) despot and tyrant, who, like the fallen angels, aspired to found another empire, symbolized in the Tower of Babel "whose top may reach to Heaven." Until that moment all men had spoken the same tongue, but as the tower rose, God in judgment sent upon Nimrod's followers confusion of tongues, so that their proud tower became a Tower of Confusion, another Pandemonium. From this time forth, men would cease to be united even by a common language. The account of the attempted usurpation by Nimrod leads Adam to sharp criticism of this "son" who will attempt to rule his brothers as a tyrant (XII. 64-78). God, says Adam, gave man dominion over animals, "but man over men he made not lord." His invective leads Michael to point out that the sin of Nimrod was implicit in the sin of Adam, and allows Milton, even more than the Angel, an op-

portunity to drive home in his most extensive passage on the sub-
ject, his central teaching about the Fall of Adam and Eve in terms
of the "faculty psychology" and the necessity for the preeminence
of Reason:

> yet know withal
> Since thy original lapse, true liberty
> Is lost, which always with right Reason dwells
> Twinned, and from her hath no dividual being.
> Reason in Man obscured or not obeyed,
> Immediately upstart passions catch the government
> From Reason, and to servitude reduce
> Man till then free.
>
> (XII. 82-90)

Milton carries over his ethical philosophy into the realm of po-
litical philosophy, in an explanation, though not justification, of
periods in history in which tyranny has reigned in various parts of
the earth:

> Therefore since he permits
> Within himself unworthy powers to reign
> Over free Reason, God in judgment just,
> Subjects him from without to violent lords
> Who oft as undeservedly enthrall
> His outward freedom. Tyranny must be,
> Though to the tyrant thereby no excuse.
> Yet sometimes nations will decline so low
> From virtue, which is Reason, that no wrong
> But justice, and some fatal curse annexed,
> Deprive them of their outward liberty,
> Their inward lost.
>
> (XII. 90-101)

As so often in this period, macrocosm and microcosm are inter-
related: disturbances in Man are reflected in the body politic,
which in turn affects the little world of Man.

The Chosen People

Even in the first generation after Noah, "the only son of light in a dark age," mankind began again to "tend from bad to worse." Wearied by the widespread iniquities of men, God withdraws Himself from the many and selects "one peculiar nation," (XII. 106-118) springing from "one faithful man," Abraham. These are the chosen people, called to go forth

> into a land
> Which He will show him, and from him will raise
> A mighty nation, and upon him shower
> His benediction so that in his seed
> All nations shall be blessed.

(XII. 122-26)

And so we begin to pass from Genesis—the book of the beginning of the world—to Exodus, the account of the deliverance from bondage. As we do so, let us listen for that word "seed" which we have just heard in the prophecy of the descendants of Abraham. We hear it twice repeated a few lines later:

> all nations of the Earth
> Shall in his seed be blessed. By that seed
> Is meant thy great Deliverer, who shall bruise
> The serpent's heel.

(XII. 148-50)

We follow the chosen people into Egypt, where Abraham dies and Moses succeeds as leader of the Israelites. We hear of their bondage under Pharaoh, who attempts to wipe them out by killing the male children (XII. 165-69) and of the visitations sent upon Pharaoh—rivers of blood, plagues of frogs and locusts, of hail and darkness, culminating in the miracle of the Passover, the destruction of the Egyptians and the safe passage of the chosen through the Red Sea (XII. 173-216). The climax of the long pil-

grimage occurs when Moses on Sinai receives the Law from God
and gives it to the people (XII. 227-44).

The Prefiguration of Christ

In this climactic passage we begin to understand why Milton has
selected—and will select—the particular Biblical characters em-
phasized in Book XII. Very early in Christianity had begun an
allegorical interpretation of the Scriptures, whereby the New Testa-
ment might be made consistent with the Old Testament and (partic-
ularly in the hands of Philo Judaeus) with Greek philosophy also.
Most important for Books XI and XII of *Paradise Lost* was the de-
velopment of what has been called "typological allegory or
symbolism," and more recently, "figuralism." By this method a per-
son or event in the Old Testament might become a "type" or "fig-
ura" of a person or event in the New Testament, and there, in turn,
might be prophetic of the Last Judgment. The past is an "umbra"
that shadows forth the future. Milton refers to this kind of alle-
gorization, and uses some of its vocabulary, as he interprets Moses'
receiving the Law on Mount Sinai:

> whose gray top
> Shall tremble, He descending, will Himself
> In thunder, lightning, and loud trumpets' sound,
> Ordain them laws; part such as appertain
> To civil justice'; part religious rites
> Of sacrifice; informing them *by types*
> *And shadows, of that destined Seed, to bruise*
> The Serpent, by which means He shall achieve
> Mankind's deliverance.
>
> (XII. 227-235)

Here again is that "destined *seed*," repeated shortly in "the land
promised to Abraham and his *seed*" (XII. 259-60) and a dozen
lines below (XII. 273) in "Just Abraham and his seed." Abraham
was a prefiguration of Christ, Moses even more so.

The idea of Moses as a "figura" of Christ seems to have begun from interpretations of Exodus XX. 19, when the people said to Moses: "Speak thou with us, and we will hear; but let not God speak with us, lest we die." It was developed further in Deuteronomy, when Moses expatiated on and interpreted the Law shortly before his death. In Deuteronomy XVIII. 15, Moses said: "Jehovah thy God will raise up unto thee a prophet from the midst of these, of thy brethren, like unto me." In Acts III.22 the verse from Deuteronomy was so interpreted by Peter, when, addressing the Israelites, he spoke of the things foreshadowed by the mouths of all the prophets, and quoted the verse in · Deuteronomy. So Milton combines Exodus and Deuteronomy:

> But the voice of God
> To mortal ears is dreadful; they beseech
> That Moses might report to them His Will,
> And terror cease. He grants what they besought,
> Instructed that *to God is no access*
> *Without Mediator, whose high office now*
> *Moses in figure bears, to introduce*
> *One greater of whose day he shall foretell;*
> And all the prophets in their age the times
> Of great Messiah shall sing.
>
> (XII. 235-44)

We understand now why Milton departs from Genesis and Exodus to introduce into his pageant of history two later Biblical characters, Joshua and David, both of whom had been interpreted "from shadowy types to truth" (XII. 303) as prefigurations of Christ. It was not Moses who led the children of Israel to the Promised Land

> But Joshua, *whom the Gentiles Jesus call,*
> *His name and office bearing,* who shall quell
> The adversary Serpent, and bring back
> Through the World's wilderness, long-wandered Man
> Safe to eternal Paradise of rest.
>
> (XII. 309-13)

Of all the prefigurations of Christ in the Old Testament, none had a more persistent and pervasive history than David, as a type of king not born to royalty but anointed by God; David the Psalmist, dancing before the Lord; David, the great exemplar of the virtues found in Christ, humility and sublimity. Milton interprets the prophecy of II Samuel VII. 10-16 as meaning that David

> both for piety renowned
> And puissant deeds, a promise shall receive
> Irrevocable that his royal throne
> For ever shall endure. The like shall sing
> All prophecy—that of the royal stock
> Of David (so I name this king) shall rise
> *A Son, the Woman's Seed to thee foretold,*
> *Foretold to Abraham,* as in whom shall trust
> All nations, and to kings foretold of kings
> The last, for of His reign shall be no end.
>
> (XII. 326-330)

The prefigurations of Christ in great historical teachers and leaders of the Old Testament are transcended by the last vision of the future Michael relates to Adam: the coming of the Christ-child, in which, as in the *Nativity Ode* so long before, Milton retells the beloved Christmas story (XII. 360-71). Michael concludes:

> A Virgin is His Mother, but His Sire
> The Power of the Most High: He shall ascend
> The throne hereditary, and bound His reign
> With Earth's wide bounds, His Glory with the Heavens.
>
> (XII. 368-71)

The mood of Adam's response to this last vision of the future is very different from that he expressed at the end of Book XI. "With such joy surcharged as had like grief been dewed in tears," he speaks, understanding at last why the word "Seed" has been so constantly reiterated:

> O Prophet of glad tidings, finisher
> Of utmost hope! now clear I understand

What oft my steadiest thoughts have searched in vain—
Why our great Expectation should be called
The Seed of Woman! Virgin Mother, hail!
High in the love of Heaven, yet from my loins
Thou shalt proceed, and from thy womb the Son
Of God most High; so Man with God unite.

(XII. 375-82)

The Paradox of the Fortunate Fall

Many of the early Christian thinkers interpreted the Fall as un-
mitigated tragedy, both for Adam and for his descendants. "In
Adam's Fall we sinned all," and presumably nothing could be done
about it, so far as Man was concerned. But there was another
strain in Christian thinking, charmingly suggested in a little medi-
eval hymn, which we sometimes still hear, particularly at Christ-
mastime:

Adam lay ibounden
 Bounden in a bond;
Four thousand winter
 Thought he not too long;
And all was for an appil,
 An appil that he tok,
As clerkes finden
 Wreten in here book.
Ne hadde the appil take ben,
 The appil taken ben,
Ne hadde never our lady
 A bene hevene quene.
Blessed be the time
 That appil take was
Therefore we moun singen
 Deo gracias.

This interpretation, usually called by the Latin phrase *Felix Culpa*
(the Fortunate Fall) is discussed in connection with Milton by

Arthur O. Lovejoy in "The Paradox of the Fortunate Fall." The belief was never heterodox though not so pervasive as the more austere position. We have heard passing references to the idea, but, as Michael finishes his prophecy with the coming of the Seed of Woman, Adam's joy bursts forth:

> O goodness infinite! goodness immense,
> That all this good of evil shall produce,
> And evil turn to good—more wonderful
> Than that which by Creation first brought forth
> Light out of darkness! Full of doubt I stand,
> Whether I should repent me now of sin
> By me done and occasioned, or rejoice
> Much more that much more good thereof shall spring—
> To God more glory, more good will to men
> From God, and over wrath grace shall abound.
>
> (XII. 469-78)

The mood of the conclusion of *Paradise Lost* is not despair but triumph. "Obscurely then foretold" it has become increasingly clear to Adam. "Go, waken Eve," Michael instructs him, and share with her your knowledge [of]

> The great deliverance by her Seed to come
> (For by the Woman's Seed) on all mankind
> That ye may live, which will be many days,
> Both in one faith unanimous, though sad,
> With cause, for evils past, yet much more cheered
> With meditation on the happy end.
>
> (XII. 600-605)

But Eve already knew, "for God is also in sleep, and dreams advise." The mood of both Adam and Eve has changed profoundly. The turbulent confusion of their period of animosity, their shocked rebellion at leaving the Garden, has given way to peace, which they had begun to feel before Michael's arrival but which the vision of the future had disturbed for some time. Adam and Eve have taken, and will continue to take, the final step in regeneration: departure from evil and conversion to good. Peace returns to Adam's breast. In answer to the Angel's penultimate speech, Adam replies:

> Greatly instructed, I shall hence depart,
> Greatly in peace of thought, and have my fill
> Of knowledge, what this vessel can contain.

(XII. 558-60)

Eve, too, calmed by gentle dreams, is ready to leave the Garden of Eden to seek with Adam a new life; her words are a paraphrase of those of Ruth to Naomi:

> But now lead on!
> In me is no delay; with thee to go
> Is to stay here; without thee here to stay
> Is to go hence unwilling.

(XII. 614-17)

The new Adam and Eve are very different from those calm, dispassionate First Parents who remained somehow aloof from us, dwelling as they did in an unreal idyllic world remote from our experience, different, too, from the man and woman who suddenly came alive in an all-too-human quarrel. Milton had written in *Areopagitica:* "I cannot praise a fugitive and cloistered virtue, unexercised and unbreathed." The virtue of Adam and Eve before the Fall had been fugitive and cloistered. Now they have become true wayfaring and warfaring Christians, setting out to encounter the perils of a world beyond the gates of Paradise. When we see them for the last time they are intensely human. In spite of their acceptance of their banishment, they linger until the "hasty Angel" takes them by the hand to the gate, and even when they have passed it, they look back to what had been their "happy seat," guarded now by Cherubim with flaming swords. As the Angel had foretold, there was to be sadness in the long days in exile: "Some natural tears they dropped"; the first steps into the unknown world were "wandering and slow." But as they wiped the tears, they were true heirs of the great age of exploration and discovery that had preceded their poetic creation. "The World was all before them where to choose."

Milton's philosophy of history is far from a cyclical or degenerative theory. Its scope and meaning are not limited to Books XI and XII, nor limited to Man. It began with Raphael's account of the exaltation of Christ; it ends with Michael's prophetic scene of the coming of Christ, and the reiterated prophecy that in time to come the Seed will crush the head of Satan. The complete scope of history was announced in the Prologue:

> Of man's first disobedience, and the fruit
> Of that forbidden tree . . .
> > *till one greater Man*
> *Restore us, and regain the blissful seat* . . .

The pilgrimage of the life of Man is only one episode in a long history that began before the Creation of our World and will not end, even when the World is destroyed at the Last Judgment

> for then the Earth
> Shall be all Paradise, far happier place
> Than this of Eden, and far happier days.
> > (XII. 463-65)

Even for Adam and Eve, life is far from being completely tragic. They have sinned and suffered, but they have learned their lesson. They have repented and set out, by deeds and faith, to work for their regeneration. The final mood, as we watch them leave Eden, is that we shall feel again at the end of *Samson Agonistes*—

> His servants He with new acquist
> Of true experience from this great event,
> With peace and consolation hath dismissed.
> > (*Samson Agonistes*, 1754-56)

It is fitting that the last word we hear from our Original Parents should be "restore," fitting, too, that the last word should be spoken, not by Adam but by Eve, the first to sin, the first to repent, from whom will come the Savior of Mankind. "By me the Promised Seed shall all restore." As our acquaintance with Adam and Eve seemed to begin in the morning, so it seems to end with evening. Dr. Margaret Byard of Columbia University, studying the reiterated harmonies and dissonances in *Paradise Lost*, finds in Adam's last speeches echoes of the *Magnificat*, in Eve's of the *Nunc Dimittis*, the last two canticles sung at Evensong. Whether Milton so intended or not, the mood of Evensong is fitting for the conclusion of *Paradise Lost*, which is not a tragedy but a divine comedy.

Paradise Regained

Paradise Regained was published in 1671, preceding *Samson Agonistes* in the same volume. Evidence for the date of composition is far from conclusive. Edward Phillips says that it "doubtless was begun and finished and printed after the other (*Paradise Lost*) was published, and that in a wonderful short space considering the sublimity of it." Few modern critics accept the statement of the Quaker, Thomas Ellwood, that he suggested the subject to Milton, after Milton had lent him the manuscript of *Paradise Lost*. When he returned that, he says that Milton asked him what he thought of it, "which I modestly but freely told him, and after some further discourse about it, I pleasantly said to him, 'Thou hast said much here of Paradise Lost, but what has thou to say of Paradise Found?'" According to Ellwood, Milton made no answer, "but sat some time in a muse, then brake off the discourse, and fell upon another subject." After the plague was over, and Milton returned to London, Ellwood says, "he showed me his second poem, called *Paradise Regained,* and in a pleasant voice said to me, 'This is owing to you; for you put it into my head by the question you put to me at Chalfont, which before I had not thought of.'" Walter Raleigh (*Milton,* New York and London, 1900, p. 161) was one of the first to question Ellwood's statement. Tillyard (*Milton,* pp. 297-99) goes further, suggesting that Milton was having fun with

the simple and literal Ellwood. Certainly if the Quaker had read
Paradise Lost with any care, he must have realized that Milton
had already had a good deal to say about "Paradise Found." The
Trinity Manuscript lists among the many dramas Milton consid-
ered "Christus Patiens." While most of us follow Hanford's inter-
pretation that the trilogy of Milton's major works is a development
of the passage in *The Reason of Church Government,* in which
Milton suggested a long epic, a short epic, and a drama, we should
not forget that in the same passage he suggested other possibilities
as well: the Apocalypse, "the majestic image of a high and stately
tragedy,"; the "magnific odes and hymns" of Pindar and Callima-
chus; "those frequent songs throughout the law and prophets."
(Words that we will do well to remember when we come to Book
IV of *Paradise Regained*.) Let us be fair to Ellwood, and at least
raise the question whether his remark might have been the deter-
mining factor to Milton who had not yet finally decided which of
all these possibilities he would attempt for his second major poem.

Style

Although Phillips spoke of the "sublimeness" of *Paradise Re-
gained,* he added: "however it is generally censured to be much
inferior to the other, though he could not hear with patience any
such thing when related to him." There is, however, little question
that to most readers *Paradise Regained* comes as an anticlimax,
particularly if read immediately after *Paradise Lost*. The "organ
voice" is stilled. The intricate tapestry of *Paradise Lost* has become
bare and unadorned. Those who found the rhetorical Latinate style
of *Paradise Lost* difficult will encounter no such problem with
Paradise Regained, in which the language is almost stark in its
simplicity. As we shall find when we come to *Samson Agonistes,*
some modern critics believe that the drama was written early—
well before *Paradise Lost*. If we follow that theory, we may believe

that the "mighty-mouthed inventor of great harmonies" lost his poetical power in old age and was no longer capable of writing sublime poetry. The majority of us, who accept *Samson* as Milton's last work, must seek elsewhere to explain the marked difference in style in *Paradise Regained*.

Self-conscious rhetorician as Milton was, he wrote in many styles, as we have seen, and always had his reason for choosing one rather than another. I may make two suggestions about the simplicity of style in *Paradise Regained,* the first of which is possible, but not in my mind probable. During the middle years of Milton's century, English literature was undergoing many transformations, the most obvious of which was a self-conscious change from the "genus grande"—the oratorical style, which came to its climax in Sir Thomas Browne—to the "genus humile," or simple style. There were many reasons for the change: a shift in models from the Ciceronian to the Senecan, from Corinthian to Attic; the growing influence of science with the insistence of Bacon, Descartes and others, that "matter" rather than "manner" was important; the Puritan emphasis upon simplicity rather than ostentation; in the pulpit, an increasing belief that the preacher should emphasize "doctrina" rather than "eloquentia," as had such sermon-orators as John Donne and Lancelot Andrewes. Something of the same sort was happening in English poetry. It is interesting to recall that T. S. Eliot, who at one period urged modern poets away from Milton on the ground that his "poetic" style was a bad influence upon poetry, went through a period in which he shifted his seventeenth-century allegiance from Donne to Dryden, praising the Restoration writer for the conversational simplicity of both his prose and his poetry. Milton could not have been unaware of what was happening to the literature of his period. It is conceivable, therefore, that in *Paradise Regained* he was deliberately writing in the "plain style" rather than the oratorical. It is conceivable, I say, but in view of Milton's invectives against the tendencies of the Restoration, I doubt that it is true. The real explanation is simpler and more obvious.

The materials of *Paradise Lost* had been drawn not only from the Old Testament but from the most "sublime" books: the first chapters of Genesis; Job; the Psalms; the Prophets. The New Testament—as the materials dictated—was sparsely used, and appears chiefly in the angelic choruses paraphrased from the Apocalypse, that "majestic image of a high and stately tragedy." The materials for *Paradise Regained* came from the New Testament, particularly the Gospels. The Christ of *Paradise Lost,* sitting at the right hand of God or setting out as His "effectual Might," could well speak the speech of angels, as, indeed, could Satan, an archangel, though fallen. But to Milton, artist, rhetorician and reverent reader of the Bible, the sublime style would have been artistically wrong for the Christ who lived in this world, a man among men, for Jesus, of whose style we have evidence in the sermons, the parables, the accounts of the apostles. The style of Jesus Christ, as it has come down to us, at least in the Synoptic Gospels, was simple, direct, clear, forceful, designed for simple men—farmers, shepherds, fishermen, workers in the vineyard. As Jesus, Christ must and does speak in his own person and in his own style. Still another explanation for the "plainness" of style may well be implied in the debate between Satan and Christ in Book IV about the superiority of Hebrew to classical literature, which we will consider later.

Sources

Since Milton's theme in all his major works, as in *Comus,* is temptation, he was chiefly indebted for his materials to the two books which treat the temptation of Christ in the wilderness. The Gospel according to Saint John does not describe the Temptation. Mark says only (Mark I. 12-13): "And straightway the Spirit driveth him forth into the wilderness. And he was in the wilderness forty days tempted of Satan, and he was with the wild beasts, and the angels ministered unto him." Both Matthew and Luke tell the same basic story, but the order of events is different. Matthew mentions first the temptation by hunger, then the pinnacle of the temple, finally the mountain from which Satan showed Christ "all the kingdoms of the world, and the glory of them." Milton adopted Luke's order, the scene on the pinnacle following that on the mountain. As in *Paradise Lost,* Milton scrupulously makes use of all the Biblical material, then feels free to elaborate and develop his sources, introducing antecedent action as well as references to Christ's subsequent life on earth, and adding to the accounts in the Gospels other Biblical material. The influence of the structure of the Book of Job is clear, as are parallels between Christ and Job which Milton draws.

Various commentators have pointed out close parallels between *Paradise Regained* and the book in the *Faerie Queene* (II. vii) to which Milton referred in *Areopagitica,* when he called Spenser "a better teacher than Scotus or Aquinas" and said that Spenser "describing true temperance under the guise of Guyon, brings him in with his palmer through the cave of Mammon and the bower of earthly bliss, that he might see and know, and yet abstain." In that scene Guyon debated with Mammon, as Christ with Satan. He was offered power and fame; he spent three days without food or sleep; after his trial, an angel was sent to care for him. Spenser developed the virtue of "temperance," one of the virtues of Christ stressed by Milton. Analogues have also been suggested with Giles Fletcher's *Christ's Victory and Triumph.*

In addition to such specific sources, Miss Elizabeth Pope points out that "by the seventeenth century an immense mass of doctrine, interpretation, and legend had gradually accumulated about that narrative (in the Gospels), and given rise to a traditional or conventional conception of the event familiar to every intelligent and instructed Christian. . . . If the seventeenth-century reader turned from the commentaries to collections of homilies, volumes of sermons, biographies of Christ, or tracts on the temptation, he found the same questions raised and the same answers given. . . . When he opened his copy of *Paradise Regained* in 1671, he must have expected to find the subject treated in conformity with the fixed principles established by the tradition." What those traditions were and the extent to which Milton adopted them, Miss Pope discusses in *Paradise Regained: The Tradition and the Poem* (Baltimore, 1947).

Main Characters

In characterization as in style, *Paradise Regained* seems anticlimactic after *Paradise Lost*. (Since it is clear that I am unsympathetic with much of *Paradise Regained,* I urge the student to read the perceptive study of it by Arnold Stein in *Heroic Knowledge.*) Although Milton picks up certain characters and episodes from the longer epic, they no longer have the vitality we felt in *Paradise Lost.* Satan the Dictator again convenes a council, and we hear an occasional familiar name, such as that of Belial; but there is no trace of the grandeur or the oratory of the Council Scene in *Paradise Lost.* Nor does Satan give the impression of latent power and passion we once felt in him. In the Satan of *Paradise Regained* there is neither development nor degeneration. He is a static character, little more than an academic disputant, much more like the Satan of the Book of Job—the devil's advocate—than the majestic fallen archangel we once knew.

What the reader makes of the Christ of *Paradise Regained* depends upon many things. Those who find anti-Trinitarianism in *Paradise Lost* may well feel that this Christ is even less a basic part of the Trinity than was the majestic character of *Paradise Lost.* Or they may go in another direction and say that, because Milton was denying the Trinity in the long epic, he is here paying his tribute to the greatness of the man, Christ,—that this Christ is the Great Exemplar to man of the life possible for a man to live. Basically, however, the Christ of the short epic is much less a theological than an ethical character. In sharp contrast to *Paradise Lost,* in which both author and characters grappled with problems of dogma, Milton enters into almost no theological discussion here. His emphasis is not upon a theological concept of Christ but upon a man who lived a perfect life. A good treatment of this ethical Christ is that of Merritt Hughes, "The Christ of *Paradise Regained* and the Renaissance Heroic Tradition," in which he shows how the idea of a "hero" had developed among Renaissance writers. Fundamentally Christ is Aristotle's "magnanimous man," (*Nichomachean Ethics,* IV.iii.16). Ironically enough, it is Satan who pays high tribute to this quality in him, when (II. 137-39) he acknowledges that Christ is

> With more than human gifts from Heaven adorned,
> Perfections absolute, graces divine,
> And *amplitude of mind* to greatest deeds.

Milton's Christ, as Mr. Hughes shows, is very similar to Spenser's Knight of Temperance, as well as to other Renaissance examples of "heroicall virtue." Arnold Stein (pp. 17-35) expands the treatment of "the virtues" represented by Christ, emphasizing temperance as of central importance, but showing that it must be considered in relationship to other virtues, magnanimity, piety, justice.

In *Paradise Regained* Milton faced a basic problem, familiar in all classical epic and drama; Since the end of the story is known from the beginning to the reader or audience, there is no possibility of suspense in our modern sense of that word. In *Samson Agonistes,* as we shall see, Milton might use various devices inherited from the classics to take the place of the suspense to which we are accustomed in novel or drama. Is there any suspense in *Paradise Regained?* Certainly at casual reading there seems to be none. The short epic is a protracted debate, often arid and barren, in which neither disputant shows much emotion. Satan, to be sure, is occasionally described as "inly racked," or "collecting all his serpent wiles," leading us to expect more action than we find, but his basic position seems that suggested at the beginning of Book III:

> Satan stood
> A while as mute confounded what to say,
> What to reply, confuted and convinced
> Of his weak arguing and fallacious drift.
>
> (III. 1-4)

The phrases most frequently reiterated about Christ are: "To whom thus Jesus *patiently* replied"; "the Son of God *unmoved* replied." Is there any way in which the epic may be read other than a rather tedious exchange of arguments in which Satan was defeated even before he began the temptation?

So far as Satan is concerned I think there is much suspense in *Paradise Regained.* He states to the first Council:

> For this ill news I bring, the Woman's Seed
> Destined to this, is late of woman born.
>
> (I. 64-65)

Satan has been present at the baptism in Jordan, has seen the dove descend (though he adds, "whate'er it meant") and has heard the voice from Heaven. But is he really persuaded that this man who was born into the world a few years earlier is the same Christ whose exaltation in Heaven had caused Satan's rebellion? Of one thing we may be sure: although Satan had heard the curse passed upon Adam and Eve and the serpent, he has no idea at what period of history that prophecy would come true. The Satan of Book X in *Paradise Lost* made light of the prophecy:

> I am to bruise his head:
> His seed (when is not set) shall bruise my heel:
> A world who would not purchase with a bruise
> Or much more grievous pain?
>
> (X. 498-501)

In the first Council Scene in *Paradise Regained,* he shows more concern. The appointed time may have come (I. 57-59). For four thousand years Satan and the fallen angels have roamed throughout the world, traducing men, worshipped by heathen, hearing and seeing nothing to indicate that the prophecy will be fulfilled. Doom

may now be at hand, if this simple man of Galilee is indeed the
foretold Seed of Woman. But is he? If we conclude that Satan is
not actually *sure* that this was the Christ he knew in Heaven un-
til that moment on the pinnacle, then there is intense force in that
simple climactic sentence: "He said, and stood."

The order of the temptations implies suspense on Satan's part as
well as the reader's. Satan's reaction to Christ's refusal to be
tempted by the earlier ones indicates that he had considered this
almost a foregone conclusion. He accepts it easily, dropping each
temptation almost abruptly. There is slightly more tension in the
scene of the temptation by earthly power than in the preceding
ones, as if Satan really felt that Christ would not be tempted be-
cause of bodily hunger, but might conceivably be by the power
of empire. Satan, however, rises to the heights of which he is capa-
ble only when he comes to the temptation by wisdom, rhetorically
the finest of all and the most moving. Here for the first time the
reader feels that Christ might have been tempted by the loveliness
of Athens, "mother of arts and eloquence." Indeed, the reader
may well feel that Satan had counted on success in this temptation
as he had not before. His final act is one of desperation, when by
his supernatural power "he caught him up" and set Christ on the
highest pinnacle of the temple. Milton's following of the order of
Luke rather than of Matthew was not only because of the spectacu-
lar ending it permitted but, much more, because this *is* the climax to
Satan, the last possible opportunity for him to prove to himself
whether or not this is the Son of God.

Is this a climax, too, so far as Christ is concerned? Does he also
experience suspense? I raise the question though I cannot answer
it, so far as theology is concerned. Did Milton's Christ *know* that he
was the Son of God? He *believed* it, to be sure. Roman Catholic
priests with whom I have discussed the matter tell me that, ac-
cording to the teaching of their Church, Christ in this world pos-
sessed all the powers He had had in Heaven, including omniscience.
If that is true, there can be no suspense on Christ's part. But
Milton was a Protestant, and differed from Roman Catholicism

on many important matters of dogma. He has not committed himself on this one, but I call attention to Christ's long autobiographical speech (I. 196-293). Christ remembers his early youth—a precocious youth—when "no childish play" was pleasing to him. Above his years, he read the Law and became so adept that he disputed with the teachers in the Temple. "Victorious deeds" inflamed his heart. He felt himself "called" to do some great thing, though he did not know what it was to be. It was his mother who first told him that he was "no son of mortal man," told him of the miracle of his birth. This led him again to study the Law and the Prophets and to learn all he could of the Messiah he was said to be. John the Baptist recognized him, though he had not recognized John. He heard the Voice from Heaven and recognized it as a sign.

> by which I knew the time
> Now full, that I no more should live obscure
> But openly begin, as best becomes
> The authority which I derived from Heaven.

> (I. 286-91)

But he seems still to be following his mother's teaching, rather than remembering his own life in Heaven. Does this speech sound as if Milton's Christ, as boy and young man on earth, had the omniscience and foreknowledge he had in Heaven—indeed, does it sound as if he had any recollection of Heaven? I think not. In that case the Temptation may have been suspense to him, as to Satan; until the moment on the pinnacle, Milton's Christ *believed*, but he did not *know*.

BOOK I

Milton begins by referring back to *Paradise Lost,* though the first
seventeen lines are not a Prologue in the sense we found in the
long epic. There is, to be sure, an invocation to a Spirit, with the
conventional classical idea that the poet is asking for inspiration.
There is also the convention that the subject-matter of this poem,
like that of the other, is "above heroic." But there is no apostrophe
to Light, as we have found it before, and no personal allusion to
his blindness. As in *Paradise Lost* he feels "more safe" when he is
standing on earth and dealing with problems of this world, not of
Heaven. Although there is a brief scene in Heaven and two in
Hell, they require little or no comment on Milton's part. We hear
the details of the Baptism, and follow Satan to Hell where he in-
forms his followers of what he has seen and heard. For a moment
the scene changes to Heaven, where God informs Gabriel that He
is deliberately exposing Christ to Satan's wiles, in order that Satan
may learn again that God cannot and will not be opposed by him.
There is a brief chorus of angelic acclamation but with no such
music as we have heard in *Paradise Lost.* After the reminiscense
of Christ, we pass with him to the wilderness, where he remained
for forty days and nights, "nor tasted human food." Although he is
among wild animals, they become as gentle in his presence as
were the prelapsarian animals in Eden. Satan approaches at last,
"an aged man in rural weeds." Knowing that Christ has hungered
for forty days, Satan urges him to command that the stones be
made bread. In the answer of Christ we feel for a moment super-
natural power: as Satan knows who Christ is, so Christ knows Sa-
tan (I. 356).

In Satan's speech we hear the familiar strain of hypocrisy, so recurrent in his actions and speeches in *Paradise Lost*. He insists that he is still the servant of God, in spite of his rebellion. Although he has lost God's love, he has not lost, he insists,

> To love, at least contemplate and admire,
> What I see excellent in good, or fair,
> Or virtuous.

(I. 380-82)

Satan protests too much. We are no more persuaded by his smooth and unctuous words than is Christ, and no more sorry to see him leave at the end of the scene.

BOOK II

The scene changes for a time back to Galilee where men like Andrew and Simon, who had accepted Christ as the Messiah, begin to doubt, because of his unexplained absence. (II. 1-57) It is possible, of course, that, as in the case of Moses, his absence will prove temporary, or even that, like Elijah, he has already been translated. His mother, too, becomes concerned (II. 60-104) as she sees many others returning from the Baptism, but not her son. Her mind goes back to the Annunciation, and for the first time since the birth of her child, she begins to wonder, though her basic attitude is meekness and resignation. Satan returns to his legions to report that so far he has had no success. For a moment we hear Belial, with whom we became well acquainted in the Council Scene of *Paradise Lost,* and hear a proposal which seems shocking and even blasphemous to many readers: "Set women in his way and in his path." To be sure, Satan peremptorily dismisses any such possibility, yet we find ourselves wondering why Milton even introduced it. It is possible that, although only three of the Seven Deadly Sins are emphasized by Milton as by Matthew and Luke—Gluttony, Covetousness, Pride—all seven may be implicit in *Paradise Regained,* as Professor Robert Fox has found them all in *Paradise Lost.* Certainly in the scenes dealing with power and glory, Satan suggests that Christ might be accused of Sloth, and he makes many attempts to arouse him to both Anger and Envy. But why then Belial's suggestion and Satan's reply, unless Milton was indicating that Christ could under no circumstances be tempted by Lust?

Satan departs, taking with him "a chosen band of spirits likest to himself in guile," who will aid him in the expansion of the temptation by hunger. The scene returns to the wilderness, where Christ, as man, is now suffering very human pangs of hunger and thirst (II. 245-59). Sleeping, he dreams of Elijah, who was fed by ravens and by an angel (I. Kings XVII. 5-6), of Daniel's refusal of the meat offered by Nebuchadnazzer (Daniel I. 8-19). He waked "and found all was but a dream." Wandering in the wilderness, he comes to a pleasant grove, where Satan again appears, with some hope that Christ, suffering as he is, may be tempted by physical appetite. Here Milton departs widely from the Scriptural account, which he had repeated almost verbatim in Book I, to describe the lavish feast set before Christ—a table laden with food and drink reminiscent of that in the enchanter's palace of *Comus.* Christ's refusal, too, reminds us of that earlier temptation when the Lady said:.

> none
> But such as are good men can give good things,
> And that which is not good is not delicious
> To a well-governed and wise appetite.
>
> (*Comus* 703-705)

In answer to Satan's question whether he would eat if food and wine were placed before him, Christ replies, "Thereafter as I like the giver." Satan's temptation by hunger, even when Christ can see and smell the lavish feast, fails, as a lesser temptation by hunger had not failed with Eve.

In the remainder of Book II Satan begins to prepare for the next temptation, by wealth, fame and glory. He reminds Christ that, as a man, he is "unknown, unfriended, low of birth," that he has been "bred up in poverty." He is clearly aware that Christ's heart is set on high actions, to which the road in Satan's mind is clear—through riches, wealth and treasure, which are within Satan's power to bestow. These, and according to Satan, these alone, lead to dominion and rule over men. Christ's answer, with his definition of a true ruler (reminding us of the speech on tyranny in *Paradise Lost*) should have warned Satan that his second temptation will prove as futile as his first:

> Yet he who reigns within himself and rules
> Passions, desires and fears, is more a king;
> Which every wise and virtuous man attains;
> And who attains not, ill aspires to rule
> Cities of men, or headstrong multitudes,
> Subject himself to anarchy within,
> Or lawless passions in him, which he serves.
> But to guide nations in the way of truth
> By saving doctrine, and from error lead
> To know, and knowing worship God aright
> Is yet more kingly.

(II. 466-76)

BOOK III

There are reminiscences in Book III of techniques and situations Milton used in Books XI and XII of *Paradise Lost,* when Raphael combined what was prophecy to Adam with what was history to us. In *Paradise Regained* the books of the Old Testament are history to both Satan, who has lived through the four thousand years, and to Jesus, well studied as he was in the Law and Prophets. There is, however, one marked difference in the historical materials Satan chooses. His illustrations are drawn from classical history even more than from the Bible. Attempting to arouse Christ's desire for glory, he goes back to Alexander the Great, to Scipio, to Pompey (III. 31-36) all of whom had become famous before they were as old as Jesus is now. To these illustrious examples, he adds Julius Caesar, who "wept that he had lived so long inglorious." (III. 41-42) Jesus replies in words reminiscent of the "fame" passage in *Lycidas,* that true glory is not found in "the blaze of fame," in the applause of the vulgar:

> This is true glory and renown, when God,
> Looking on the Earth, with approbation marks
> The just man, and divulges him through Heaven
> To all his angels, who with true applause
> Recount his praises.

(III. 60-64)

In opposition to Satan's classical heroes, he emphasizes Job, famous in Heaven, though "on Earth less known."

Since Jesus was not moved by examples of Greek and Roman conquerors (we should remember this when we come to the scenes of Rome and Greece in Book IV) the devil, who can quote Scripture to his purpose, returns to the Old Testament. If Christ believes that he is the true heir to the throne of David, let him not forget that Judea is now in the hands of Roman usurpers, "reduced a province under Roman yoke" under Tiberius, and reminds him of Judas Maccabeus, who also had "retired unto the desert, but with arms," and who succeeded in putting his family on the throne of David.

The second part of Book III is particularly reminiscent of Book XI of *Paradise Lost.* Reminding Jesus that he has lived "a private life," with no experience of the greater world, he leads Christ "up to a mountain high." Here, as I have suggested elsewhere (*Mountain Gloom and Mountain Glory,* pp. 274-76), the blind Milton's imagination carried over to earth the sense of vastness he had felt in the cosmic heavens. The technique is, I believe "telescopic," as are the great scenes of "cosmic perspective" in *Paradise Lost,* particularly implied in his reference to "my airy microscope" (IV. 56-58) and the lines

> By what strange parallax, or optic skill
> Of vision, multiplied through air or glass
> Of telescope, were curious to inquire.

> (IV. 40-42)

The description (III. 262-309) is the most extensive terrestrial panorama in seventeenth-century literature. "Turning with easy eye," Christ beholds Nineveh, Babylon, Persepolis, Bactra, Araxata, Teredon, Ctesipon. As so often, too, in *Paradise Lost,* we feel the love of proper names Milton shared with many of his contemporaries. In the long pageant of Biblical history, Christ, like Adam before him, is shown many *exempla* of conquerors who, through their conquests, had left behind them names long remembered in history.

BOOK IV

The last book of *Paradise Regained* is the only one by which most modern readers are moved. This is, in part, because the scenes Satan shows Christ are much more familiar to us (whether we have seen them with our eyes or not), our literary heritage from classical civilization, in part because Milton himself responded emotionally to his materials as he has not seemed to do in the earlier books. Here alone he rises to the poetic heights we have known so long, which have not been approached in the previous dialogues between Satan and Christ. Far more than in Book III, we feel the temptation of "all the kingdoms of the world," in the glory that was Greece and the grandeur that was Rome. In the first vision of the "great and glorious Rome, Queen of the Earth," there may be personal reminiscence on Milton's part of the city he had come to know well during his periods of residence there. He was familiar enough with the capitol

> Above the rest lifting his stately head
> On the Tarpeian rock, her citadel
> Impregnable.
>
> (IV. 48-50)

He had seen many of the "turrets and terraces, and glittering spires . . . pillars and roofs" that remained from the past, and he himself must have traversed the Appian and the Aemilian Ways. At the time of the Temptation, the tyrant Tiberius still officially ruled Rome, though he had withdrawn to Capri—Satan says, "his horrid lusts in private to enjoy"—leaving the real command to "a wicked favorite," Sejanus. In such a period of degeneration, Satan urges, what more probable than that the emergence of such a young man as Jesus, "endowed with royal virtue as thou art," might "expel this monster from his throne," and set the people "free from servile yoke?" (IV. 90-102) Christ is no more moved by scenes of "Roman luxury though called magnificence" than he had been by the earlier pageants of conquest by arms, nor has he been sent into the world to free a people who have brought their vassalage upon themselves:

> That people victor once, now vile and base,
> Deservedly made vassal; who once just,
> Frugal, and mild, and temperate, conquered well,
> But govern ill the nations under yoke. . . .
> These thus degenerate, by themselves enslaved.
>
> (IV. 132-45)

Clearly Christ is not to be moved by visions of conquest by arms, of magnificence and luxury, by the possibility of being Emperor of Rome.

Satan sees one penultimate possibility: he has heard the story of Jesus disputing in the Temple with the Rabbis. "Be famous, then," he suggests, "by wisdom." (IV. 221). But if that is Christ's ambition, knowledge of the Law and Prophets will not prove enough:

> All knowledge is not couched in Moses' law,
> The Pentateuch or what the Prophets wrote;
> The Gentiles also know, and write, and teach
> To admiration, led by Nature's light.
>
> (IV. 225-28)

If Christ is to achieve fame through wisdom, he must set himself to school to Gentiles as to Jews, and to do so, must add their wisdom to his Hebrew knowledge.

This is the transition to the beautiful and moving scene of Athens, "the eye of Greece, mother of arts and eloquence," with its "sweet recess," its "studious walks and shades," and the nostalgic charm of

> the olive-grove of Academe,
> Plato's retirement, where the Attic bird
> Trills her thick-warbled notes the summer long.
> There flowery hill Hymettus with the sound
> Of bees' industrious murmur oft invites
> To studious musing; there Ilissus rolls
> His whispering stream.
>
> (IV. 244-50)

Here is the great tribute to Greek philosophy—to Plato, Aristotle, Socrates, Zeno, the Peripatetics, the Epicureans, the Stoics, the tribute, too, to Greek literature, the "Aeolian charms" of such poets as Sappho, the "Dorian lyric odes" of Pindar, the epics of blind Homer, the lofty tragedians, "teachers of moral prudence," and the orators with their "resistless eloquence."

Christ's reply to the speech in which Satan has paid such homage to the classics is the one passage in *Paradise Regained* which has torn modern critics asunder, and so must be discussed in some detail. Is the most "classical" of all our English poets here repudiating his goodly heritage, the great tradition in which all his earlier poetry has had its roots? At first reading, Christ's speech comes as a shock to modern readers who, even if they are not so deeply versed as was Milton in Latin and Greek, have been educated in the humanistic tradition. In answer to Satan's praise of Greek thought, Christ dismisses the philosophers, one after another: Socrates, whom Satan had exalted as the "wisest of men," whose teaching had "watered all the schools," was, indeed, "the first and wisest of them all," but, Christ reminds Satan, his wisdom lay in his profession "to know that only, that he nothing knew." Plato "to fabling fell, and smooth conceits." The Sceptics "doubted all things, though plain sense." Aristotle joined "virtues . . . with riches and long life." The Epicureans found the end of life in bodily pleasure and "careless ease." The "philosophic pride" of the Stoics is treated in the most detail of all, "as fearing God nor man." Whoever seeks true wisdom in any of these Schools will not find it.

Christ's dismissal of Greek literature is not quite so complete as that of Greek philosophy, though it sounds devastating to those who read it as Milton's dismissal of the "lyric odes" he had adapted, of the blind Homer with whom he had asked to be remembered, the "lofty great tragedians" he had considered among the best teachers of moral philosophy, and the great orators upon whom he had modelled much of his prose. Anything worthy of praise was merely imitated—"ill imitated," Christ says—from "Hebrew songs and harps in Babylon." Their vices—and they were many—were their own: "their gods ridiculous"; their swelling epithets "thick laid" like "varnish on a harlot's cheek." The orators, as a group, come off a little better. They were statesmen and lovers of their country but still far inferior to Hebrews who taught in "unaffected" style. The persistent emphasis in the passage upon Hebraic "plainness" as opposed to Greek elaboration of style is particularly interesting in view of the strikingly "plain style" of *Paradise Regained* and may imply Milton's *apologia* for that style. If this is Milton speaking, however, he has indeed de-

342 👹 JOHN MILTON

parted from the "old ways" that once were the "good ways" he had followed so long.

Various modern commentators on the passage are conveniently quoted by Merritt Hughes from whom I borrow a few. (Headnotes 12-14, pp. 475-76.) J. H. Hanford reads into the passage "a half reconciliation between (Milton's) Puritanism and his love of learning." Robert Adams speaks of "that provincial contempt for the classics, which resounds throughout *Paradise Regained.*" Malcolm Ross sees Christ denying "the philosophic spirit, the searching mind of the Greeks (once so dear to Milton)." Douglas Bush refuses to believe "that in old age the puritan had conquered the humanist," though he finds it "painful to watch Milton turn and rend some main roots of his being." Read in this way, *Paradise Regained* should be the last of Milton's works, his farewell to humanism, his final repudiation of the glory and the grandeur. To read Christ's speech as reflecting Milton's own attitude, and yet to accept *Samson Agonistes* as Milton's final work, (as most of these critics do) seems to me "to make strange contradiction."

If we must persist in the perversity of reading an author's personal position and convictions into a particular speech of his characters, let us be fair (particularly to such a fair-minded disputant as Milton has proved in his many poetic debates) and let John Milton speak not only Christ's lines but also Satan's on Greek philosophy and literature. Here I cannot agree with what Merritt Hughes (Headnote 12) says and others imply: "Christ's reply to Satan is too clear and passionate to reflect anything but the poet's actual state of mind." Satan's speech is just as clear, and much more filled with characteristic Miltonic overtones and rhythms— indeed, they are some of the loveliest lines he ever wrote. I will go farther and say that in the tribute to the classics, the words are Satan's but the music and language are Milton's. Are we to believe that in the few moments, hours or days that elapsed between Milton's dictating the lovely lines on Academe and the Attic bird, the murmuring bees and whispering stream, surcharged as they are with deep emotion—that in that short time, Milton lost his love and his faith? Or did Milton dictate one of the speeches and his amanuensis write the other!

If I seem impatient with the tendency to read Milton's position into Christ's speech it is in part because such argument makes us forget that Christ is a speaker in a poem, and that he is saying what he ought to have said, and undoubtedly would have said even if it had not been Satan to whom he was replying. Bred in a pious family, he early read the Law and Story "and found it sweet, Made it my whole delight." Even if he had been only human, with his background, his education and his religion, he *should* have believed that the Law, the Psalms, the Prophets, *were* far superior to Greek literature and philosophy. In addition, altercations over Milton's own beliefs carry us away from the importance of what Christ is saying about knowledge and wisdom. "Be famous then by wisdom," Satan had said, and had gone on to imply that if Christ's empire was to be that of the mind, he must read and study Greek philosophy and literature, since "The Gentiles also know, and write and teach To admiration." Christ replies to Satan on three counts. I shall take the simplest one first.

Although Satan used the word "wisdom," he was actually talking about "knowledge," as Christ makes clear:

> However, many books
> Wise men have said, are wearisome; who reads
> Incessantly, and to his reading brings not
> A spirit and judgment equal or superior,
> (And what he brings, what needs he elsewhere seek?)
> Uncertain and unsettled yet remains,
> Deep versed in books, and shallow in himself,
> Crude or intoxicate, collecting toys
> And trifles for choice matters, worth a sponge,
> As children gathering pebbles on the shore.
>
> (IV. 321-30)

Now let us consider what—to Christ—made the inferiority of Greek to Hebraic philosophy and literature. For all their metaphysics, the Greeks did not know how the world or man began.

They did not know the Bible, did not know the one true God. The hymns and psalms of the Old Testament are inevitably superior to the fables and odes of the Greeks, because

> God is praised aright, and godlike men,
> The Holiest of Holies, and his saints,
> Such are from God inspired.
>
> (IV. 348-50)

The Peripatetics, the Epicureans, the Stoics, even Socrates, shared in common an insuperable barrier to true wisdom:

> Ignorant of themselves, of God much more,
> And how the world began and how man fell.
>
> (IV. 310-11)

Pagans as they were, they did not know the true religion, were not illuminated by the one true Fountain, did not know God. This is what Milton's Christ said, and it is exactly what Jesus should and would have said.

I have left the most difficult passage until the end. Christ begins his speech:

> Think that I know these things, or think
> I know them not. . . .
>
> (IV. 286-87)

Milton did not know, nor do we know today, the extent to which the historical Jesus had been exposed to Hellenistic culture, though Christ's reply seems to indicate an extensive acquaintance with both Greek philosophy and literature. But, as Christ says, that is not the important point:

> not therefore am I short
> Of knowing what I ought. He who receives
> Light from above, from the Fountain of Light,
> No other doctrine needs, though granted true.
>
> (IV. 287-90)

The Greeks did not have true illumination because they did not know the Fountain of Light. In place of God, they could acknowledge only Fortune or Fate:

> who therefore seeks in these
> True wisdom, finds her not, or by delusion
> Far worse, her false resemblance only meets,
> An empty cloud.

> (IV. 318-21)

The Hebrew prophets and psalmists by whom "God is praised aright, and godlike men," were "from God inspired." The distinction Christ makes between learning and wisdom is similar in some ways to the distinction Raphael made to Adam between the "discursive" and the "intuitive" Reason. The angels had no need of learning, no need for ratiocination. They were wise intuitively; they knew by illumination. Adam, lying on the ground, strove to justify the ways of God to men intellectually, using his "discursive Reason" but Eve's was a change not of mind but of heart; she intuitively *felt* the justice of God toward the sins of men. Wisdom comes not from the making or reading of many books, of which there is no end. It comes through the Light of Nature, which is "not in all quite lost" (IV. 352). That light is in kind if not in degree the Light from above, from the Fountain of Light. Satan's temptation, "Be famous then by wisdom" is no temptation at all to Christ, who as man has within himself the Light of Nature, the kingdom of the mind which comes from the Fountain of Light. As Son of God, he has come into the world to lighten its darkness, to bring to men the illumination of the one true Light.

The Final Temptation

Between the last two scenes, a night elapses. Back in the wilderness, Christ finds his sleep disturbed. As with Eve, Satan, unseen, is close beside him, disturbing his sleep "with ugly dreams." Then a great storm rises, thunder, lightning, rain, torrential gales that tore up great trees in the forest. "Nor stayed the terror there." Presumably at Satan's summons, "infernal ghosts and hellish furies" howled and shrieked. A dark and troubled night indeed, which would have proved to another than Christ "the dark night of the soul," Satan had hoped to produce. Yet through it, as Satan himself says, Christ remained "unappalled in calm and sinless peace." The night is followed by a most beautiful morning, during which Satan appears again. Since we are approaching the climax, we must consider the situation carefully. Even now, Satan is not certain of Christ's identity. "For Son of God to me," he says, "is yet in doubt." He is not entirely sure

> In what degree or meaning thou art called
> The Son of God, which bears no single sense;
> The Son of God I also am, or was,
> And if I was, I am; relation stands;
> All men are sons of God.
>
> (IV. 516-20)

Satan is so often a hypocrite that it is dangerous to take him at face-value, but I see no reason to doubt what he says: he is still not finally persuaded of Christ's identity. He is about to make his last desperate attempt, which will clinch the matter, one way or the other. Catching up Christ and, by his supernatural power, carrying him above the city of Jerusalem, he sets Christ on the highest pinnacle of the Temple, saying with bitter irony:

> I to thy Father's house
> Have brought thee, and highest placed; highest is best.
>
> (IV. 552-53)

To stand upright on that pinnacle "will ask thy skill." If he cannot stand, let him cast himself down and ask his God to give His angels charge over him, as the Psalms prophesied. The devil can quote Scripture to his purpose; so too Christ:

> To whom thus Jesus, "Also it is written,
> "Tempt not the Lord thy God." He said, and stood.
>
> (IV. 560-61)

This is the climax of *Paradise Regained,* and, if we are persuaded that Satan has not really known that this is the Son of God, a very dramatic climax, as Satan falls and Christ stands, until the angels, as in the prophecy, come to bear him gently down to earth. More and more I am persuaded that this is a climax too for Christ.

Through the heavenly anthems of the angelic hosts we hear the words which again, as in the opening lines, link *Paradise Regained* with *Paradist Lost:*

> thou hast avenged
> Supplanted Adam, and by vanquishing
> Temptation hast regained lost Paradise. . . . .
> A fairer Paradise is founded now
> For Adam and his chosen sons, whom thou
> A Savior, art come down to reinstall. . . .
> Hail, Son of the Most High, heir of both worlds,
> Queller of Satan, on thy glorious work
> Now enter and begin to save mankind.
>
> (IV. 606-35)

But the history of the life of Christ in this world is not yet over; indeed his mission on earth is only now beginning. Even while the angels are singing

> he unobserved
> Home to his mother's house private returned.

Samson Agonistes

GENERAL INTRODUCTION

Samson Agonistes was published in 1671 (following the epic), in the same volume with *Paradise Regained*. Until the last few years it was generally considered Milton's last work. There is no external evidence for or against that theory. Edward Phillips said only: "It cannot be concluded when he wrote his excellent tragedy." David Masson took for granted that it was composed between 1666 and 1670. Some recent critics have tended to put it much further back, William Riley Parker to "the period between 1647-53," and Allan Gilbert further still. He thinks it may have been composed not long after the drafts of five possible plays on Samson of which we have record in the Trinity Manuscript. If his suggestion is accepted, *Samson* would become the first of Milton's major works. Between the extremes of Masson and Gilbert is the theory of A. S. P. Woodhouse that the mood of the drama seems to reflect Milton's in the Restoration years 1660-61, when he was struggling between despair and hope, rather than the last years after *Paradise Regained,* when he had presumably found peace. Recent stylistic studies, however (notably that of Ants Oras, "Milton's Blank Verse and the Chronology of his Major Poems") dealing with feminine endings, strong pauses and other prosodic matters, tend to reestablish the belief that *Paradise Regained* followed *Paradise Lost* and that *Samson Agonistes* is Milton's last work.

We remember that in *The Reason of Church Government,* when Milton was pondering the form best suited for the great poem he wished to write, he discussed a long epic in the manner of Homer, Virgil and Tasso, a short epic for which the Book of Job might "be a brief model," and went on to question "whether those dramatic constitutions, wherein Sophocles and Euripides reign, shall be found more doctrinal and exemplary to a nation." The prose-preface to *Samson Agonistes* begins with the words: "Tragedy, as it was anciently composed, hath been ever held the gravest, moralest, and most profitable of all other Poems." Milton had various reasons for adding the preface to his drama, one of which undoubtedly was that the Puritans had prohibited "stage plays" and the theatres had been closed for many years. As if in reply to his own party, he calls attention to the fact that St. Paul did not hesitate to quote Euripides in the Holy Scriptures; that the Book of Revelation (as Milton himself had suggested in *The Reason of Church Government*), might be considered a classical tragedy, with acts divided by choruses; that Gregory Nazianzen, Bishop of Constantinople, had written a tragedy called *Christ Suffering,* a belief widely accepted in Milton's time though now doubted.

To Milton drama inevitably implied Greek tragedy, rather than the forms developed by the Elizabethan, Jacobean and Restoration dramatists who, as he says in the preface, made the "error of intermixing comic stuff with tragic sadness and gravity; or introducing trivial and vulgar persons." It implied, too, the supposed "Aristotelian unities" of time, place and action, though the "unity of time," particularly mentioned by Milton, was not Aristotelian but had been read into the *Poetics* by much later critics. In addition Milton followed the classical practice of using a Chorus. "The Chorus," he says, "is here introduced after the Greek manner, not ancient only but modern, and still in use among the Italians." The sources and analogues of *Samson Agonistes* in Greek tragedy are many. Aeschylus, Sophocles and Euripides all played a part in its making, as William Riley Parker has shown in the most comprehensive study of the subject, *Milton's Debt to Greek Tragedy in Samson Agonistes*. Euripides, according to Mr. Parker, was Milton's favorite Greek dramatist, but *Samson Agonistes* is closer to the other two in various ways. It resembles Aeschylus, particularly *Prometheus Bound,* in its stark simplicity—few characters, a simple plot, concentration on a main figure. But it is close to Sophocles also. As Samson was the strong man of Hebraic legend, so Heracles in Greek tradition was strong in himself but weak in his relation to women. There are reminiscences of the *Trachiniae* of Sophocles, in which the story of Heracles is told. Even more, *Samson* recalls Sophocles' *Oedipus at Colonnus,* in which Oedipus, blind and helpless through his own fault, is visited by a succession of friends and enemies, the contrast between his former greatness and his present ignominy stressed by the chorus and commentators. There are various other analogues but these are the closest.

The form of *Samson Agonistes* and many of its characteristics are Greek, but what of the characters? These, of course, are basically Hebraic, drawn from Judges XIII-XVI, chapters that should be in the minds of all students before they begin to read the drama. As in *Paradise Lost,* Milton carefully follows the Scriptures: there is no detail of the original account that he fails to introduce either through Samson's reminiscences or those of his father and friends. But as in *Paradise Lost,* he does not hesitate to transcend his source by elaboration and development—and, indeed, in two instances by actual changes from the Biblical account: in the Bible, Dalilah was not Samson's wife, as Milton makes her, but a mistress, with whom his relation was apparently casual. A lesser addition is in the account of Manoa, since the Bible gives no authority for the idea that Samson's father was approaching the Philistian lords in an attempt to arrange his son's ransom from slavery. The final impression of Milton's Samson is very different from that of the Biblical character. Samson in Judges is basically a very simple person: a giant of folklore who has gathered around himself all sorts of legends of gods and demigods. In Milton's hands he comes alive as an intensely suffering human being, struggling with God, struggling with himself—much more like Job than the legendary giant of Judges. The Bible emphasizes his strength; Milton his psychology. Classical drama though *Samson* is, it is in structure also close to the Book of Job, in which we see Job lying upon the ground, questioning himself and his Maker, in which, too, we watch the psychological effect upon him of "Job's comforters." In the Book of Job, as in *Samson Agonistes,* we feel a descending line in the first part, as the "comfort" of his friends serves only to deepen the suffering of the chief character; in the last part we are conscious of a rising line of confidence and trust.

Hellenism and Hebraism are combined in *Samson Agonistes.* What of Christianity? The most extensive treatment of supposed Christian elements in the drama is Michael Krouse's *Milton's Samson and the Christian Tradition,* in which the author develops the thesis that in Milton's mind Samson has been allegorized in such a way that he has become not only a saint, but a prototype of Christ in the sense we have found Moses, Abraham, and David prefigurations of Christ in Book XII of *Paradise Lost.* From this point of view the title of the drama becomes very significant: to a Greek, Samson *Agonistes* might have meant only "Samson Struggling," as an athlete competing in the Olympic games might have struggled. As time went on, the meaning of the title broadened to imply that Samson was a champion for truth, until it finally took on a Christian connotation, such as it has in Augustine's *De Agone Christiano,*—Samson is the "true warfaring Christian" of whom Milton wrote in the *Areopagitica.* T. Scott Craig goes even further with the Christianity of Samson ("Concerning Milton's Samson," *Renaissance News* V [1952] 43-53) "Samson Agonistes is really Christus Agonistes," he says. The drama is a typological representation of the agony of Christ in Gethsemane, "a liturgical orchestration of the major themes of Calvinist scholasticism." The drama is liturgy; the "agony of Samson is a surrogate for the unbloody sacrifice of the mass." The climax of the liturgy is in the choral ode in which Samson's regeneration is compared to the resurrection of the phoenix. (ll. 1704 ff)

Classical, Hebraic, Christian—so *Samson Agonistes* has been interpreted by one commentator or another. I myself do not feel the drama Christian. Its great power in my mind lies in the very fact that it is the least Christian of all Milton's major works, indeed that Christianity plays almost no part in it. Milton is at his greatest when he treats the Old Testament rather than the New (with a few exceptions when he paraphrases the Book of Revelation). A great deal of the weakness of *Paradise Regained* rises from the fact that it *is* Christian and that both the classical and Hebraic elements which made the majesty of *Paradise Lost* are almost lacking except in the two passages which have been discussed. *Samson Agonistes* combines the two great cultures to which Milton was most responsive.

As this is a Greek drama, it involves certain conventions which we must accept and keep in mind while reading it. The "unities" Milton took for granted require great compression, since the action must cover not more than one day, and usually only a few hours, as does *Samson.* In my analysis I have indicated a division into Acts, a word the Greek might not recognize. The division into scenes—if one prefers that word—is marked by the Chorus which in Milton's hands was somewhat different from the Chorus customary in Greek tragedy, though the Chorus was used in varying ways by different dramatists. Milton himself mentions the fact that the Chorus was still used in modern drama and a number of commentators (see particularly Gretchen Finney, "The Choruses in *Samson Agonistes"* in *Musical Backgrounds for English Literature*), have suggested that Milton's chorus is more Italian than classical. The Chorus has various uses; it may and often does tell the antecedent action, reminding us of episodes in Samson's life which took place before the play begins. It acts as commentary upon what other characters say and do. In *Samson,* it plays a part as one of the various "provocative incidents" which arouse Samson from his lethargy and assist in changing his attitude. One of its chief functions is to set a mood, indicating a change of one sort or another from the preceding act or scene.

One of the customary conventions of Greek tragedy seems strange to modern audiences, accustomed to the "star system," and expecting the last scene to be the climactic one for the chief character. In classical tragedy the "star" does not appear in the last act. The principle of "decorum" demanded that no scene of bloodshed, death, or physical suffering be shown on the stage. The technique is very different from that of many "tragedies of blood" of the Elizabethan period in which one dead body after another is carried out, and diametrically opposed to that of the modern cinema, in which climactic scenes of murder and bloodshed are treated as if they were linked sweetness long drawn out. The chief speeches in the last scene of a classical tragedy are those of a Messenger who in graphic rhetoric describes the scene we have not seen, as the Messenger in *Samson* holds the actors in suspense for many lines before telling them what has happened to Samson. (For the comfort of modern amateur actors who may resent the anticlimax for the "star," let it be said that in Greek drama, when there were usually only two or three actors, the "star" doubled the parts of hero and Messenger, thus getting the best of both worlds.)

Greek drama differs from modern drama in another important way. The materials used by the Greeks were always familiar, drawn from history, Homeric epic, legend, mythology. The audience at a Greek play knew the end from the beginning. There is therefore no possibility of suspense in the modern sense, when the outcome of the story is presumably unknown until the very end. The audience at a Greek play, as has often been said, was in a godlike position (like the fore-knowing God of *Paradise Lost*), knowing what is concealed from the characters. They experience suspense, as we do not. In place of suspense, the Greek dramatist used various devices, which we shall find in *Samson Agonistes*. Dramatic irony is very important; the audience will catch "double talk" on the part of the author when none is meant by the character who is unconscious of any double meaning in his words. Mr. Tillyard (*Milton,* pp. 343-45) has rightly made a strong point of Milton's use of *peripeteia,* using as a classical example the scene in *Oedipus Rex* in which "the messenger comes to cheer Oedipus and free him from his alarms about his mother, but by revealing who he is, produces the opposite effect." Mr. Tillyard adds: "A *peripeteia* happens, not when there is mere change of fortune, but when an intention or action brings about the opposite of what was meant." In 'Samson's case, each of his actions which seem to lead to greater ignominy, proves to lead ultimately to triumph. In the same way, the Philistines, who call Samson in to make them sport, actually call him in to destroy them.

The most subtle substitute for suspense in classical drama lies in the development of *catharsis:* the author's so involving us with the development of character that, in spite of our foreknowledge of what is to happen, we feel the emotions of pity and fear, so that we involve ourselves with the character, suffering in his suffering, experiencing intense pity for him. It is this *catharsis* which Milton discusses in the prose-preface, when he paraphrases Aristotle, saying that tragedy has "power by raising pity and fear, or terror, to purge the mind of those and such-like passions, that is to temper and reduce them to just measure with a kind of delight, stirred up by reading or seeing those passions well imitated." Even though we know from the beginning that Samson will pull down the temple, and that he will be killed with his enemies, we follow the play with a growing feeling of intensity, as Milton brings to life a character, lets us see him suffering yet sense his gradually growing moral power, lets us feel his nobility and the rightness of his life and death. Milton's is the finest expression of *catharsis* in our language, as fine as that in any Greek drama.

The basic theme of *Samson* is the one Milton first used so long ago in *Comus,* repeated in *Paradise Lost* and *Paradise Regained:* temptation. His purpose in the drama, as in the long epic, is to justify the ways of God to men. Similar though the themes and problems are, there is one important difference. In *Paradise Lost,* Satan was tempted and fell. Adam and Eve, too, were tempted and fell. But Satan was an Archangel, and although Adam and Eve were human beings, before the Fall they were prototypes, rather than man and woman as we know them. Christ in *Paradise Regained,* whatever he may be theologically, cannot be tempted. Samson is the first character—since the Lady in *Comus*—who is a human being on a par with ourselves, subject to the frailties familiar to us. Temperate though he may have been in all appetites except the sexual, he differs from other human beings only in his gigantic size and strength. Those modern commentators who would make *Samson* the first, rather than the last of the major works, might have made a stronger case than they do by suggesting a progress in Milton's treatment of temptation: from the simple Lady in *Comus,* he passed to another basically simple human being, Samson; then rose to show us temptation first in an angel of God, then in the originals of man and woman. Finally, in *Paradise Regained,* he offered us the Great Exemplar: a man living the life of men in this world, but a Man who could not be tempted.

Prologue

Various Greek dramas began (as, indeed, did *Comus*) with a Prologue, a device used by the author to set the scene and mood, and to give the audience a certain amount of antecedent action. The Prologue of *Samson Agonistes* recalls particularly the opening scene of Sophocles' *Oedipus at Colonnus,* in which the blind Oedipus is led on to the stage by his daughter, Antigone, and the scene in Euripides' *Phoenissiae* in which the blind Tiresias is also led in by his daughter. We know at once that Samson is blind; we are aware that he is a prisoner of the Philistines, "eyeless in Gaza, at the mill with slaves." This is a holiday on which the people are holding a feast to their God Dagon, that "twice battered God of Palestine," of whom we first heard in the *Nativity Ode.*

In various ways, the Prologue recalls both Adam's soliloquy in Book X of *Paradise Lost* and various prologues in the epic. Like Adam and like Satan, Samson is intensely conscious of the contrast between "what once I was, and what am now." Like Adam, in effect, he ponders why he has been born, and particularly why his birth was foretold by an Angel and his

> breeding ordained and prescribed
> As of a person separate to God,
> Designed for great exploits.

With Adam, too, he feels it imperative that he justify the ways of God to men, and particularly to face the problem of his own responsibility for what has happened. Again, like Adam, he feels the terror of a "living death." (79. ff.) But like prologues in *Paradise Lost,* and even more than any one of them, this is a lament on blindness. In *Paradise Lost,* when he was speaking *in propria persona,* Milton could say only a little about his own infirmity. Now that he is speaking for Samson, he is free to say much more. It is inevitable that we should read many lines in Samson's Prologue as autobiographical, remembering (if, indeed, Milton wrote *Samson Agonistes* late in life) that Milton had also known what it meant to be "blind among enemies," perhaps even, "dark" as he was, exposed

> To daily fraud, contempt, abuse and wrong,
> Within doors, as without, still as a fool
> In power of others, never in my own,
> Scarce half I seem to live, dead more than half.

(76-79)

ACT I

Samuel Johnson said that *Samson Agonistes* has a beginning and
an end but that it has "no middle, since nothing passes between
the first act and the last, that either hastens or delays the death of
Samson." As so often when he wrote about Milton, Johnson
seemed to go out of his way to be perversely wrong. He failed to
see that *Samson Agonistes* is preeminently a psychological study
of the development of a human being. Each "act" or "episode"
plays an integral part, as we shall see. Each one serves as what has
been called "a provocative incident." Each one has its effect upon
Samson.

The Chorus—as in the Book of Job a group of former friends—
speak at first to each other, Samson not yet aware who they are.
They too comment on the great contrast between what Samson *was*
and *is,* as he "lies at random, carelessly diffused . . . as one past
hope." (120-22) Their memories go back to give us further an-
tecedent action, reminding us of heroic feats for which Samson was
famous, of a man of prodigious strength who tore a lion, as a lion
tears a kid, who ran weaponless on armies to make "arms ridicu-
lous," who slew a thousand with the jawbone of an ass, who tore
up the gates of Gaza, and carried them off to a hill (130-50). They
too comment upon Samson's blindness by which he has become
the dungeon of himself.

So far Samson has not distinguished their words nor is he sure
who the visitors are. When he understands that they are friends, he
can unburden himself somewhat, and particularly discuss the
treachery of his wives.

ACT II

The Chorus' announcement to Samson that his father is coming awakens in Samson "another inward grief," which deepens as Manoa, like the Chorus, emphasizes the "miserable change" between what Samson was and what he is. Manoa's mind goes back to his own prayers for a son, the descent of an Angel prophesying Samson's birth and ordaining his "nurture holy." Is it not unjust of God, Manoa asks in effect, that after all Samson's great deeds for his nation, he should be ignominiously punished for one error? (368-71) Manoa's words are close to Samson's own in his soliloquy, but as he hears his father questioning God's ways to men, Samson turns to God's defence:

> Appoint not heavenly dispensation, Father,.
> Nothing of all these evils hath befallen me
> But justly; I myself have brought them on,
> Sole author, I, sole cause.

(373-76)

Again he goes back in his memory to his own "foul effeminancy," (a charge some modern commentators bring against Adam) in his betrayal of the secret of his strength to Dalilah. The servitude he suffers from the Philistines is only servitude he has brought upon himself, his "servile mind Rewarded well with servile punishment." (ll. 412-13)

So far, Samson, the Chorus and Manoa have concerned themselves chiefly with reminiscences of Samson's past. Now Manoa introduces a new circumstance of which Samson has not known. On this holiday, the Philistines are holding a great feast, honoring their god Dagon, who has delivered Samson, that arch-enemy, into their hands:

> So Dagon shall be magnified, and God,
> Besides whom is no god, compared with idols,
> Disglorified, blasphemed, and had in scorn
> By the idolatrous amidst their wine.

(440-43)

Of all punishments, this is the most shameful, as his father knows, not only to Samson but to his father's house. His fall has resulted in his personal shame and that of his family; but it has brought about even more the fall of the true God. (462-63) It is all very well for Samson to insist that Jehovah will arise and "His great Name assert." The fact remains that in the eyes of the carousing Philistines Jehovah has fallen in his servant's fall.

Manoa unintentionally rubs salt into Samson's wound by telling him that he has already approached "some Philistian lords," in an attempt to arrange ransom for his son. Manoa is speaking and acting only as a father might well speak and act. For all his own suffering and the blow to his family pride, the safety and physical comfort of his son are paramount in his mind. As a father, he is looking forward to caring physically for his son. As he says later, "It shall be my delight to tend his eyes And view him sitting in his house." (1490-91) Manoa, we notice, lays great stress upon the preservation of Samson's physical life, even though that life may be lived in ignominy:

> Better at home lie bedrid, not only idle,
> Inglorious, unemployed, with age outworn.

(579-80)

At one moment (we shall understand this better later in the play) he warns his son against any thought of ending his own life. (502-507) The father's solicitude is bitter medicine for his son. The father is old; Samson should be at the height of his physical strength; as a good Hebrew son, he should have tended his father. The irony is apparent to him, if not to the father. Life, as such, seems to him little or nothing. "As for life, To what end shall I seek it?" (521-22) Again we hear the reiterated contrast between what he *is* and what he *was,* leading Samson now to interpret his fall—as a Greek dramatist might have interpreted it—as a result of *Hybris,* that Pride of mortals so often published by the gods:

> Fearless of danger, like a petty god
> I walked about, admired of all, and dreaded
> On hostile ground, none daring my affront,
> Then swollen with pride into the snare I fell.
>
> (529-32)

The Chorus, too, comments upon the irony of a single weakness in a man otherwise so strong, not only bodily, but mentally strong, for Samson, temperate in all matters but one, had shown himself proof against the temptations which most often cause man's downfall: "desire of wine and all delicious drinks." (541 ff.) But, as Samson himself replied, "What availed this temperance, not complete?" (559)

Manoa's visit has served as one of a series of "provocative incidents" upon his son. Samson is even more poignantly aware than before of the blow suffered by family-pride; he has let his family down; still worse, he has let his God down. He has subjected his proud elderly father to the ignominy of abasing himself before the enemy and suing for the ransom of his son in order to tend him at home in indefinite ignominy. As Manoa leaves, again with unconscious irony emphasizing the fact that with "a father's timely care" he is setting out to prosecute the means of ransom, the Chorus and Samson again ponder God's ways to men in the choral ode, "God of our fathers, what is man!" (668-689) Like Adam in his soliloquy, Samson acquits God and accepts the responsibility for his downfall. But like Adam, he still speaks from the lips rather than the heart, which seems to echo Adam's, "Inexplicable Thy justice seems." Samson is still in a state of lethargy. No matter whether he has sat or stood while conversing with his friends, he is still metaphorically lying on the ground. Even though he has insisted that Jehovah will not remain subservient to Dagon, he accepts the fact that this will come about with no assistance from him. The comfort of "Job's comforters" has served only to deepen his despair. Until this moment he has remained passively quiescent to what seems his fate. It is the entrance of his wife that first begins to arouse him from lethargy, that begins to bring about the change from the passive to the active Samson.

ACT III

The Dalilah scene is highly ironic, but if there is bitterness, there is also saltiness from the moment the Chorus sees her approaching:

> But who is this, what thing of sea or land,
> Female of sex *it seems*.
> (710-11)

Decked out in all possible finery, Dalilah appears on the scene "like a stately ship of Tarsus"—an Old Testament symbol of pride—

> With all her bravery on, and tackle trim,
> Sails filled and streamers waving,
> Courted by all the winds that hold them play,
> An amber scent of odorous perfume
> Her harbinger, a damsel train behind.
> (717-21)

Were there memories here, I wonder, of two very different scenes in Shakespeare: the entrance of the Nurse in *Romeo and Juliet,* and of Cleopatra on her barge? Dalilah is indeed a "rich Philistian matron"—richer because of money paid her for the betrayal of her husband. Whatever his position before, Samson literally and physically springs to his feet as he hears her name. "My wife! My traitress! Let her not come near." Like Satan in his temptation of

Eve, Dalilah begins with hypocrisy. "Like a fair flower surcharged with dew, she weeps." Her "conjugal affection," is stronger than her doubt and fear of Samson's reception of her. Her one desire is to lighten his suffering and make whatever amends may lie in her power. As Adam turned upon Eve with a savage, "Out of my sight, thou Serpent," so Samson turns upon Dalilah, "Out, out, Hyena!" Step by step, Dalilah attempts his defences (766-820) as Satan step by step had tempted Eve's. Her weakness was only the frailty common to all women: she was curious and inquisitive. When this evokes no response, she tries another, again reminiscent of Eve, who after she had eaten the apple was afraid lest Adam take another wife:

> I saw thee mutable
> Of fancy, feared lest one day thou wouldst leave me
> As her at Timna, sought by all means therefore
> How to endear.
>
> (793 ff.)

Jealous not only of other women but of the sense of adventure that so often sent Samson forth, she had sought to make him "mine and love's prison." Forgive a poor wretch, who did what she did only because she was a woman, and a woman who loved her husband!

Samson's vigor is returning momentarily, more than he knows. "Weakness, indeed," he says savagely, "I can well believe it— weakness to resist Philistian gold." Not for a moment does the disillusioned Samson believe that Dalilah did what she did for love:

> But love constrained thee; call it furious rage
> To satisfy thy lust: Love seeks to have love;
> My love how couldst thou hope, who tookest the way
> To raise in me inexpiable hate.
>
> (837-40)

Her opening gambits having failed, Dalilah attempts another. The magistrates had insisted that her duty was to the state, "to entrap a common enemy" of her people. "And the Priest was not behind, but ever at my ear." For the first time Dalilah has come close to the truth, rising from that "levity"—as Samson calls it—of frivolous arguments to a basic one which raised a profound question. In Samson's reply we come to understand why Milton made Dalilah Samson's wife rather than his mistress, as she had been in the Scriptures. The Biblical Dalilah could have justified her actions far more readily than could the Miltonic. Milton puts the legal and moral problem thus:

> Being once a wife, for me thou wast to leave
> Parents and country; nor was I their subject,
> Nor under their protection, but my own,
> Thou mine, not theirs; if aught against my life
> Thy country sought of thee, it sought unjustly,
> Against the Law of Nature, Law of Nations.
>
> (885-90)

As an orthodox Hebrew, Samson might have confined himself to Genesis: "Therefore shall a man leave his father and his mother, and shall cleave unto his wife." Had he known it, he might have added the example of Ruth and Naomi, But Milton has gone farther, adding to the Hebraic teaching basic ideas of Roman law. The Law of Nature had had a long history, the Law of Nations one, which if not so long, was sometimes more perplexing. On this problem Milton held that both the Law of Nature and the Law of Nations agreed with Genesis that the first duty of a wife was not to her country but to her husband.

Dalilah is not yet discouraged. She has two further possibilities, the first similar to Manoa's plan for Samson: she will intercede with the Philistines for his release with every hope of success. She will take him home from this loathsome prison, and with "nursing diligence" care for him all the rest of his life. Manoa's proffer of physical care had been hard enough for his son; Dalilah's is intolerable. When he remembers what she had been able to do while he still had both strength and sight, what might he expect now, blind, helpless, as easily deceived as a child? Prison seems liberty in comparison with what he would find in her house, which he will never enter.

Dalilah has one last card to play, the one that had proved her trump card in the past—her physical attraction to Samson. She plays it with her briefest speech, one line only: "Let me approach at least, and touch thy hand." The violence of Samson's response proves the extent to which Dalilah has roused him from his lethargy:

Not for thy life, lest fierce remembrance wake
My sudden rage to tear thee joint from joint.

(952-53)

Dalilah has lost the game, but she has done for Samson what neither his father nor his friends was able to do, brought him to life, made him conscious of his manhood. If we may use a modern medical analogy, Samson's adrenal glands have been stimulated, have suddenly become active. Vigor returns to his body.

Commentators differ greatly in their interpretations of Dalilah. To some she is little more than still another example of Milton's misogyny. She has usually been considered only in her effect upon Samson, not as a character with her own complex psychology. Professor Hanford says (*Poems of John Milton,* p. 577): "In the whole dialogue Dalilah's psychology seems less intelligible than Samson's. The portrayal is remarkably in contrast to that of Eve in *Paradise Lost,* where we seem to have no difficulty in following all the complications of thought and feeling." He makes a statement, extraordinary to me at least, about the speech beginning in line 928: "The momentary softening of Samson's tone as he rejects Dalilah's kindly proposal is as subtle as it is moving." "Softening," indeed, couched in such diction as "gins and toils," "fair enchanted cup and warbling charms," "adder's wisdom." Remembering Milton's use of animal imagery in tracing the degeneration of Satan, we may notice particularly "adder's wisdom," Samson's "Hyena," and the later chorus in which Dalilah is called both "serpent" and "viper."

The most thoroughgoing Devil's advocate for Dalilah is the perversely amusing William Empson in *Milton's God* (pp. 211-228), from which I can offer only a few samples: "Any number of people have defended the Devil, in their various ways, but I do not know that anyone has defended Delilah and yet her case is even easier to defend than Adam's—it's a push-over. . . . Critics have become accustomed to say that the poem shows a deep trust in God; but they would be shocked if they read the story in their newspapers, and a modern jury would at once regard Delilah as a deeply wronged wife." Mr. Empson finds in her lines "a cool though generous-minded assurance of being in the right." Of her last speech he says: "There she does speak of herself a little; she can at least save her pride. But even then she does it with such large-mindedness, such inability merely to call the kettle black, that she gives us no cause for calling her earlier professions of love insincere."

To be sure, Mr. Empson added his chapter on Dalilah as an epilogue to his book on *Milton's God,* professedly because Milton's treatment of her "proves, I think, that the moral generosity of *Paradise Lost* is not due to accident, muddle-headedness or split personality." (What Mr. Empson gives Milton with one hand, he frequently takes away with the other.) Suspicious as he often is of Milton's motives, he curiously seems to accept Dalilah at face-value: "It would be wilful to doubt that she still loves him and wants to keep him, because we are given no other reason for her visit." This seems a problem to other critics as well. Mr. Tillyard says (*Milton,* p. 341): "As a person Dalilah is credible: a fine woman impelled by cruelty and curiosity to visit Samson." Mr. Hanford (*Poems of John Milton,* p. 579), interpreting lines 1000 ff. writes: "Her motivation in coming to visit Samson would therefore be, like his own in going to the Philistian feast, 'of God.' But this formulation does not prevent speculation as to why, in human terms, she did come to him."

Dalilah came to Samson, I think, just as Harapha is to come, as an emissary of the Philistian magistrates, both instructed to report back their findings about Samson's general condition before the lords go so far as to demand Samson's attendance as a mountebank at their feast. We must remember that Samson had long been their scourge; with their foxes as firebrands he had burned their grain and their olives; with the jawbone of an ass, he had smitten a thousand men. When they bound him, the ropes became like flax and dropped from his arms. More than once he had lied to them through Dalilah about the secret of his strength. Temporarily they have reduced him to slavery by cutting his hair; but hair grows, and may not strength return? The magistrates and lords were taking no chances. What better spies could they have than the wife who had successfully tempted him once, and their own giant, in their eyes next to Samson in strength and valor?

Dalilah is on the stage for less than three hundred lines. Perhaps the very compression aided Milton in making her one of the most complex and powerful characters in all his works. We have seen her showing much the same subtlety as Satan in his temptation of Eve, and indeed her basic approach is very similar, based as it is on hypocrisy. When she has played her last card, she throws aside all hypocrisy, and becomes what she is and has been throughout Samson's whole acquaintance with her—a Philistian patriot,

> who to save
> Her country from a fierce destroyer, chose
> Above the faith of wedlock bands.
>
> (984-86)

Dalilah's last speech is one of Milton's greatest. That long training in debate had never served him better. He could and did give the Devil his due to such an extent as to persuade Blake that he was of the Devil's party. As he paraphrased the Psalms to make them great English poetry, so he paraphrased songs of triumph in the Old Testament, particularly the Song of Deborah in Judges, exulting after another woman had killed Sisera, the enemy of her people. Dalilah's last speech makes us momentarily believe that

> in my country where I most desire . . .
> I shall be named among the famousest
> Of women, sung at solemn festivals,
> Living and dead recorded.
>
> (980-84)

Yet as we listen to the triumphal strain, let us not forget that, of all the passages of tragic irony in *Samson Agonistes,* this is the most poignant. Within the space of a few hours, there will be none of her countrymen to bring flowers to adorn her tomb, no magistrates or priests to confer upon her "the public marks of honor and renown" which she has undoubtedly earned from them. Before evening, the husband she betrayed will pull down the roof of the temple

> Upon the heads of all who sat beneath,
> Lords, Ladies, Captains, Counsellors or Priests,
> Their choice nobility and flower, not only
> Of this but each Philistian city round.

(1652-55)

Samson will lie with them—and presumably Dalilah herself, who would have been the last to absent herself from the celebration she had done so much to bring about.

ACT IV

This act is divided into two scenes, having in common the theme of "trial by physical strength." Harapha is the strong man of the Philistians, as Samson had been of the Hebrews, a taunting braggart prize-fighter, who has come to gloat over a fallen champion. From the beginning his tone is insolent: "I thought gyves and the mill had tamed thee!" When Samson suggests that Harapha act rather than merely boast of what he might have done, Harapha adds still further insult. Not only does he disdain to fight with a blind man, but Samson needs a bath before he is fit to be touched. (1106-07) Samson is in full command of himself. Whether the

Chorus knows it or not, indeed, whether he himself fully realizes it, we, the audience are aware that his physical strength is returning and his moral strength at the full. When "like a petty god" he had strutted over the earth in those earlier days, he would not have had the moral strength to take insolence as calmly as he does now. If Harapha wants to try his strength, let them find some narrow room, where blindness will not be such a handicap; let Harapha put on all his magnificent accoutrement. Samson will meet him with only an oaken staff, and Harapha will discover what true strength is. Harapha has clearly no intention of fighting. A *miles gloriosus,* a boasting braggart, he wishes only to taunt a fallen foe, and suggest that Samson had done what he did not by his own strength, but by black magic. (1130-35) "I know no spells," Samson answers quietly, "use no forbidden aids. My strength is in the living God who gave me at my nativity this strength." His God, indeed! Harapha throws back at him. What kind of God is this that he has delivered Samson into the hands of his enemies? It was one thing for Harapha to taunt Samson. It is quite another for Harapha to dare taunt the True God. Samson is morally strong, but Harapha is a coward, and when Samson again challenges him to combat (1233-35) he skulks off the stage. The Chorus remarks: "His Giantship is gone somewhat crestfallen."

Although the Chorus is not fully aware of the change that has come over Samson, they realize something of it, as the tone of their choral ode implies:

O how comely it is, and how reviving
To the spirits of just men long oppressed.

(1269-70)

But to the Chorus, Samson's self-control in the face of insult that would once have aroused him to fury, may be only the result of the patience Samson has learned, that Patience that once replied to Milton: "They also serve who only stand and wait."

The second scene, which follows with the entrance of a Philistian Officer, continues the "trial by physical strength." The Officer has been sent to command Samson to appear at the feast to Dagon officially to show his feats of strength, actually to give the Philistines a chance to exult publicly over the ignominy of their once most dangerous foe. Still Samson retains his self-control. He reminds them that he is a Hebrew, and that his law forbids his taking part in the rites of other religions. (1319-21) Have they not swordplayers and gymnasts of every sort to make them sport? "I will not come," he says flatly. The Chorus is concerned. Surely the Philistines will not accept this categorical reply. For the first time Samson tells his friends what we have been realizing for some time: that his physical strength is returning. While he will not be constrained to go to the Temple of Dagon, he may do so voluntarily. What he will do when he gets there he does not yet know, but the "rousing motions" he is experiencing make him feel that this day which began in profound despair may lead to "something extraordinary." We, the audience, recognize, as his friends cannot, the dramatic irony of his words:

> This day will be remarkable in my life
> By some great act, or of my days the last.
>
> (1388-89)

Since this is classical drama, we see the hero for the last time well before the end of the play, and say our farewell to Samson as, of his own volition, not by force, he goes quietly away with the Officer, saying to his friends

> Happen what may, of me expect to hear
> Nothing dishonorable, impure, unworthy
> Our God, our Law, my Nation, or myself;
> The last of me or not I cannot warrant.
>
> (1423-26)

ACT V

The irony increases as Manoa enters, just after the departure of Samson, happy in the success of his efforts to ransom his son. He has experienced ignominy with some of the Philistines, "wondrous harsh, contemptuous, proud." But on the whole he has reason to believe that if the ransom can be raised, Samson will be released. At this moment he hears a great shout—presumably as Samson appears before the revellers. While the Chorus comments on the irony that the father should tend his son rather than the son his father, and while Manoa looks happily forward to bringing his son home, there comes a far greater noise:

> Noise call you it or universal groan
> As if the whole inhabitation perished.

(1512-13)

As in all Greek tragedies, the climax of the story is told by a Messenger. The tension mounts as the Messenger holds the other characters in suspense by double-talk, so that, though they know that Gaza has fallen, they do not learn Samson's fate for twenty-nine lines. Even then the double-talk continues:

Manoa: Yet ere I give the reins to grief, say first,
           How died he? death to life is crown or shame.
           All by him fell, thou sayest, by whom fell he? . . .
Mess: Unwounded of his enemies he fell.
Manoa: Wearied with slaughter then or how? Explain.
Mess: By his own hands.
Manoa: Self-violence? What cause
           Brought him so soon at variance with himself?

Only now do we hear in detail all that has happened since Samson left the stage. The feats of strength he performed (which should have given the Philistines warning); his request for an intermission; his leaning, as if tired, against the two massy pillars that supported the roof; his last speech, and the spectacular catastrophe as the great temple fell with the sound of thunder and earthquake upon the nobility and flower of the Philistines.

The mood of the ending of *Samson Agonistes* is predominantly Hebraic, though it is a mood which the Greeks too would have understood and shared. One reflection only may be interpreted as Christian, the comment of the Chorus that Samson lies victorious

> Among thy slain self-killed
> Not willingly, but tangled in the fold
> Of dire necessity, whose law in death conjoined
> Thee with thy slaughtered foes.
>
> (1664-67)

Here Milton indicates the position that Samson's death was not suicide in the usual sense of the word, a matter that had been debated *pro* and *con* by Christians long before Milton wrote. Apart from this passing reference, the mood of the ending is another Hebraic song of exultation rather than mourning over the death of a great conqueror who had "slaughtered foes in number more Than all thy life had slain before," a man who had justified himself and even more had justified his God. It is noticeable that in all the choral odes and in Manoa's speeches, there is no suggestion (as in *Lycidas*) of the Christian idea of immortality, of the Resurrection of body or soul, certainly no Christian sense of the forgiveness of enemies in that exultant epitaph of a father for his dead son:

> Come, come, no time for lamentation now,
> Nor much more cause. Samson hath quit himself
> Like Samson, and heroically hath finished
> A life heroic, on his enemies
> Fully revenged, hath left them years of mourning
> And lamentation to the sons of Caphtor

Through all Philistian bounds. To Israel
Honor hath left, and freedom.

(1708-15)

Manoa is not to spend his age, as he had anticipated, tending a helpless son. Rather he will summon his kindred, his friends to attend the dead son "with obsequy and funeral train," home to his father's house. There his monument will be built of laurel and palm. Youths will continue to come to praise his valor and his strength, and virgins will visit his tomb with flowers.

The final chorus, as has often been pointed out, is very close to the choruses of five of Euripides' plays: *Bacchae, Alcestis, Andromache, Helen, Medea,* all of which comment upon the fact that the gods appear in many forms and do many things which man cannot foresee. There had been moments in the mind of Samson and his friends when God had seemed to hide his face, when man had questioned God's ways. But the true meaning of the highest wisdom is "ever best found in the close." Samson has justified his ways to God and God his ways to men. The effect of great tragedy which Milton had sought and found is *catharsis,* "by raising pity and fear, or terror, to purge the mind of those and such-like passions." Milton has given the finest expression in our language of such *catharsis:*

Nothing is here for tears, nothing to wail
Or knock the breast, no weakness, no contempt,
Dispraise or blame, nothing but well and fair
And what may quiet us in a death so noble. . . .
　　His servants he with new acquist
　　Of true experience from this great event,
　　With peace and consolation hath dismissed,
　　And calm of mind, all passion spent.

A number of years ago, President William Allan Neilson persuaded his old friend, Sir Herbert Grierson, retired from his professorship at Edinburgh, to conduct a Milton course with me at Smith College. After the last meeting of the class, when he had read the end of *Samson* aloud in his rich Scottish brogue to a hushed hall of undergraduates, he said to me: "I am glad now that you and Neilson persuaded me to teach Milton once more. In youth we often find him a difficult poet because we have not yet the experience or the background fully to appreciate his art. In middle life, we critics often quarrel with him because his 'doxy' is not our 'doxy,' and we think we know all the answers better than he. Before I die, I want to write just one more essay, 'On Re-Reading Milton in Old Age.' I shall say then what I have tried to express this term to your students, which they cannot yet understand: that Milton is the one great English poet who lasts a lifetime."

Sir Herbert had no reason to doubt that *Samson Agonistes* was Milton's last work and these words his final statement of the wisdom he had learned from life. There are many of us who will continue to believe that these were Milton's last poetic words, and who in age have found with Sir Herbert that Milton, indeed, lasts a lifetime.

Selected Bibliography

❦

[This list includes all books and articles mentioned in the text, with a few others of general interest.]

GENERAL REFERENCE WORKS

The Oxford Classical Dictionary. Oxford: Clarendon, 1957 (or more recent ed.)

AVERY, CATHERINE B., New Century Classical Handbook. New York: Appleton-Century-Crofts, 1962.

BRADSHAW, JOHN, A Concordance to the Poetical Works of John Milton. London: Sonnenschein; New York: Macmillan, 1894

CLEVELAND, CHARLES D., A Complete Concordance to the Poetical Works of John Milton. London: Sampson, Low, Marsh, 1867.

GILBERT, ALLEN H., A Geographical Dictionary of Milton. New Haven: Yale Yale University Press, 1919.

HUCKABAY, CALVIN, John Milton: A Bibliographical Supplement, 1929-1957. Pittsburgh: Duquesne University Press, 1960.

LE COMTE, EDWARD, A Milton Dictionary. New York: Philosophical Library, 1961.

LOCKWOOD, LAURA, Lexicon to the English Poetical Works of John Milton. New York: Macmillan, 1907.

OSGOOD, CHARLES G., The Classical Mythology of Milton's English Poems. New York: Holt, 1900.

STEVENS, DAVID H., Reference Guide to Milton, 1800-1929. Chicago: University of Chicago Press, 1930.

EDITIONS
(lists only editions referred to in this volume)

The definitive edition of Milton's Works is still the "Columbia Milton": The Works of John Milton, ed. Frank Allen Patterson and others. New York: Columbia University Press, 1931-38. 19 vols. in 21.

Complete Poetry and Selected Prose of John Milton, ed. Merritt Y. Hughes. New York: Odyssey Press, 1957. (This is the most completely annotated one-volume edition, indispensable for teachers and advanced students. I have referred to it throughout this volume as "Hughes." A volume containing *Paradise Lost* has just appeared in paperback, other volumes presumably to follow.)

Complete Prose Works of John Milton, ed. Don M. Wolfe. New Haven: Yale University Press, 1953—. To be published in 8 vols. Vols. I and II have appeared.

The Complete Poetical Works of John Milton, ed. William Vaughan Moody. Cambridge Edition. Boston: Houghton Mifflin, 1899. (Various later editions)

The Poems of John Milton, ed. James Holly Hanford. New York: Ronald Press, 1936, second ed. 1953.

The Poetical Works of John Milton, ed. Helen Darbishire. Oxford: Clarendon Press, 1952-55, 2 vols.

Poems of Mr. John Milton: the 1645 Edition, with Essays and Analysis by Cleanth Brooks and John Edward Hardy. New York: Harcourt Brace. 1951.

Milton's Comus, being the Bridgewater Mss. with Notes, and a Short Family Memoir, by the Lady Alex Egerton. London: Dent, 1910.

BIOGRAPHICAL

The definitive biography of Milton still remains David Masson, The Life of John Milton: Narrated in Connection with the Political, Ecclesiastical and Literary History of his Times. Cambridge and London: Macmillan, 1859-94, 7 vols. This must, however, be supplemented and corrected by various of the following:

BRENNECKE, ERNEST JR., John Milton the Elder and his Music. New York: Columbia University Press, 1938.

BROWN, ELEANOR, Milton's Blindness. New York: Columbia University Press, 1934.

CLARK, DONALD, Milton at St. Paul's School. New York: Columbia University Press, 1948.

DARBISHIRE, HELEN, ED., The Early Lives of Milton. London: Constable, 1932.

DIEKHOFF, JOHN S., ED., Milton on Himself. New York: Oxford University Press, 1939.

DORIAN, DONALD, The English Diodatis. New Brunswick: Rutgers University Press, 1950.

FRENCH, J. MILTON, "The Powell-Milton Bond," Harvard Studies and Notes. XXIX (1938) 61-73.

The Life Records of John Milton. New Brunswick: Rutgers University Press, 1949-53.

HANFORD, JAMES HOLLY, A Milton Handbook. New York: Appleton-Century-Crofts, fourth ed. 1946, reprinted 1954. An indispensable book for the Milton teacher or student.

John Milton, Englishman. New York: Crown Publishers, 1944.

GENERAL CRITICISM
(*treating more than one of Milton's works*)

ADAMS, ROBERT M., Ikon: John Milton and his Modern Critics. Ithaca: Cornell University Press, 1955.

ALLEN, DON CAMERON, The Harmonious Vision: Studies in Milton's Poetry. Baltimore: Johns Hopkins Press, 1954.

BUSH, DOUGLAS, Mythology and the Renaissance Tradition in English Poetry. Minneapolis: University of Minnesota Press.

The Renaissance and English Humanism. Toronto: University of Toronto Press, 1939, 1941.

Classical Influences in Renaissance Lietrature. Cambridge: Harvard University Press, 1952.

ELIOT, T. S., "A Note on the Verse of John Milton"; "Milton," in On Poetry and Poets. London: Faber, 1957, 156-83.

FINNEY, GRETCHEN LUDKE, Musical Backgrounds for English Literature, 1580-1650. New Brunswick: Rutgers University Press, 1962.

GRIERSON, H. J. C., Milton and Wordsworth: Poets and Prophets. Cambridge: Cambridge University Press, 1937.

HIGHET, GILBERT, The Classical Tradition: Greek and Roman Influences on Western Literature. New York: Oxford University Press, 1949.

ORAS, ANTS, Milton's Blank Verse and the Chronology of his Major Poems. Gainesville: University of Florida Press, 1953.

PRINCE, F. T., The Italian Element in Milton's Verse. Oxford: Clarendon Press, 1954.

SAURAT, DENIS, Milton: Man and Thinker. New York: Dial Press, 1925; second ed., London: Dent, 1944; reprinted 1946.

SVENDSEN, KESTER, Milton and Science. Cambridge: Harvard University Press, 1956.

TILLYARD, E. M. W., Milton. New York: Dial Press, 1930.

WHALER, JAMES, Counterpoint and Symbol. Anglistica 6. Copenhagen: Rosenkilde and Bagger, 1956.

WHITING, GEORGE W., Milton's Intellectual Milieu. Chapel Hill: University of North Carolina Press, 1939.

JUVENILIA AND MINOR POEMS

ALLEN, DON CAMERON, "Milton's Comus as a Failure in Artistic Compromise." ELH XVI (1949) 104-19.

BARKER, ARTHUR, "The Pattern of Milton's Nativity Ode," UTQ X (1941) 167-81

BROOKS, CLEANTH, "The Light Symbolism in L'Allegro and Il Penseroso," The Well Wrought Urn. New York: Royal and Hitchcock; London: Dobson, 1949, 47-61.

EVANS, WILLA M., Henry Lawes: Musician and Friend of Poets. New York: Modern Language Association; London: Oxford University Press, 1941.

HANFORD, J. H., "The Pastoral Elegy and Milton's Lycidas," PMLA XXV (1910) 403-47.

JAYNE, SEARS, "Subject of Milton's Ludlow Mask," PMLA LXXIV (1959) 533-43.

LE COMTE, EDWARD, "New Light on the Haemony Passage," PQ XXI (1942) 283-98.

MADDISON, CAROL, Apollo and the Nine: A History of the Ode. London: Kegan Paul, 1960.

MAXWELL, J. C., "The Pseudo-Problem of Comus," CJ I (1948) 376-80.

NEILSON, WILLIAM ALLAN, "The Scottish Psalter," The Bible and its Literary Associations, ed. Margaret Crook. New York: Abington Press, 1937.

PATRIDES, C. A., Lycidas: The Tradition and the Poem. New York: Holt, Rinehart, Winston, 1961. Contains essays of F. T. Prince and Wayne Shumaker, referred to in discussion of Lycidas.

ROBERTSON, DAVID M., Pindar: A Poet of Eternal Ideas. Baltimore: Johns Hopkins Press, 1936.

THOMPSON, CLAUDE, "That Two-Handed Engine Will Smite," SP XIX (1962) 184-200.

TILLYARD, E. M. W., "L'Allegro and Il Penseroso," The Miltonic Setting. Cambridge: Cambridge University Press, 1938, 1-38.

"The Action of Comus," Studies in Milton. London: Chatto and Windus, 1951, 82-99.

TUVE, ROSAMUND, Images and Themes in Five Poems by John Milton. Cambridge: Harvard University Press, 1957.

WELSFORD, ENID, The Court Masque. Cambridge: Cambridge University Press, 1927.

WOODHOUSE, A. S. P., "The Argument of Milton's Comus," UTQ XI (1941) 46-71.

MIDDLE YEARS AND SONNETS

BARKER, ARTHUR, Milton and the Puritan Dilemma, 1641-1660. Toronto: University of Toronto Press; London: Milford, 1942.

FINK, ZERA, The Classical Republicans. Evanston: Northwestern University Press, 1945.

HALLER, WILLIAM, The Rise of Puritanism. New York: Columbia University Press, 1938.

Liberty and Reformation in the Puritan Revolution. New York: Columbia University Press, 1955.

"For the Liberty of Unlicenc'd Printing," Amer. Sch. XIV (1945) 326-33.

"The Puritan Art of Love," HLQ V (1942) 235-72.

LASKI, HAROLD, "Areopagitica after Three Hundred Years," Freedom of Expression, ed. Herman Ould. London: Hutchinson Intl. Authors, 1945.

PARKER, WILLIAM, "Milton's Last Sonnet," RES XXI (1945) 235-38; "Milton's Last Sonnet Again," RES n.s. 2, (1951) 147-52.

PYLE, FITZROY, "Milton's Sonnet on his Late Espoused Saint," RES XXV (1949) 57-60.

READ, HERBERT, The Areopagitica: A Coat of Many Colors. London: Routledge, 1945.

SEWELL, ARTHUR, A Study of Milton's Christian Doctrine. London: Oxford University Press, 1939.

SPITZER, LEO, "Understanding Milton," Hopkins Review (Summer 1951) 17-25.

STEVENS, DAVID H., "The Order of Milton's Sonnets," MP XVII (1919) 25-33.

WOODHOUSE, A. S. P., Puritanism and Liberty. London: Dent, 1938.

PARADISE LOST

BOWRA, C. M., From Virgil to Milton. London: Macmillan, 1943.

BRINKLEY, ROBERTA F., Arthurian Legend in the Seventeenth Century. Baltimore: Johns Hopkins Press, 1932.

BROADBENT, J. B., Some Graver Subject: An Essay on Paradise Lost. New York: Barnes and Noble, 1960.

BUSH, DOUGLAS, The Renaissance and English Humanism. Toronto: University of Toronto Press, 1939; reprinted 1941.
Paradise Lost in Our Time: Some Comments. Toronto: University of Toronto Press, 1945.

DAITCHES, DAVID, Milton. London: Hutchinson Univ. Library, 1957.

DIEKHOFF, JOHN S., Milton's Paradise Lost: A Commentary on the Argument. New York: Columbia University Press; London: Oxford University Press, 1946.

EMPSON, WILLIAM, Milton's God. London: Chatto Windus, 1961.

FERRY, ANN D., Milton's Epic Voice. Cambridge: Harvard University Press, 1963.

GILBERT, ALLEN H., On the Composition of Paradise Lost. Chapel Hill: University of North Carolina Press, 1947.

HALLER, WILLIAM, "Hail, Wedded Love!" ELH XIII (1946) 79-97.

HUNTLY, F. L., "A Justification of Milton's Paradise of Fools," ELH XXI (1954) 107-113.

KELLEY, MAURICE, This Great Argument: A Study of Milton's De Doctrina Christiana as a Gloss upon Paradise Lost. Princeton: Princeton University Press, 1941.

KERMODE, FRANK, ED., The Living Milton. London: Routledge Paul, 1960.

KIVETTE, RUTH M., Milton on the Trinity. Columbia University Doctoral Dissertation. Ann Arbor Microfilms, 1960.

LEAVIS, F. R., The Common Pursuit. London: Chatto Windus, 1952.
LEWIS, C. S., A Preface to Paradise Lost. London: Oxford University Press, 1941.
MC COLLEY, GRANT, "Milton's Dialogue on Astronomy," PMLA LII (1937) 180-91. "The Epic Catalogue in Paradise Lost," ELH IV (1937) 180-191.
MURRAY, GILBERT, The Classical Tradition in Poetry. Cambridge: Harvard University Press, 1927.
NICOLSON, MARJORIE, Science and Imagination. Ithaca: Cornell University Press, 1956. (Contains essays on "Milton and the Telescope" "Kepler, John Donne and the Somnium," 58-109.
"Milton's Hell and the Phelegraean Fields," UTQ VII (1938) 500-13.
Breaking of the Circle. New York: Columbia University Press, rev. ed. 1960.
Voyages to the Moon. New York: Macmillan, 1948, 1960.
Mountain Gloom and Mountain Glory. Ithaca: Cornell University Press, 1959.
PETER, JOHN, A Critique of Paradise Lost. New York: Columbia University Press, 1960.
RAJAN, B., Paradise Lost and the Seventeenth Century Reader. London: Chatto Windus, 1947.
SMITH, REBECCA W., "The Source of Milton's Pandemonium," MP XXIX (1941) 187-98.
STEIN, ARNOLD, Answerable Style, Minneapolis: University of Minnesota Press, 1953.
SUMMERS, JOSEPH, The Muse's Method: An Introduction to Paradise Lost. Cambridge: Harvard University Press, 1962.
TILLYARD, E. M. W., The English Epic and its Background. New York: Oxford University Press, 1954.
WALDOCK, A. J. A., Paradise Lost and its Critics. Cambridge: Cambridge University Press, 1947.
WRIGHT, BERNARD, Milton's Paradise Lost: A Reassessment of the Poem. London: Methuen, 1962.

PARADISE REGAINED

FRYE, NORTHROP, "The Typology of Paradise Regained," MP LIII (1956) 227-38.
HUGHES, MERRITT, "The Christ of Paradise Regained and the Renaissance Heroic Tradition," SP XXXV (1938) 254-77.
POPE, ELIZABETH, Paradise Regained: The Tradition and the Poem. Baltimore: Johns Hopkins Press, 1947.
STEIN, ARNOLD, Heroic Knowledge: An Interpretation of Paradise Regained and Samson Agonistes. Minneapolis: University of Minnesota Press, 1957.

TILLYARD, E. M. W., "The Christ of Paradise Regained," Studies in Milton. London: Chatto Windus, 1951, 100-106.
WOODHOUSE, A. S. P., "Theme and Pattern in Paradise Regained," UTQ XXV (1956) 167-82.

SAMSON AGONISTES

BOWRA, C. M., "Samson Agonistes," Inspiration and Poetry. London: Macmillan, 1955.
CRAIG, T. SCOTT, "Concerning Milton's Samson," Renaissance News V (1952) 43-53.
ELLIS-FERMOR, UNA, "Samson Agonistes and Religious Drama," The Frontiers of Drama. London: Methuen, 1945, 17-30.
GILBERT, ALLEN, "Is Samson Agonistes Unfinished?" PQ XXVIII (1949) 98-106.
KROUSE, F. MICHAEL, Milton's Samson and the Christian Tradition. Princeton: Princeton University Press, 1949.
PARKER, WILLIAM R., Milton's Debt to Greek Tragedy in Samson Agonistes. Baltimore: Johns Hopkins Press, 1937.

STYLE AND VERSIFICATION

BRIDGES, ROBERT, Milton's Prosody. Oxford: Oxford University Press, 1893.
MILES, JOSEPHINE, The Continuity of Poetic Language. Berkeley: University of California Press. 1951.
ORAS, ANTS, "Metre and Chronology in the Epitaph on the Duchess of Winchester," NQ 198 (1953) 332-33.
SPROTT, S. ERNEST, Milton's Art of Prosody. Oxford: Blackwell, 1953.

ABBREVIATIONS USED ABOVE

Amer. Sch.—American Scholar
C.J.—Cambridge Journal
ELH—English Literary History
HLQ—Huntington Library Quarterly
MP—Modern Philology
NQ—Notes and Queries
PMLA—Publications of the Modern Language Association
PQ—Philological Quarterly
RES—Review of English Studies

Index

[Note: Names and titles listed in the Bibliography have been repeated here only when the author, book or article is discussed in the text.]

Noyes, Alfred, 119
Nye, Phillip, 168

Odyssey, xii, 4, 28, 78, 178, 252, 255
Of Education, 12, 15, 120-23, 126,
1. 1, 165
Of Reformation in England, 130
On Shakespeare, 30-31
On the Death of a Fair Infant, 25-26
On the University Carrier, 28-9
On Time, 44-5, 46, 104
Ovid, 4, 148, 165

Palmer, Herbert, 165
Paradise Lost, xi, xiii, 16, 24, 31,
36, 38, 39, 43, 46, 59, 78, 100,
118, 126, 128, 137, 140, 151,
154, 155, 160, 170, 177-322,
323, 324, 325, 326, 327, 328,
329, 330, 333, 334, 335, 336,
337, 338, 347, 350, 352, 353,
354, 356, 364, 365
Paradise Regained, 8, 16, 308, 323-
347, 348, 352, 355
Parker, William Riley, 123, 150,
157-161, 348, 350
Passion, The, 43-4, 45
Paulet, John, 47
Peter, John, 223, 228, 236
Petrarch, 142, 143, 144, 159
Pindar, 4, 31, 32, 162
Phillips, Edward, 120, 121, 122, 123,
124, 125, 135, 136, 146, 158-9,
180, 323
Phillips, John, 121, 150
Plutarch, 162
Pope, Alexander, 184, 190, 215, 256
Pope, Elizabeth, 327, 328
Prince, F. T., 104
Prynne, William, 168
Psalms, paraphrases of, 9, 22-25

Raleigh, Walter, 323
Ravenscroft, Thomas, 23
Reason of Church Government, 6,
19, 130, 179, 324, 349
Rossetti, Dante Gabriel, 143
Ruskin, John, 98-9
Rutherford, Samuel, 167

Saintsbury, George, 105
Salmasius (Claude Saumaise), 134
Samson Agonistes, 39, 44, 128, 151,
155, 156, 224, 299, 323, 324,
325, 329, 343, 348-73
Sandys, George, 195
Sappho, 4
Saurat, Denis, 263
Scott-Craig, T. S. K., 351
Scotus, Duns, 302
Scudamore, Thomas, 116
Second Defence, 5, 12, 115, 117, 125,
138, 151, 153, 168
Shakespeare, xi, xii, 5, 7, 64, 100,
141, 144, 186, 205, 207, 235,
361
Shelley, Percy Bysshe, 15, 181, 186
Shirley, James, 70
Shumaker, Wayne, 100
Simpson, Sidrach, 168
Skinner, Cyriak, 150-51, 155-57
Smart, John S., 145, 149, 150, 153
162, 164
Smith, Rebecca, 197
Socrates, 344
Sonnets, 140-74
A Book was Writ, 162-4
Avenge, O Lord, 173-4
Because you have thrown off, 144,
166-9
Captain or Colonel, 131, 161-2
Cromwell, 171-2
Cyriack, this three years day,
155-6
Cyriack, whose Grandsire, 150-51
Fairfax, 169-71
Henry Lawes, 147-8
How Soon hath time, 18
I did but prompt, 165-6
Lady that in the prime, 145
Lawrence of virtuous father, 149-
150
Lady Margaret Ley, 146-7
Mrs. Catharine Thomason, 148-9
Sir Henry Vane, 172-3
When I consider, 157-61
Sophocles, 4, 58, 90, 222, 349, 350,
354
Spencer, Lady Alice, 66-7
Spenser, Edmund, viii, ix, 66, 83, 85.